Mary Jones and Geoff Jones

Cambridge IGCSE™
Biology
Coursebook
Third edition

CAMBRIDGE
UNIVERSITY PRESS

CAMBRIDGE
UNIVERSITY PRESS

University Printing House, Cambridge CB2 8BS, United Kingdom

One Liberty Plaza, 20th Floor, New York, NY 10006, USA

477 Williamstown Road, Port Melbourne, VIC 3207, Australia

314–321, 3rd Floor, Plot 3, Splendor Forum, Jasola District Centre, New Delhi – 110025, India

79 Anson Road, #06–04/06, Singapore 079906

Cambridge University Press is part of the University of Cambridge.

It furthers the University's mission by disseminating knowledge in the pursuit of education, learning and research at the highest international levels of excellence.

Information on this title:
www.cambridge.org/9781107614796 (Paperback + CD-ROM)
www.cambridge.org/9781316637692 (Paperback + CD-ROM + Cambridge Elevate Enhanced edition, 2 years)
www.cambridge.org/9781107503014 (Cambridge Elevate Enhanced edition, 2 years)

© Cambridge University Press 2002, 2014

First published 2002
Second edition 2010
Third edition 2014

40 39 38 37 36 35 34 33 32 31 30 29 28 27 26 25 24 23 22 21

Printed in Malaysia by Vivar Printing

A catalogue record for this publication is available from the British Library

ISBN 978-1-107-61479-6 Paperback with CD-ROM for Windows® and Mac®
ISBN 978-1-316-63769-2 Paperback with CD-ROM for Windows
and Mac Paperback + Cambridge Elevate enhanced edition, 2 years
ISBN 978-1-107-50301-4 Cambridge Elevate enhanced edition, 2 years

Additional resources for this publication at www.cambridge.org/education

Contents

Introduction   v

Acknowledgements   vi

1 Classification   1
1.1 Characteristics of living things   1
1.2 Classification   2
1.3 The kingdoms of living organisms   6
1.4 Viruses   9
1.5 Classifying animals   9
1.6 Classifying plants   12
1.7 Keys   15

2 Cells   18
2.1 Cell structure   19
2.2 Cells and organisms   25

3 Movement in and out of cells   28
3.1 Diffusion   29
3.2 Osmosis   30
3.3 Active transport   35

4 The chemicals of life   40
4.1 What are you made of?   41
4.2 Carbohydrates   41
4.3 Fats   44
4.4 Proteins   45
4.5 DNA   47

5 Enzymes   49
5.1 Biological catalysts   50
5.2 Properties of enzymes   51

6 Plant nutrition   58
6.1 Types of nutrition   59
6.2 Photosynthesis   59
6.3 Leaves   59
6.4 Uses of glucose   64
6.5 Testing leaves for starch   65
6.6 Limiting factors   69
6.7 The importance of photosynthesis   70

7 Animal nutrition   73
7.1 Diet   74
7.2 Digestion   78
7.3 Teeth   80
7.4 The alimentary canal   82
7.5 Assimilation   89

8 Transport in plants   93
8.1 Plant transport systems   94
8.2 Water uptake   96
8.3 Transpiration   97
8.4 Transport of manufactured food   102

9 Transport in animals   106
9.1 Circulatory systems   108
9.2 The heart   109
9.3 Blood vessels   113
9.4 Blood   117
9.5 Lymph and tissue fluid   122

10 Pathogens and immunity   127
10.1 Pathogens   128
10.2 Body defences   129
10.3 The immune system   133

11 Respiration and gas exchange   140
11.1 Respiration   141
11.2 Gas exchange in humans   143
11.3 Breathing movements   146

12 Excretion   153
12.1 Excretory products   154
12.2 Nitrogenous waste   154
12.3 The human excretory system   156

13 Coordination and response   161
13.1 Coordination in animals   162
13.2 The human nervous system   162
13.3 Receptors   165
13.4 The endocrine system   170
13.5 Coordination and response in plants   172

14 Homeostasis   178
14.1 Maintaining the internal environment   179
14.2 Control of body temperature   179
14.3 Control of blood glucose concentration   184

15 Drugs   188
15.1 What is a drug?   189
15.2 Medicinal drugs   189
15.3 Misuse of drugs   190
15.4 Tobacco smoking   192

16 Reproduction in plants   197
16.1 Asexual reproduction   198
16.2 Sexual reproduction   198
16.3 Sexual reproduction in flowering plants   200
16.4 Comparing sexual and asexual reproduction   208

17 Reproduction in humans   212
17.1 Human reproductive organs   213
17.2 Fertilisation and development   215
17.3 The menstrual cycle   220
17.4 Birth control   222
17.5 Sexually transmitted infections   225

18 Inheritance   230
18.1 Chromosomes   231
18.2 Cell division   231
18.3 Inheritance   235
18.4 DNA and protein synthesis   243

19 Variation and natural selection   247
19.1 Variation   248
19.2 Adaptive features   250
19.3 Selection   253

20 Organisms and their environment   264
20.1 Ecology   265
20.2 Energy flow   265
20.3 Nutrient cycles   270
20.4 Population size   272

21 Biotechnology   280
21.1 What is biotechnology?   281
21.2 Using yeast   281
21.3 Making use of enzymes   282
21.4 Penicillin   284
21.5 Genetic engineering   286

22 Humans and the environment   292
22.1 Food production   293
22.2 Habitat destruction   296
22.3 Pollution   299
22.4 Conservation   307

Answers to questions   318

Glossary   330

Index   339

Terms and Conditions of use for the CD-ROM   347

CD-ROM
Study and revision skills
Multiple choice tests
Practice exam-style papers and marking schemes
Glossary
Notes on Activities for Teachers/Technicians
Self-assessment checklists
Activities
Answers to Coursebook end-of-chapter questions
Revision checklists
Animations

Introduction

This book has been written to help you study IGCSE Biology. We hope that you enjoy using it.

The book can also be used with the Cambridge 'O' level Biology syllabus (5090).

Core and Supplement

Your teacher will tell you whether you are studying just the Core part of the Biology syllabus, or whether you are studying the Supplement as well. If you study the Core only, you will be entered for Papers 1 and 3 and either Paper 5 or 6, and can get a maximum of Grade C. If you also study the Supplement, you may be entered for Papers 2 and 4, and either Paper 5 or 6, and will be able to get a maximum of Grade A*. The Supplement material in this book is marked by a letter 'S' and brown bars in the margin, like this.

Definitions

There are quite a lot of definitions in the IGCSE syllabus that you need to learn by heart. These are all in this book, at appropriate points in each chapter, inside boxes with a heading 'Key definition'. Make sure you learn these carefully.

Questions

Each chapter has several sets of Questions within it. Most of these require quite short answers, and simply test if you have understood what you have just read (or what you have just been taught).

At the end of each chapter, there are some longer questions testing a range of material from the chapter. Some of these are past questions from Cambridge exam papers, or are in a similar style to Cambridge questions.

Activities

Each chapter contains Activities. These will help you to develop the practical skills that will be tested in your IGCSE Biology examination. There are more Activities on the CD-ROM. These are marked with this symbol:

There are two possible exams to test your practical skills, called Paper 5 and Paper 6. Your teacher will tell you which of these you will be entered for. They are equally difficult, and you can get up to Grade A* on either of them. You should try to do the Activities no matter which of these papers you are entered for.

Summary

At the end of each chapter, there is a short list of the main points covered in the chapter. Remember, though, that these are only very short summaries, and you'll need to know more detail than this to do really well in the exam.

The CD-ROM

There is a CD-ROM in the back of the book. You'll also find the Summaries on the CD-ROM. You can use the revision checklists on the CD-ROM to check off how far you have got with learning and understanding each idea.

The CD-ROM also contains a set of interactive multiple-choice questions testing whether you know and understand the material from each chapter.

You'll find some self-assessment checklists on the CD-ROM too, which you can print off and use to assess yourself each time you observe and draw a specimen, construct a results chart, draw a graph from a set of results or plan an experiment. These are all very important skills, and by using these checklists you should be able to improve your performance until you can do them almost perfectly every time.

There are some suggestions on the CD-ROM about how you can give yourself the very best chance of doing well in your exams, by studying and revising carefully. There are also some practice exam papers.

Workbook

There is a workbook to go with this textbook. If you have one, you will find it really helpful in developing your skills, such as handling information and solving problems, as well as some of the practical skills.

Acknowledgements

Cover image/Frans Lanting, Mint Images/SPL, p. 1 Alamy; 2 Geoff Jones; pp. 7*t*, 7*b* Alamy; p. 11 Geoff Jones; p.15 Geoff Jones; p. 17 Geoff Jones; p. 18 SPL; pp. 20*t*, 20*b* Eleanor Jones; p. 21 Biophoto Associates/SPL; p.22*t*, 22*b*,22*br* SPL; p. 26 SPL; p. 28 Alamy; p. 34 Geoff Jones; p. 40 SPL; p. 42 SPL; p. 43 SPL; p. 44 Alamy; p.45 SPL; 46*t*, 46*b* SPL; p. 49 Alamy; p. 58 SPL; p. 61*t* Biophoto Associates/SPL; p.61*b* SPL; p. 61*r* Andrew Syred/SPL; p. 65 Nigel Cattlin/Alamy; p. 67 Alamy; p. 73 SPL; p. 75 7.3–7.6 Geoff Jones; p. 77*l* Alex Segre/Alamy; p. 77*r* Images of Africa Photobank/Alamy; p. 87 Biophoto Associates/SPL; p. 88*l* SPL; p.88*r* SPL; p. 93 Alamy; p. 94 Andrew Syred/SPL; p. 95 J.C. Revy/SPL; p.96*t* SPL; p. 96*b* SPL; p. 106 Alamy; p. 110 Alamy; p. 112 Alamy; p. 114 Janine Photolibrary/Alamy; p. 115 Prof. P. Motta/Dept. of Anatomy/University "La Sapienza", Rome/SPL; pp. 118, 120, 121 Phototake Inc./Alamy; p. 127 Alamy;p. 129*t* Alamy; p. 129*b* Alamy; p. 130 Alamy; p. 131 Alamy; p. 132*l* Alamy; p. 132*r* Alamy; p. 136 Alamy; p. 137 Alamy; p. 140 Alamy; p. 150 Rick Rickman/NewSport/Corbis; p. 153 Alamy; p. 161 SPL; p. 164 Wendy Lee; p. 165 Visual Ideas/Nora/Corbis; p. 175 SPL; p. 178 Alamy; p.185*l* SPL; p. 186*r* SPL; p. 188 Alamy; p. 189*t* CNRI/SPL; p.189*b* Alamy; p. 191*l* Zuma Press/Zuma/Corbis; 191*r* St Bartholomew's Hospital/SPL; p. 192 SPL; pp 194*l*, 194*r* Biophoto Associates/SPL; p. 195 SPL; p. 197 Alamy; p. 201 Geoff Jones; p. 202*t* Alamy: p. 202*b* Pictox/Alamy; p. 204 SPL; p. 208 Alamy; p. 212*t* SPL; p. 212*b* SPL; p. 215 Alamy; p. 219 Alamy; p. 225 SPL; p. 230 Alamy; p. 231*l* Chery Power/SPL; 231*r* CNRI/SPL; p. 232 Leonard Lessin/FBPA/SPL;p. 239 Alamy; p. 247*l* Alamy; p. 247*r* Alamy; p. 248 *tr* Wendy Lee; p. 248*t* Imagebroker/Alamy; p. 248*b* Sam Sangster/Alamy; p. 251*l* Alamy; p 251*tr* Alamy; p. 251*br* Geoff Jones; p. 253*l* Jayanta Dey/epa/Corbis; p 253*r* Mary Evans Picture Library/Alamy; p.254 Pat & Tom Leeson/SPL; p. 255 Stephen Dalton/NHPA; p. 257 Agence Nature/NHPA; p. 259*tb* Geoff Jones; p. 259*br* Terry Matthews/Alamy; p. 262 Alamy; p. 264 SPL; p. 278 SPL; p. 280 SPL; p. 281 SPL; p. 282*l* SPL; p. 282*r* SPL; p. 283 SPL; p. 287 SPL; p. 292 Alamy; p. 293*bl* David South/Alamy; 293*tr* David R. Frazier Photolibrary, Inc/Alamy; p. 294*tl* SPL; p. 294*tr* Alamy; p. 294*bl* SPL; p. 295*t* Alamy; p295*b* Alamy; p. 296*l* Gideon Mendel for Action Aid/Corbis; p. 296*r* Alamy; p. 297*tl* Alamy; 297*bl* Sylvia Cordaiy Photo Library Ltd/Alamy; p. 297*tr* Geoff Jones; p.297*br* Geoff Jones; p. 301*l* Lou Linwei/Alamy; p. 301*r* Jim West/Alamy; p. 303 Blickwinkel/Alamy; p. 305 Nigel Cattlin/Alamy; p. 306 Alamy; p. 308 Alamy; p. 312 Alamy; p. 313 Alamy; p.314*l* Alamy; p. 314*tr* Alamy; p. 314*br* Alamy; p. 315 Alamy

Abbreviations
SPL = Science Photo Library
t = top, *b* = bottom, *l* = left, *r* = right

Layout and illustration by Greenhill Wood Studios

1 Classification

In this chapter, you will find out about:

♦ the characteristics of living things
♦ naming organisms using the binomial system
♦ how living organisms are classified
♦ how to use dichotomous keys to identify organisms.

The puzzle of the platypus

In 1788, British settlers arrived in Australia. They were amazed by many of the animals that they saw, and a strange animal with fur, webbed feet and a beak was among the most puzzling (Figure 1.1).

People had already been living in Australia for almost 50 000 years, and different groups of these indigenous people had various names for this animal, such as dulawarrung. But the British arrivals were not satisfied with just giving the animal a name. They wanted to classify it – to decide which group of animals it belonged in.

And this was where the problem began. The animal had a beak and webbed feet, like a duck. It had fur, like a mole. No-one knew whether it laid eggs or gave birth to live young. So was it a bird? Was it a mammal? No-one could decide.

In 1799, a dead specimen of this strange animal was taken to England, where it was studied by Dr George Shaw. To begin with, he thought it was a hoax. He looked very carefully to see if someone had stitched the beak onto the head, but no – it was clearly a genuine part of the animal.

Dr Shaw gave the animal a Latin name, *Platypus anatinus*. 'Platypus' means 'flat-footed' and 'anatinus' means 'like a duck'. However, someone then pointed out that the name *Platypus* had already been taken, and belonged to a species of beetle. So another name was suggested by a German scientist, who gave it the name *Ornithorhynchus paradoxus*. The first word means 'nose like a bird' and the second means 'puzzling'. This is the Latin name that is used for the animal today.

Although the Latin name *Platypus* could not be used, people still called the animal a platypus. In the following years, proof was found that platypuses lay eggs, rather than giving birth to live young. However, they feed their young on milk, which is a characteristic feature of mammals. Scientists eventually decided to classify the platypus as a mammal, despite its odd beak and the fact that it lays eggs. It was put into a new group of mammals, called monotremes, which also includes the echidnas (spiny anteaters).

Figure 1.1 The platypus is superbly adapted for hunting prey in water.

1.1 Characteristics of living things

Biology is the study of living things, which are often called **organisms**. Living organisms have seven features or characteristics which make them different from objects that are not alive (Figure **1.2**). The definitions of these characteristics are shown in the boxes below and on the opposite page. You should learn these definitions now, but you will find out much more about each of them later in this book.

Growth All organisms begin small and get larger, by the growth of their cells and by adding new cells to their bodies.

Movement All organisms are able to move to some extent. Most animals can move their whole body from place to place, and plants can slowly move parts of themselves.

Sensitivity All organisms pick up information about changes in their environment, and react to the changes.

Excretion All organisms produce unwanted or toxic waste products as a result of their metabolic reactions, and these must be removed from the body.

Reproduction Organisms are able to make new organisms of the same species as themselves.

Nutrition Organisms take substances from their environment and use them to provide energy or materials to make new cells.

Respiration All organisms break down glucose and other substances inside their cells, to release energy that they can use.

Figure 1.2 Characteristics of living organisms.

Key definitions

movement – an action by an organism causing a change of position or place

respiration – the chemical reactions in cells that break down nutrient molecules and release energy

sensitivity – the ability to detect and respond to changes in the environment

growth – a permanent increase in size

reproduction – the processes that make more of the same kind of organism

excretion – removal from organisms of toxic materials and substances in excess of requirements

nutrition – taking in of materials for energy, growth and development

In addition to these seven characteristics, living organisms have another feature in common. When we study living organisms under a microscope, we can see that they are all made of cells. These cells all have:

♦ cytoplasm
♦ a cell membrane
♦ a chemical called DNA, making up their genetic material
♦ ribosomes, which are used for making proteins inside the cell
♦ enzymes that are used to help the cell to carry out anaerobic respiration.

You can find out more about the structure of cells in Chapter **2**.

1.2 Classification

Classification means putting things into groups. There are many possible ways in which we could group living organisms. For example, we could put all the organisms with legs into one group, and all those without legs into another. Or we could put all red organisms into one group, and all blue ones into another. The first of these ideas would be much more useful to biologists than the second.

The main reason for classifying living things is to make it easier to study them. For example, we put humans, dogs, horses and mice into one group (the mammals) because they share certain features (for example, having hair) that are not found in other groups. We think that all mammals share these features because they have all descended from the same ancestor that lived long ago. The ancestor that they all share is called a **common ancestor**. The common ancestor that gave rise to all the mammals lived more than 200 million years ago.

We would therefore expect all mammals to have bodies that have similar structures and that work in similar ways. If we find a new animal that has hair and suckles its young on milk, then we know that it belongs in the mammal group. We will already know a lot about it, even before we have studied it at all.

Using DNA to help with classification

In the past, the only ways that biologists could decide which organisms were most closely related to each other was to study the structure of their bodies. They looked carefully at their **morphology** (the overall form and shape of their bodies, such as whether they had legs or wings) and their **anatomy** (the detailed body structure, which could be determined by dissection). We still use these methods of classification today. But we now have new tools to help to work out evolutionary relationships, and one of the most powerful of these is the study of **DNA**.

DNA is the chemical from which our chromosomes are made. It is the genetic material, passed on from one generation to the next. You can read more about its structure in Chapter **4**, where you will find out that each DNA molecule is made up of strings of smaller molecules, containing four different **bases**. These bases, called A, C, G and T, can be arranged in any order. Biologists can compare the sequences of bases

S in the DNA of organisms from two different species. The more similar the base sequences, the more closely related the species are to one another. They have a more recent common ancestor than species that have DNA base sequences that are less similar. The similarities in sequences of amino acids in proteins can be used in the same way.

The classification system

The first person to try to classify organisms in a scientific way was a Swedish naturalist called Linnaeus. He introduced his system of classification in 1735. He divided all the different kinds of living things into groups called **species**. He recognised 12 000 different species. Linnaeus's species were groups of organisms that shared the same appearance and behaviour. We still use this system today. Biologists do not always agree on exactly how to define a species, but usually we say that organisms belong to the same species if they can breed together successfully, and the offspring that they produce can also breed.

Species are grouped into larger groups called genera (singular: **genus**). Each genus contains several species with similar characteristics (Figure **1.3**). Several genera are then grouped into a family, families into orders, orders into classes, classes into phyla and finally phyla into **kingdoms**. Some of the more important groups are described in this chapter.

Figure **1.3** shows five animals that all belong to the mammal order. You can see that they all have hair, which is a characteristic feature of mammals. The animals have been classified into two groups – horse-like mammals and dog-like mammals. (What features do you think differ between these two groups?) The horse-like mammals all belong to the genus *Equus*. The dog-like ones belong to the genus *Canis*.

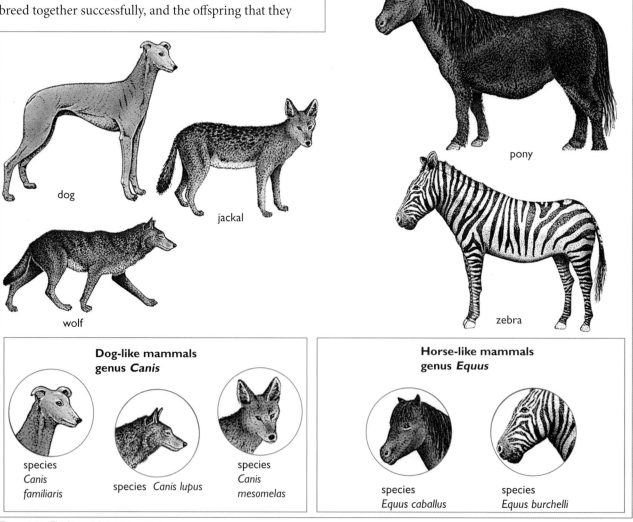

Figure 1.3   The binomial naming system.

The binomial naming system

Linnaeus gave every species of living organism two names, written in Latin. This is called the **binomial system**. The first name is the name of the genus the organism belongs to, and always has a capital letter. The second name is the name of its species, and always has a small letter. This two-word name is called a **binomial**.

For example, a wolf belongs to the genus *Canis* and the species *lupus*. Its binomial is *Canis lupus*. These names are printed in italics. When you write a Latin name, you cannot write in italics, so you should underline it instead. The genus name can be abbreviated like this: *C. lupus*.

 Question

1.1 The table shows how two organisms – a monarch butterfly and a giant pangolin – are classified.

   a Use the informatiton in the table to suggest whether these two organisms are not related at all, distantly related or closely related. Explain how you made your decision.

   b Write down the genus of the giant pangolin.

   c Use the Internet or a textbook to find out how a human is classified. Write it down in a table like the one shown on the right.

Kingdom	animal	animal
Phylum	arthropods	vertebrates
Class	insects	mammals
Order	Lepidoptera (butterflies and moths)	Pholidota
Family	Danaidae	Manidae
Genus	*Danaus*	*Manis*
Species	*Danaus plexippus*	*Manis gigantea*

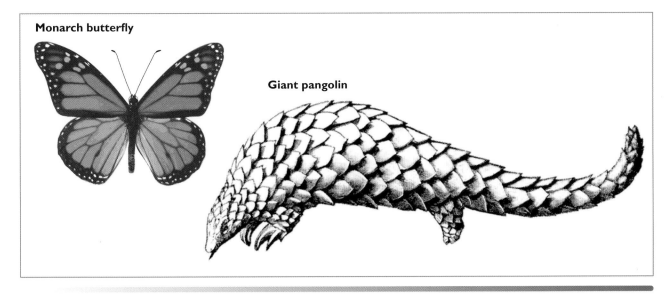

Monarch butterfly

Giant pangolin

1.3 The kingdoms of living organisms

Animals

Animals (Figure 1.4) are usually easy to recognise. Most animals can move actively, hunting for food. Under the microscope, we can see that their cells have no cell walls.

Some animals have, in the past, been confused with plants. For a very long time, sea anemones were classified as plants, because they tend to stay fixed in one place, and their tentacles look rather like flower petals. Now we know that they are animals.

Characteristics:
◆ multicellular (their bodies contain many cells)
◆ cells have a nucleus, but no cell walls or chloroplasts
◆ feed on organic substances made by other living organisms.

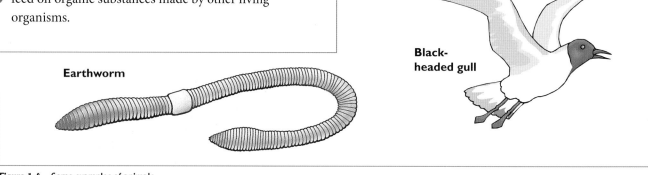

Figure 1.4   Some examples of animals.

Plants

The plants that are most familiar to us are the flowering plants, which include most kinds of trees. These plants have leaves, stems, roots and flowers (Figure 1.5). However, there are other types of plants – including ferns and mosses – that do not have flowers. What all of them have in common is the green colour, caused by a pigment called chlorophyll. This pigment absorbs energy from sunlight, and the plant can use this energy to make sugars, by the process of photosynthesis.

As they do not need to move around to get their food, plants are adapted to remain in one place. They often have a spreading shape, enabling them to capture as much sunlight energy as possible.

Characteristics:
◆ multicellular
◆ cells have a nucleus, cell walls made of cellulose and often contain chloroplasts
◆ feed by photosynthesis
◆ may have roots, stems and leaves.

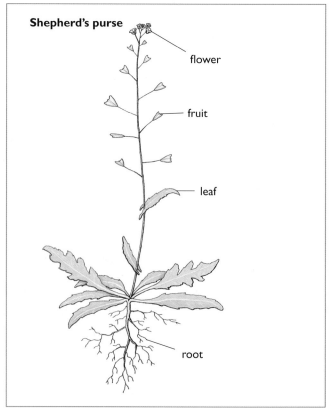

Figure 1.5.   An example of a plant.

❓ Questions

1.2 The photograph below shows a sea anemone.
   a Explain why people used to think that sea anemones were plants.
   b Explain how using a microscope could help you to confirm that sea anemones are animals.

1.3 The photograph below shows a plant called a liverwort. Liverworts do not have roots or proper leaves. They do not have flowers. Suggest how you could show that a liverwort belongs to the plant kingdom.

Fungi

For a very long time, fungi were classified as plants. However, we now know that they are really very different, and belong in their own kingdom. Figure **1.6** shows the characteristic features of fungi.

We have found many different uses to make of fungi. We eat them as mushrooms. We use the unusual fungus yeast to make ethanol and bread. We obtain antibiotics such as penicillin from various different fungi.

Some fungi, however, are harmful. Some of these cause food decay, while a few cause diseases, including ringworm and athlete's foot.

Fungi do not have chlorophyll and do not photosynthesise. Instead they feed saprophytically, or parasitically, on organic material like faeces, human foods and dead plants or animals.

Characteristics:
♦ usually multicellular (many-celled)
♦ have nuclei
♦ have cell walls, not made of cellulose
♦ do not have chlorophyll
♦ feed by saprophytic or parasitic nutrition.

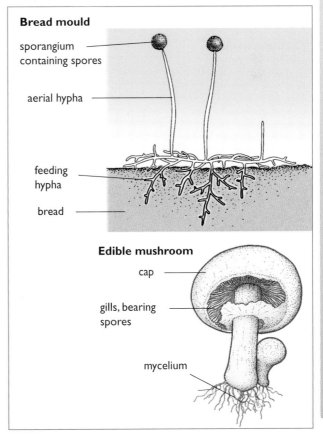

Figure 1.6 Some examples of fungi.

⑤ Protoctista

The kingdom Protoctista (Figure **1.7**) contains quite a mixture of organisms. They all have cells with a nucleus, but some have plant-like cells with chloroplasts and cellulose cell walls, while others have animal-like cells without these features. Most protoctists are unicellular (made of just a single cell) but some, such as seaweeds, are multicellular.

Characteristics:

♦ multicellular or unicellular
♦ cells have a nucleus
♦ cells may or may not have a cell wall and chloroplasts
♦ some feed by photosynthesis and others feed on organic substances made by other organisms.

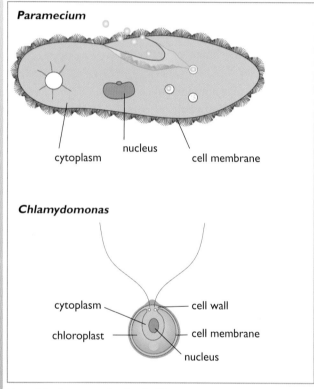

Figure 1.7 Some examples of protoctists.

Prokaryotes ⑤

Figure **1.8** shows some bacteria. Bacteria have cells that are very different from the cells of all other kinds of organism. The most important difference is that they do not have a nucleus.

You will meet bacteria at various stages in your biology course. Some of them are harmful to us and cause diseases such as tuberculosis (TB) and cholera. Many more, however, are helpful. You will find out about their useful roles in the carbon cycle and the nitrogen cycle, in biotechnology, in the treatment of sewage to make it safe to release into the environment and in making insulin for the treatment of people with diabetes.

Some bacteria can carry out photosynthesis. The oldest fossils belong to this kingdom, so we think that they were the first kinds of organism to evolve.

Characteristics:

♦ often unicellular (single-celled)
♦ have no nucleus
♦ have cell walls, not made of cellulose
♦ have no mitochondria.

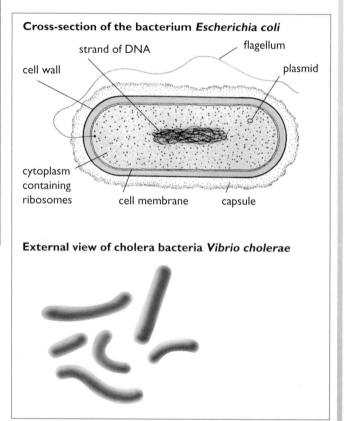

Figure 1.8 Some examples of bacteria.

⑤ 1.4 Viruses

You have almost certainly had an illness caused by a virus. Viruses cause common diseases such as colds and influenza, and also more serious ones such as AIDS.

Viruses are not normally considered to be alive, because they cannot do anything other than just exist, until they get inside a living cell. They then take over the cell's machinery to make multiple copies of themselves. These new viruses burst out of the cell and invade others, where the process is repeated. The host cell is usually killed when this happens. On their own, viruses cannot move, feed, excrete, show sensitivity, grow or reproduce.

Figure **1.9** shows one kind of virus. It is not made of a cell – it is simply a piece of DNA or RNA (a chemical similar to DNA) surrounded by a protein coat. It is hugely magnified in this diagram. The scale bar represents a length of 10 nanometres. One nanometre is 1×10^{-9} mm. In other words, you could line up more than 15 000 of these viruses between two of the millimetre marks on your ruler.

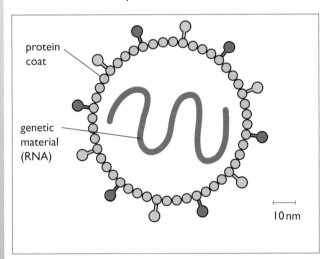

Figure 1.9 The structure of a simple virus

❓ Questions

⑤ **1.4** Why are viruses not generally considered to be living things?

1.5 State **one** similarity and **one** difference between the cells of a fungus and the cells of a plant.

1.6 How do the cells of bacteria differ from the cells of plants and animals?

1.5 Classifying animals

Figure **1.10** shows some of the major groups into which the animal kingdom is classified.

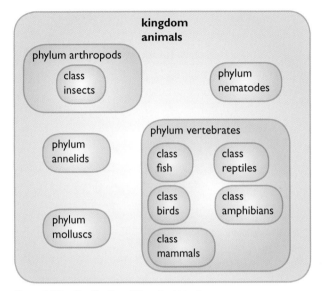

Figure 1.10 Classification of the animal kingdom.

Phylum Vertebrates

These are animals with a supporting rod running along the length of the body. The most familiar ones have a backbone and are called vertebrates.

Class Fish

The fish (Figure **1.11**) all live in water, except for one or two like the mudskipper, which can spend short periods of time breathing air.

Characteristics:

♦ vertebrates with scaly skin
♦ have gills
♦ have fins.

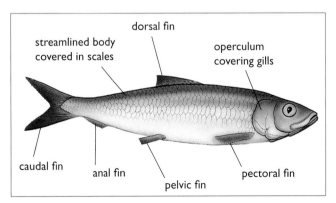

Figure 1.11 A fish.

Class Amphibians

Although most adult amphibians live on land, they always go back to the water to breed. Frogs, toads and salamanders are amphibians (Figure **1.12**).

Characteristics:

♦ vertebrates with moist, scale-less skin
♦ eggs laid in water, larva (tadpole) lives in water
♦ adult often lives on land
♦ larva has gills, adult has lungs.

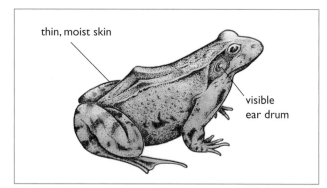

Figure 1.12   A frog.

Class Reptiles

These are the crocodiles, lizards, snakes, turtles and tortoises (Figure **1.13**). Reptiles do not need to go back to the water to breed because their eggs have a waterproof shell which stops them from drying out.

Characteristics:

♦ vertebrates with scaly skin
♦ lay eggs with rubbery shells.

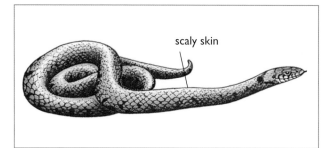

Figure 1.13   A snake.

Class Birds

The birds (Figure **1.14**), like reptiles, lay eggs with waterproof shells.

Characteristics:

♦ vertebrates with feathers
♦ forelimbs have become wings
♦ lay eggs with hard shells
♦ endothermic
♦ have a beak
♦ heart has four chambers.

Figure 1.14   A bird.

Class Mammals

This is the group that humans belong to (Figure **1.15**).

Characteristics:

♦ vertebrates with hair
♦ have a placenta
♦ young feed on milk from mammary glands
♦ endothermic
♦ have a diaphragm
♦ heart has four chambers
♦ have different types of teeth (incisors, canines premolars and molars).

Figure 1.15   An ocelot, an example of a mammal.

Phylum Arthropods

Arthropods are animals with jointed legs, but no backbone. They are a very successful group, because they have a waterproof exoskeleton that has allowed them to live on dry land. There are more kinds of arthropod in the world than all the other kinds of animal put together.

Characteristics:

♦ several pairs of jointed legs
♦ exoskeleton.

Insects

Insects (Figure **1.16**) are a very successful group of animals. Their success is mostly due to their exoskeleton and tracheae, which are very good at stopping water from evaporating from the insects' bodies, so they can live in very dry places. They are mainly terrestrial (land-living).

Characteristics:

♦ arthropods with three pairs of jointed legs
♦ two pairs of wings (one or both may be vestigial)
♦ breathe through tracheae
♦ body divided into head, thorax and abdomen.

Figure 1.16   Some examples of insects.

Crustaceans

These are the crabs, lobsters and woodlice. They breathe through gills, so most of them live in wet places and many are aquatic.

Characteristics:

♦ arthropods with more than four pairs of jointed legs
♦ not millipedes or centipedes
♦ breathe through gills.

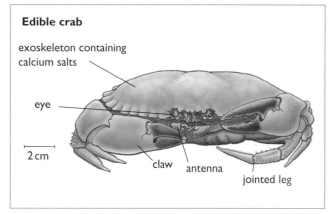

Figure 1.17   An example of a crustacean.

Arachnids

These are the spiders, ticks and scorpions. They are land-dwelling organisms.

Characteristics:

♦ arthropods with four pairs of jointed legs
♦ breathe through gills called book lungs.

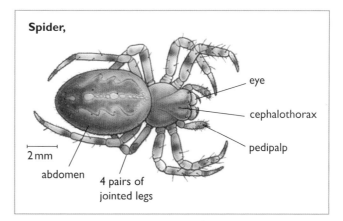

Figure 1.18   An example of an arachnid.

Myriapods

These are the centipedes and millipedes.

Characteristics:

♦ body consists of many segments
♦ each segment has jointed legs.

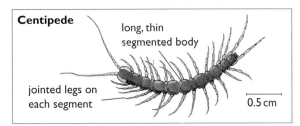

Figure 1.19   An example of a myriapod.

⓺ Questions

Ⓢ 1.7 List **three** ways in which all mammals differ from all birds.

1.8 Explain why bats are classified as mammals, even though they have wings.

1.6 Classifying plants

We have seen that plants are organisms that have cells with cell walls made of cellulose. At least some parts of a plant are green. The green colour is caused by a pigment called chlorophyll, which absorbs energy from sunlight. The plant uses this energy to make glucose, using carbon dioxide and water from its environment. This is called photosynthesis.

Plants include small organisms such as mosses, as well as ferns (Figure **1.20**) and flowering plants (Figure **1.21**).

Ⓢ Ferns

Ferns have leaves called fronds. They do not produce flowers, but reproduce by means of spores produced on the underside of the fronds.

Characteristics:

♦ plants with roots, stems and leaves
♦ have leaves called fronds
♦ do not produce flowers
♦ reproduce by spores

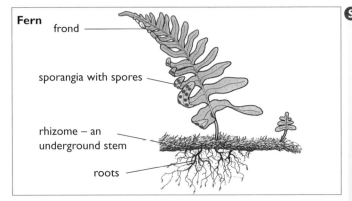

Figure 1.20   An example of a fern.

Flowering plants

These are the plants that are most familiar to us. They can be tiny, or very large – many trees are flowering plants.

Characteristics:

♦ plants with roots, stems and leaves
♦ reproduce sexually by means of flowers and seeds
♦ seeds are produced inside the ovary, in the flower

Flowering plants can be divided into two main groups, the monocotyledonous plants and the dicotyledonous plants, often abbreviated to monocots and dicots (Figure **1.21**). Monocots have only one cotyledon in their seeds (page 205). They usually have a branching root system, and often have leaves in which the veins run in parallel to one another. Dicots have two cotyledons in their seeds. They frequently have a tap root system, and their leaves are often broader than those of monocots, and have a network of branching veins.

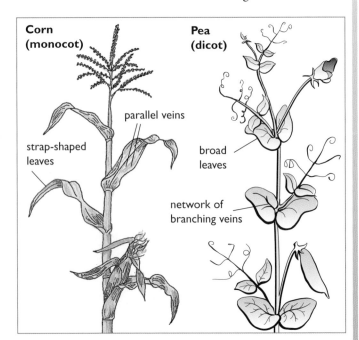

Figure 1.21   Flowering plants.

Activity 1.1
Making biological drawings

Skill
AO3.3 Observing, measuring and recording

Biologists need to be able to look closely at specimens – which might be whole organisms, or just part of an organism – and note significant features of them. It is also important to be able to make simple drawings to record these features. You don't have be good at art to be good at biological drawings. A biological drawing needs to be simple but clear.

You will be provided with a specimen of an animal to draw.

1   Look carefully at the specimen, and decide what group of animals it belongs to. Jot down the features of the organism that helped you to classify it.

2   Make a large, clear drawing of your organism.

Here are some points to bear in mind when you draw.

♦ Make good use of the space on your sheet of paper – your drawing should be large. However, do leave space around it so that you have room for labels.

♦ Always use a sharp HB pencil and have a good eraser with you.

♦ Keep all lines single and clear.

♦ Don't use shading unless it is absolutely necessary.

♦ Don't use colours.

♦ Take time to get the outline of your drawing correct first, showing the right proportions.

♦ Now label your drawing to show the features of the organism that are characteristic of its classification group. You could also label any features that help the organism to survive in its environment. These are called **adaptations**. For example, if your organism is a fish, you could label 'scales overlapping backwards, to provide a smooth, streamlined surface for sliding through the water'.

Here are some points to bear in mind when you label a diagram.

♦ Use a ruler to draw each label line.

♦ Make sure the end of the label line actually touches the structure being labelled.

♦ Write the labels horizontally.

♦ Keep the labels well away from the edges of your drawing.

Activity 1.2
Calculating magnification

Skill
A03.3 Observing, measuring and recording

Drawings of biological specimens are usually made at a different size from the real thing. It is important to show this on the diagram. The magnification of a diagram is how much larger it is than the real thing.

$$\text{magnification} = \frac{\text{size of drawing}}{\text{size of real object}}$$

For example, measure the length of the spider's body in the diagram below. You should find that it is 40 mm long.

The real spider was 8 mm long. So we can calculate the magnification like this:

$$\text{magnification} = \frac{\text{length in drawing}}{\text{length of real spider}}$$

$$= \frac{40}{8}$$

$$= \times 5$$

The following are two very important things to notice.

♦ You must use the same units for all the measurements. Usually, millimetres are the best units to use.
♦ You should not include any units with the final answer. Magnification does not have a unit. However, you *must* include the 'times' sign. If you read it out loud, you would say 'times five'.

❓ Questions

A1 Measure the length of the lowest 'tail' (it is really called an appendage) on the centipede below. Write your answer in millimetres.
A2 The real length of the appendage was 10 mm. Use this, and your answer to question **A1**, to calculate the magnification of the drawing of the centipede.

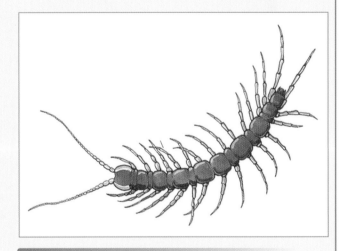

Study tip

Be prepared to use the magnification equation organised in a different way:

$$\text{size of real object} = \frac{\text{size of drawing}}{\text{magnification}}.$$

1.7 Keys

If you want to identify an organism whose name you do not know, you may be able to find a picture of it in a book. However, not every organism may be pictured, or your organism may not look exactly like any of the pictures. If this happens, you can often find a key that you can use to work out what your organism is.

A key is a way of leading you through to the name of your organism by giving you two descriptions at a time, and asking you to choose between them. Each choice you make then leads you on to another pair of descriptions, until you end up with the name of your organism. This kind of key is called a dichotomous key. 'Dichotomous' means 'branching into two', and refers to the fact that you have two descriptions to choose from at each step.

Here is a key that you could use to identify the organisms shown in Figure 1.22.

1	jointed limbs	2
	no jointed limbs	earthworm
2	more than 5 pairs of jointed limbs	centipede
	5 or fewer pairs of jointed limbs	3
3	first pair of limbs form large claws	crab
	no large claws	4
4	3 pairs of limbs	locust
	4 pairs of limbs	spider

To use the key, pick **one** of the animals that you are going to identify. Let's say you choose organism **B**. Decide which description in step **1** matches your organism. It has jointed limbs, so the key tells us to go to step **2**. Decide which description in step **2** matches organism **B**. It has more than 5 pairs of jointed limbs, so it is a centipede.

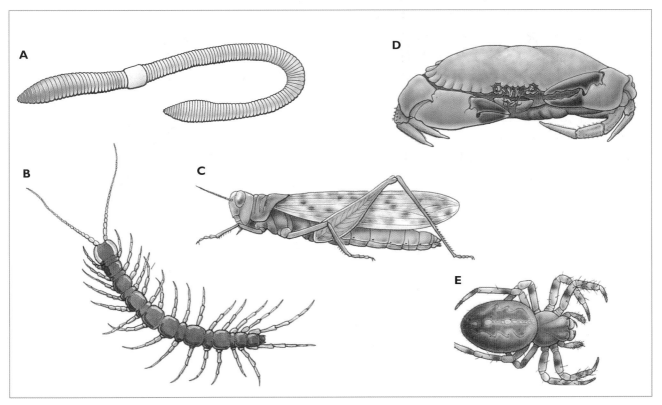

Figure 1.22 Organisms for practising using a key.

Constructing keys

Using a key is quite easy, but writing your own key is much more of a challenge.

Let's say you want to write a key to enable someone to identify each of the four flowers in Figure **1.20**.

First, make a list of features that clearly vary between the flowers. They should be features that cannot possibly be mistaken. Remember that the person using the key will probably only have one of the flowers to look at, so they cannot necessarily compare it with another kind of flower. So the number of petals or the colour is a good choice, but the size (large or small) is not, because different people might have different ideas about what is 'large' or 'small'.

Now choose one of these features that can split the flowers into two groups. The two groups don't have to be the same size – you could have two in one group and two in the other, or perhaps one in one group and the rest in the other.

Now concentrate on a group that contains more than one flower. Choose another feature that will allow you to split the flowers into two further groups. Keep doing this until each 'group' contains only one flower.

Now go back and refine your key. Think carefully about the wording of each pair of statements. Make sure that each pair is made up of two clear alternatives. Try to reduce your key to the smallest possible number of statement pairs.

Finally, try your key out on a friend. If they have any problems with it, then try to reword or restructure your key to make it easier to use.

Figure 1.23 Can you write a key to identify these flowers?

Summary

You should know:

♦ the seven characteristics that distinguish living things from non-living objects
♦ why it is important to classify organisms
♦ about the binomial system of naming organisms
Ⓢ ♦ how DNA base sequences help with classification
♦ the characteristic features of animals (including arthropods and vertebrates) and plants
Ⓢ ♦ the features of ferns and flowering plants (dicotyledons and monocotyledons)
♦ the features of bacteria, fungi and protoctists, and the problems of classifying viruses
♦ how to make good biological drawings and calculate magnification
♦ how to use a dichotomous key to identify an unknown organism
♦ how to construct a dichotomous key.

End-of-chapter questions

1   a   Without looking back at the beginning of this chapter, decide which **five** of these characteristics are found in all living things.

movement	blood system	sight	growth	photosynthesis
nutrition	sensitivity	speech	excretion	

   b   List the other **two** characteristics of all living organisms.

2   Three species of tree have the following binomials: *Carpodiptera africana, Commiphora africana, Commiphora angolensis*

Which **two** of these species do biologists consider to be the most closely related?
Explain your answer.

3   Construct a table to compare the characteristic features of animals and plants.

S 4   Construct a dichotomous key to help someone to identify **five** of your teachers.
Try to meet these criteria:

- each pair of characteristics describes one contrasting feature
- each person could be identified without having to compare them with another person
- the key contains no more than four pairs of points (you may be able to do it with just three pairs).

When you have finished, swap your key with someone else to check if it works. If not, make adjustments to it.

5   The photograph shows a section through a fruit.

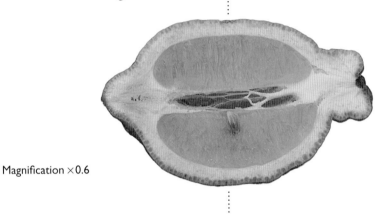

Magnification ×0.6

   a   Make a large diagram of the fruit. You do not need to label your diagram.   [5]
   b   Calculate the diameter of the actual fruit at the point indicated by the dotted line.
       Show your working, and remember to include the unit.   [3]

S 6   The diagram shows a virus.

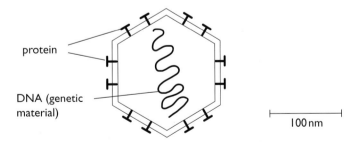

protein

DNA (genetic
material)

100 nm

   a   With reference to the diagram, and your own knowledge, discuss whether or not viruses can
       be considered to be living organisms.   [5]
   b   1 nm (nanometre) is 10^{-9} m. Measure the length of the scale bar. Use this, and the label on the
       scale bar, to calculate the magnification of the diagram. Show your working.   [3]

2 Cells

In this chapter, you will find out about:

♦ the structure of plant cells and animal cells
♦ the functions of the different parts of cells
♦ tissues, organs and organ systems.

Cells from deep time

If a long, thin spike of limestone hanging down from the roof of a cave is called a stalactite, what do you call a long, thin drip of bacteria-filled slime?

Caver Jim Pisarowicz decided to call them snottites, and the name stuck (Figure 2.1). Snottites are studied by biologists interested in organisms that can live in environments so strange that almost nothing else can live there. These organisms are called extremophiles, which means 'lovers of extreme conditions'.

Snottites are found in caves where the atmosphere contains large amounts of the smelly, toxic gas hydrogen sulfide. The bacteria in the slimy threads, far from being poisoned by the gas, actually use it to make their food. In the middle of the threads, there is virtually no oxygen, yet some kinds of bacteria live even here.

Similar conditions – a lot of hydrogen sulfide, almost no oxygen – were found in the Earth's very early atmosphere, more than 3.5 billion years ago, and this is probably when these extremophile bacteria first evolved. At that time, the cells of all organisms were much less complex than those of plants and animals (which did not appear on Earth until around 2 billion years ago). They had no nucleus, for example. Yet bacteria made of these seemingly simple cells are clearly very successful, if they have managed to survive almost unchanged through such an unimaginably long period of time.

Figure 2.1 Snottites hanging from the roof of a cave.

2.1 Cell structure

All organisms are made of cells. Cells are very small, so large organisms contain millions of cells. Some organisms are unicellular, which means that they are made of just a single cell. Bacteria and yeast are examples of single-celled organisms.

Microscopes

To see cells clearly, you need to use a microscope (Figure 2.2). The kind of microscope used in a school laboratory is called a light microscope because it shines light through the piece of animal or plant you are looking at. It uses glass lenses to magnify and focus the image. A very good light microscope can magnify about 1500 times, so that all the structures in Figures 2.3 and 2.4 can be seen.

Photomicrographs of plant and animal cells are shown in Figure 2.5 and Figure 2.6. A photomicrograph is a picture made using a light microscope.

To see even smaller things inside a cell, an electron microscope is used. This uses a beam of electrons instead of light, and can magnify up to 500 000 times. This means that a lot more detail can be seen inside a cell. We can see many structures more clearly, and also some structures that could not be seen at all with a light microscope.

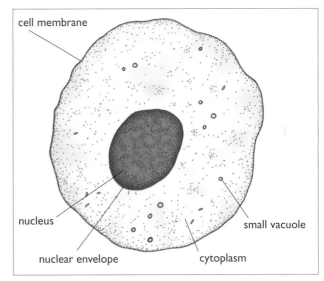

Figure 2.3 A typical animal cell – a liver cell – as seen with a light microscope.

? Questions

2.1 How many times can a good light microscope magnify?

2.2 If an object was 1mm across, how big would it look if it was magnified 10 times?

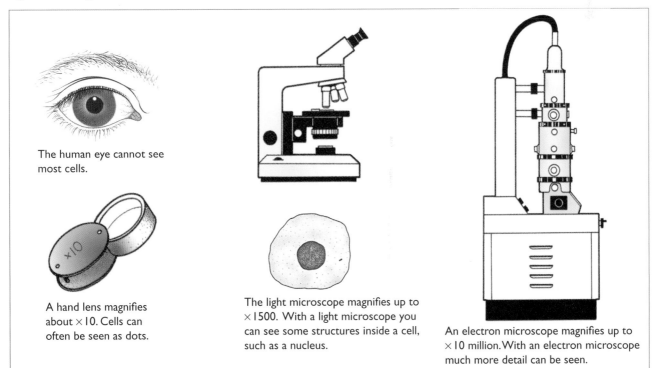

The human eye cannot see most cells.

A hand lens magnifies about ×10. Cells can often be seen as dots.

The light microscope magnifies up to ×1500. With a light microscope you can see some structures inside a cell, such as a nucleus.

An electron microscope magnifies up to ×10 million. With an electron microscope much more detail can be seen.

Figure 2.2 Equipment used for looking at biological material.

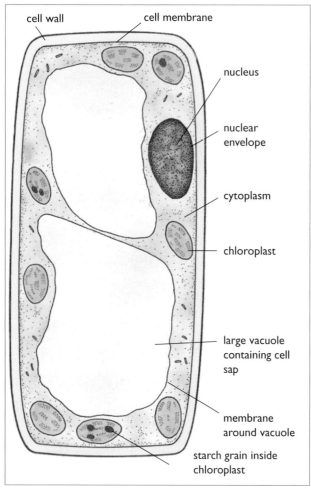

Figure 2.4 A typical plant cell – a palisade mesophyll cell – as seen with a light microscope.

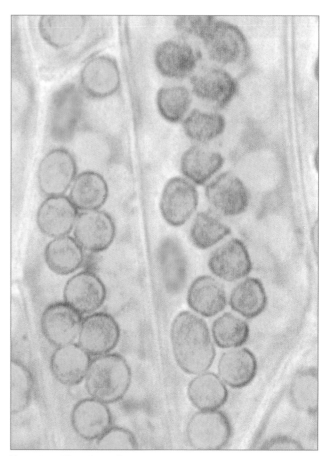

Figure 2.5 Many plant cells contain green structures, called chloroplasts. Even if it does not have any chloroplasts, you can still identify a plant cell because it has a cell wall around it (×2000).

Cell membrane

Whatever sort of animal or plant they come from, all cells have a **cell membrane** (sometimes called the cell surface membrane) around the outside. Inside the cell membrane is a jelly-like substance called **cytoplasm**, in which are found many small structures called **organelles**. The most obvious of these organelles is usually the **nucleus**. In a plant cell, it is very difficult to see, because it is right against the cell wall.

The cell membrane is a very thin layer of protein and fat. It is very important to the cell because it controls what goes in and out of it. It is said to be **partially permeable**, which means that it will let some substances through but not others.

Cell wall

All plant cells are surrounded by a cell wall made mainly of **cellulose**. Paper, which is made from cell walls, is

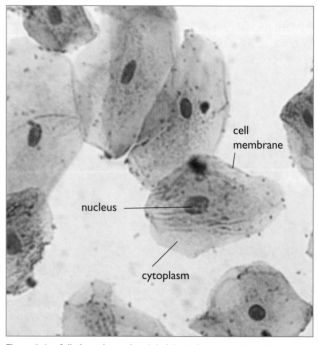

Figure 2.6 Cells from the trachea (windpipe) of a mammal, seen through a light microscope (×300).

also made of cellulose. Animal cells never have cell walls made of cellulose. Cellulose belongs to a group of substances called polysaccharides, which are described in Chapter 4. Cellulose forms fibres which criss-cross over one another to form a very strong covering to the cell (Figure 2.7). This helps to protect and support the cell. If the cell absorbs a lot of water and swells, the cell wall stops it bursting.

Because of the spaces between fibres, even very large molecules are able to go through the cellulose cell wall. It is therefore said to be fully permeable.

Cytoplasm

Cytoplasm is a clear jelly. It is nearly all water; about 70% is water in many cells. It contains many substances dissolved in it, especially proteins. Many different metabolic reactions (the chemical reactions of life) take place in the cytoplasm.

Vacuoles

A vacuole is a space in a cell, surrounded by a membrane, and containing a solution. Plant cells have very large vacuoles, which contain a solution of sugars and other substances, called cell sap. A full vacuole presses outwards on the rest of the cell, and helps to keep it in shape. Animal cells have much smaller membrane-bound spaces, called vesicles, which may contain food or water.

Chloroplasts

Chloroplasts are never found in animal cells, but most of the cells in the green parts of plants have them. They contain the green colouring or pigment called chlorophyll. Chlorophyll absorbs energy from sunlight, and this energy is then used for making food for the plant by photosynthesis (Chapter 6).

Chloroplasts often contain starch grains, which have been made by photosynthesis. Animal cells never contain starch grains. Some animal cells, however, do have granules (tiny grains) of another substance similar to starch, called glycogen. These granules are found in the cytoplasm, not inside chloroplasts.

Nucleus

The nucleus is where the genetic information is stored. This helps the cell to make the right sorts of proteins. The information is kept on the chromosomes, which are inherited from the organism's parents. The chromosomes are made of DNA.

Chromosomes are very long, but so thin that they cannot easily be seen even using the electron microscope. However, when the cell is dividing, they become short and thick, and can be seen with a good light microscope.

Table 2.1 compares some features of plant cells and animal cells.

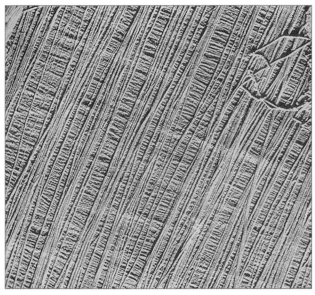

Figure 2.7   Cellulose fibres from a plant cell wall. This picture was taken using an electron microscope (×50 000).

Plant cells	Animal cells
have a cellulose cell wall outside the cell membrane	have no cell wall
have a cell membrane	have a cell membrane
have cytoplasm	have cytoplasm
have a nucleus	have a nucleus
often have chloroplasts containing chlorophyll	have no chloroplasts
often have large vacuoles containing cell sap	have only small vacuoles
often have starch grains	never have starch grains; sometimes have glycogen granules
often regular in shape	often irregular in shape

Table 2.1   A comparison of plant and animal cells.

Ⓢ Mitochondria

Photographs of cells taken using an electron microscope, called electronmicrographs, show tiny structures that are almost invisible with a light microscope. They are called mitochondria (singular: mitochondrion). Mitochondria are found in almost all cells, except those of prokaryotes. Figures **2.8** and **2.9** show electronmicrographs of mitochondria.

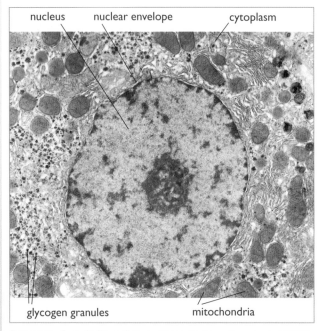

Figure 2.8 Part of a liver cell seen using an electron microscope (×20 000).

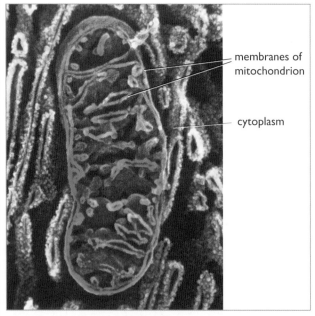

Figure 2.9 Close-up of a mitochondrion. Electron microscopes only show images in black and white, so this photo has been artificially coloured (×30 000).

Mitochondria are the powerhouses of the cell. Inside Ⓢ them, oxygen is used to release energy from glucose, in the process called aerobic respiration. You will find out more about aerobic respiration in Chapter **11**.

Not surprisingly, cells that use a lot of energy have a lot of mitochondria. Muscle cells, for example, are tightly packed with mitochondria. Sperm cells, which need energy to swim to the egg, and neurones (nerve cells), which need energy to transmit impulses, also have large numbers of mitochondria.

The black spots in the electron micrograph in Figure **2.8** are granules of a carbohydrate called glycogen. This is similar to starch. (Starch is never found in animal cells – they store glycogen instead.) Glycogen is a reserve fuel. When required, it can be broken down to glucose, to be used as a fuel by the mitochondria in the liver cell, or transported in the blood to other cells that need it.

Ribosomes

Even tinier structures than mitochondria can just be seen with an electron microscope (Figure **2.10**). They are called ribosomes. They look like tiny dots attached to a network of membranes that runs throughout the cytoplasm. This network is called the rough endoplasmic reticulum. Ribosomes may also just be scattered freely in the cytoplasm. Ribosomes are found in all types of cells – bacteria, protoctists, fungi, animals and plants all have ribosomes in their cells.

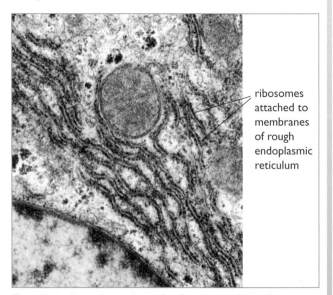

Figure 2.10 You can just make out tiny ribosomes attached to the membranes in this electron micrograph of a cell (×30 000).

Although they are so tiny that we can scarcely see them even with an electron microscope, ribosomes have a very important function in a cell. They are the places where proteins are made, by joining amino acids together in a long chain. This is done according to instructions carried on the DNA in the cell's nucleus, which specify the sequence of amino acids that should be strung together to make a particular protein. You can read more about this in Chapter 4.

Micrometres

Cells, and structures inside them such as mitochondria and ribosomes, are so small that we need a very small unit in which to measure them. The most useful one is the micrometre, symbol μm.

$$1\,\mu m = 1 \times 10^{-6}\,m$$
$$1\,m = 10^{6}\,\mu m$$

Questions

2.3 How many micrometres are there in 1 cm?

2.4 How many micrometres are there in 1 mm?

2.5 The mitochondrion in Figure **2.9** is magnified 20 000 times.

  a Using a ruler, carefully measure the maximum length of the mitochondrion. Record your measurement in mm (millimetres).

  b Convert your answer to μm (micrometres).

  c Use the formula:

$$\text{real size in }\mu m = \frac{\text{size of the image in }\mu m}{\text{magnification}}$$

to calculate the real size of the mitochondrion in μm.

  d How many of these mitochondria could you line up end to end between two of the mm marks on your ruler?

Activity 2.1
Using a microscope

Practise using a microscope to look at very small things.

Activity 2.2
Looking at animal cells

Skills
AO3.1 Using techniques, apparatus and materials
AO3.3 Observing, measuring and recording

⚠ Wash your hands thoroughly after handling the trachea and cells.

Some simple animal cells line the mouth and trachea (or windpipe). If you colour or stain the cells, they are quite easy to see using a light microscope (see Figure **2.6** and Figure **2.11**).

1 Using a section lifter, gently rub off a little of the lining from the inside of the trachea provided.

2 Put your cells onto the middle of a clean microscope slide, and gently spread them out. You will probably not be able to see anything at all at this stage.

3 Put on a few drops of methylene blue.

4 Gently lower a coverslip over the stained cells, trying not to trap any air bubbles.

5 Use filter paper or blotting paper to clean up the slide, and then look at it under the low power of a microscope.

6 Make a labelled drawing of a few cells.

Questions

A1 Which part of the cell stained the darkest blue?

A2 Is the cell membrane permeable or impermeable to methylene blue? Explain how you worked out your answer.

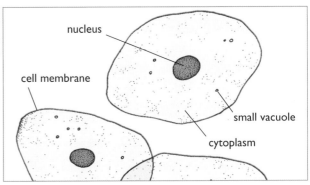

Figure 2.11 A drawing of tracheal cells seen through a light microscope.

Activity 2.3
Looking at plant cells

Skills
AO3.1 Using techniques, apparatus and materials
AO3.3 Observing, measuring and recording

 Take care with the sharp blade when cutting the onion.

To be able to see cells clearly under a microscope, you need a very thin layer. It is best if it is only one cell thick. An easy place to find such a layer is inside an onion bulb.

1   Cut a small piece from an onion bulb, and use forceps to peel a small piece of thin skin, called epidermis, from the inside of it. Do not let it get dry.
2   Put a drop or two of water onto the centre of a clean microscope slide. Put the piece of epidermis into it, and spread it flat.
3   Gently lower a coverslip onto it.
4   Use filter paper or blotting paper to clean up the slide, and then look at it under the low power of a microscope.
5   Make a labelled drawing of a few cells. Figure **2.12** may help you, but do not just copy it. Do remember not to colour your drawing.
6   Using a pipette, take up a small amount of iodine solution. Very carefully place some iodine solution next to the edge of the coverslip. The iodine solution will seep under the edge of the coverslip. To help it do this, you can place a small piece of filter paper next to the opposite side of the coverslip, which will soak up some of the liquid and draw it through.
7   Look at the slide under the low power of the microscope. Note any differences between what you can see now and what it looked like before adding the iodine solution.

Questions

A1 Name **two** structures which you can see in these cells, but which you could not see in the tracheal cells (Activity **2.2**).
A2 Most plant cells have chloroplasts, but these onion cells do not. Suggest a reason for this.
A3 Iodine solution turns blue-black in the presence of starch. Did any of the onion cells contain starch?

Questions

2.6   What sort of cells are surrounded by a cell membrane?
2.7   What are plant cell walls made of?
2.8   What does fully permeable mean?
2.9   What does partially permeable mean?
2.10 What is the main constituent of cytoplasm?
2.11 What is a vacuole?
2.12 What is cell sap?
2.13 Chloroplasts contain chlorophyll. What does chlorophyll do?
2.14 What is stored in the nucleus?
2.15 Why can chromosomes be seen only when a cell is dividing?

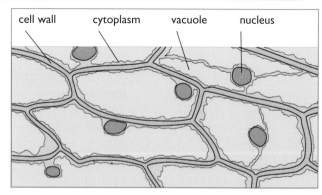

Figure 2.12   A drawing of onion epidermis cells seen through a light microscope after staining with iodine.

Questions

2.16 Which types of cells contain mitochondria?
2.17 Outline the function of mitochondria.
2.18 Which types of cells contain ribosomes?
2.19 Outline the function of ribosomes.

2.2 Cells and organisms

A large organism such as yourself may contain many millions of cells, but not all the cells are alike. Almost all of them can carry out the activities which are characteristic of living things, but many of them specialise in doing some of these better than other cells do. Muscle cells, for example, are specially adapted for movement. Most cells in the leaf of a plant are specially adapted for making food by photosynthesis.

Table **2.2** lists examples of specialised cells, and the parts of the book where you will find information about how their structures help them to carry out their functions.

Tissues

Often, cells which specialise in the same activity are found together. A group of cells like this is called a tissue. An example of a tissue is a layer of cells lining your stomach. These cells make enzymes to help to digest your food (Figure **2.13**).

The stomach also contains other tissues. For example, there is a layer of muscle in the stomach wall, made of cells which can move. This muscle tissue makes the wall of the stomach move in and out, churning the food and mixing it up with the enzymes.

Plants also have tissues. You may already have looked at some epidermis tissue from an onion bulb. Inside a leaf, a layer of cells makes up the palisade tissue, in which the cells are specialised to carry out photosynthesis.

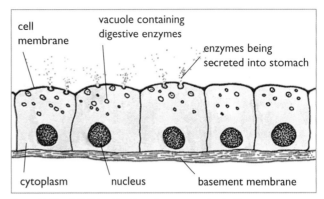

Figure 2.13 Cells lining the stomach – an example of a tissue.

Organs

All tissues in the stomach work together, although each has its own job to do. A group of tissues like this makes up an organ. The stomach is an organ. Other organs include the heart, the kidneys and the lungs.

In a plant, an onion bulb is an organ. A leaf is another example of a plant organ.

Organ systems

The stomach is only one of the organs which help in the digestion of food. The mouth, the intestines and the stomach are all part of the digestive system. The heart is part of the circulatory system, while each kidney is part of the excretory system.

The way in which organisms are built up can be summarised like this: cells make up tissues, which make up organs, which make up organ systems, which make up organisms. For example, the ciliated cells in Figure **2.14** make up a tissue that is part of an organ (the bronchus), which is part of the respiratory system which is part of the organism or person.

Type of cell	Where it is found	Function	Where you can find out more
ciliated cell	lining the trachea and bronchi	move mucus upward	page 145
root hair cells	near the ends of plant roots	absorb water and mineral salts	page 96–97
xylem vessels	in stems, roots and leaves of plants	transport water and mineral salts; help in support	page 94
palisade mesophyll cells	beneath the epidermis of a leaf	photosynthesis	page 60
nerve cells	throughout the bodies of animals	transmit information in the form of electrical impulses	page 162
red blood cells	in the blood of mammals	transport oxygen	page 117
sperm and egg cells	in testes and ovaries	fuse together to produce a zygote	page 214

Table 2.2 Some examples of specialised cells.

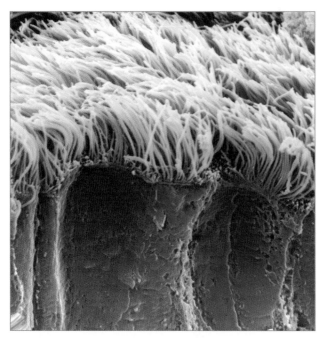

Figure 2.14 These cells make up a tissue lining the bronchus (a tube that carries air into the lungs). The tiny 'hairs' are called cilia.

Key definitions

tissue – a group of cells with similar structures, working together to perform a shared function

organ – a structure made up of a group of tissues, working together to perform specific functions

organ system – a group of organs with related functions, working together to perform body functions

Summary

You should know:
- ◆ the structure of an animal cell and a plant cell as seen using a microscope, and be able to compare them
- ◆ the functions of the different parts of animal cells and plant cells
- ◆ how cells are organised into tissues, organs and organ systems
- Ⓢ ◆ how to calculate magnification using μm (micrometres).

End-of-chapter questions

1 Arrange these structures in order of size, beginning with the smallest:

   stomach   mitochondrion   starch grain   tracheal cell   nucleus

2 For each of the following, state whether it is an organelle, a cell, a tissue, an organ, an organ system, or an organism.

  a   heart
  b   trachea
  c   onion epidermis
  d   onion bulb
  e   onion plant
  f   human being
  g   lung

3   State which part of a plant cell:
    a   makes food by photosynthesis
    b   releases energy from food
    c   controls what goes in and out of the cell
    d   stores information about making proteins
    e   contains cell sap
    f   protects the outside of the cell.

4   Distinguish between each pair of terms.
    a   chloroplast, chlorophyll
    b   cell wall, cell membrane
    c   organelle, organ

5   The diagram shows two cells.

Cell **A**

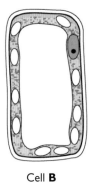

Cell **B**

    a   i   State where, in a human, a cell of type **A** would normally be found.   [1]
         ii   State where, in a plant, a cell of type **B** would be found.   [1]
    b   Use only words from the list to copy and complete the statements about cell **B**.

air	cellulose	chloroplasts	membrane	mitochondria
nucleus	starch	vacuole	wall	cell sap

         Cell **B** has a thick outer layer called the cell .... This is made of .... The cytoplasm
         of cell **B** contains many .... that are used in the process of photosynthesis. The large
         permanent .... is full of .... and this helps to maintain the shape of the cell.   [5]

    [Adapted from Cambridge IGCSE® Biology 0610/21, Question 1, May/June 2010]

3 Movement in and out of cells

In this chapter, you will find out about:

♦ diffusion
♦ osmosis
♦ why diffusion and osmosis are important to cells and organisms
♦ active transport.

Diffusion spreads a deceptive scent

Like most brightly-coloured flowers, fly orchids rely on insects to transfer their pollen from one flower to another (Figure 3.1). The pollen contains the male gametes, so the insects help the male gametes to reach the female gametes in another flower, so that fertilisation can take place.

But insects do not perform this service out of kindness. Many flowers persuade insects to pollinate them by providing sweet nectar, or lots of spare protein-rich pollen for the insects to eat.

Not so the fly orchid. This flower uses deception to attract male digger wasps.

Female digger wasps produce a chemical whose molecules diffuse through the air for long distances. The chemical, called a pheromone, is sensed by male digger wasps, which follow it up its concentration gradient to its source. There, hopefully, they will find a female wasp with which they can mate.

Fly orchids produce a very similar chemical, which diffuses outwards from the flower. Male digger wasps sense and react to it just as they do to the pheromone of the female wasps. When they arrive at its source, they try to mate – but unfortunately for the males, this source isn't a female wasp, but an orchid flower.

As they try to mate, the wasps pick up pollen from the flower. They don't seem to learn by their mistake, but continue to visit other orchid flowers, leaving orchid pollen behind as they try to mate with them.

Figure 3.1 A male digger wasp tries to mate with a fly orchid flower.

3.1 Diffusion

Atoms, molecules and ions are always moving. The higher the temperature, the faster they move. In a solid substance the particles cannot move very far, because they are held together by attractive forces between them. In a liquid they can move more freely, knocking into one another and rebounding. In a gas they are freer still, with no attractive forces between the molecules or atoms. Molecules and ions can also move freely when they are in solution.

When they can move freely, particles tend to spread themselves out as evenly as they can (Figure **3.2**). This happens with gases, solutions, and mixtures of liquids. Imagine, for example, a rotten egg in one corner of a room, giving off hydrogen sulfide gas. To begin with, there will be a very high concentration of the gas near the egg, but none in the rest of the room. However, before long the hydrogen sulfide molecules have spread throughout the air in the room. Soon, you will not be able to tell where the smell first came from – the whole room will smell of hydrogen sulfide.

The hydrogen sulfide molecules have spread out, or diffused, through the air.

Diffusion and living organisms.

Living organisms obtain many of their requirements by diffusion. They also get rid of many of their waste products in this way. For example, plants need carbon

dioxide for photosynthesis. This diffuses from the air into the leaves, through the stomata. It does this because there is a lower concentration of carbon dioxide inside the leaf, as the cells are using it up. Outside the leaf in the air, there is a higher concentration. Carbon dioxide molecules therefore diffuse into the leaf, down this concentration gradient.

Oxygen, which is a waste product of photosynthesis, diffuses out in the same way. There is a higher concentration of oxygen inside the leaf, because it is being made there. Oxygen therefore diffuses out through the stomata into the air.

Diffusion is also important in gas exchange for respiration in animals and plants (Figure **3.3**). Cell membranes are freely permeable to oxygen and carbon dioxide, so these easily diffuse into and out of cells.

Some of the products of digestion are absorbed from the ileum of mammals by diffusion (page **85–86**), and we have already seen that flowering plants use diffusion to attract pollinators like bees and wasps.

Figure 3.2 Diffusion is the result of the random movement of particles.

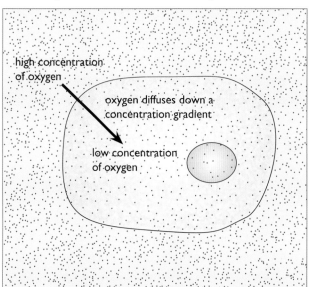

Figure 3.3 Diffusion of oxygen into a cell. The red dots represent oxygen molecules.

Questions

⑤ 3.1 Define diffusion.

3.2 List **three** examples of diffusion in living organisms.

3.3 You will need to think about your knowledge of particle theory to answer this question.

   a What effect does an increase in temperature have on the kinetic energy of molecules of a gas or a solute?

   b Predict and explain how an increase in temperature will affect the rate of diffusion of a solute.

Activity 3.1
Demonstrating diffusion in a solution

Skill

AO3.3 Observing, measuring and recording

1 Fill a gas jar with water. Leave it for several hours to let the water become very still.
2 Carefully place a small crystal of potassium permanganate into the water.
3 Make a labelled drawing of the gas jar to show how the colour is distributed at the start of your experiment.
4 Leave the gas jar completely undisturbed for several days.
5 Make a second drawing to show how the colour is distributed.

You can try this with other coloured salts as well, such as copper sulfate or potassium dichromate.

Questions

A1 Why was it important to leave the water to become completely still before the crystal was put in?

A2 Why had the colour spread through the water at the end of your experiment?

A3 Suggest **three** things that you could have done to make the colour spread more quickly.

Activity 3.2
Investigating factors that affect the rate ⑤ of diffusion

3.2 Osmosis

Water is one of the most important compounds in living organisms. It can make up around 80% of some organisms' bodies. It has many functions, including acting as a **solvent** for many different substances. For example, substances are transported around the body dissolved in the water in blood plasma.

Every cell in an organism's body has water inside it and outside it. Various substances are dissolved in this water, and their concentrations may be different inside and outside the cell. This creates concentration gradients, down which water and solutes will diffuse, if they are able to pass through the membrane.

It's easiest to think about this if we consider a simple situation involving just one solute.

Figure **3.4** illustrates a concentrated sugar solution, separated from a dilute sugar solution by a membrane. The membrane has holes or pores in it which are very small. An example of a membrane like this is Visking tubing.

Water molecules are also very small. Each one is made of two hydrogen atoms and one oxygen atom. Sugar molecules are many times larger than this. In Visking tubing, the holes are big enough to let the water molecules through, but not the sugar molecules. Visking tubing is called a **partially permeable** membrane because it will let some molecules through but not others.

There is a higher concentration of sugar molecules on the right-hand side of the membrane in Figure **3.4**, and a lower concentration on the left-hand side. If the membrane was not there, the sugar molecules would diffuse from the concentrated solution into the dilute one until they were evenly spread out. However, they cannot do this because the pores in the membrane are too small for them to get through.

There is also a concentration gradient for the water molecules. On the left-hand side of the membrane, there is a high concentration of water molecules. On the

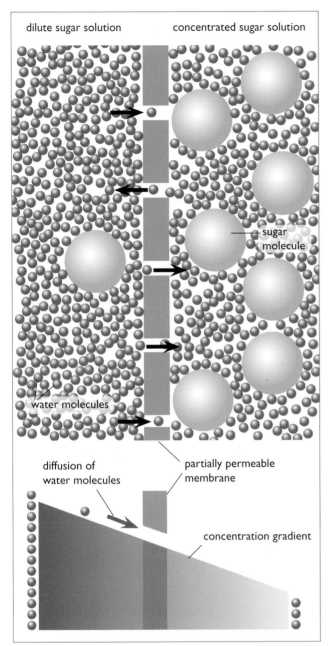

dilute sugar solution   concentrated sugar solution

sugar
molecule

water molecules

diffusion of
water molecules

partially permeable
membrane

concentration gradient

Figure 3.4 Osmosis.

right-hand side, the concentration of water molecules is lower because a lot of space is taken up by sugar molecules.

Because there are more water molecules on the left hand side, at any one moment more of them will 'hit' a hole in the membrane and move through to the other side than will go the other way (right to left). Over time, there will be an overall, or net, movement of water from left to right. This is called osmosis.

You can see that osmosis is really just a kind of diffusion. It is the diffusion of water molecules, in a situation where the water molecules but not the solute molecules can pass through a membrane.

It is actually rather confusing to talk about the 'concentration' of water molecules, because the term 'concentration' is normally used to mean the concentration of the solute dissolved in the water. It is much better to use a different term instead. We say that a dilute solution (where there is a lot of water) has a high water potential. A concentrated solution (where there is less water) has a low water potential.

In Figure **3.4**, there is a high water potential on the left-hand side and a low water potential on the right-hand side. There is a water potential gradient between the two sides. The water molecules diffuse down this gradient, from a high water potential to a low water potential.

⑤

❓ Questions

3.4 Which is larger – a water molecule or a sugar molecule?

3.5 What is meant by a partially permeable membrane?

3.6 Give **two** examples of partially permeable membranes.

3.7 How would you describe a solution that has a high concentration of water molecules?

Key definition

⑤ osmosis – the diffusion of water molecules from a region of higher water potential (dilute solution) to a region of lower water potential (concentrated solution), through a partially permeable membrane

Cell membranes

Cell membranes behave very much like Visking tubing. They let some substances pass through them, but not others. They are partially permeable membranes.

There is always cytoplasm on one side of any cell membrane. Cytoplasm is a solution of proteins and other substances in water. There is usually a solution on the other side of the membrane, too. Inside large animals, cells are surrounded by tissue fluid (page 122). In the soil, the roots of plants are often surrounded by a film of water.

So, cell membranes often separate two different solutions – the cytoplasm, and the solution around the cell. If the solutions are of different concentrations, then osmosis will occur.

Activity 3.3
Diffusion of substances through a membrane

Skills
AO3.1 Using techniques, apparatus and materials
AO3.3 Observing, measuring and recording
AO3.4 Interpreting and evaluating observations and data

You are going to investigate diffusion of two different substances dissolved in water (solutes). When a substance is dissolved, its particles are free to move around.

In this investigation, you will use starch solution and iodine solution. The solutions will be separated by a membrane made out of Visking tubing. Visking tubing has microscopic holes in it. The holes are big enough to let water molecules and iodine molecules through, but not starch molecules, which are bigger than the holes.

1   Collect a piece of Visking tubing. Moisten it and rub it until it opens.
2   Tie a knot in one end of the tubing.
3   Using a pipette, carefully fill the tubing with some starch solution.
4   Tie the top of the tubing very tightly, using thread.
5   Rinse the tubing in water, just in case you got any starch on the outside of it.
6   Put some iodine solution into a beaker.
7   Gently put the Visking tubing into the iodine solution, so that it is completely covered, as shown in the diagram.
8   Leave the apparatus for about 10 minutes.

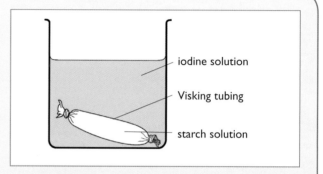

iodine solution

Visking tubing

starch solution

? Questions

A1 What colour were the liquids inside and outside the tubing at the start of the experiment?
A2 What colour were the liquids inside and outside the tubing at the end of the investigation?
A3 When starch and iodine mix, a blue-black colour is produced. Where did the starch and iodine mix in your experiment?
A4 Did either the starch particles or the iodine particles diffuse through the Visking tubing? How can you tell?
A5 Copy and complete these sentences.
    At the start of the experiment, there were starch molecules inside the tubing but none outside the tubing. Starch particles are too .... to go through Visking tubing.
    At the start of the experiment, there were iodine molecules .... the tubing but none .... the tubing. The iodine molecules diffused into the tubing, down their .... gradient.
    When the starch and iodine molecules mixed, a .... colour was produced.

Osmosis and animal cells

Figure **3.5** illustrates an animal cell in pure water. The cytoplasm inside the cell is a fairly concentrated solution. The proteins and many other substances dissolved in it are too large to get through the cell membrane. Water molecules, though, can get through.

If you compare this situation with Figure **3.4** (page **31**), you will see that they are similar. The dilute solution in Figure **3.4** and the pure water in Figure **3.5** are each separated from a concentrated solution by a partially permeable membrane. In Figure **3.5**, the concentrated solution is the cytoplasm and the partially permeable membrane is the cell membrane. Therefore, osmosis will occur.

Water molecules will diffuse from the dilute solution into the concentrated solution. What happens to the cell? As more and more water enters the cell, it swells. The cell membrane has to stretch as the cell gets bigger, until eventually the strain is too much, and the cell bursts.

Figure **3.6** illustrates an animal cell in a concentrated solution. If this solution is more concentrated than the cytoplasm, then water molecules will diffuse out of the cell. Look at Figure **3.4** (page **31**) to see why.

As the water molecules go out through the cell membrane, the cytoplasm shrinks. The cell shrivels up.

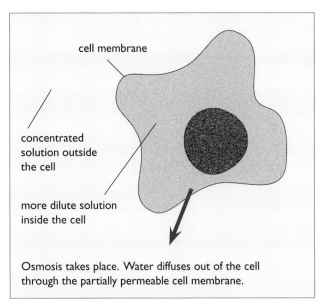

Osmosis takes place. Water diffuses out of the cell through the partially permeable cell membrane.

Figure 3.6 Animal cells shrink in a concentrated solution.

Osmosis and plant cells

Plant cells do not burst in pure water. Figure **3.7** illustrates a plant cell in pure water. Plant cells are surrounded by a cell wall. This is fully permeable, which means that it will let any molecules go through it.

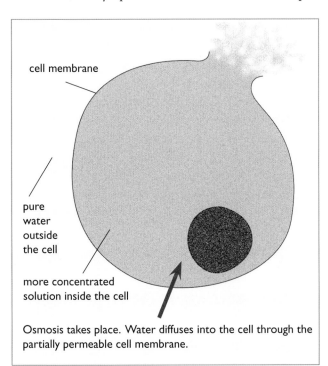

Osmosis takes place. Water diffuses into the cell through the partially permeable cell membrane.

Figure 3.5 Animal cells burst in pure water.

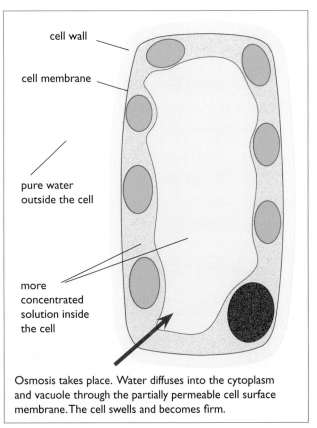

Osmosis takes place. Water diffuses into the cytoplasm and vacuole through the partially permeable cell surface membrane. The cell swells and becomes firm.

Figure 3.7 Plant cells become swollen and firm in pure water.

Although it is not easy to see, a plant cell also has a cell surface membrane just like an animal cell. The cell membrane is partially permeable. A plant cell in pure water will take in water by osmosis through its partially permeable cell membrane in the same way as an animal cell. As the water goes in, the cytoplasm and vacuole will swell.

However, the plant cell has a very strong cell wall around it. The cell wall is much stronger than the cell membrane and it stops the plant cell from bursting. The cytoplasm presses out against the cell wall, but the wall resists and presses back on the contents.

S A plant cell in this state is rather like a blown-up tyre – tight and firm. It is said to be **turgid**. The turgidity of its cells helps a plant that has no wood in it to stay upright, and keeps the leaves firm. Plant cells are usually turgid.

Figure **3.8** and Figure **3.9** illustrate a plant cell in a concentrated solution. Like the animal cell in Figure **3.6**, it will lose water by osmosis. The cytoplasm shrinks, and stops pushing outwards on the cell wall. Like a tyre when some of the air has leaked out, the cell becomes floppy. It is said to be **flaccid**. If the cells in a plant become flaccid, the plant loses its firmness and begins to wilt.

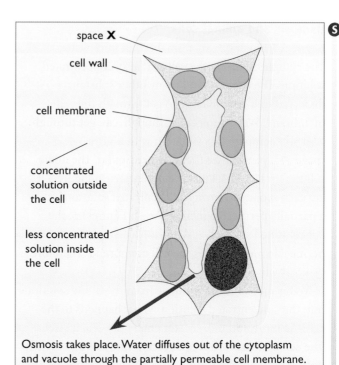

Osmosis takes place. Water diffuses out of the cytoplasm and vacuole through the partially permeable cell membrane. First, the cell shrinks slightly and becomes flaccid. Then the cell membrane pulls away from the cell wall, and the cell is plasmolysed.

Figure 3.9 Plant cells become flaccid and may plasmolyse in a concentrated solution.

If the solution is very concentrated, then a lot of water will diffuse out of the cell. The cytoplasm and vacuole go on shrinking. The cell wall, though, is too stiff to be able to shrink much. As the cytoplasm shrinks further and further into the centre of the cell, the cell wall gets left behind. The cell membrane, surrounding the cytoplasm, tears away from the cell wall.

A cell like this is said to be **plasmolysed**. This does not normally happen because plant cells are not usually surrounded by very concentrated solutions. However, you can make cells become plasmolysed if you do Activity **3.4**. Plasmolysis usually kills a plant cell because the cell membrane is damaged as it tears away from the cell wall.

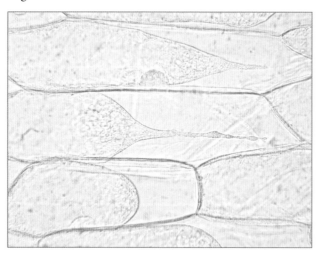

Figure 3.8 These onion cells have been placed in a concentrated solution. The cytoplasm has shrunk inwards, leaving big gaps between itself and the cell walls (×300).

Activity 3.4
Investigate and describe the effects on plant tissue of immersing them in different solutions

❓ Questions

3.8 What happens to an animal cell in pure water?

3.9 Explain why this does not happen to a plant cell in pure water.

3.10 Which part of a plant cell is:
  a fully permeable?
  b partially permeable?

❓ Questions ━━━━━━━━━━

Ⓢ 3.11 What is meant by a turgid cell?

3.12 What is plasmolysis?

3.13 How can plasmolysis be brought about?

3.14 In Figure **3.9**, what fills space **X**?
Explain your answer.

3.15 Describe the events shown in Figures **3.5** and **3.6** in terms of water potential.

3.3 Active transport

There are many occasions when cells need to take in substances which are only present in small quantities around them. Root hair cells in plants, for example, take in nitrate ions from the soil. Very often, the concentration of nitrate ions inside the root hair cell is higher than the concentration in the soil. The diffusion gradient for the nitrate ions is out of the root hair, and into the soil.

Despite this, the root hair cells are still able to take nitrate ions in. They do it by a process called **active transport**. Active transport is an energy-consuming process by which substances are transported against their concentration gradient. The energy is provided by respiration in the cell.

In the cell membrane of the root hair cells are special transport proteins. These proteins pick up nitrate ions from outside the cell, and then change shape in such a way that they push the nitrate ions through the cell membrane and into the cytoplasm of the cell.

As its name suggests, active transport uses energy. The energy is provided by respiration inside the root hair cells. (You can find out about respiration in Chapter **11**.) Energy is needed to produce the shape change in the transport protein. You can think of active transport as a process in which chemical energy that has been released from glucose (by respiration) is converted into kinetic energy of molecules and ions.

Ⓢ Most other cells can carry out active transport. In the human small intestine, for example, glucose can be actively transported from the lumen of the intestine into the cells of the villi. In kidney tubules, glucose is actively transported out of the tubule and into the blood.

Figure **3.10** shows how active transport of glucose takes place.

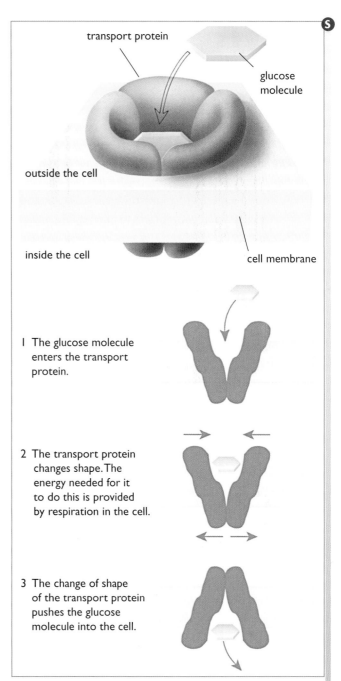

I The glucose molecule enters the transport protein.

2 The transport protein changes shape. The energy needed for it to do this is provided by respiration in the cell.

3 The change of shape of the transport protein pushes the glucose molecule into the cell.

Figure 3.10 Active transport.

Key definition

active transport – the movement of molecules Ⓢ and ions in or out of a cell through the cell membrane against a concentration gradient, using energy from respiration

Activity 3.5
Measuring the rate of osmosis

Skills
AO3.1 Using techniques, apparatus and materials
AO3.2 Planning
AO3.3 Observing, measuring and recording
AO3.4 Interpreting and evaluating observations and data

1 Collect a piece of Visking tubing. Moisten it and rub it between your fingers to open it. Tie one end tightly.
2 Use a dropper pipette to put some concentrated sugar solution into the tubing.
3 Place a long, narrow glass tube into the tubing, as shown in the diagram. Tie it very, very tightly, using thread.
4 Place the tubing inside a beaker of water, as shown in the diagram.

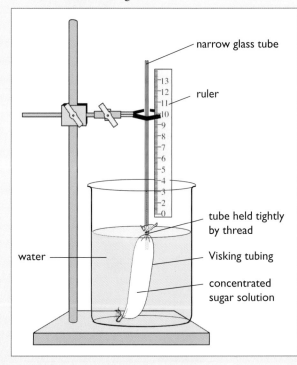

5 Mark the level of liquid inside the glass tube.
6 Make a copy of this results chart.

Time in minutes	0	2	4	6	8	10	12	14	16
Height of liquid in mm									

Every 2 minutes, record the level of the liquid in the glass tube.
7 Collect a sheet of graph paper. Draw a line graph of your results. Put *time in minutes* on the *x*-axis, and *height in mm* on the *y*-axis.

Questions

A1 Describe what happened to the liquid level inside the glass tube.
A2 Explain why this happened.
A3 Use your graph to work out the mean (average) rate at which the liquid moved up the tube, in mm per second. (Ask your teacher for help if you are not sure how to do this.)
A4 Predict what would have happened to the rate of osmosis in this experiment if you had used a kind of Visking tubing with ridges and grooves in it, giving it a larger surface area. Explain your answer.
A5 When temperature rises, particles move more quickly. Describe how you could use this apparatus to carry out an experiment to investigate the effect of temperature on the rate of osmosis. Think about the following things.
   ◆ What will you vary in your experiment?
   ◆ What will you keep the same?
   ◆ What will you measure, when will you measure it and how will you measure it?
   ◆ How will you record and display your results?
   ◆ Predict the results that you would expect.

Activity 3.6
Osmosis and potato strips

Summary

You should know:

- ♦ how diffusion results from the random movement of particles
- ♦ the factors that affect the rate of diffusion
- ♦ why diffusion is important to cells and living organisms
- ♦ the importance of water as a solvent
- ♦ about osmosis, which is a special kind of diffusion, involving water molecules
- ♦ how osmosis affects animal cells and plant cells
- ♦ about active transport, and why it is important to cells.

End-of-chapter questions

1   Which of a–d below is an example of **i** diffusion, **ii** osmosis, or **iii** neither?
    Explain your answer in each case.

    a   Water moves from a dilute solution in the soil into the cells in a plant's roots.

    b   Saliva flows out of the salivary glands into your mouth.

    c   A spot of blue ink dropped into a glass of still water quickly colours all the water blue.

    d   Carbon dioxide goes into a plant's leaves when it is photosynthesising.

2   Each of these statements was made by a candidate in an examination. Each one contains at least one error.
    Decide what is wrong with each statement, and rewrite it correctly.

    a   If Visking tubing containing a sugar solution is put into a beaker of water, the sugar solution moves out
    of the tubing by osmosis.

    b   Plant cells do not burst in pure water because the cell wall stops water getting into the cell.

    c   When a plant cell is placed in a concentrated sugar solution, water moves out of the cell by osmosis,
    through the partially permeable cell wall.

S   **d**   Animal cells plasmolyse in a concentrated sugar solution.

3   Explain each of the following.

    a   Diffusion happens faster when the temperature rises.

    b   Oxygen diffuses out of a plant leaf during daylight hours.

    c   Water molecules can pass through Visking tubing, but starch molecules cannot.

    d   An animal cell bursts if placed in pure water.

    e   If a plant is short of water, its leaves lose their firmness and the plant wilts.

4 a Define diffusion. [2]

  b The diagram below shows an apparatus that was set up to investigate diffusion.

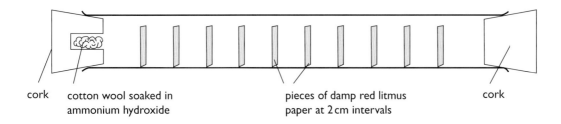

cork   cotton wool soaked in   pieces of damp red litmus   cork
        ammonium hydroxide   paper at 2 cm intervals

The graph below shows the results for two samples of ammonium hydroxide that were investigated.

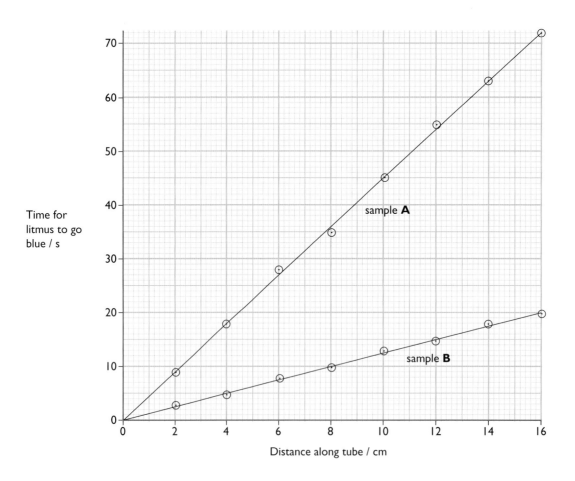

The table below gives data for a third sample, **C**, of ammonium hydroxide that was investigated.

Distance of red litmus paper along tube / cm	Time for red litmus paper to go blue / s
2	6
4	10
6	15
8	21
10	25
12	29
14	35
16	41

  i   Plot the data in the table on a copy of the graph.   [3]
  ii Suggest what has caused the litmus paper to go blue.   [1]
  iii State which sample of ammonium hydroxide took longest to travel 10 cm
      along the tube.   [1]
  iv What can you suggest about the concentration of sample **C**?
      Explain your answer.   [2]

[Cambridge IGCSE® Biology 0610/2, Question 8, October/November 2004]

5 The bar chart shows the concentration of potassium ions and sodium ions in a sample of pond water,
   and in the cells of a plant growing in the water.

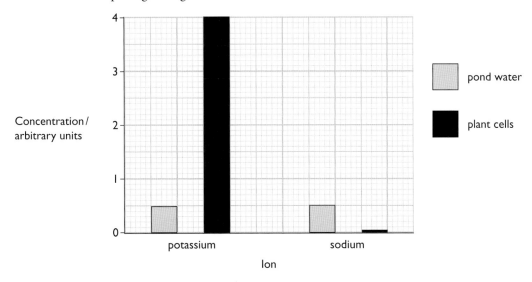

  a   Describe the differences between the concentrations of the ions in the pond water
      and in the plant cells.   [3]
  b   Suggest the process by which the ions move beweeen the pond water and the plant cells.
      Explain why you think this process is involved.   [2]
  c   Describe how the process that you have described in your answer to **b** takes place. [4]

4 The chemicals of life

In this chapter, you will find out about:

♦ why water is so important to living organisms
♦ what carbohydrates, fats (lipids) and proteins are made of, and their properties
♦ the roles of carbohydrates, fats and proteins in living organisms
♦ how to test for the presence of carbohydrates, lipids and proteins
♦ the structure of DNA.

Did meteorites spark the beginning of life on Earth?

On the morning of September 26th, 1969, the people of Murchison, in Australia, were surprised by a roaring noise and bright lights in the sky. Many people rushed out of their homes and offices to see what was happening. They were witnessing the fall of what is now known as the Murchison meteorite.

The meteorite broke up as it entered the Earth's atmosphere, so that when the pieces hit the ground they were spread over an area of 13 km². The largest fragment that was picked up had a mass of 7 kg, but it is estimated the mass of the original meteorite was probably more than 100 kg.

The meteorite was especially useful for research because people had seen it fall, so scientists knew exactly when and how it had reached the Earth. Studies of the meteorite suggest that it formed about 4.6 billion years ago – the time at which the Sun was forming.

Chemists have analysed the substances that the meteorite fragments are made of. They contain a lot of carbon. And some of this carbon is in molecules of amino acids. There are 15 different amino acids in the meteorite.

We think we understand how amino acids can form in space – for example from hydrogen, carbon monoxide and nitrogen in a hot, newly-formed asteroid as it cools. Many meteorites are known to contain amino acids. And this has made scientists wonder if perhaps these amino acids, brought to Earth from outer space, might have been important in the origin of life on Earth. In the early history of the Earth, before it had developed an atmosphere, many more meteorites hit the surface than happens today, and they could have brought quite large quantities of amino acids to our planet.

Today, all living organisms contain 20 different amino acids, which are used to build proteins. It's intriguing to think that perhaps life would not have evolved without these deliveries from outer space (Figure 4.1).

Figure 4.1 A huge meteor fell near Chelyabinsk in Russia in February 2013, producing a shock wave that shattered windows and injured more than 1500 people. This photo was taken from a car dashboard video camera.

4.1 What are you made of?

The bodies of all living things are made of many different kinds of chemicals. Most of our bodies are made up of water. We also contain carbohydrates, proteins and fats. These substances are what our cells are made of. Each of them is vital for life.

In this chapter, we will look at each of these kinds of substances in turn. As you work through your biology course, you will keep meeting them over and over again.

It will help if you have a basic understanding of the meanings of the terms atom, element and molecule. If you are not sure about these, ask your biology or chemistry teacher to explain them to you.

Water

In most organisms, almost 80% of the body is made up of water. We have seen that cytoplasm is a solution of many different substances in water. The spaces between our cells are also filled with a watery liquid.

Inside every living organism, chemical reactions are going on all the time. These reactions are called metabolism. Metabolic reactions can only take place if the chemicals which are reacting are dissolved in water. Water is an important solvent. This is one reason why water is so important to living organisms. If their cells dry out, the reactions stop, and the organism dies.

Water is also needed for other reasons. For example, plasma, the liquid part of blood, contains a lot of water, so that substances like glucose can dissolve in it. These dissolved substances are transported around the body. Water is also need to dissolve enzymes and nutrients in the alimentary canal, so that digestion can take place.

We also need water to help us to get rid of waste products. As you will see in Chapter 12, the kidneys remove the waste product, urea, from the body. The urea is dissolved in water, forming urine.

Study tip

When asked why water is important to organisms, many students answer 'so that they do not dry out'. This is not a good answer – make sure you explain *why* the water is needed.

4.2 Carbohydrates

Carbohydrates include starches and sugars. Their molecules contain three kinds of atom – carbon (C), hydrogen (H), and oxygen (O). A carbohydrate molecule has about twice as many hydrogen atoms as carbon or oxygen atoms.

Sugars

The simplest kinds of carbohydrates are the simple sugars or monosaccharides. Glucose is a simple sugar. A glucose molecule is made of six carbon atoms joined in a ring, with the hydrogen and oxygen atoms pointing out from and into the ring (Figure 4.2).

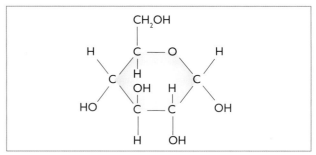

Figure 4.2 The structure of a glucose molecule.

A glucose molecule contains six carbon atoms, twelve hydrogen atoms, and six oxygen atoms. To show this, its molecular formula can be written $C_6H_{12}O_6$. This formula stands for one molecule of this simple sugar, and tells you which atoms it contains, and how many of each kind.

Although they contain many atoms, simple sugar molecules are very small (Figure 4.3). They are soluble in water, and they taste sweet.

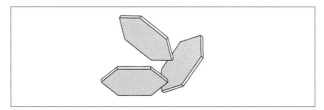

Figure 4.3 Simple sugars, or monosaccharides, have small molecules and are soluble.

If two simple sugar molecules join together, a larger molecule called a complex sugar or disaccharide is made (Figure 4.4). Two examples of complex sugars are sucrose (the sugar we use in hot drinks, or on breakfast cereal, for example) and maltose (malt sugar). Like simple sugars, they are soluble in water and taste sweet.

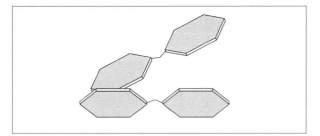

Figure 4.4 Complex sugars (disaccharides), such as maltose, are made from two simple sugars that have been joined together.

Polysaccharides

If many simple sugars join together, a very large molecule called a **polysaccharide** is made. Some polysaccharide molecules contain thousands of sugar molecules joined together in a long chain. The **cellulose** of plant cell walls is a polysaccharide and so is **starch**, which is often found inside plant cells (Figure 4.5). Animal cells often contain a polysaccharide called **glycogen**. Most polysaccharides are insoluble, and they do not taste sweet.

Functions of carbohydrates

Carbohydrates are needed for energy. One gram of carbohydrate releases 17 kJ (kilojoules) of energy. The energy is released by respiration (Chapter 11).

The carbohydrate that is normally used in respiration is glucose. This is also the form in which carbohydrate is transported around an animal's body. Human blood plasma contains dissolved glucose, being transported to all the cells. The cells then use the glucose to release the energy that they need to carry out the processes of life.

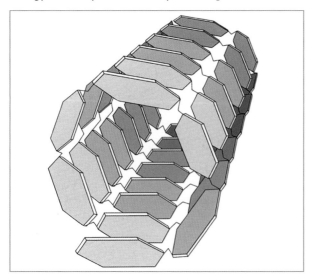

Figure 4.5 This is just a small part of a molecule of a polysaccharide, like starch.

Plants also use glucose in respiration, to provide them with energy. However, they do not transport glucose around their bodies. Instead, they transport sucrose. The cells change the sucrose to glucose when they need to use it.

Plants store carbohydrates as starch. It is quick and easy to change glucose into starch, or starch into glucose. Some plants store large quantities of starch in their seeds or tubers, and we use these as food.

Animals do not store starch. Instead, they store carbohydrates in the form of the polysaccharide glycogen. However, only small quantities of glycogen can be stored. It is mostly stored in the cells in the liver and the muscles.

The polysaccharide cellulose is used to make the criss-crossing fibres from which plant cell walls are constructed. Cellulose fibres are very strong, so the cell wall helps to maintain the shape of the plant cell.

Testing for carbohydrates

We can test for the presence of sugars by adding Benedict's solution to a food, and heating it. If the food contains **reducing sugar** (such as glucose or maltose), then a brick-red colour will be produced. The mixture changes gradually from blue, through green, yellow and orange, and finally brick red (Figure 4.6). If there is no reducing sugar, then the Benedict's solution remains blue.

Figure 4.6 Positive results of the Benedict's test. The tube on the left contained a small amount of reducing sugar, and the one on the right a larger amount.

Activity 4.1
Testing foods for sugars

Skills
AO3.1 Using techniques, apparatus and materials
AO3.3 Observing, measuring and recording

⚠ Wear eye protection if available.
If possible, heat the tubes using a water bath. If you have to heat directly over a Bunsen flame, use a test-tube holder and point the opening of the tube away from people.
Take care if using a sharp blade to cut the food.

All simple sugars, and some complex sugars such as maltose, are **reducing sugars**. This means that they will react with a blue liquid called Benedict's solution. We can use this reaction to find out if a food or other substance contains a reducing sugar.

1   Draw a results chart.

Food	Colour with Benedict's solution	Simple sugar present

2   Cut or grind a little of the food into very small pieces. Put these into a test tube. Add some water, and shake it up to try to dissolve it.
3   Add some Benedict's solution. Benedict's solution is blue, because it contains copper salts.
4   Heat the tube to about 80 °C, in a water bath. If there is reducing sugar in the food, a brick-red precipitate will form.
5   Record your result in your results chart. If the Benedict's solution does not change colour, do not write 'no change'. Write down the actual colour that you see – for example, blue. Then write down your conclusion from the result of the test.

This test works because the reducing sugar reduces the blue copper salts to a red compound.

The test for starch is easier, as it does not involve heating. You simply add iodine solution to a sample of the food. If there is starch present, a blue-black colour is obtained (Figure 4.7). If there is no starch, the iodine solution remains orange-brown.

Figure 4.7   The black colour shows that the potato contains starch.

Activity 4.2
Testing foods for starch

Skills
AO3.1 Using techniques, apparatus and materials
AO3.3 Observing, measuring and recording

There is no need to dissolve the food for this test.
1   Draw a results chart.
2   Put a small piece of the food onto a white tile.
3   Add a drop or two of iodine solution. Iodine solution is brown, but it turns blue-black if there is starch in the food. Record each of your results and conclusions.

❓ Question
A1   How could you test a solution to see if it contained iodine?

4.1 What is metabolism?

4.2 Why do organisms die if they do not have enough water?

4.3 Which **three** elements are contained in all carbohydrates?

4.4 The molecular formula for glucose is $C_6H_{12}O_6$. What does this tell you about a glucose molecule?

4.5 To which group of carbohydrates does each of these substances belong: **a** glucose, **b** starch and **c** glycogen?

4.6 In what form:

   a   do most organisms use carbohydrates in respiration?

   b   do animals transport carbohydrates in their blood?

   c   do animals store carbohydrates in their cells?

   d   do plants transport carbohydrates round their bodies?

   e   do plants store carbohydrates in their cells?

4.3 Fats

Fats are also known as lipids. Like carbohydrates, fats contain only three kinds of atom – carbon, hydrogen and oxygen. A fat molecule is made of four smaller molecules joined together. One of these is glycerol. Attached to the glycerol are three long molecules called fatty acids (Figure **4.8**).

Fats are insoluble in water. Fats that are liquid at room temperature are called oils.

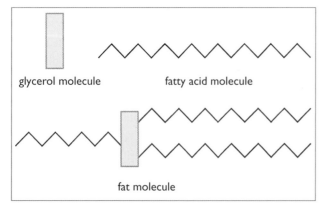

Figure 4.8   The structure of a fat molecule.

Functions of fats

Like carbohydrates, fats and oils can be used in a cell to release energy. A gram of fat gives about 39 kJ of energy. This is more than twice as much energy as that released by a gram of carbohydrate. However, most cells use carbohydrates first when they need energy, and only use fats when all the available carbohydrates have been used.

The extra energy that fats contain makes them very useful for storing energy. In mammals, some cells, particularly ones underneath the skin, become filled with large drops of fats or oils. These stores can be used to release energy when needed. This layer of cells is called adipose tissue. Adipose tissue also helps to keep heat inside the body – that is, it insulates the body. Animals such as walruses, which live in very cold places, often have especially thick layers of adipose tissue, called blubber (Figure **4.9**). Many plants store oils in their seeds – for example, peanut, coconut and castor oil. The oils provide a good store of energy for germination.

Figure 4.9   A walrus on the Arctic island, Spitzbergen.

Testing for fats and oils

There are several different tests for fats. One of the best is the ethanol emulsion test.

Firstly, you chop the food and shake it up with ethanol. Although fats will not dissolve in water, they do dissolve in ethanol. Next, you pour the ethanol into water. If there was any fat in the food, then the fat–ethanol mixture breaks up into millions of tiny droplets when it is mixed with the water. This mixture is called an emulsion. It looks white and opaque, like milk (Figure **4.10**). If there was no fat in the food, the mixture of water and ethanol remains transparent.

Activity 4.3
Testing foods for fats

Skills
A03.1 Using techniques, apparatus and materials
A03.3 Observing, measuring and recording

1 Draw a results chart.
2 Chop or grind a small amount of food, and put some into a very clean, dry test tube. Add some absolute (pure) ethanol. Shake it thoroughly.
3 Put some distilled water in another tube.
4 Pour some of the liquid part, but not any solid, from the first tube into the water. A milky appearance shows that there is fat in the food.

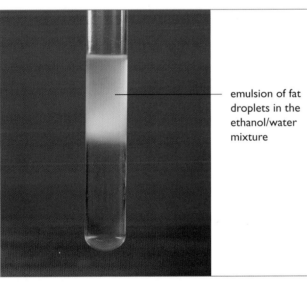

— emulsion of fat droplets in the ethanol/water mixture

Figure 4.10   A positive result for the emulsion test.

 Questions

4.7 Which **three** elements are found in all fats and oils?
4.8 State **two** uses of fats to living organisms.
4.9 We get cooking oil mostly from the seeds of plants. Why do plant seeds contain oil?

4.4 Proteins

Protein molecules contain some kinds of atoms which carbohydrates and fats do not (Figure **4.11**). As well as carbon, hydrogen and oxygen, they also contain nitrogen (N) and small amounts of sulfur (S).

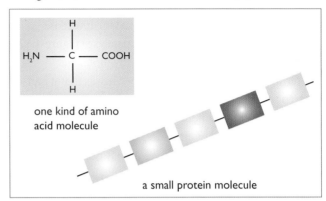

one kind of amino acid molecule

a small protein molecule

Figure 4.11   Structure of a protein molecule.

Like polysaccharides, protein molecules are made of long chains of smaller molecules joined end to end. These smaller molecules are called **amino acids**. There are about 20 different kinds of amino acid. Any of these 20 can be joined together in any order to make a protein molecule. Each protein is made of molecules with amino acids in a precise order. Even a small difference in the order of amino acids makes a different protein, so there are millions of different proteins which could be made.

Functions of proteins

Some proteins are soluble in water; an example is haemoglobin, the red pigment in blood. Others are insoluble in water; for example, keratin. Hair and fingernails are made of keratin.

Unlike carbohydrates, proteins are not normally used to provide energy. Many of the proteins in the food you eat are used for making new cells. New cells are needed for growing, and for repairing damaged parts of the body. In particular, cell membranes and cytoplasm contain a lot of protein.

Proteins are also needed to make antibodies. These help to kill bacteria and viruses inside the body. Enzymes are also proteins.

The long chains of amino acids from which protein molecules are formed can curl up into different shapes. The way in which the chain curls up, and therefore the three-dimensional shape of the protein molecule, is

⑤ determined by the sequence of amino acids in the chain. Different sequences of amino acids result in different shapes of protein molecules.

For most protein molecules, their shape directly affects their function. For example, as you will see in Chapter 5, some protein molecules, called enzymes, act as catalysts. The shape of the enzyme molecule determines which reactions it can catalyse (Figure 4.12).

Similarly, the shape of an antibody molecule determines the kinds of bacteria or viruses that it can attach to. Different shapes of antibody molecules are needed to bind to different kinds of bacteria and viruses. Each different kind of antibody therefore has a different sequence of amino acids from which it is built.

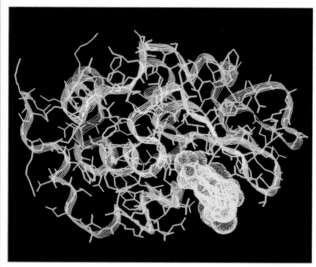

Figure 4.12 This is a model of an enzyme called lysozyme, which is found in saliva and tears. The purple band represents the chain of amino acids, which is coiled up to produce a small depression called the active site. The yellow part is another molecule, the substrate, that fits perfectly into the active site.

❓ Questions

4.10 Name **two** elements found in proteins that are not found in carbohydrates.

4.11 How many different amino acids are there?

4.12 In what way are protein molecules similar to polysaccharides?

4.13 Give **two** examples of proteins.

4.14 State **three** functions of proteins in living organisms.

Testing for proteins

The test for proteins is called the biuret test (Figure 4.13). This involves mixing the food in water, and then adding dilute copper sulfate solution. Then dilute potassium hydroxide solution is gently added. A purple colour indicates that protein is present. If there is no protein, the mixture stays blue.

Activity 4.4
Testing foods for protein

Skills
AO3.1 Using techniques, apparatus and materials
AO3.3 Observing, measuring and recording

⚠️ Wear eye protection if available. Potassium hydroxide is a strong alkali. If you get it on your skin, wash with plenty of cold water.
Take care if using a sharp blade to cut the food.

The biuret test
The biuret test uses potassium hydroxide solution and copper sulfate solution. You can also use a ready-mixed reagent called biuret reagent, which contains these two substances already mixed together.

1 Draw a results chart.
2 Put the food into a test tube, and add a little water.
3 Add some potassium hydroxide solution.
4 Add two drops of copper sulfate solution.
5 Shake the tube gently. If a purple colour appears, then protein is present.

Figure 4.13 The tube on the left shows a negative result for the biuret test. The tube on the right shows a positive result.

Table **4.1** compares some properties of carbohydrates, fats and proteins.

	Carbohydrates	Fats	Proteins
Elements they contain	C, H, O	C, H, O	C, H, O, N
Smaller molecules of which they are made	simple sugars (monosaccharides)	fatty acids and glycerol	amino acids
Solubility in water	sugars are soluble; polysaccharides are insoluble	insoluble	some are soluble and some are insoluble
Why organisms need them	easily available energy (17 kJ/g)	storage of energy (39 kJ/g); insulation; making cell membranes	making cells, antibodies, enzymes, haemoglobin; also used for energy

Table 4.1   A comparison of carbohydrates, fats and proteins.

Ⓢ 4.5 DNA

DNA stands for deoxyribonucleic acid. DNA is the chemical that makes up our genes and chromosomes. It is the material that we inherit from our parents, which gives us many of our characteristics.

Figure **4.14** shows the structure of a very small part of a DNA molecule. It is made of two long strands, each with a series of bases arranged along it. The bases on the two strands are held together by bonds, forming cross links. The two strands then twist together into a kind of spiral called a helix.

There are four kinds of bases, known by the letters A, C, G and T. If you look carefully at Figure **4.14**, you will see that T and A always link up with each other, and also C and G. The bases always pair up in this way.

The sequence of the bases in our DNA provides a code that is used to determine the kinds of proteins that are made in our cells. This, in turn, determines how our cells, tissues and organs develop. The sequence determines that you are a human and not a tree, as well as many of your personal characteristics such as your hair colour and your blood group. In Chapter **18**, you will find out more about how DNA does this.

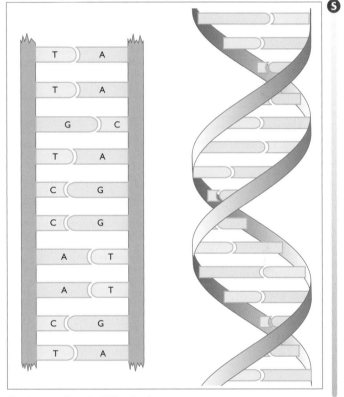

Figure 4.14   Part of a DNA molecule.

Summary

You should know:
- ♦ the functions of water in living organisms
- ♦ the structure and uses of carbohydrates, and the Benedict's test and iodine test to identify them
- ♦ the structure and uses of fats, and the ethanol emulsion test
- ♦ the structure and uses of proteins, and the biuret test
- Ⓢ ♦ the relationship between the amino acid sequence, structure and function of a protein
- ♦ the structure of DNA and the importance of its base sequence.

End-of-chapter questions

1   For each of these carbohydrates, state: **i** whether it is a monosaccharide, disaccharide or polysaccharide; **ii** whether it is found in plants only, animals only or in both plants and animals; **iii** one function.

    a   glucose
    b   starch
    c   cellulose
    d   glycogen

2   Name:

    a   an element found in proteins but not in carbohydrates or lipids
    b   the small molecules that are linked together to form a protein molecule
    c   the reagent used for testing for reducing sugars
    d   the substance which the emulsion test detects
    e   the form in which carbohydrate is transported in a plant
    f   the term that describes all the chemical reactions taking place in an organism.

3   Imagine that you have been given two colourless solutions.

Describe how you could find out which of them contains the greater concentration of reducing sugar. You will need to think carefully about all the different variables that you would need to keep constant.

4   Copy and complete the table below. Do not write anything in the box that is shaded grey.

Substance	Carbohydrate, fat or protein?	Elements it contains	How to test for it	One function
haemoglobin				
glucose				
cellulose				
starch				
enzyme				

[5]

S 5   A sample of DNA was tested to find out which bases were present.
It was found that 30% of the bases in the DNA were T.

    a   What percentage of the bases in the DNA would you expect to be A? Explain your answer. [2]
    b   What percentage of the bases in the DNA would you expect to be C? Explain your answer. [2]
    c   Explain why two organisms that have different sequences of bases in their DNA may look different from each other. [2]

5 Enzymes

In this chapter, you will find out about:

♦ enzymes and what they do
♦ how enzymes are affected by temperature and pH
Ⓢ ♦ why enzymes are affected by temperature and pH
♦ how to investigate the effects of temperature and pH on enzyme activity
♦ how to plan, carry out and evaluate your own experiments on enzyme activity.

Forensics and salivary amylase

Forensic science is the use of scientific techniques to obtain evidence relating to crimes (Figure 5.1).

Human saliva contains an enzyme, called salivary amylase, that helps to digest starch in the mouth. Forensic scientists can test surfaces for the presence of human salivary amylase. This can help to determine whether a person was present at the scene of a crime.

When the test first came in, it was only able to detect the activity of amylase – that is, whether starch was digested. Although this could be useful, a positive result did not prove that a person had left saliva at the scene. This is because amylase is also produced by many other organisms, such as bacteria and fungi.

In the late 1980s, a new test that could detect human amylase directly was introduced. However, this test can still give positive results for amylase from other organisms, including rats and gorillas. Although it is very unlikely that a gorilla was present at the scene of a crime, it is often possible that a rat might have left the saliva behind.

Today, forensic scientists are also able to search for cheek cells within a saliva sample. If they can find any, then they can test the DNA in them. This can then provide evidence that can link a particular person to the crime scene.

Figure 5.1   Forensic scientists at a crime scene. Can you suggest why they are wearing clothing that covers most of the their bodies?

5.1 Biological catalysts

Many chemical reactions can be speeded up by substances called catalysts. A catalyst alters the rate of a chemical reaction, without being changed itself.

Within any living organism, chemical reactions take place all the time. They are sometimes called metabolic reactions. Almost every metabolic reaction is controlled by catalysts called enzymes. Without enzymes, the reactions would take place very slowly, or not at all. Enzymes ensure that the rates of metabolic reactions are great enough to sustain life.

Key definitions

catalyst – a substance that increases the rate of a chemical reaction and is not changed by the reaction

enzymes – proteins that function as biological catalysts

For example, inside the alimentary canal, large molecules are broken down to smaller ones in the process of digestion. These reactions are speeded up by enzymes. A different enzyme is needed for each kind of food. For example, starch is digested to the sugar maltose by an enzyme called amylase. Protein is digested to amino acids by protease.

These enzymes are also found in plants – for example, in germinating seeds, where they digest the food stores for the growing seedling. Many seeds contain stores of starch. As the seed soaks up water, the amylase is activated and breaks down the starch to maltose. The maltose is soluble, and is transported to the embryo in the seed. The embryo uses it to provide energy for growth, and also to provide glucose molecules that can be strung together to make cellulose molecules, for the cell walls of the new cells produced as it grows.

Another enzyme which speeds up the breakdown of a substance is catalase. Catalase works inside the cells of living organisms – both animals and plants – for example, in liver cells or potato cells. It breaks down hydrogen peroxide to water and oxygen. This is necessary because hydrogen peroxide is produced by many of the chemical reactions which take place inside

cells. Hydrogen peroxide is a very dangerous substance, and must be broken down immediately.

Not all enzymes help to break things down. Many enzymes help to make large molecules from small ones. One example of this kind of enzyme is starch phosphorylase, which builds starch molecules from glucose molecules inside plant cells.

Naming enzymes

Enzymes are named according to the reaction that they catalyse. For example, enzymes which catalyse the breakdown of carbohydrates are called carbohydrases. If they break down proteins, they are proteases. If they break down fats (lipids) they are lipases.

Sometimes, they are given more specific names than this. For example, we have seen that the carbohydrase that breaks down starch is called amylase. One that breaks down maltose is called maltase. One that breaks down sucrose is called sucrase.

The lock and key mechanism

An enzyme works by allowing the molecule of the substance on which it is acting to fit into it. The fit has to be perfect. The enzyme is like a lock, into which another molecule fits like a key. We say that the shape of the enzyme and the shape of the substrate are complementary to one another. Figure 5.2 shows how this works.

The active site

A chemical reaction always involves one substance changing into another. In an enzyme-controlled reaction, the substance which is present at the beginning of the reaction is called the substrate. The substance which is made by the reaction is called the product.

For example, in saliva there is an enzyme called amylase. It catalyses the breakdown of starch to the complex sugar maltose. In this reaction, starch is the substrate, and maltose is the product.

$$\text{starch} \xrightarrow{\text{amylase}} \text{maltose}$$

Figure 5.3 shows how amylase does this. An amylase molecule has a dent in it called its active site. This has a shape that is complementary to the shape of part of a starch molecule. The starch (the substrate) fits into the active site of amylase (the enzyme), forming an enzyme-substrate complex. When the starch molecule is in the active site, the enzyme breaks it apart.

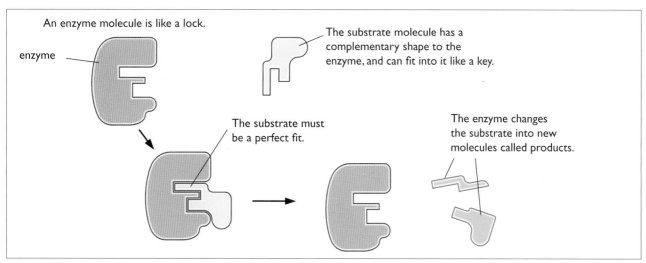

An enzyme molecule is like a lock.

enzyme

The substrate molecule has a complementary shape to the enzyme, and can fit into it like a key.

The substrate must be a perfect fit.

The enzyme changes the substrate into new molecules called products.

Figure 5.2 The lock and key mechanism.

S All enzymes have active sites. Each enzyme has an active site that exactly fits its substrate. This means that each enzyme can only act on a particular kind of substrate. Amylase, for example, cannot break down protein molecules, because they do not fit into its active site.

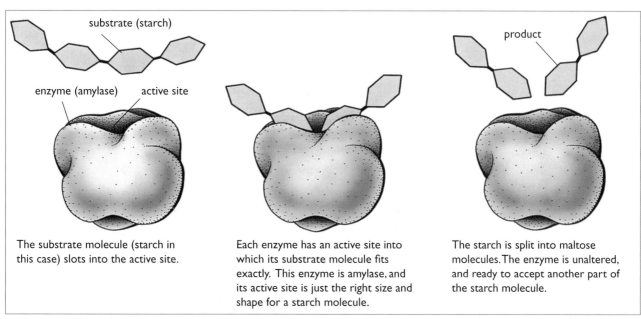

substrate (starch)

product

enzyme (amylase)　active site

The substrate molecule (starch in this case) slots into the active site.

Each enzyme has an active site into which its substrate molecule fits exactly. This enzyme is amylase, and its active site is just the right size and shape for a starch molecule.

The starch is split into maltose molecules. The enzyme is unaltered, and ready to accept another part of the starch molecule.

Figure 5.3 How an enzyme works.

 **Questions**

5.1 What is a catalyst?

5.2 What are the catalysts inside a living organism called?

5.3 Which kinds of reaction inside a living organism are controlled by enzymes?

5.4 What is meant by a carbohydrase?

5.5 Give **one** example of a carbohydrase.

5.6 Name the substrate and product of a reaction involving a carbohydrase.

5.2 Properties of enzymes

1 **All enzymes are proteins** This may seem rather odd, because some enzymes actually digest proteins.

2 **Enzymes are made inactive by high temperature** This is because they are protein molecules, which are damaged by heat.

3 **Enzymes work best at a particular temperature** Enzymes which are found in the human body usually work best at about 37 °C (Figure 5.4).

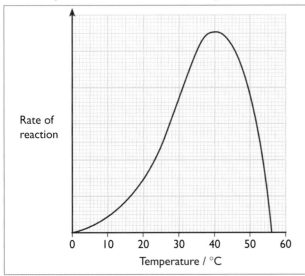

Figure 5.4 How temperature affects enzyme activity.

4 **Enzymes work best at a particular pH** pH is a measure of how acid or alkaline a solution is. Some enzymes work best in acid conditions (low pH). Others work best in neutral or alkaline conditions (high pH) (Figure 5.5).

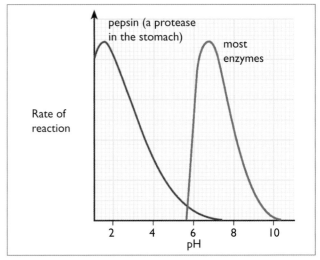

Figure 5.5 How pH affects enzyme activity.

5 **Enzymes are catalysts** They are not changed in the chemical reactions which they control. They can be used over and over again, so a small amount of enzyme can change a lot of substrate into product.

6 **Enzymes are specific** This means that each kind of enzyme will only catalyse one kind of chemical reaction.

Activity 5.1
The effect of catalase on hydrogen peroxide

Skills
AO3.1 Using techniques, apparatus and materials
AO3.3 Observing, measuring and recording
AO3.4 Interpreting and evaluating observations and data

 Wear eye protection if available.
Hydrogen peroxide is a powerful bleach. Wash it off with plenty of water if you get it on your skin.

Catalase is found in almost every kind of living cell. It catalyses this reaction:

$$\text{hydrogen peroxide} \xrightarrow{\text{catalase}} \text{water} + \text{oxygen}$$

1 Read through the instructions. Decide what you will observe and measure, and draw a results table.

2 Measure 10 cm³ of hydrogen peroxide into each of five test tubes or boiling tubes.

3 To each tube, add one of the following substances:
   a some chopped raw potato
   b some chopped boiled potato
   c some fruit juice
   d a small piece of liver
   e some yeast suspension.

4 Light a wooden splint, and then blow it out so that it is glowing. Gently push the glowing splint down through the bubbles in your tubes.

5 Record your observations, and explain them as fully as you can.

Temperature and enzyme activity

Most chemical reactions happen faster at higher temperatures. This is because the molecules have more kinetic energy – they are moving around faster, so they bump into each other more frequently. This means that at higher temperatures an enzyme is likely to bump into its substrate more often than at lower temperatures. They will also hit each other with more energy, so the reaction is more likely to take place (Figure **5.4**).

However, enzymes are damaged by high temperatures. For most human enzymes, this begins to happen from about 40 °C upwards. As the temperature increases beyond this, the enzyme molecules start to lose their shape. The active site no longer fits perfectly with the substrate. The enzyme is said to be denatured. It can no longer catalyse the reaction.

The temperature at which an enzyme works fastest is called its optimum temperature. Different enzymes have different optimum temperatures. For example, enzymes from the human digestive system generally have an optimum of around 37 °C. Enzymes from plants often have optimums around 28 °C to 30 °C. Enzymes from bacteria that live in hot springs may have optimums as high as 75 °C.

pH and enzyme activity

The pH of a solution affects the shape of an enzyme. Most enzymes are their correct shape at a pH of about 7 – that is, neutral. If the pH becomes very acidic or very alkaline, then they are denatured. This means that the active site no longer fits the substrate, so the enzyme can no longer catalyse its reaction (Figure **5.5**).

Some enzymes have an optimum pH that is not neutral. For example, there is a protease enzyme in the human stomach that has an optimum pH of about 2. This is because we have hydrochloric acid in our stomachs. This protease must be able to work well in these very acidic conditions.

Study tip

Do not say that enzymes are 'killed' by high temperatures. Enzymes are chemicals, not living organisms.

Questions

5.7 What is meant by an optimum temperature?

5.8 What is the optimum temperature for the enzyme in Figure **5.4**?

5.9 Why are enzymes damaged by high temperatures? S

Activity 5.2
Investigating the effect of pH on the activity of catalase

Skills
AO3.1 Using techniques, apparatus and materials
AO3.3 Observing, measuring and recording
AO3.4 Interpreting and evaluating observations and data

 Wear eye protection if available.
Hydrogen peroxide is a powerful bleach. Wash it off with plenty of water if you get it on your skin.

Catalase is a common enzyme which is the catalyst in the breakdown of hydrogen peroxide, H_2O_2. Catalase is found in almost every kind of living cell. Hydrogen peroxide is a toxic substance formed in cells.

The breakdown reaction is as follows:

$$2H_2O_2 \longrightarrow 2H_2O + O_2$$

The rate of the reaction can be determined from the rate of oxygen production.

One indirect but simple way to measure rate of oxygen production is to soak up a catalase solution onto a little square of filter paper and then drop it into a beaker containing a solution of H_2O_2. The paper sinks at first, but as the reaction proceeds, bubbles of oxygen collect on its surface and it floats up.

(continued ...)

(... continued)

The time between placing the paper in the beaker and it floating to the surface is a measure of the rate of the reaction.

In this investigation, you will test this hypothesis:

Catalase works best at a pH of 7 (neutral).

1   Label five $50 \, cm^3$ beakers pH 5.6, 6.2, 6.8, 7.4, 8.0.
2   Measure $5 \, cm^3$ of 3% hydrogen peroxide solution into each beaker.
3   Add $10 \, cm^3$ of the correct buffer solution to each beaker. (A buffer solution keeps the pH constant at a particular value.)
4   Cut out 20 squares of filter paper exactly $5 \, mm \times 5 \, mm$. Alternatively, use a hole punch to cut out circles of filter paper all exactly the same size. Avoid handling the paper with your fingers, as you may get grease onto it. Use forceps (tweezers) instead.
5   Prepare a leaf extract by grinding the leaves in a pestle and mortar. Add $25 \, cm^3$ of water and stir well.
6   Allow the remains of the leaves to settle and then pour the fluid into a beaker. This fluid contains catalase.
7   Prepare a results table like the one below.
8   Pick up a filter paper square with forceps and dip it into the leaf extract.
9   Make sure you are ready to start timing. Then place the filter paper square at the bottom of the beaker containing H_2O_2 and pH 5.6 buffer solution. (Do not let it fall near the side of the beaker.) As you put the square into the beaker, start a stopwatch. Stop the watch when the paper floats horizontally at the surface.
10   Record the time in your table and repeat steps 8 and 9 twice more.
11   Follow steps 8–10 for each of the other pHs.

12   Pour some of the remaining leaf extract into a test tube and boil for 2 minutes. Cool under a tap.
13   Repeat steps 8–10, using the boiled extract.
14   Calculate the mean (average) time taken at each pH and enter it into your table.
15   Draw a graph to show time taken for flotation plotted against pH and compare with Figure 5.5.

	Time taken for paper to float in seconds				
pH	5.6	6.2	6.8	7.4	8.0
Tests 1					
2					
3					
Mean					
Boiled extract					

Questions

A1   Does the enzyme have an optimum pH? If it does, what do your results suggest it to be?
A2   Do your results support the hypothesis you were testing, or do they disprove it? Explain your answer.
A3   What is the effect of boiling the extract?
A4   Why do the filter paper squares have to be exactly the same size?
A5   In most experiments in biology, we can never be quite sure that we would get exactly the same results if we did it again. There are always some limitations on the reliability of the data that we collect. Can you think of any reasons why the results you got in your experiment might not be absolutely reliable? For example:
  ♦ Might there have been any variables that were not controlled and that might have affected the results?
  ♦ Were you able to measure the volumes and times as accurately as you would have liked?

Activity 5.3
Investigate the effect of temperature on the activity of amylase

Activity 5.4
Investigating the effect of temperature on the activity of catalase

Summary

You should know:

- ◆ how enzymes work as biological catalysts
- ◆ how enzymes are named
- Ⓢ ◆ about active sites, substrates and products
- ◆ why enzymes are specific for their particular substrates
- ◆ how temperature affects enzyme activity
- Ⓢ ◆ why temperature affects enzyme activity
- ◆ how pH affects enzyme activity
- Ⓢ ◆ why pH affects enzyme activity
- ◆ how to investigate the effect of temperature and pH on enzyme activity
- ◆ how to plan and carry out an investigation into enzyme activity.

End-of-chapter questions

1 Explain the meaning of each of these terms:

    a   enzyme

    b   denatured

Ⓢ   c   substrate

    d   product

    e   active site.

2 A protease enzyme is found in the stomachs of humans. It catalyses the breakdown of long chains of amino acids (proteins) into individual amino acid molecules.

    a   Suggest the optimum temperature for the activity of this protease enzyme.

    b   The stomach contains hydrochloric acid. Suggest the optimum pH for the activity of this protease enzyme.

Ⓢ   c   Explain why the rate of an enzyme-controlled reaction is relatively slow at low temperatures.

    d   Explain why the rate of the reaction slows down above the enzyme's optimum temperature.

3 Students investigated samples of amylase from 100 goats. 100 small filter paper discs were each soaked in a different sample of goat amylase. The students tested the activity of these amylase samples using plain paper. Plain paper contains starch.

    A circle of plain paper was placed into a Petri dish as shown in the diagram below. Iodine solution was used to stain the starch in the plain paper.

    a   When iodine solution reacts with the starch in the plain paper, what colour would you see?   [1]

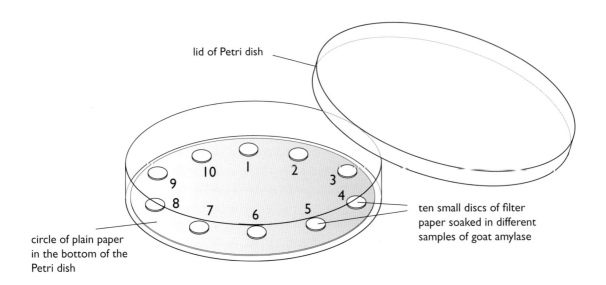

lid of Petri dish

ten small discs of filter paper soaked in different samples of goat amylase

circle of plain paper in the bottom of the Petri dish

Ten amylase soaked filter paper discs were placed into one of the Petri dishes as shown in the diagram above.

Ten Petri dishes were set up as in the diagram.

The students lifted the filter paper discs at one-minute intervals and recorded the number of areas where there had been a reaction.

b   How would the students know that a reaction had taken place?   [1]

If a reaction had not taken place, the students replaced the disc of filter paper for another minute. This procedure was repeated for five minutes.

Their results are recorded in the table below.

Time / minutes	Number of **new** areas where there had been a reaction	**Total** number of areas where there had been a reaction
1	14	14
2	28	42
3	18	60
4	12	...
5	6	...

c   **i**   Copy and complete the table by calculating the total number of areas where there had been a reaction after 4 and 5 minutes.

Show your working.   [2]

ii   Plot a graph using the data from the **first two columns**, to show the differences in the activity of amylase.   [5]

iii   Suggest **two** reasons for the differences in amylase activity of the samples.   [2]

d   Suggest **three** ways in which you could improve this investigation.   [3]

[Cambridge IGCSE® Biology 0610/61, Question 1, May/June 2011]

⑤ 4 Enzymes are biological catalysts. The diagram below shows how the enzyme, sucrase, breaks down a molecule of sucrose.

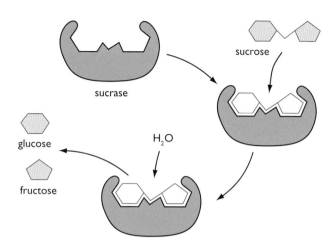

a Describe how sucrase catalyses the breakdown of sucrose. You should refer to the diagram above in your answer.   [3]

b Three enzymes, **P**, **Q** and **R**, were extracted from different regions of the alimentary canal of a mammal. The effect of pH on the activity of the enzymes was investigated at 40 °C. The results are shown in the diagram below.

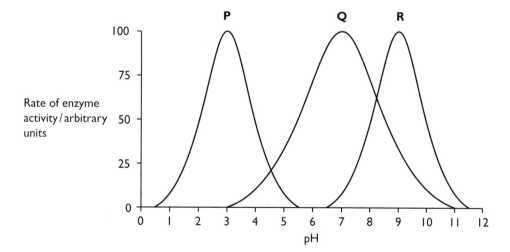

    i Explain why the investigation was carried out at 40 °C.   [2]
    ii Using information in the diagram above, describe the effects of increasing pH on the rate of activity of enzyme **Q**.   [3]

[Cambridge IGCSE® Biology 0610/33, Question 3, October/November 2010]

6 Plant nutrition

In this chapter, you will find out about:

♦ how plants make carbohydrates by photosynthesis
♦ the structure of leaves
♦ how plants use the glucose they produce in photosynthesis
♦ how to carry out investigations into photosynthesis
(S) ♦ the factors that affect the rate of photosynthesis
♦ why plants need nitrate and magnesium ions.

Using solar energy to make fuels

As the human population continues to grow, we are using more and more fuel to provide energy for our homes, industries and vehicles. A lot of this energy comes from burning fossil fuels, which produces carbon dioxide. The quantity of carbon dioxide

in the atmosphere is increasing, contributing to global warming. We need to find alternative ways of providing energy.

Can we take a lesson from plants? Plants use energy from sunlight to make food that fuels their bodies. They actually use up carbon dioxide in this process. Already, in many parts of the world, plants are being grown not to provide us with food, but to provide us with fuel that can be burnt to produce electricity, or to move vehicles. But this takes up a large amount of land that may be needed to grow food crops, or that would be better left as natural forests or other habitats for wildlife.

So scientists are looking into ways in which we might use a kind of 'artificial photosynthesis' to make hydrogen, which can be used as a fuel (Figure **6.1**).

Plants have an amazing substance called chlorophyll, which captures energy from sunlight and helps to transfer this energy into carbohydrates. Research into artificial photosynthesis is exploring potential substances that might be able to perform the same role, particularly semi-conductors like tungsten diselenide or silicon. The process would use light, water and carbon dioxide – just like plants do. However, instead of producing carbohydrates, we could use artificial photosynthesis to produce hydrogen from water. Hydrogen is a good fuel because it produces only water and not carbon dioxide when it is burnt.

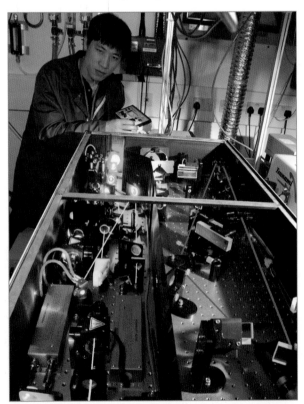

Figure 6.1 Research is being carried out into ways of using solar energy to make hydrogen.

6.1 Types of nutrition

All living organisms need to take many different substances into their bodies. Some of these may be used to make new parts, or repair old parts. Others may be used to release energy. Taking in useful substances is called feeding, or nutrition.

Animals and fungi cannot make their own food. They feed on organic substances that have originally been made by plants. Some animals eat other animals, but all the substances passing from one animal to another were first made by plants. Animal nutrition is described in Chapter 7.

Green plants make their own food. They use simple inorganic substances – carbon dioxide, water and minerals – from the air and soil. Plants build these substances into complex materials, making all the carbohydrates, lipids, proteins and vitamins that they need. Substances made by living things are said to be organic.

6.2 Photosynthesis

Green plants make the carbohydrate glucose from carbon dioxide and water. At the same time, oxygen is produced.

If you just mix carbon dioxide and water together, they will not make glucose. They have to be given energy before they will combine. Green plants use the energy of sunlight for this. The reaction is therefore called photosynthesis ('photo' means light, and 'synthesis' means manufacture).

Key definition

photosynthesis   the process by which plants manufacture carbohydrates from raw materials using energy from light

Chlorophyll

However, sunlight shining onto water and carbon dioxide still will not make them react together to make glucose. The sunlight energy has to be trapped, and then used in the reaction. Green plants have a substance which does this. It is called chlorophyll.

S Chlorophyll is the pigment which makes plants look green. It is kept inside the chloroplasts of plant cells.

S When sunlight falls on a chlorophyll molecule, some of the energy in the light is absorbed. The chlorophyll molecule then releases the energy. The released energy makes carbon dioxide combine with water, with the help of enzymes inside the chloroplast. The glucose that is made contains energy that was originally in the sunlight. So, in this processs, light energy is transferred to chemical energy.

The photosynthesis equation

The full equation for photosynthesis is written like this:

$$\text{carbon dioxide} + \text{water} \xrightarrow[\text{chlorophyll}]{\text{sunlight}} \text{glucose} + \text{oxygen}$$

S To show the number of molecules involved in the reaction, a balanced equation needs to be written. Carbon dioxide contains two atoms of oxygen, and one of carbon, so its molecular formula is CO_2. Water has the formula H_2O. Glucose has the formula $C_6H_{12}O_6$. Oxygen molecules contain two atoms of oxygen, and so they are written O_2.

The balanced equation for photosynthesis is this:

$$6CO_2 + 6H_2O \xrightarrow[\text{chlorophyll}]{\text{sunlight}} C_6H_{12}O_6 + 6O_2$$

❓ Questions

6.1 Give **one** example of an organic substance.
6.2 Which inorganic substances does a plant use to make carbohydrates?
6.3 What is chlorophyll, and how does it help the plant?

6.3 Leaves

Photosynthesis happens inside chloroplasts. This is where the enzymes and chlorophyll are that catalyse and supply energy for the reaction. In a typical plant, most chloroplasts are in the cells in the leaves. A leaf is a factory for making carbohydrates.

Leaves are therefore specially adapted to allow photosynthesis to take place as quickly and efficiently as possible.

Leaf structure

A leaf consists of a broad, flat part called the lamina (Figure 6.2), which is joined to the rest of the plant by a leaf stalk or petiole. Running through the petiole are vascular bundles, which then form the veins in the leaf. These contain tubes which carry substances to and from the leaf.

Although a leaf looks thin, it is in fact made up of several layers of cells. You can see these if you look at a transverse section (TS) of a leaf under a microscope (Figures 6.3, 6.4 and 6.5).

The top and bottom of the leaf are covered with a layer of closely fitting cells called the epidermis (Figures 6.6 and 6.7). These cells do not contain chloroplasts. Their function is to protect the inner layers of cells in the leaf. The cells of the upper epidermis often secrete a waxy substance, that lies on top of them. It is called the cuticle, and it helps to stop water evaporating from the leaf. There is sometimes a cuticle on the underside of the leaf as well.

In the lower epidermis, there are small openings called stomata (singular: stoma). Each stoma is surrounded by a pair of sausage-shaped guard cells which can open or close the hole. Guard cells, unlike other cells in the epidermis, do contain chloroplasts.

The middle layers of the leaf are called the mesophyll ('meso' means middle, and 'phyll' means leaf). These cells all contain chloroplasts. The cells nearer to the top of the leaf are arranged like a fence or palisade, and they form the palisade layer. The cells beneath them are rounder, and arranged quite loosely, with large air spaces between them. They form the spongy layer (Figure 6.3).

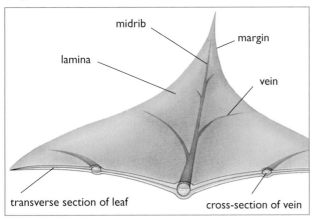

Figure 6.2 The structure of a leaf.

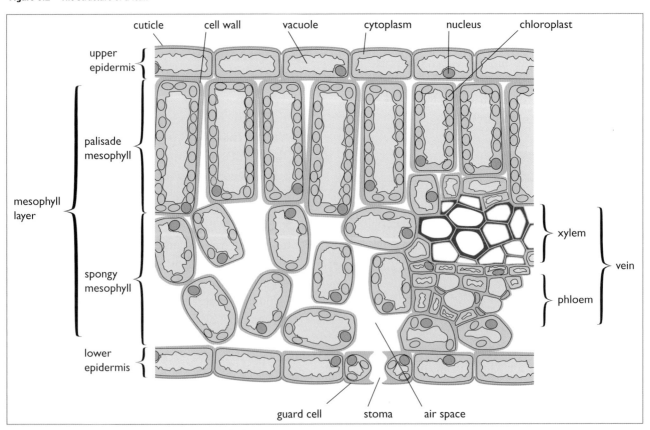

Figure 6.3 Transverse section through a small part of a leaf.

Running through the mesophyll are veins or vascular bundles. Each vein contains large, thick-walled xylem vessels (Figure 8.3) for carrying water. There are also smaller, thin-walled phloem tubes (Figure 8.5) for carrying away sucrose and other substances that the leaf has made.

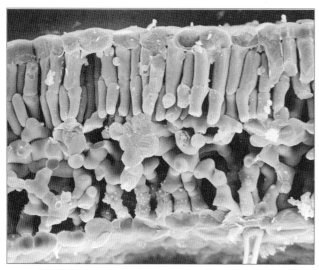

Figure 6.4 A photograph taken with a scanning electron microscope, showing the cells inside a leaf. Scanning electron microscopes provide 3D images. (× 400).

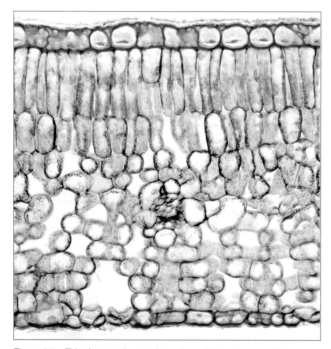

Figure 6.5 This photograph was taken using a light microscope. It shows a transverse section of a leaf from a tea plant. Can you identify all the tissues labelled in Figure 6.3? (× 400).

Leaf adaptations

Leaves are adapted to obtain carbon dioxide, water and sunlight.

Carbon dioxide

Carbon dioxide is obtained from the air. There is not very much available, because only about 0.04% of the air is carbon dioxide. Therefore, the leaf must be very efficient at absorbing it. The leaf is held out into the air by the stem and the leaf stalk, and its large surface area helps to expose it to as much air as possible.

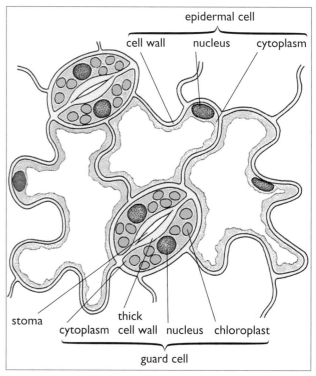

Figure 6.6 Surface view of the lower epidermis of a leaf.

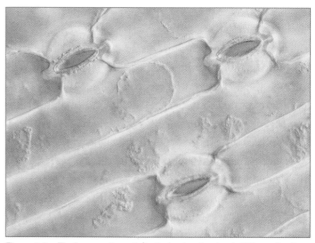

Figure 6.7 The lower surface of a leaf, showing the closely fitting cells of the epidermis. The oval openings are stomata, and the two curved cells around each stoma are guard cells (× 450).

Activity 6.1

Use a microscope to observe the cells that cover a leaf.

❓ Questions

6.4 What is another name for a leaf stalk?

6.5 Which kind of cell makes the cuticle on a leaf?

6.6 What is the function of the cuticle?

6.7 What are stomata?

6.8 What are guard cells?

6.9 List **three** kinds of cell in a leaf which contain chloroplasts, and **one** kind which does not.

S The cells which need the carbon dioxide are the mesophyll cells, inside the leaf. The carbon dioxide can get into the leaf through the stomata. It does this by diffusion, which is described in Chapter 3. Behind each stoma is an air space (Figure **6.3**) which connects up with other air spaces between the spongy mesophyll cells. The carbon dioxide can therefore diffuse to all the cells in the leaf. It can then diffuse through the cell wall and cell membrane of each cell, and into the chloroplasts.

Water

Water is obtained from the soil. It is absorbed by the root hairs, and carried up to the leaf in the xylem vessels. It then travels from the xylem vessels to the mesophyll cells by osmosis, which was described in Chapter 3. The path it takes is shown in Figures **6.8** and **6.9**.

Sunlight

The position of a leaf and its broad, flat surface help it to obtain as much sunlight as possible. If you look up through the branches of a tree, you will see that the leaves are arranged so that they do not cut off light from one another more than necessary. Plants that live in shady places often have particularly big leaves.

The cells that need the sunlight are the mesophyll cells. The thinness of the leaf allows the sunlight to penetrate right through it, and reach all the cells. To help this, the epidermal cells are transparent, with no chloroplasts.

In the mesophyll cells, the chloroplasts are arranged to get as much sunlight as possible, particularly those in the palisade cells. The chloroplasts can lie broadside

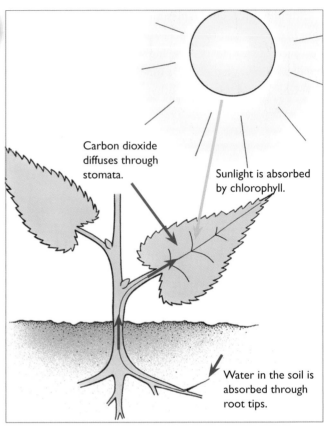

Figure 6.8 How the materials for photosynthesis get into a leaf.

Carbon dioxide diffuses through stomata.

Sunlight is absorbed by chlorophyll.

Water in the soil is absorbed through root tips.

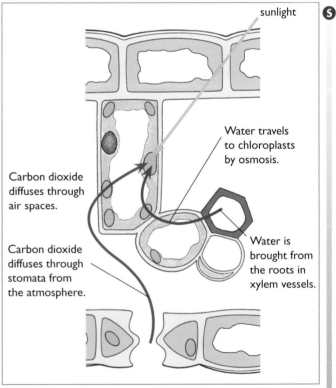

Figure 6.9 How the raw materials for photosynthesis get into a palisade cell.

sunlight **S**

Carbon dioxide diffuses through air spaces.

Carbon dioxide diffuses through stomata from the atmosphere.

Water travels to chloroplasts by osmosis.

Water is brought from the roots in xylem vessels.

on to do this, but in strong sunlight, they often arrange themselves end on. This reduces the amount of light absorbed. Inside them, the chlorophyll is arranged on flat membranes (Figure **6.10**) to expose as much as possible to the sunlight.

Adaptations of leaves for photosynthesis are shown in Table **6.1**.

Study tip

Note that chlorophyll does not 'attract' light. It absorbs energy from light.

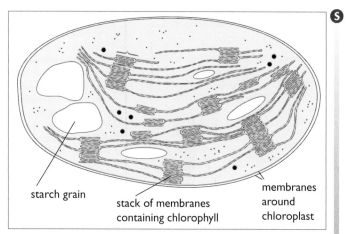

Figure 6.10　The structure of a chloroplast.

Adaptation	Function
supported by stem and petiole	to expose as much of the leaf as possible to the sunlight and air
large surface area	to expose as large an area as possible to the sunlight and air
thin	to allow sunlight to penetrate to all cells; to allow CO_2 to diffuse in and O_2 to diffuse out as quickly as possible
stomata in lower epidermis	to allow CO_2 to diffuse in and O_2 to diffuse out
air spaces in spongy mesophyll	to allow CO_2 and O_2 to diffuse to and from all cells
no chloroplasts in epidermal cells	to allow sunlight to penetrate to the mesophyll layer
chloroplasts containing chlorophyll present in the mesophyll layer	to absorb energy from sunlight, so that CO_2 will combine with H_2O
palisade cells arranged end on	to keep as few cell walls as possible between sunlight and the chloroplasts
chloroplasts inside palisade cells often arranged broadside on	to expose as much chlorophyll as possible to sunlight
chlorophyll arranged on flat membranes inside the chloroplasts	to expose as much chlorophyll as possible to sunlight
xylem vessels within short distance of every mesophyll cell	to supply water to the cells in the leaf, some of which will be used in photosynthesis
phloem tubes within short distance of every mesophyll cell	to take away sucrose and other organic products of photosynthesis

Table 6.1　Adaptations of leaves for photosynthesis.

❓ Questions

6.10 What are the raw materials needed for photosynthesis?

6.11 What percentage of the air is carbon dioxide?

6.12 How does carbon dioxide get into a leaf?

6.13 How does a leaf obtain its water?

6.14 Give **two** reasons why the large surface area of leaves is advantageous to the plant. Ⓢ

6.15 Leaves are thin. What purpose does this serve?

⑤ 6.4 Uses of glucose

One of the first carbohydrates to be made in photosynthesis is glucose. There are several things that may then happen to it (Figure **6.11**).

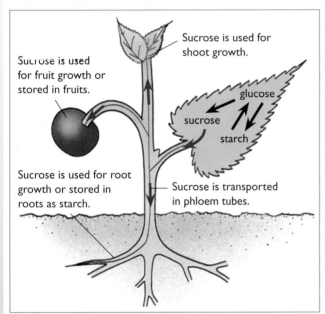

Sucrose is used for shoot growth.

Sucrose is used for fruit growth or stored in fruits.

glucose

sucrose

starch

Sucrose is used for root growth or stored in roots as starch.

Sucrose is transported in phloem tubes.

Figure 6.11 The products of photosynthesis.

Used for energy

Energy may be released from glucose in the leaf. All cells need energy, which they obtain by the process of respiration (Chapter **11**). Some of the glucose which a leaf makes will be broken down by respiration, to release energy.

Stored as starch

Glucose may be turned into starch and stored in the leaf. Glucose is a simple sugar (page **41**). It is soluble in water, and quite a reactive substance. It is not, therefore, a very good storage molecule. First, being reactive, it might get involved in chemical reactions where it is not wanted. Secondly, it would dissolve in the water in and around the plant cells, and might be lost from the cell. Thirdly, when dissolved, it would increase the concentration of the solution in the cell, which could cause damage.

The glucose is therefore converted into starch to be stored. Starch is a polysaccharide, made of many glucose molecules joined together. Being such a large molecule, it is not very reactive, and not very soluble. It can be made into granules which can be easily stored inside the chloroplasts.

Used to make proteins and other organic substances ⑤

Glucose may be used to make other organic substances. The plant can use glucose as a starting point for making all the other organic substances it needs. These include the carbohydrates sucrose and cellulose. Plants also make fats and oils.

Plants can also use the sugars they have made in photosynthesis to make amino acids, which can be built up into proteins. To do this, they need nitrogen. Unfortunately, even though the air around us is 78 % nitrogen, this is completely useless to plants because it is very unreactive. Plants have to be supplied with nitrogen in a more reactive form, usually as nitrate ions. They absorb nitrate ions from the soil, through their root hairs, by diffusion and active transport. The nitrate ions combine with glucose to make amino acids. The amino acids are then strung together to form protein molecules.

Another substance that plants make is chlorophyll. Once again, they need nitrogen to do this, and also another element – magnesium. The magnesium, like the nitrate ions, is obtained from the soil.

Table **6.2** shows what happens to a plant if it does not have enough of these ions. Figure **6.12** shows what happens when a plant does not have enough nitrogen. Farmers often add extra mineral ions to the soil in which their crops are growing, to make sure that they do not run short of these essential substances.

Changed to sucrose for transport

A molecule has to be small and soluble to be transported easily. Glucose has both of these properties, but it is also rather reactive. It is therefore converted to the complex sugar sucrose to be transported to other parts of the plant. Sucrose molecules are also quite small and soluble, but less reactive than glucose. They dissolve in the sap in the phloem vessels, and can be distributed to

Element	nitrogen	magnesium
Mineral salt	nitrates or ammonium ions	magnesium ions
Why needed	to make proteins	to make chlorophyll
Deficiency	weak growth, yellow leaves	yellowing between the veins of leaves

Table 6.2 Mineral ions required by plants.

Figure 6.12 This stunted, yellow maize seedling is suffering from nitrogen deficiency.

whichever parts of the plant need them (Figure 6.11).

The sucrose may later be turned back into glucose again, to be broken down to release energy, or turned into starch and stored, or used to make other substances which are needed for growth.

Questions

6.16 Why is glucose not very good for storage in a leaf?

6.17 What substances does a plant need to be able to convert glucose into proteins?

6.18 Explain why a plant that does not get enough nitrate has weak growth.

6.19 How do parts of the plant such as the roots, which cannot photosynthesise, obtain food?

6.5 Testing leaves for starch

Iodine solution is used to test for starch. A blue-black colour shows that starch is present. However, if you put iodine solution onto a leaf which contains starch, it will not immediately turn black. This is because the starch is inside the chloroplasts in the cells. The iodine solution cannot get through the cell membranes to reach the starch and react with it.

Another difficulty is that the green colour of the leaf and the brown iodine solution can look black together.

Therefore, before testing a leaf for starch, you must break down the cell membranes, and get rid of the green colour (chlorophyll). The way this is done is described in Activity 6.2. The cell membranes are first broken down by boiling water, and then the chlorophyll is removed by dissolving it out with alcohol.

Activity 6.2
Testing a leaf for starch

Skills
AO3.1 Using techniques, apparatus and materials

Leaves turn some of the glucose that they make in photosynthesis into starch. If we find starch in a leaf, that tells us if it has been photosynthesising.

 Wear eye protection if available.
Take care with the boiling water.
Alcohol is *very flammable*. Turn out your Bunsen flame *before* putting the tube of alcohol into the hot water.
Use forceps to handle the leaf.

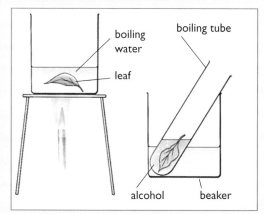

1 Take a leaf from a healthy plant, and drop it into boiling water in a water bath. Leave for about 30 s. Turn out the Bunsen flame.

2 Remove the leaf, which will be very soft, and drop it into a tube of alcohol in the water bath. Leave it until all the chlorophyll has come out of the leaf.

3 The leaf will now be brittle. Remove it from the alcohol, and dip it into hot water again to soften it.

4 Spread out the leaf on a white tile, and cover it with iodine solution. A blue-black colour shows that the leaf contains starch.

Questions

A1 Why was the leaf put into boiling water?

A2 Why did the alcohol become green?

A3 Why was the leaf put into alcohol after being put into boiling water?

Controls

If you do Activities **6.3**, **6.4** and **6.5**, you can find out for yourself which substances a plant needs for photosynthesis. In each investigation, the plant is given everything it needs, except for one substance. Another plant is used at the same time. This is a control. The control is given everything it needs, including the substance being tested for. Sometimes the control is a leaf, or even a part of a leaf, from the experimental plant. The important thing is that the control has all the substances it needs, while the experimental plant – or leaf – is lacking one substance.

Both plants (or leaves) are then treated in exactly the same way. Any differences between them at the end of the investigation, therefore, must be because of the substance being tested.

At the end of the investigation, test a leaf from your experimental plant and one from your control to see if they have made starch. By comparing them,

you can find out which substances are necessary for photosynthesis.

Destarching plants

It is very important that the leaves you are testing should not have any starch in them at the beginning of the investigation. If they did, and you found that the leaves contained starch at the end of the investigation, you could not be sure that they had been photosynthesising. The starch might have been made before the investigation began.

So, before doing any of these investigations, you must destarch the plants. The easiest way to do this is to leave them in a dark cupboard for at least 24 hours. The plants cannot photosynthesise while they are in the cupboard because there is no light. So they use up their stores of starch. To be certain that they are thoroughly destarched, test a leaf for starch before you begin.

Activity 6.3
To see if light is needed for photosynthesis

Skills
AO3.1 Using techniques, apparatus and materials
AO3.3 Observing, measuring and recording
AO3.4 Interpreting and evaluating observations and data

 Wear eye protection if available.
Take care with the boiling water.
Alcohol is *very flammable*. Turn out your Bunsen flame *before* putting the tube of alcohol into the hot water.
Use forceps to handle the leaf.

1   Take a healthy bean or Pelargonium plant, growing in a pot. Leave it in a cupboard for a few days, to destarch it.
2   Test one of its leaves for starch, to check that it does not contain any.
3   Using a folded piece of black paper or aluminium foil, a little larger than a leaf, cut out a shape (see diagram). Fasten the paper or foil over both sides of a leaf on your plant, making sure that the edges are held firmly together. Don't take the leaf off the plant!

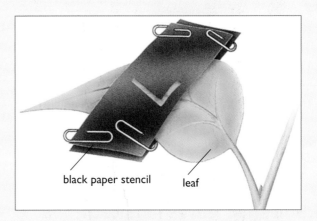

black paper stencil   leaf

4   Leave the plant near a warm, sunny window for a few days.
5   Remove the cover from your leaf, and test the leaf for starch.
6   Make a labelled drawing of the appearance of your leaf after testing for starch.

❓ Questions

A1 Why was the plant destarched before the beginning of the experiment?
A2 Why was part of the leaf left uncovered?
A3 What do your results tell you about light and photosynthesis?

Activity 6.4
To see if chlorophyll is needed for photosynthesis

Skills
AO3.1 Using techniques, apparatus and materials
AO3.3 Observing, measuring and recording
AO3.4 Interpreting and evaluating observations and data

 Wear eye protection if available. Take care with the boiling water. Alcohol is *very flammable*. Turn out your Bunsen flame *before* putting the tube of alcohol into the hot water. Use forceps to handle the leaf.

1 Destarch a plant with variegated (green and white) leaves. Then leave your plant in a warm, sunny spot for a few days.

2 Test one of the leaves for starch (Activity **6.2**).

3 Make a drawing of your leaf before and after testing.

? Questions

A1 What was the control in this investigation?

A2 What do your results tell you about chlorophyll and photosynthesis?

Activity 6.5
To show that oxygen is produced in photosynthesis

Skills
AO3.1 Using techniques, apparatus and materials
AO3.3 Observing, measuring and recording

1 Set up the apparatus shown in the diagram. Make sure that the test tube is completely full of water.

2 Leave the apparatus near a warm, sunny window for a few days.

3 Carefully remove the test tube from the top of the funnel, allowing the water to run out, but not allowing the gas to escape.

4 Light a wooden splint, and then blow it out so that it is just glowing. Carefully put it into the gas in the test tube. If it bursts into flame, then the gas is oxygen.

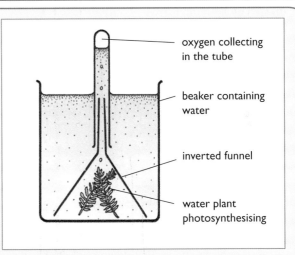

oxygen collecting in the tube

beaker containing water

inverted funnel

water plant photosynthesising

? Questions

A1 Why was this investigation done under water?

A2 This investigation has no control. Try to design one.

Activity 6.6
To see if carbon dioxide is needed for photosynthesis

Activity 6.7
Photosynthesis in a pond weed

⑤ Activity 6.8
Investigating the effect of light intensity on photosynthesis

Skills
AO3.1 Using techniques, apparatus and materials
AO3.2 Planning
AO3.3 Observing, measuring and recording
AO3.4 Interpreting and evaluating observations and data
AO3.5 Evaluating methods

 If you use an electric lamp, keep water well away from it.

If you did Activity **6.6**, you may have noticed that the plant seemed to produce more bubbles in bright sunlight than when it was in the shade. This could mean that the rate of photosynthesis is affected by light intensity.

1   Write down a hypothesis that you will investigate. The hypothesis should be one sentence, and it should describe the relationship that you think exists between light intensity and the rate of photosynthesis. You can vary light intensity by moving a light source closer to the plant. The shorter the distance between the light and the plant, the greater the light intensity.
You can use a water plant in your investigation.

2   Once you have an idea about how you will do your experiment, write it down as a list of points. Then think through it again, and make improvements to your plan. Once you are fairly happy with it, show your teacher. You must not try to do your experiment until your teacher says that you may begin.
 ♦ What apparatus and other materials will you need for your experiment?
 ♦ What will you vary in your experiment? How will you vary it?
 ♦ What will you keep the same in all the tubes or beakers in your experiment? How will you do this?

 ♦ What will you measure in your experiment? How will you measure it? When will you measure it? Will you do repeat measurements and calculate a mean?
 ♦ How will you record your results? (You can sketch out a results chart, ready to fill in.)
 ♦ How will you display your results? (You can sketch the axes of the graph you plan to draw.)
 ♦ What will your results be if your hypothesis is correct? (You can sketch the shape of the graph you think you will get.)

3   Once you have approval from your teacher, you should do your experiment. Most scientific researchers find that they want to make changes to their experiment once they actually begin doing it.
This is a good thing to do. Make careful notes about all the changes that you make.

4   Finally, write up your experiment in the usual way, including:
 ♦ a heading, and the hypothesis that you tested
 ♦ a diagram of the apparatus that you used, and a full description of your method
 ♦ a neat and carefully headed table of results, including means if you decided to do repeats
 ♦ a neat and carefully headed line graph of your results
 ♦ a conclusion, in which you say whether or not your results support your hypothesis
 ♦ a discussion, in which you use what you know about photosynthesis to try to explain the pattern in your results
 ♦ an evaluation of the reliability of your data
 ♦ an evaluation of your method.

⑤ 6.6 Limiting factors

If a plant is given plenty of sunlight, carbon dioxide and water, the limit on the rate at which it can photosynthesise is its own ability to absorb these materials, and make them react. However, quite often plants do not have unlimited supplies of these materials, and so their rate of photosynthesis is not as high as it might be.

Sunlight

In the dark, a plant cannot photosynthesise at all. In dim light, it can photosynthesise slowly. As light intensity increases, the rate of photosynthesis will increase, until the plant is photosynthesising as fast as it can. At this point, even if the light becomes brighter, the plant cannot photosynthesise any faster (Figure **6.13**).

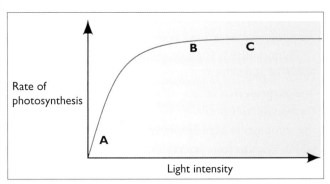

Figure 6.13 The effect of light intensity on the rate of photosynthesis.

Over the first part of the curve in Figure **6.13**, between A and B, light is a limiting factor. The plant is limited in how fast it can photosynthesise because it does not have enough light. You can see this because when the plant is given more light it photosynthesises faster.

Between B and C, however, light is not a limiting factor. You can show this because, even if more light is shone on the plant, it still cannot photosynthesise any faster. It already has as much light as it can use.

Carbon dioxide

Carbon dioxide can also be a limiting factor (Figure **6.14**). The more carbon dioxide a plant is given, the faster it can photosynthesise up to a point, but then a maximum is reached.

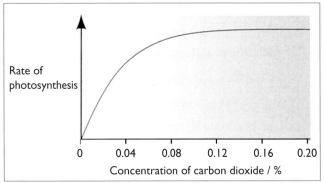

Figure 6.14 The effect of carbon dioxide concentration on the rate of photosynthesis.

Temperature

The chemical reactions of photosynthesis can only take place very slowly at low temperatures, so a plant can photosynthesise faster on a warm day than on a cold one.

Stomata

The carbon dioxide which a plant uses diffuses into the leaf through the stomata. If the stomata are closed, then photosynthesis cannot take place. Stomata often close if the weather is very hot and sunny, to prevent too much water being lost. This means that on a really hot day photosynthesis may slow down.

Growing crops in glasshouses

When plants are growing outside, we cannot do much about changing the conditions that they need for photosynthesis. If a field of sorghum does not get enough sunshine, or is short of carbon dioxide, then it just has to stay that way. But if crops are grown in glasshouses, then it is possible to control the conditions so that they are photosynthesising as fast as possible.

For example, in parts of the world where it is often too cold for good growth of some crop plants, they

---

Key definition

limiting factor – something present in the environment in such short supply that it restricts life processes

---

Activity 6.9
Investigating the effect of carbon dioxide concentration on the rate of photosynthesis.

(S) can be grown in heated glasshouses. This is done, for example, with tomatoes. The temperature in the glasshouse can be kept at the optimum level to encourage the tomatoes to grow fast and strongly, and to produce a large yield of fruit that ripens quickly.

Light can also be controlled. In cloudy or dark conditions, extra lighting can be provided, so that light is not limiting the rate of photosynthesis. The kind of lights that are used can be chosen carefully so that they provide just the right wavelengths that the plants need.

In tropical countries, the problem may be that temperature and light intensity are too high. Both of these can be reduced by shading the plants from direct sunlight. This could be inside a closed glasshouse, but this will usually need to have windows or parts of the roof that can be opened, to allow hot air to escape. It is often simpler, and just as effective, to provide shade by growing taller plants nearby, or by providing a simple roof over the crop plants.

Carbon dioxide concentration can also be controlled. Carbon dioxide is often a limiting factor for photosynthesis, because its natural concentration in the air is so very low. In a closed glasshouse, it is possible to provide extra carbon dioxide for the plants.

(?) Questions

6.20 What is meant by a limiting factor?   (S)
6.21 Name **two** factors which may limit the rate of photosynthesis of a healthy plant.
6.22 Why do plants sometimes stop photosynthesising on a very hot, dry day?

6.7 The importance of photosynthesis

Photosynthesis is of importance, not only to green plants, but to all living organisms. It is the basic reaction which brings the energy of the Sun into ecosystems (page 266). The flow of energy in ecosystems is one-way. So there is a constant need for replenishment from the energy source, and therefore a constant need for photosynthesis.

Photosynthesis is also essential for maintaining a constant global level of oxygen and carbon dioxide. The oxygen given off is available for respiration. Carbon dioxide produced by respiration and from the combustion of fuels is used in photosynthesis, which helps to stop the levels of carbon dioxide in the atmosphere from rising too high.

(S) Activity 6.10
Investigating the effect of temperature on the rate of photosynthesis.

Summary

You should know:

♦ the equation for photosynthesis
♦ the role of chlorophyll in photosynthesis
(S) ♦ the structure of a leaf
♦ how a leaf is adapted to carry out photosynthesis efficiently
♦ how a plant uses and stores the carbohydrates made in photosynthesis
♦ why plants need nitrate ions and magnesium ions
♦ how to test a leaf for starch
♦ how to do experiments to investigate the need for chlorophyll, light and carbon dioxide for photosynthesis
(S) ♦ about the importance of a control in an experiment
♦ about factors that can limit the rate of photosynthesis
♦ how to investigate the effect of light intensity, temperature and carbon dioxide on the rate of photosynthesis
♦ how glasshouses can be used to provide optimum conditions for photosynthesis of crop plants.

End-of-chapter questions

1 Copy and complete this table to show how, and for what purpose, plants obtain these substances.

	Obtained from	Used for
Nitrates		
Water		
Magnesium		
Carbon dioxide		

2 Explain the difference between each of these pairs of terms.

    a   chloroplast and chlorophyll
    b   palisade layer and spongy layer
    c   organic substances and inorganic substances
    d   guard cell and stoma

3 **a**   Write the word equation for photosynthesis.
    b   Describe how a leaf obtains the two substances on the left hand side of your equation.
    c   Describe what happens to the two substances on the right hand side of your equation.

S 4 Explain how each of the following helps a leaf to photosynthesise.

    a   There is an air space behind each stoma.
    b   The epidermal cells of a leaf do not have chloroplasts.
    c   Leaves have a large surface area.
    d   The veins in a leaf branch repeatedly.
    e   Chloroplasts have many membranes in them.

5 Which carbohydrate does a plant use for each of these purposes? Explain why.

    a   transport
    b   storage

6 Describe how a carbon atom in a carbon dioxide molecule in the air could become part of a starch molecule in a carrot root. Mention all the structures it would pass through, and what would happen to it at each stage.

7 The diagram shows a section through a leaf.

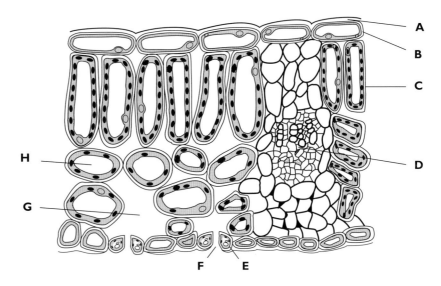

S **a** Give the letters that indicate **i** a stoma, **ii** the cuticle and **iii** a vascular bundle. [3]

  b **i** The upper layers of a leaf are transparent. Suggest an advantage to a plant of this feature. [1]

    ii The cuticle is made of a waxy material. Suggest an advantage to a plant of this feature. [1]

    iii State **two** functions of vascular bundles in leaves. [2]

  c Most photosynthesis in plants happens in leaves.

    i Name the **two** raw materials needed for photosynthesis. [2]

    ii Photosynthesis produces glucose.

      Describe how plants make use of this glucose. [4]

8 A student set up the apparatus shown in the diagram to investigate the effect of carbon dioxide concentration on the rate of photosynthesis of a pond plant. The student used five similar pieces of pond plant and five different concentrations of sodium hydrogencarbonate ($NaHCO_3$) solution, which provides the carbon dioxide. The student counted the number of bubbles produced by the pond plant over a period of five minutes.

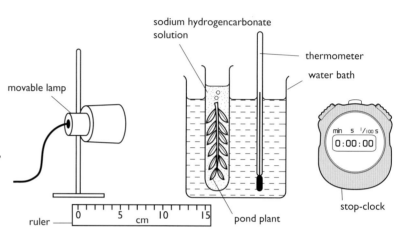

  a Explain how the student made sure that the results were due only to the change in carbon dioxide concentration. [4]

The student repeated the investigation at each concentration and calculated the rate of photosynthesis. The student's results are shown in the table below.

Carbon dioxide concentration / %	Rate of photosynthesis / number of bubbles per minute			
	1st	2nd	3rd	mean
0	3	2	4	3
0.1	6	4	5	5
0.2	12	7	11	
0.3	14	15	16	15
0.4	18	22	21	20
0.5	19	23	21	21

  b **i** Calculate the mean rate of photosynthesis when the carbon dioxide concentration was 0.2%. [1]

    ii Plot the results from the table on graph paper. Draw an appropriate line on the graph to show the relationship between carbon dioxide concentration and the rate of photosynthesis. [2]

  c Explain the effect of increasing carbon dioxide concentration on the rate of photosynthesis up to 0.4% as shown in your graph. [2]

  d Suggest the result that the student would get if a carbon dioxide concentration of 0.6% was used and explain your answer. [3]

  e The student used tap water as the 0% carbon dioxide concentration. Explain why the student recorded some bubbles being produced. [1]

[*Cambridge IGCSE® Biology 0610/32, Question 3, October/November 2009*]

7 Animal nutrition

In this chapter, you will find out about:

♦ a balanced diet
♦ nutrients and their sources
♦ that different people need different amounts of energy in their diet
♦ why we need to digest the food that we eat
♦ teeth
♦ the structure of the alimentary canal, and the functions of each of its parts
♦ how digested food is absorbed and assimilated.

Stomach acid

Figure 7.1 is a photograph taken through an endoscope, showing the inside of a person's stomach. An endoscope is a tube that can be swallowed. Light is shone down the tube, so that doctors can view the stomach lining.

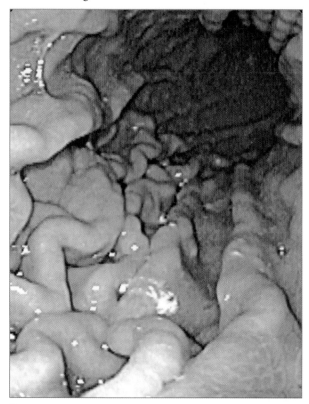

Figure 7.1 This is what the inside of a human stomach looks like.

The stomach is part of the digestive system – a long tube along which the food that you eat travels after you swallow it. You can see that the stomach has many folds inside it. The cells covering these folds secrete enzymes and hydrochloric acid. Both of these substances help in digestion – the breakdown of your food into small molecules. These small molecules then have to travel through the walls of the digestive system to get into the blood, which delivers them to any of your cells that need them.

The hydrochloric acid in your stomach has a concentration of about $0.1\,mol\,dm^{-3}$. If you dipped a piece of blue litmus paper into it, it would turn bright red. This acid helps to activate the enzymes in the stomach. It also helps to unravel folded-up protein molecules in our food (it denatures them), making it easier for enzymes to digest them by chopping up their long chains of amino acids. And it also destroys many of the bacteria that are present in our food, reducing the chance of these breeding inside us and making us ill.

The stomach doesn't secrete acid all the time. Acid secretion is switched on when we see, smell or taste food. The brain reacts to these stimuli by sending impulses along nerves to the acid-secreting cells in the stomach wall, switching them on. Once the food has moved out of the stomach, into the next part of the digestive system, acid secretion stops.

7.1 Diet

Animals get their food from other organisms – from plants or other animals. They cannot make their own food as plants do.

The food an animal eats every day is called its diet. Most animals need seven types of nutrient in their diet. These are:

♦ carbohydrates
♦ proteins
♦ fats
♦ vitamins
♦ minerals
♦ water
♦ fibre.

A diet which contains all of these things, in the correct amounts and proportions, is called a balanced diet.

Energy needs

Every day, a person uses up energy. The amount you use partly depends on how old you are, which sex you are and what job you do. A few examples are shown in Figure 7.2.

The energy you use each day comes from the food you eat. If you eat too much food, some of the extra will probably be stored as fat. If you eat too little, you may not be able to obtain as much energy as you need. This will make you feel tired.

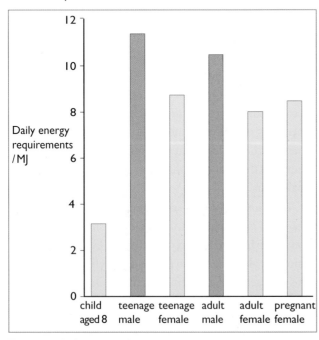

Figure 7.2 Daily energy requirements.

All food contains some energy. Scientists have worked out how much energy there is in particular kinds of food. You can look up this information. A few examples are given in Table 7.1. You may remember that one gram of fat contains about twice as much energy as one gram of protein or carbohydrate (page 47). This is why fried foods should be avoided if you are worried about putting on weight.

A person's diet may need to change at different times of their life. For example, a woman will need to eat a little more each day when she is pregnant, and make sure that she has extra calcium and iron in her diet, to help to build her baby's bones, teeth and blood. She will also need to eat more while she is breast feeding. Most people find that they need to eat less as they reach their 50s and 60s, because their metabolism slows down.

Nutrients

As well as providing you with energy, food is needed for many other reasons. To make sure that you eat a balanced diet you must eat foods containing carbohydrate, fat and protein. You also need each kind of vitamin and mineral, fibre and water. These substances are called nutrients. If your diet doesn't contain all of these nutrients, your body will not be able to work properly.

The structures of molecules of carbohydrates, fats and proteins, and their uses in the body, are described in sections 4.2 to 4.4, on pages 41 to 46. Figures 7.3, 7.4, 7.5 and 7.6 show foods that are good sources of these nutrients.

Vitamins

Vitamins are organic substances which are only needed in tiny amounts. If you do not have enough of a vitamin, you may get a deficiency disease. Table 7.2 on page 76 provides information about vitamins C and D.

Minerals

Minerals are inorganic substances. Once again, only small amounts of them are needed in the diet. Table 7.3 on page 76 shows two of the most important ones.

Fibre

Fibre helps to keep the alimentary canal working properly. Food moves through the alimentary canal (page 82) because the muscles contract and relax to

Food	kJ / 100 g
baked beans	270
bananas	326
boiled egg	612
boiled white (Irish) potatoes	339
brown bread	948
cabbage	66
canned peaches	373
carrots	98
cheddar cheese	1682
chocolate	2214
chocolate biscuits	2197
cornflakes	1567
cottage cheese	402
custard	496
fish (dried, salt)	1016
fish (fresh)	340
french fries	1065
fried liver	1016
fruit yoghurt	405
ice cream	698
lentils	1293
lettuce	36
marmalade	1035
melon	96
milk	272
oatmeal	1698
oranges	150
pawpaw	160
peas	161
plain biscuits	1925
rice	1536
roast chicken	599
roast peanuts	2364
sardines	906
spaghetti	1612
stewed steak	932
sugar	1682
tomatoes	60
unsweetened fruit juice	143
white bread	991

Table 7.1   Energy content of some different kinds of food.

Figure 7.3   Some good sources of carbohydrates.

Figure 7.4   Some good sources of proteins.

Figure 7.5   Some good sources of fats.

Figure 7.6   Some good sources of fibre.

squeeze it along. This is called peristalsis. The muscles are stimulated to do this when there is food in the alimentary canal. Soft foods do not stimulate the muscles very much. The muscles work more strongly when there is harder, less digestible food, like fibre, in the alimentary canal. Fibre keeps the digestive system in good working order, and helps to prevent constipation.

All plant foods, such as fruits and vegetables, contain fibre (Figure 7.6). This is because the plant cells have cellulose cell walls. Humans cannot digest cellulose.

One common form of fibre is the outer husk of cereal grains, such as oats, wheat and barley. This is called bran. Some of this husk is found in wholemeal bread. Brown or unpolished rice is also a good source of fibre.

Fat and heart disease

The kind of fat found in animal foods is called saturated fat. These foods also contain cholesterol. Some research suggests that people who eat a lot of saturated fat and cholesterol are more likely to get heart disease than people who do not. This is because fat deposits build up on the inside of arteries, making them stiffer and narrower. If this happens in the coronary arteries supplying the heart muscle with blood, then not enough blood can get through. The heart muscles run short of oxygen and cannot work properly. This is called coronary heart disease. The deposits can also cause a blood clot, which results in a heart attack (page 109).

Dairy products such as milk, cream, butter and cheese contain a lot of saturated fat. So do red meat and eggs. But vegetable oils are usually unsaturated fats. These, and also oils from fish, do not increase the risk of heart disease, so it is sensible to use these instead of animal fats when possible.

Vegetable oil can be used for frying instead of butter or lard. Polyunsaturated spreads can be used instead of butter.

Fish and white meat such as chicken do not contain much saturated fat, so eating more of these and less red meat may help to cut down the risk of heart disease.

Obesity

People who take in more energy than they use up get fat. Being very fat is called obesity (Figure 7.7). Obesity is dangerous to health. Obese people are more likely to get heart disease, strokes and, diabetes. The extra weight placed on the legs can cause problems with the joints, especially knees.

Most people can control their weight by eating normal, well-balanced meals and taking regular exercise. Crash diets are not a good idea, except for someone who is very overweight. Although a person

Vitamin	Foods that contain it	Why it is needed	Deficiency disease
C	citrus fruits (such as oranges, limes), raw vegetables	to make the stretchy protein collagen, found in skin and other tissues; keeps tissues in good repair	scurvy, which causes pain in joints and muscles, and bleeding from gums and other places; this used to be a common disease of sailors, who had no fresh vegetables during long voyages
D	butter, egg yolk (and can be made by the skin when sunlight falls on it)	helps calcium to be absorbed, for making bones and teeth	**S** rickets, in which the bones become soft and deformed; this disease was common in young children in industrial areas, who rarely got out into the sunshine

Table 7.2 Vitamins.

Mineral element	Foods that contain it	Why it is needed	Deficiency disease
calcium, Ca	milk and other dairy products, bread	for bones and teeth; for blood clotting	brittle bones and teeth; poor blood clotting
iron, Fe	liver, red meat, egg yolk, dark green vegetables	for making haemoglobin, the red pigment in blood which carries oxygen	**S** anaemia, in which there are not enough red blood cells so the tissues do not get enough oxygen delivered to them

Table 7.3 Minerals.

may manage to lose a lot of weight quickly, he or she will almost certainly put it on again once he or she stops dieting.

Starvation and malnutrition

In many countries in the world, there is no danger of people suffering from obesity. In some parts of Africa, for example, several years of drought can mean that the harvests do not provide enough food to feed all the people. Despite help from other countries, many people have died from starvation. Even if there is enough food to keep people alive, they may suffer from malnutrition.

Ⓢ Malnutrition is caused by not eating a balanced diet. One common form of malnutrition is **kwashiorkor** (Figure 7.8). This is caused by a lack of protein in the diet. It is most common in children between the ages of nine months and two years, after they have stopped feeding on breast milk.

Kwashiorkor is often caused by poverty, because the child's carers do not have any high-protein food to give to the child. But sometimes it is caused by a lack of knowledge about the right kinds of food that should be eaten.

Children suffering from kwashiorkor are always underweight for their age. But they may often look quite fat, because their diet may contain a lot of carbohydrate. If they are put onto a high-protein diet, they usually begin to grow normally again.

Figure 7.7 Being very overweight increases the risk of many different, and serious, health problems. Weight around your middle has been shown to be clearly linked to heart disease.

Figure 7.8 The older boy is thin, but has a swollen abdomen, suggesting he is suffering from kwashiorkor. This photo was taken at a refugee camp in Ethiopa.

The most severe forms of malnutrition result from a lack of both protein and energy in the diet. Severe shortage of energy in the diet causes **marasmus**, in which a child has body weight much lower than normal, and looks emaciated. Ⓢ

Activity 7.1
Testing foods for vitamin C

Skills
AO3.1 Using techniques, apparatus and materials
AO3.2 Planning
AO3.3 Observing, measuring and recording
AO3.4 Interpreting and evaluating observations and data
AO3.5 Evaluating methods

The DCPIP test is used to find out if a food contains vitamin C. DCPIP is a blue liquid. Vitamin C causes DCPIP to lose this colour.

First, try out the test:

1 Measure 2 cm³ of DCPIP into a clean test tube.
2 Use a dropper pipette to add lemon juice to the DCPIP. Count how many drops you need to add before the DCPIP loses its colour.

You can use this test to compare the concentration of vitamin C in different liquids. The less liquid you have to add to the DCPIP to make it lose its colour, the more vitamin C there is in the liquid.

3 Plan and carry out an experiment to test **one** of the following hypotheses.
   a Fresh lemon juice contains more vitamin C than other types of lemon juice.
   b Raw potato contains more vitamin C per g than boiled or baked potato.
   c Freezing vegetables or fruit juices reduces their vitamin C content.
   d Storing vegetables in a refrigerator retains more vitamin C than storing them at room temperature.

❓ Questions

7.1 A balanced diet contains these nutrients:

carbohydrates   fats   proteins
vitamins   minerals   water

   a   Which of these nutrients are organic, and
which are inorganic?

   b   Which of these nutrients can provide energy?

   c   What is the role of fibre in the diet?

7.2 List **three** health problems associated with obesity.

7.3 What is coronary heart disease?

7.4 What is the difference between starvation and
malnutrition?

7.5 What is meant by a deficiency disease?

7.6 Give **two** examples of deficiency diseases.

7.2 Digestion

The **alimentary canal** of a mammal is a long tube
running from one end of its body to the other (Figure
7.9). Before food can be of any use to the animal, it
has to get out of the alimentary canal and into the
bloodstream. This is called **absorption**. To be absorbed,
molecules of food have to get through the walls of the
alimentary canal. They need to be quite small to be able
to do this.

The food that is eaten by mammals usually contains
some large molecules of protein, carbohydrate and fat.
Before these molecules can be absorbed, they must be
broken down into small ones. This is called **digestion**.

Figure **7.10** shows what happens to the three kinds
of nutrients that need to be digested – fats, proteins and
carbohydrates. Look at one column at a time, and work
down it, to follow what happens to that type of food as it
passes through the alimentary canal.

Large carbohydrate molecules, such as polysaccharides,
have to be broken down into simple sugars
(monosaccharides). Proteins are broken down to amino
acids. Fats are broken down to fatty acids and glycerol
(Table 7.4).

Simple sugars, water, vitamins and minerals are
already small molecules, and they can be absorbed just
as they are. They do not need to be digested.

Nutrient	Enzyme that breaks it down	Small molecules produced
starch	amylase	simple sugars
protein	protease	amino acids
fat	lipase	fatty acids and glycerol

Table 7.4   Functions of digestive enzymes.

Mechanical and chemical digestion

Often the food an animal eats is in quite large pieces.
These pieces of food need to be broken up by teeth, and
by churning movements of the alimentary canal. This is
called **mechanical digestion**.

Once pieces of food have been ground up, the large
molecules present are then broken down into small

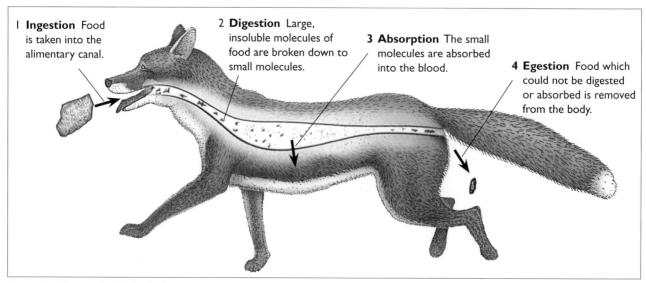

1 **Ingestion** Food is taken into the alimentary canal.

2 **Digestion** Large, insoluble molecules of food are broken down to small molecules.

3 **Absorption** The small molecules are absorbed into the blood.

4 **Egestion** Food which could not be digested or absorbed is removed from the body.

Figure 7.9   How an animal deals with food.

ones. This is called chemical digestion. It involves a chemical change from one sort of molecule to another. Enzymes are involved in this process (Chapter 5). Figure 7.10 summarises how mechanical and chemical digestion work together to produce small molecules the body can use.

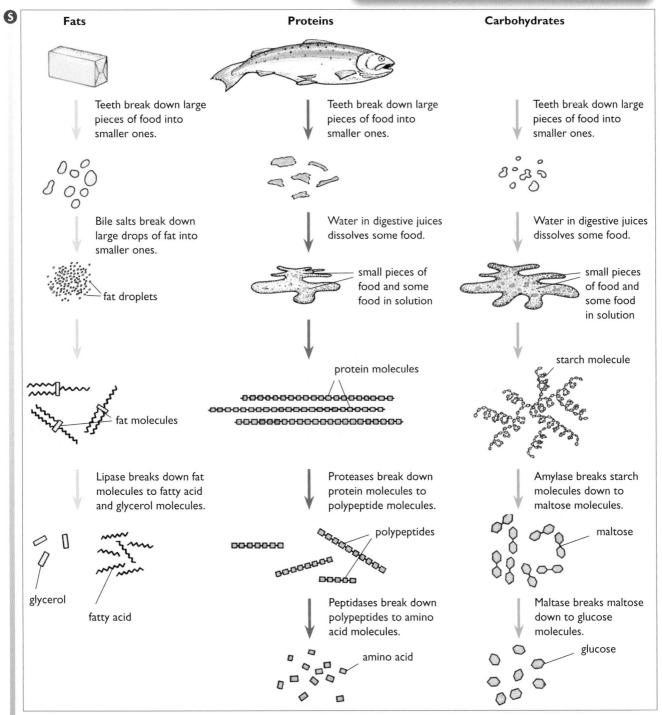

Figure 7.10 Digestion.

7.7 What is digestion?

7.8 Name **two** groups of food that do not need to be digested.

7.9 What does digestion change each of these kinds of food into: **a** polysaccharides, **b** proteins and **c** fats?

7.10 What is meant by chemical digestion?

7.3 Teeth

Teeth help with the **ingestion** and mechanical digestion of the food we eat.

Teeth can be used to bite off pieces of food. They then chop, crush or grind them into smaller pieces. This gives the food a larger surface area, which makes it easier for enzymes to work on the food in the digestive system. It also helps soluble parts of the food to dissolve.

The structure of a tooth is shown in Figure 7.11. The part of the tooth which is embedded in the gum is called the root. The part which can be seen is the crown. The crown is covered with enamel. Enamel is the hardest substance made by animals. It is very difficult to break or chip it. However, it can be dissolved by acids. Bacteria feed on sweet foods left on the teeth. This makes acids, which dissolve the enamel and decay sets in.

Under the enamel is a layer of dentine, which is rather like bone. Dentine is quite hard, but not as hard as enamel. It has channels in it which contain living cytoplasm.

In the middle of the tooth is the pulp cavity. It contains nerves and blood vessels. These supply the cytoplasm in the dentine with food and oxygen.

The root of the tooth is covered with cement. This has fibres growing out of it. These attach the tooth to the jawbone, but allow it to move slightly when biting or chewing.

Key definition

ingestion – taking of substances, e.g. food and drink, into the body through mouth

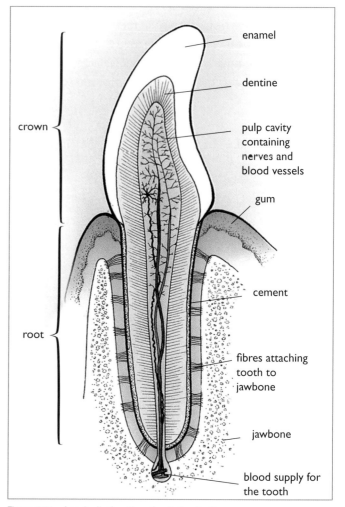

Figure 7.11 Longitudinal section of an incisor tooth.

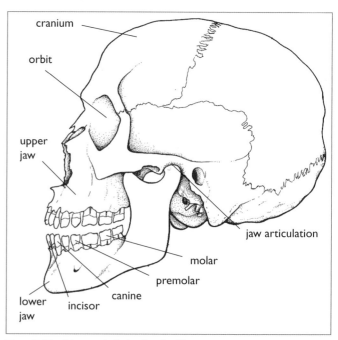

Figure 7.12 A human skull, showing the different types of teeth.

Types of teeth

Most mammals have four kinds of teeth (Figures **7.12** and **7.13**). Incisors are the sharp-edged, chisel-shaped teeth at the front of the mouth. They are used for biting off pieces of food. Canines are the more pointed teeth at either side of the incisors. Premolars and molars are the large teeth towards the back of the mouth. They are used for chewing food. In humans, the ones right at the back are sometimes called wisdom teeth. They do not grow until much later in the person's development than the others.

Mammals also differ from other animals in having two sets of teeth. The first set is called the milk teeth or deciduous teeth. In humans, these start to grow through the gum, one or two at a time, when a child is about five months old. By the age of 24 to 30 months, most children have a set of 20 teeth.

This first set of teeth begins to fall out when the child is about seven years old. Twenty teeth to replace the ones which fall out, plus 12 new teeth, make up the complete set of permanent teeth. There are 32

altogether. Most people have all their permanent teeth by about 17 years of age.

Dental decay

Tooth decay and gum disease are common problems. Both are caused by bacteria. You have large numbers of bacteria living in your mouth, most of which are harmless. However, some of these bacteria, together with substances from your saliva, form a sticky film over your teeth, especially next to the gums and in between the teeth. This is called plaque.

Plaque is soft and easy to remove at first, but if it is left it hardens to form tartar, which cannot be removed by brushing.

Gum disease

If plaque is not removed, the bacteria in it may infect the gums. The gums swell, become inflamed, and may bleed when you brush your teeth. This is usually painless, but if the bacteria are allowed to spread they may work down around the root of the tooth. The tooth becomes loose, and needs removing (Figure **7.14**).

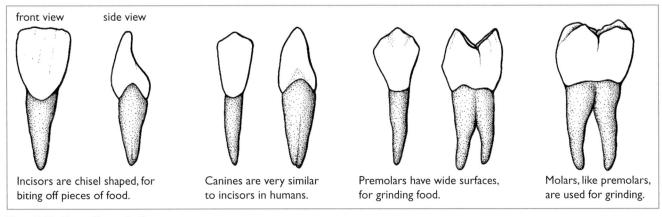

Incisors are chisel shaped, for biting off pieces of food.

Canines are very similar to incisors in humans.

Premolars have wide surfaces, for grinding food.

Molars, like premolars, are used for grinding.

Figure 7.13 Types of human teeth.

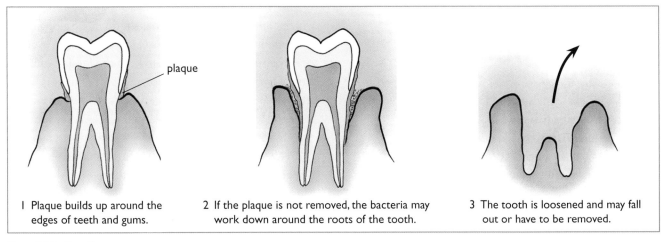

1 Plaque builds up around the edges of teeth and gums.

2 If the plaque is not removed, the bacteria may work down around the roots of the tooth.

3 The tooth is loosened and may fall out or have to be removed.

Figure 7.14 Gum disease.

Activity 7.2
Checking your teeth

Tooth decay

If sugar is left on the teeth, bacteria in the plaque will feed on it. They use it in respiration, changing it into acid. The acid gradually dissolves the enamel covering the tooth, and works its way into the dentine (Figure 7.15). Dentine is dissolved away more rapidly than the enamel. If nothing is done about it, the tooth will eventually have to be taken out.

There are several easy things which you can do to keep your teeth and gums healthy and free from pain.

1 Don't eat too much sugar. If you never eat any sugar, you will not have tooth decay. But nearly everyone enjoys sweet foods, and if you are careful you can still eat them without damaging your teeth. The rule is to eat sweet things only once or twice a day, preferably with your meals. The worst thing you can do is to suck or chew sweet things all day long. And don't forget that many drinks also contain a lot of sugar.

2 Use a fluoride toothpaste regularly. Fluoride makes your teeth more resistant to decay. Drinking water which contains fluoride, or brushing teeth with a fluoride toothpaste, makes it much less likely that you will have to have teeth filled or extracted. Regular and thorough brushing also helps to remove plaque, which will prevent gum disease and reduce decay.

3 Make regular visits to a dentist. Regular dental check-ups will make sure that any gum disease or tooth decay is stopped before it really gets a hold.

Questions

7.11 What are incisors, and what are they used for?

7.12 Describe **two** ways in which mammals' teeth differ from those of other animals.

7.13 What is plaque?

7.14 Explain how plaque can cause:
a gum disease and b tooth decay.

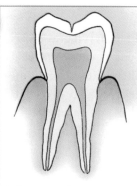
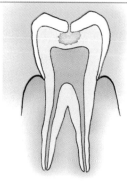

1 Particles of sugary foods get trapped in cracks in the teeth.

2 Bacteria feeding on the sugar form acids, which dissolve a hole in the enamel and dentine.

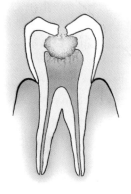
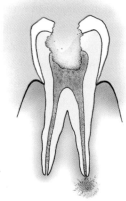

3 There are nerves in the pulp cavity, so the tooth becomes very painful if the infection gets this far.

4 The infection can spread rapidly through the pulp cavity, and may form an abscess at the root of the tooth.

Figure 7.15 Tooth decay.

7.4 The alimentary canal

The alimentary canal is a long tube which runs from the mouth to the anus. It is part of the digestive system. The digestive system also includes the liver and the pancreas.

The wall of the alimentary canal contains muscles, which contract and relax to make food move along. This movement is called peristalsis (Figure 7.16).

Sometimes, it is necessary to keep the food in one part of the alimentary canal for a while, before it is allowed to move to the next part. Special muscles can close the tube completely in certain places. They are called sphincter muscles.

To help the food to slide easily through the alimentary canal, it is lubricated with mucus. Mucus is made in goblet cells which occur along the alimentary canal.

Each section of the alimentary canal has its own

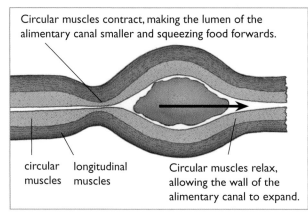

Circular muscles contract, making the lumen of the alimentary canal smaller and squeezing food forwards.

circular muscles   longitudinal muscles

Circular muscles relax, allowing the wall of the alimentary canal to expand.

Figure 7.16   Peristalsis.

part to play in the digestion, absorption, and egestion of food. Figure 7.17 shows the main organs of the digestive system.

The mouth

Food is ingested using the teeth, lips and tongue. The teeth then bite or grind the food into smaller pieces, increasing its surface area.

The tongue mixes the food with saliva, and forms it into a bolus. The bolus is then swallowed.

Saliva is made in the salivary glands. It is a mixture

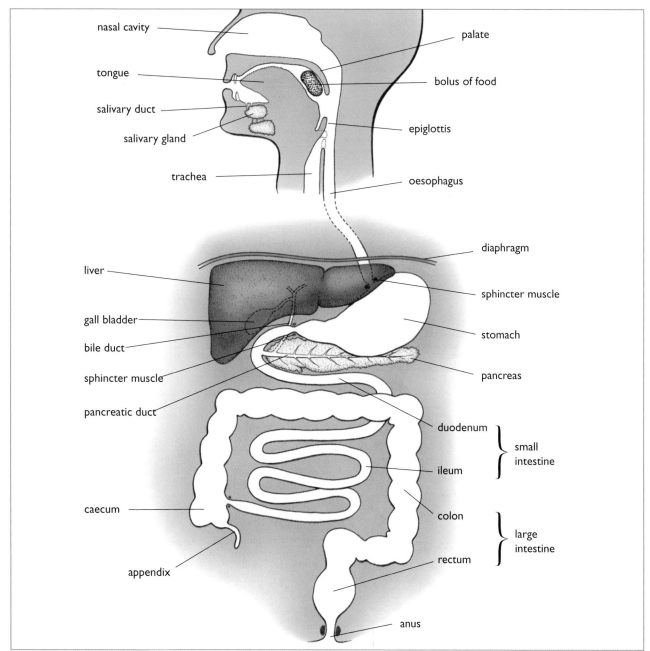

Figure 7.17   The human digestive system.

of water, mucus and the enzyme amylase. The water helps to dissolve substances in the food, allowing us to taste them. The mucus helps the chewed food to bind together to form a bolus, and lubricates it so that it slides easily down the oesophagus when it is swallowed. Amylase begins to digest starch in the food to the sugar maltose. Usually, it does not have time to finish this because the food is not kept in the mouth for very long. However, if you chew something starchy (such as a piece of bread) for a long time, you may be able to taste the sweet maltose that is produced.

The oesophagus

There are two tubes leading down from the back of the mouth. The one in front is the trachea or windpipe, which takes air down to the lungs. Behind the trachea is the oesophagus, which takes food down to the stomach.

When you swallow, a piece of cartilage covers the entrance to the trachea. It is called the epiglottis, and it stops food from going down into the lungs.

The entrance to the stomach from the oesophagus is guarded by a ring of muscle called a sphincter. This muscle relaxes to let the food pass into the stomach.

The stomach

The stomach has strong, muscular walls. The muscles contract and relax to churn the food and mix it with the enzymes and mucus. The mixture is called chyme.

Like all parts of the alimentary canal, the stomach wall contains goblet cells which secrete mucus. It also contains other cells which produce protease enzymes and others which make hydrochloric acid. These are situated in pits in the stomach wall (Figure 7.18).

The main protease enzyme in the stomach is pepsin. It begins to digest proteins by breaking them down into polypeptides. Pepsin works best in acid conditions. The acid also helps to kill any bacteria in the food.

Rennin is only produced in the stomach of young mammals. It causes milk that they get from their mothers to clot. The milk proteins are then broken down by pepsin.

The stomach can store food for quite a long time. After one or two hours, the sphincter at the bottom of the stomach opens and lets the chyme into the duodenum.

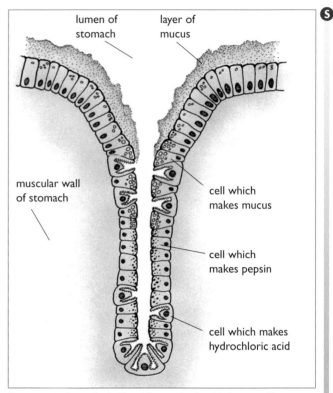

Figure 7.18 A gastric pit. 'Gastric' means 'to do with the stomach'.

The small intestine

The small intestine is the part of the alimentary canal between the stomach and the colon. It is about 5 m long. It is called the small intestine because it is quite narrow.

Different parts of the small intestine have different names. The first part, nearest to the stomach, is the duodenum. The last part, nearest to the colon, is the ileum.

Several enzymes are secreted into the duodenum. They are made in the pancreas, which is a cream-coloured gland, lying just underneath the stomach. A tube called the pancreatic duct leads from the pancreas into the duodenum. Pancreatic juice, which is a fluid made by the pancreas, flows along this tube.

This fluid contains many enzymes, including amylase, protease and lipase. Amylase breaks down starch to maltose. Trypsin is a protease, which breaks down proteins to polypeptides. Lipase breaks down fats (lipids) to fatty acids and glycerol.

These enzymes do not work well in acid environments, but the chyme which has come from the stomach contains hydrochloric acid. Pancreatic juice contains sodium hydrogencarbonate which partially neutralises the acid.

Bile

As well as pancreatic juice, another fluid flows into the duodenum. It is called bile. Bile is a yellowish green, alkaline, watery liquid, which helps to neutralise the acidic mixture from the stomach. It is made in the liver, and then stored in the gall bladder. It flows to the duodenum along the bile duct.

Bile does not contain any enzymes. It does, however, help to digest fats. It does this by breaking up the large drops of fat into very small ones, making it easier for the lipase in the pancreatic juice to digest them into fatty acids and glycerol. This is called emulsification, and is done by salts in the bile called bile salts. Emulsification is a type of mechanical digestion.

Bile also contains yellowish bile pigments. These are made by the liver when it breaks down old red blood cells. The bile pigments are made from haemoglobin. The pigments are not needed by the body, so they are eventually excreted in the faeces.

Villi

As well as receiving enzymes made in the pancreas, the small intestine makes some enzymes itself. They are made by cells in its walls.

The inner wall of all parts of the small intestine – the duodenum and ileum – is covered with millions of tiny projections. They are called villi (singular: villus). Each villus is about 1 mm long (Figures 7.19, 7.20, 7.21 (overleaf) and 7.22 on page 86). Cells covering the villi make enzymes. The enzymes do not come out into the lumen of the small intestine, but stay close to the cells which make them. These enzymes complete the digestion of food.

The carbohydrase enzyme maltase breaks down maltose to glucose. Proteases finish breaking down any polypeptides into amino acids. Lipase completes the breakdown of fats to fatty acids and glycerol.

Absorption of digested food

By now, most carbohydrates have been broken down to simple sugars, proteins to amino acids, and fats to fatty acids and glycerol. These molecules are small enough to pass through the wall of the small intestine and into the blood. This is called absorption.

The small intestine is especially adapted to allow absorption to take place very efficiently. Some of its features are listed in Table 7.5.

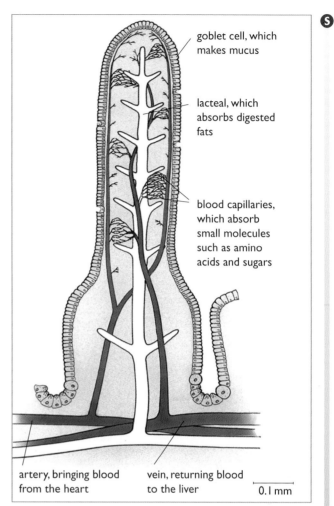

goblet cell, which makes mucus

lacteal, which absorbs digested fats

blood capillaries, which absorb small molecules such as amino acids and sugars

artery, bringing blood from the heart

vein, returning blood to the liver

0.1 mm

Figure 7.19 Longitudinal section through a villus.

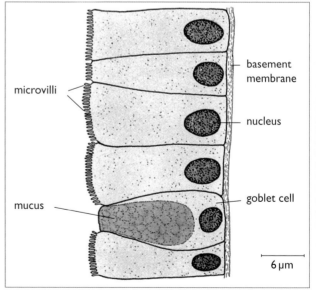

microvilli

mucus

basement membrane

nucleus

goblet cell

6 μm

Figure 7.20 Detail of the surface of a villus.

Water, mineral salts and vitamins are also absorbed in the small intestine. The small intestine absorbs between 5 and 10 dm³ of water each day.

Table **7.6** gives a summary of digestion in the human alimentary canal.

The large intestine

The colon and rectum are sometimes called the large intestine, because they are wider tubes than the duodenum and ileum.

Not all the food that is eaten can be digested, and this undigested food cannot be absorbed in the small intestine. It travels on, through the caecum, past the appendix and into the colon. In humans, the caecum and appendix have no function. In the colon, more water and salt are absorbed. However, the colon absorbs much less water than the small intestine.

By the time the food reaches the rectum, most of the substances which can be absorbed have gone into the blood. All that remains is indigestible food (fibre, or roughage), bacteria, and some dead cells from the inside of the alimentary canal. This mixture forms the faeces, which are passed out at intervals through the anus. This process is called egestion.

Activity 7.3
A model of absorption

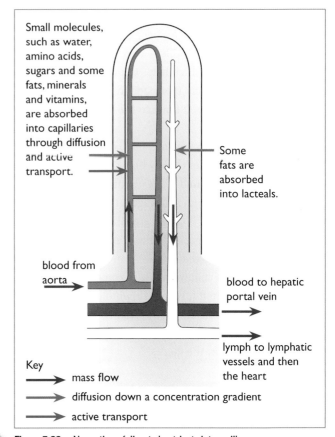

Figure 7.22   Absorption of digested nutrients into a villus.

Feature	How this helps absorption take place
It is very long, about 5 m in an adult human.	This gives plenty of time for digestion to be completed, and for digested food to be absorbed as it slowly passes through.
It has villi. Each villus is covered with cells which have even smaller projections on them, called microvilli.	This gives the inner surface of the small intestine a very large surface area. The larger the surface area, the faster nutrients can be absorbed.
Villi contain blood capillaries.	Monosaccharides, amino acids, water, minerals and vitamins, and some fats, pass into the blood, to be taken to the liver and then round the body.
Villi contain lacteals, which are part of the lymphatic system.	Fats are absorbed into lacteals.
Villi have walls only one cell thick.	The digested nutrients can easily cross the wall to reach the blood capillaries and lacteals.

Table 7.5   How the small intestine is adapted for absorbing digested nutrients.

Figure 7.21 This micrograph shows thousands of villi covering the inner wall of the small intestine. It is magnified about 20 times.

Part of the canal	Juices secreted	Where made	Enzymes in juice	Substrate	Product	Other substances in juice	Functions of other substances
mouth	saliva	salivary glands	amylase	starch	maltose		
oesophagus	none						
stomach	gastric juice	in pits in wall of stomach	pepsin	proteins	polypeptides	hydrochloric acid	acid environment for pepsin; kills bacteria in food
			rennin (only in young mammals)	milk protein	curdled milk protein		
duodenum	pancreatic juice	pancreas	amylase	starch	maltose	sodium hydrogencarbonate	reduces acidity of chyme
			trypsin	proteins	polypeptides		
			lipase	fats	fatty acids and glycerol		
	bile	liver, stored in gall bladder	none			bile salts	emulsify fats
						bile pigments	excretory products
ileum	no juice secreted; enzymes remain in or on the cells covering the villi	by cells covering the villi	maltase	maltose	glucose		
			sucrase	sucrose	glucose and fructose		
			lactase	lactose	glucose and galactose		
			peptidase	polypeptides	amino acids		
			lipase	fats	fatty acids and glycerol		

All of the digestive juices contain water and mucus. The water is used for the digestion of large molecules to small ones. It is also a solvent for the nutrients and enzymes. Mucus acts as a lubricant. It also forms a covering over the inner surface of the alimentary canal, preventing enzymes from digesting the cells.

Table 7.6 Summary of digestion in the human alimentary canal.

Diarrhoea

Diarrhoea is the loss of watery faeces. It happens when not enough water is absorbed from the faeces.

In most people, a bout of diarrhoea is just an annoyance. But if it is severe and goes on for a long time, it is a dangerous illness. Diarrhoea is the second largest cause of death of young children in the world. (The greatest cause is pneumonia.) A person with severe diarrhoea can lose dangerous amounts of water and salts from their body, causing some of their tissues and organs to stop working.

The simplest and most effective way to treat a person suffering from severe diarrhoea is to give oral rehydration therapy. This involves giving a drink containing water with a small amount of salt and sugar dissolved in it. Although there are commercially available liquids designed specially for oral rehydration, many home-made remedies work just as well. For example, green coconut water, or a drink made from yoghurt and salt, can be very effective.

There are many different causes of diarrhoea. One of these is infection by a bacterium, which causes the disease cholera (Figure 7.23). This bacterium can be spread through water and food that has been contaminated with faeces from an infected person. In places where people are forced to live in unhygienic conditions, such as in refugee camps, cholera can spread very rapidly (Figure 7.24). The worst cholera outbreak in recent times happened in Haiti in 2010, following a major earthquake that displaced thousands of people from their homes. At least 8000 people were killed by this disease.

The cholera bacterium lives and breeds in the small intestine. The bacteria produce a toxin (poison) that stimulates the cells lining the intestine to secrete chloride ions (Figure 7.25). These ions accumulate in the lumen of the small intestine. This increases the concentration of the fluid in the lumen, lowering its water potential. Once this water potential becomes lower than the water potential of the blood flowing through the vessels in the walls of the intestine, water moves out of the blood and into the lumen of the intestine, by osmosis.

This is why cholera is so dangerous. Large quantities of water are lost from the body in the watery faeces. However, so long as enough fluids can be given to replace these losses, almost every person suffering from cholera will eventually recover.

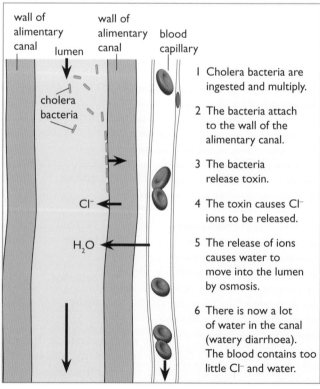

Figure 7.24 Cholera treatment in Haiti. When fluid losses are very great, rehydration therapy can be given through a drip directly into the blood stream, rather than by giving fluids to drink.

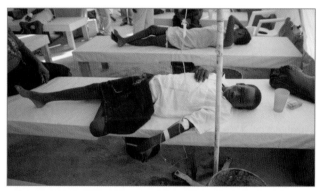

wall of alimentary canal   lumen   wall of alimentary canal   blood capillary

cholera bacteria

Cl^-

H_2O

1 Cholera bacteria are ingested and multiply.

2 The bacteria attach to the wall of the alimentary canal.

3 The bacteria release toxin.

4 The toxin causes Cl^- ions to be released.

5 The release of ions causes water to move into the lumen by osmosis.

6 There is now a lot of water in the canal (watery diarrhoea). The blood contains too little Cl^- and water.

Figure 7.25 How the cholera toxin causes diarrhoea.

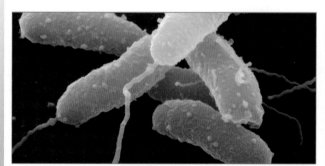

Figure 7.23 Cholera bacteria, seen using a scanning electron microscope. They are magnified about 23 000 times.

7.5 Assimilation

After they have been absorbed into the blood, the nutrients are taken to the liver, in the **hepatic portal vein** (Figure 7.26). The liver processes some of them, before they go any further (page **184**). Some of these nutrients can be broken down, some converted into other substances, some stored and the remainder left unchanged.

The nutrients, dissolved in the blood plasma, are then taken to other parts of the body where they may become assimilated as part of a cell.

The liver has an especially important role in the metabolism of glucose. If there is more glucose than necessary in the blood, the liver will convert some of it to the polysaccharide **glycogen**, and store it. You can find out more about this on page **184**.

Key definition

> assimilation – the movement of digested food molecules into the cells of the body where they are used, becoming part of the cells

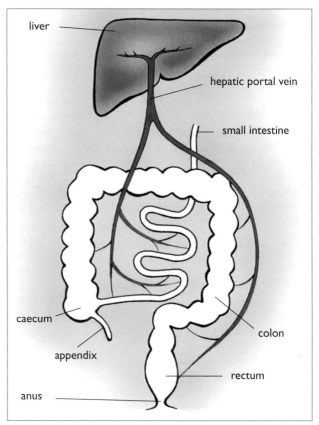

Figure 7.26 The hepatic portal vein transports absorbed nutrients from the small intestine to the liver.

? Questions

7.15 What is a sphincter muscle?

7.16 Name **two** places in the alimentary canal where sphincter muscles are found.

7.17 In which parts of the alimentary canal is mucus secreted? Explain why.

7.18 Name **two** parts of the alimentary canal where amylase is secreted. What does it do?

7.19 What is the epiglottis?

7.20 Why do the walls of the stomach secrete hydrochloric acid?

7.21 Which **two** parts of the alimentary canal make up the small intestine?

7.22 Which **two** digestive juices are secreted into the duodenum?

7.23 How do bile salts help in digestion?

7.24 What is diarrhoea, and how can it be treated?

7.25 How does the cholera bacterium cause diarrhoea?

Summary

You should know:
♦ that balanced diets differ for different people
Ⓢ ♦ how poor diet can affect health, including starvation, obesity and coronary heart disease
♦ the causes and effects of protein-energy malnutrition
♦ why food needs to be digested before it can be absorbed
♦ the functions of amylase, protease and lipase
♦ the structure and functions of the alimentary canal and other organs of the digestive system
♦ the structure and functions of teeth, and the causes of dental decay
♦ the causes, effects and treatment of cholera
♦ how nutrients are assimilated into body cells.

End-of-chapter questions

1   With the aid of examples wherever possible, explain the differences between each of the following pairs of terms.

   a   enamel, dentine
   b   digestion, absorption
   c   small intestine, large intestine
Ⓢ d   bile, pancreatic juice

2   a   What is meant by a balanced diet?
    b   Using Table **7.1** and Figure **7.2**, plan menus for one day which would provide a balanced diet for:
        i   a teenage boy, and
        ii   a pregnant woman.
        For each food you include, state how much energy, and which types of nutrients it contains.

3   The diagram below shows the human digestive system.

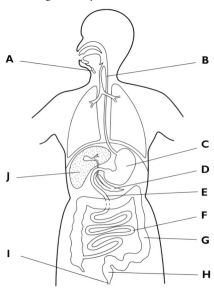

a Name each of the parts labelled **A** to **J** on the diagram.
b Give the letters (not the name) of each of the following parts:
  i **two** parts where amylase is secreted
  ii **two** parts where protease is secreted
  iii **one** part where lipase is secreted
  iv the part where hydrochloric acid is secreted
  v the **two** parts that make up the small intestine
  vi **two** parts where water is absorbed
  vii the part where egestion takes place.

4 Copy and complete these sentences about digestion, using words from the list. You may use each word once, more than once or not at all.

acids	amino	amylase	carbohydrates	duodenum	fatty
fats	gall	glycerol	hydrochloric	ileum	ingestion
large	mucus	oesophagus	pancreas	proteins	small
starch	trachea	urinary			

The teeth, lips and tongue help to take food into the mouth. This is called ....
The food is mixed with saliva from the salivary glands. Saliva contains the enzyme .... ,
which digests .... to the sugar, maltose. Saliva also contains .... , which lubricates
the chewed food making it easy to swallow.

The food travels down the .... to the stomach. Here, ... acid is secreted,
which provides ideal conditions for the enzyme pepsin to work. Pepsin is a protease, and begins
the digestion of ....

After leaving the stomach, the food enters the .... , which is the first part of the
.... intestine. Here, juices from the .... and .... bladder flow in. They contain
amylase, protease and lipase. Lipase digests fats to .... and ....

5 Calcium, iron, vitamin C and vitamin D are nutrients required in small amounts in the diet.
a Which **two** of these nutrients are organic substances? [1]
b Explain why none of these nutrients need to be digested before they are absorbed. [2]
c Name **two** foods that contain calcium. [1]
d Describe and explain the deficiency symptoms of a lack of iron in the diet. [3]
e Describe the role of vitamin D in the body. [2]

6   The diagram shows the teeth in the upper jaw of a human.

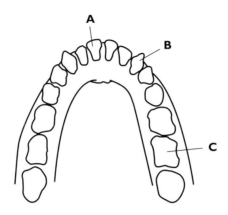

a   Name the teeth labelled **A**, **B** and **C**.   [3]
b   Draw and label a diagram to show the internal structure of the tooth labelled **C**.   [6]
c   Outline the functions of tooth **A** and tooth **C**.   [4]

7   A student was given three solutions of vitamin C, labelled **X**, **Y** and **Z**.
    She was told that solution **X** had a concentration of 0.4% vitamin C, and that solution **Y** had
    a concentration of 0.1% vitamin C.

    The student was asked to estimate the concentration of vitamin C in solution **Z**.

    •   First, she measured 2 cm³ of each solution into separate test tubes.

    •   Next, she added DCPIP solution to solution X tube, drop by drop. At first, the blue DCPIP
         was decolourised when it mixed with solution X. Eventually, a drop kept its blue colour
         when it was added. The student recorded how many drops she added before this happened.

    •   She repeated the DCPIP test with solutions Y and Z.

    These are the results the student recorded.

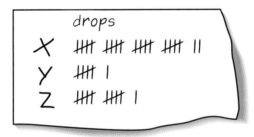

a   Record the student's observations in a suitable table.   [4]
b   Use these results to suggest the approximate vitamin C concentration of solution **Z**.
     Explain your answer.   [3]

8 Transport in plants

In this chapter, you will find out about:

♦ why plants need transport systems
♦ the structure and function of xylem
♦ how plants absorb and transport water
♦ transpiration and the factors that affect its rate
ⓢ♦ how sucrose and amino acids are transported through a plant.

The tallest trees

Is there any limit to the height to which a tree can grow? The world's tallest trees are the coastal redwoods, *Sequoia sempervirens*, that can be found in some parts of California in the USA (Figure **8.1**). The very tallest one is 116 m tall, growing in the Redwood National Park.

Scientists think that it would not be possible for a tree to grow taller than about 130 m. This all comes to down to the xylem that makes up most of a tree's trunk.

Xylem (pronounced zi-lem) is what wood is made of. Xylem vessels are long tubes, made out of dead, empty cells joined end to end. They run all the way up through a tree's trunk and out into its branches. Xylem vessels have walls made of a very strong substance called lignin. These vessels serve two purposes – they help to hold the tree up, and they provide a pathway for water to move from the roots all the way up to the very topmost leaves.

Lignin is so strong that it would certainly be possible for a tree to grow taller than 116 m and still stand up, especially if its trunk was very wide. But there is a limit on how far up water can travel. Water is pulled up through the xylem vessels in long, continuous columns, drawn upwards by the 'sucking' effect of water evaporating from the tree's leaves. This creates an upward force, but there is also a downwards force caused by the weight of the water. Past a certain height, the water column would just

break, and the leaves at the top of the tree would rapidly run out of water and die.

Figure 8.1 Giant redwoods grow in California.

8.1 Plant transport systems

All organisms need to obtain various substances from their environment. For plants, these substances are carbon dioxide and water for photosynthesis, and mineral ions which they absorb from the ground.

Plants have branching shapes. This gives them a large surface area in relation to their volume. It means that most cells are close to the surface. As we saw in Chapter 6, leaves are adapted to ensure that no cell is far away from the air, so carbon dioxide can simply diffuse in through the stomata and air spaces, easily reaching the photosynthesising mesophyll cells.

Water, though, comes from further away. Plants absorb water through their roots, and this water must be transported up to the leaves. The transport system that does this is made up of a tissue called xylem.

Plants also have a second transport system, made up of a tissue called phloem. Phloem transports sucrose and amino acids from the leaves where they are made, to other parts of the plant such as its roots and flowers.

Xylem

A xylem vessel is like a long drainpipe (Figures 8.2 and 8.3). It is made of many hollow, dead cells, joined end to end. The end walls of the cells have disappeared, so a long, open tube is formed. Xylem vessels run from the roots of the plant, right up through the stem. They branch out into every leaf.

Xylem vessels contain no cytoplasm or nuclei. Their walls are made of cellulose and lignin. Lignin is very strong, so xylem vessels help to keep plants upright. Wood is made almost entirely of lignified xylem vessels.

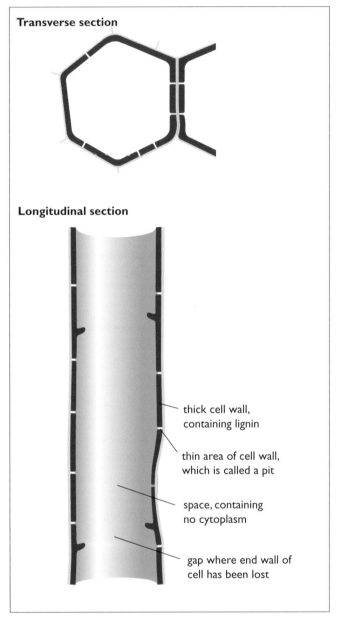

Transverse section

Longitudinal section

thick cell wall, containing lignin

thin area of cell wall, which is called a pit

space, containing no cytoplasm

gap where end wall of cell has been lost

Figure 8.3 Xylem vessels.

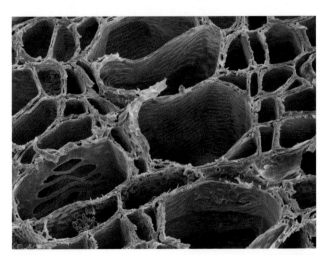

Figure 8.2 This is a scanning electron micrograph of xylem vessels (×1800).

Activity 8.1
Identify the positions of xylem vessels in roots, stems and leaves.

Phloem

You do not need to know anything about the structure of phloem, but you may find it interesting to compare with xylem. Like xylem vessels, phloem tubes are made of many cells joined end to end. However, their end walls have not completely broken down. Instead, they form sieve plates (Figures **8.4** and **8.5**), which have small holes in them. The cells are called sieve tube elements. Sieve tube elements contain cytoplasm, but no nucleus. They do not have lignin in their cell walls.

Each sieve tube element has a companion cell next to it. The companion cell does have a nucleus, and also contains many other organelles. Companion cells probably supply sieve tube elements with some of their requirements.

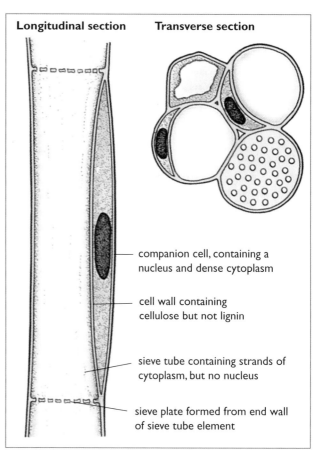

Figure 8.5 Phloem tubes. Note that you do not need to learn the structure of phloem.

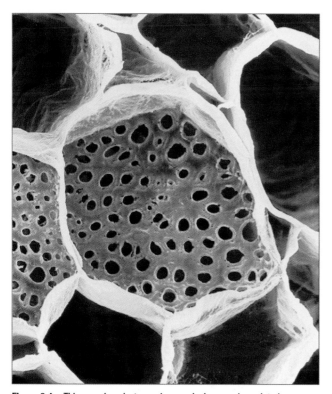

Figure 8.4 This scanning electron micrograph shows a sieve plate in a phloem sieve tube (×1300).

Vascular bundles

Xylem vessels and phloem tubes are usually found close together. A group of xylem vessels and phloem tubes is called a **vascular bundle**.

The positions of vascular bundles in roots and shoots are shown in Figures **8.6** and **8.7** (overleaf). In a root, vascular tissue is found at the centre, whereas in a shoot vascular bundles are arranged in a ring near the outside edge. Vascular bundles are also found in leaves (Figure **6.2**). They help to support the plant.

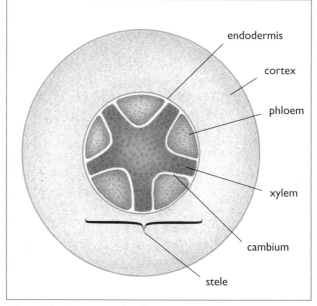

Figure 8.6 Transverse section of a root.

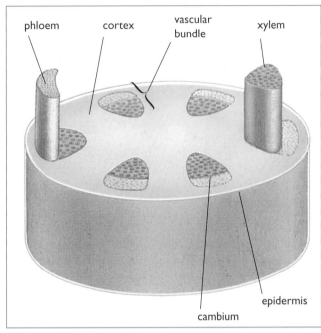

Figure 8.7   Transverse section of a stem.

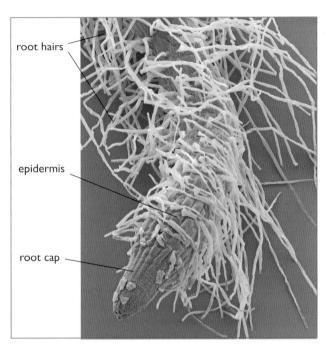

Figure 8.8   A root tip (×70).

❓ Questions

8.1 What do xylem vessels carry?

8.2 What substance makes up the cell walls of xylem vessels?

8.3 What do phloem tubes carry?

8.4 Give **three** ways in which phloem tubes differ from xylem vessels.

8.5 What is a vascular bundle?

8.2 Water uptake

Plants take in water from the soil, through their root hairs. The water is carried by the xylem vessels to all parts of the plant. Figure **8.8** shows the end of a root, magnified. At the very tip is a **root cap**. This is a layer of cells which protects the root as it grows through the soil. The rest of the root is covered by a layer of cells called the **epidermis**.

The root hairs are a little way up from the root tip. Each root hair is a long epidermal cell (Figures **8.9** and **8.10**). Root hairs do not live for very long. As the root grows, they are replaced by new ones.

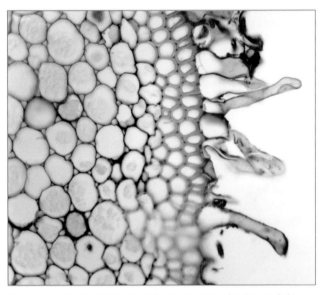

Figure 8.9   Part of a transverse section across a root, showing root hairs (×100).

The function of root hairs is to absorb water and minerals from the soil. Water moves into a root hair by **osmosis**. The cytoplasm and cell sap inside it are quite concentrated solutions. The water in the soil is normally a more dilute solution. Water therefore diffuses into the root hair, down its concentration gradient, through the partially permeable cell surface membrane (page **33**).

The root hairs are on the edge of the root. The xylem vessels are in the centre. Before the water can be taken to the rest of the plant, it must travel to these xylem vessels.

The path it takes is shown in Figure **8.10**. It travels by osmosis through the cortex, from cell to cell. Some of it may also just seep through the spaces between the cells, or through the cell walls, never actually entering a cell at all. Eventually it reaches the xylem vessels in the middle of the root. These transport it all the way up through the stem and into the leaves.

Once water reaches the xylem, it moves up xylem vessels in the same way that a drink moves up a straw when you suck it. When you suck a straw, you are reducing the pressure at the top of the straw. The liquid at the bottom of the straw is at a higher pressure, so it flows up the straw into your mouth.

The same thing happens with the water in xylem vessels. The pressure at the top of the vessels is lowered, while the pressure at the bottom stays high. Water therefore flows up the xylem vessels.

How is the pressure at the top of the xylem vessels reduced? It happens because of **transpiration**.

8.3 Transpiration

Transpiration is the evaporation of water from a plant. Most of this evaporation takes place from the leaves.

If you look back at Figure **6.6** (page **61**), you will see that there are openings on the surface of the leaf called stomata. There are usually more stomata on the underside of the leaf, in the lower epidermis. The mesophyll cells inside the leaf are each covered with a thin film of moisture.

Some of this film of moisture evaporates from the cells, and this water vapour diffuses out of the leaf through the stomata. Water from the xylem vessels in the leaf will travel to the cells by osmosis to replace it.

Water is constantly being taken from the top of the xylem vessels, to supply the cells in the leaves. This reduces the effective pressure at the top of the xylem vessels, so that water flows up them. This process is known as the **transpiration stream** (Figure **8.11**).

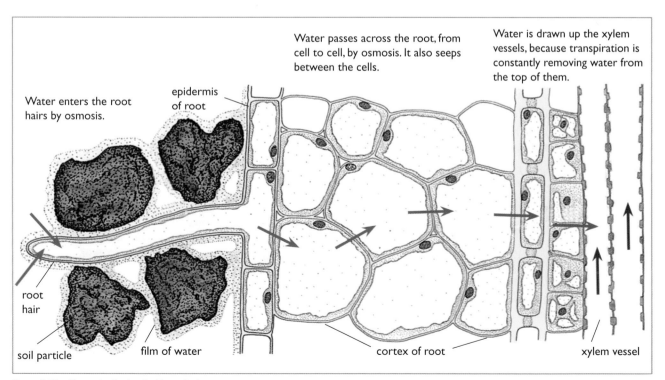

Figure 8.10 How water is absorbed by a plant.

Water enters the root hairs by osmosis.

epidermis of root

Water passes across the root, from cell to cell, by osmosis. It also seeps between the cells.

Water is drawn up the xylem vessels, because transpiration is constantly removing water from the top of them.

root hair

soil particle

film of water

cortex of root

xylem vessel

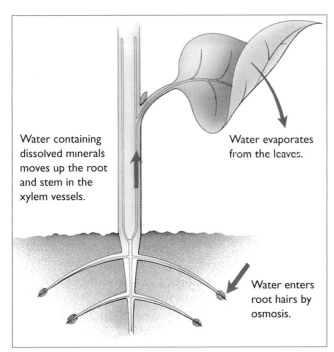

Water containing dissolved minerals moves up the root and stem in the xylem vessels.

Water evaporates from the leaves.

Water enters root hairs by osmosis.

Figure 8.11 The transpiration stream.

> ## Key definition
>
> transpiration – loss of water from plant leaves by evaporation of water at the surfaces of the mesophyll cells followed by loss of water vapour through the stomata

S Water potential gradient

You can think of the way that water moves into a root hair, across to the xylem vessels, up to the leaves and then out into the air in terms of water potential.

You may remember that water moves down a water potential gradient, from a high water potential to a low water potential (page 31). All along this pathway, the water is moving down a water potential gradient from one place to another. The highest water potential is in the solution in the soil, and the lower water potential is in the air.

The low water potential in the leaves is caused by the loss of water vapour from the leaves by transpiration. This produces a 'pull' from above, drawing water up the plant.

Water molecules have a strong tendency to stick together. This is called cohesion. When the water is 'pulled' up the xylem vessels, the whole column of water

stays together. Without cohesion, the water column would break apart and the whole system would not work.

We can now see how well the structure of a plant is adapted to help it to take up water and move it up through the plant.

♦ The root hair cells provide a huge surface area through which water can be absorbed. This increases the quantity of water that can move into the plant at any one moment.

♦ The hollow, narrow xylem vessels provide an easy pathway for water to flow all the way up from the roots to the very top of the plant.

♦ The many air spaces inside the leaf mean that there is a large surface area of wet cells from which water can evaporate into the air. This increases the rate of evaporation, drawing more water out of the xylem and speeding up the flow of water up the plant.

♦ The stomata, when open, allow water vapour to diffuse easily out of the leaf. This reduces the water potential inside the leaf, which encourages more water to evaporate from the surfaces of the mesophyll cells.

Measuring transpiration rates

It is not easy to measure how much water is lost from the leaves of a plant. It is much easier to measure how fast the plant takes up water. The rate at which a plant takes up water depends on the rate of transpiration – the faster a plant transpires, the faster it takes up water.

Figure **8.12** illustrates apparatus which can be used to compare the rate of transpiration in different conditions. It is called a potometer. By recording how fast the air/water meniscus moves along the capillary tube you can compare how fast the plant takes up water in different conditions.

There are many different kinds of potometer, so yours may not look like this. The simplest kind is just a long glass tube which you can fill with water. A piece of rubber tubing slid over one end allows you to fix the cut end of a shoot into it, making an air-tight connection. This works just as well as the one in Figure **8.12**, but is much harder to refill with water.

Conditions that affect transpiration rate

Temperature

On a hot day, water will evaporate quickly from the leaves of a plant. Transpiration increases as temperature increases.

Humidity

Humidity means the moisture content of the air. The higher the humidity, the less water will evaporate from the leaves. This is because there is not much of a diffusion gradient for the water between the air spaces inside the leaf, and the wet air outside it. Transpiration decreases as humidity increases.

Wind speed

On a windy day, water evaporates more quickly than on a still day. Transpiration increases as wind speed increases.

Light intensity

In bright sunlight, a plant may open its stomata to supply plenty of carbon dioxide for photosynthesis. More water can therefore evaporate from the leaves.

Water supply

If water is in short supply, then the plant will close its stomata. This will cut down the rate of transpiration. Transpiration decreases when water supply decreases below a certain level.

Transpiration is useful to plants, because it keeps water moving up the xylem vessels and evaporation helps to cool the leaves. But if the leaves lose too much water, the roots may not be able to take up enough to replace it. If this happens, the plant wilts, because the cells lose water by osmosis and become flaccid (page 34).

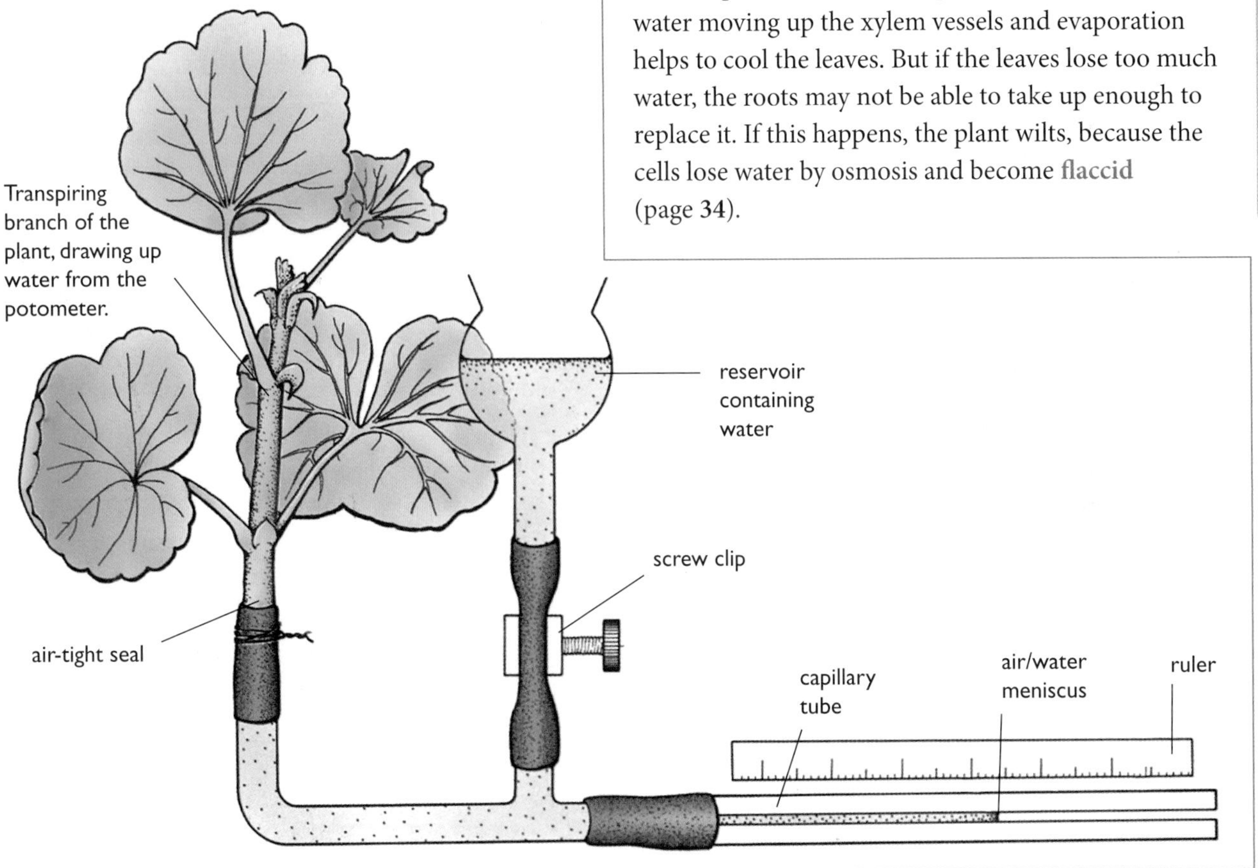

Figure 8.12 A potometer.

❓ Questions

8.6 What is the function of a root cap?

8.7 Explain how water goes into root hairs. How does this process differ from the way in which minerals enter?

8.8 What is transpiration?

8.9 What are stomata?

8.10 What is a potometer used for?

8.11 Explain how **a** temperature, and **b** light intensity affect the rate of transpiration.

Activity 8.2
To see which part of a stem transports water and solutes

Skills
AO3.1 Using techniques, apparatus and materials
AO3.2 Planning
AO3.3 Observing, measuring and recording
AO3.4 Interpreting and evaluating observations and data
AO3.5 Evaluating methods

 Take care with the sharp blade when cutting the stem sections.

1 Take a plant, such as *Impatiens*, with a root system intact. Wash the roots thoroughly.
2 Put the roots of the plant into eosin solution. Leave overnight.
3 Set up a microscope.
4 Remove the plant from the eosin solution, and wash the roots thoroughly.
5 Use a razor blade to cut across the stem of the plant about half-way up. Take great care when using a razor blade and do not touch its edges.
6 Now cut very thin sections across the stem. Try to get them so thin that you can see through them. It does not matter if your section is not a complete circle.
7 Choose your thinnest section, and mount it in a drop of water on a microscope slide. Cover with a coverslip.
8 Observe the section under a microscope. Make a labelled drawing of your section.

❓ Questions
A1 Which part of the stem contained the dye? What does this tell you about the transport of water and solutes (substances dissolved in water) up a stem?
A2 Why was it important to wash the roots of the plant:
   a before putting it into the eosin solution, and
   b before cutting sections?
A3 Design an experiment to investigate the effect of one factor (for example, light intensity, temperature, wind speed) on the rate at which the dye is transported up the stem. Remember to write down your hypothesis, and to think about variables. When you have completed your plan, ask your teacher to check it for you. Then carry out your experiment and record and display your results. Write down your conclusions, and discuss them in the light of your knowledge about transport in plants. You should also evaluate the reliability of your results and suggest how you could improve your experiment if you were able to do it again.

Activity 8.3
To see which surface of a leaf loses most water

Skills
AO3.1 Observing, measuring and recording
AO3.4 Interpreting and evaluating observations and data

Cobalt chloride paper is blue when dry and pink when wet. Use forceps to handle it.

1 Use a healthy, well-watered potted plant, with leaves which are not too hairy. Fix a small square of blue cobalt chloride paper onto each surface of one leaf, using clear sticky tape. Make sure there are no air spaces around the paper.
2 Leave the paper on the leaf for a few minutes.

❓ Questions
A1 Which piece of cobalt chloride paper turned pink first? What does this tell you about the loss of water from a leaf?
A2 Why does this surface lose water faster than the other?
A3 Why is it important to use forceps, not fingers, for handling cobalt chloride paper?

Activity 8.4
To measure the rate of transpiration of a potted plant

Skills
AO3.3 Observing, measuring and recording
AO3.4 Interpreting and evaluating observations and data

1. Use two similar well-watered potted plants. Enclose one plant entirely in a polythene bag, including its pot. This is the control.
2. Enclose only the pot of the second plant in a polythene bag. Fix the bag firmly around the stem of the plant, as in the diagram, and seal with petroleum jelly.
3. Place both plants on balances, and record their masses.
4. Record the mass of each plant every day, at the same time, for at least a week.

❓ Questions
A1 Which plant lost mass? Why?
A2 Do you think this is a good method of measuring transpiration rate? How could it be improved?

Activity 8.5
Using a potometer to compare rates of transpiration under different conditions

Skills
AO3.1 Using techniques, apparatus and materials
AO3.3 Observing, measuring and recording
AO3.4 Interpreting and evaluating observations and data

1. Set up the potometer as in Figure **8.12** (page **99**). The stem of the plant must fit exactly into the rubber tubing, with no air gaps. Petroleum jelly will help to make an air-tight seal.
2. Fill the apparatus with water, by opening the clip.
3. Close the clip again, and leave the apparatus in a light, airy place. As the plant transpires, the water it loses is replaced by water taken up the stem. Air will be drawn in at the end of the capillary tube.
4. When the air/water meniscus reaches the scale, begin to record the position of the meniscus every two minutes.
5. When the meniscus reaches the end of the scale, refill the apparatus with water from the reservoir as before.
6. Now repeat the investigation, but with the apparatus in a different situation. You could try each of these:
   ♦ blowing it with a fan
   ♦ putting it in a cupboard
   ♦ putting it in a refrigerator.
7. Draw graphs of your results.

❓ Questions
A1 Under which conditions did the plant transpire **a** most quickly, and **b** most slowly?
A2 You have been using the potometer to compare the rate of uptake of water under different conditions. Does this really give you a good measurement of the rate of transpiration? Explain your answer.

As well as absorbing water by osmosis, root hairs absorb mineral salts. These are in the form of ions dissolved in the water in the soil. They travel to the xylem vessels along with the water which is absorbed, and are transported to all parts of the plant.

These minerals are usually present in the soil in quite low concentrations. The concentration inside the root hairs is higher. In this situation the mineral ions would normally diffuse out of the root hair into the soil. Root hairs can, however, take up mineral salts against their concentration gradient. It is the cell surface membrane which does this. Special carrier molecules in the cell membrane of the root hair carry the mineral ions across the cell membrane into the cell, against their concentration gradient. This is called active transport, and is described on page 35.

8.4 Transport of manufactured food

Leaves make carbohydrates by photosynthesis. They also use some of these carbohydrates to make amino acids, proteins, oils and other organic substances.

Some of the organic food material, especially sugar, that the plant makes is transported in the phloem tubes. It is carried from the leaves to whichever part of the plant needs it. This is called translocation. The sap inside the phloem tubes therefore contains a lot of sugar, particularly sucrose.

Sources and sinks

The part of a plant from which sucrose and amino acids are being translocated is called a source. The part of the plant to which they are being translocated is called a sink.

> ### Key definition
>
> translocation – the movement of sucrose and amino acids in phloem, from regions of production (source) to regions of storage, or to regions of utilisation in respiration or growth (sink)

When a plant is actively photosynthesising and growing, the leaves are generally the major sources of translocated material. They are constantly producing sucrose, which is carried in the phloem to all other parts of the plant. These parts – the sinks – include the roots and flowers. The roots may change some of the sucrose to starch and store it. The flowers use the sucrose to make fructose (an especially sweet-tasting sugar found in nectar). Later, when the fruits are developing, quite large amounts of sucrose may be used to produce sweet, juicy fruits ready to attract animals.

But many plants have a time of year when they become dormant. During this stage, they wait out harsh conditions in a state of reduced activity. In a hot climate, this may be during the hottest, driest season. In temperate countries, it may be during the winter.

Dormant plants do not photosynthesise, but survive on their stored starch, oils and other materials. When the seasons change, they begin to grow again. Now the stored materials are converted to sucrose and transported to the growing regions.

For example, potato plants (Figure 8.13) grow in temperate regions, and are not able to survive the cold frosts of winter. During the summer, the leaves photosynthesise and send sucrose down into underground stems. Here, swellings called stem tubers develop. The cells in the root tubers change the sucrose to starch and store it.

In autumn, the leaves die. Nothing is left of the potato plant above ground – just the stem tubers beneath the soil. In spring, they begin to grow new shoots and leaves. The starch in the tubers is changed back to sucrose, and transported in the phloem to the growing stems and leaves. This will continue until the leaves are above ground and photosynthesising.

So, in summer the leaves are sources and the growing stem tubers are sinks. In spring, the stem tubers are sources and the growing leaves are sinks.

You can see from this example that phloem can transfer sucrose in either direction – up or down the plant. This isn't true for the transport of water in the xylem vessels. That can only go upwards, because transpiration always happens at the leaf surface, and it is this that provides the 'pull' to draw water up the plant.

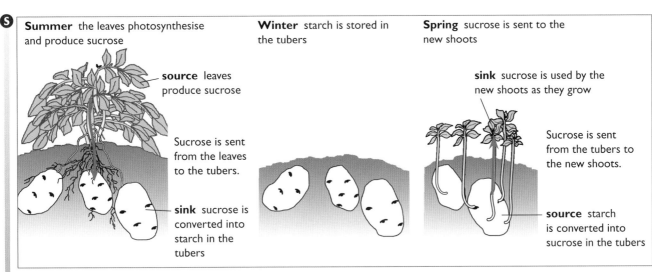

Summer the leaves photosynthesise and produce sucrose

Winter starch is stored in the tubers

Spring sucrose is sent to the new shoots

source leaves produce sucrose

Sucrose is sent from the leaves to the tubers.

sink sucrose is converted into starch in the tubers

sink sucrose is used by the new shoots as they grow

Sucrose is sent from the tubers to the new shoots.

source starch is converted into sucrose in the tubers

Figure 8.13 Potato plants in summer and spring.

Summary

You should know:

- ♦ why plants need transport systems
- ♦ the structure of xylem vessels
- ♦ where xylem and phloem are found in roots, stems and leaves
- ♦ how xylem vessels help to support a plant and transport water and mineral ions
- **S** ♦ the adaptations of root hairs for rapid uptake of water and ions
- ♦ about transpiration and the conditions that affect its rate
- **S** ♦ how transpiration causes water to move up xylem vessels
- ♦ how and why wilting occurs
- ♦ the structure of phloem tubes
- ♦ the role of phloem tubes in translocation of sucrose and amino acids
- ♦ about sources and sinks, and how they may vary at different times.

End-of-chapter questions

1   Match each of the following terms with its description. For some of the terms, there may be more than one description that matches them.

lignin	root hair	potometer
stoma	transpiration	xylem vessel

a   a long tube made of empty cells joined end to end

b   hard, strong tubes that help to support a plant

c   a strong , hard substance that makes up the walls of xylem vessels

d   an extension from a cell near the tip of a root, which absorbs water from the soil

e   the loss of water vapour from the leaves of a plant

f   a small gap between the cells of the epidermis of a plant

g   a piece of apparatus used for measuring the rate at which a plant shoot takes up water

S 2   Give the correct technical term that matches each of these descriptions.

   a   the movement of sucrose and amino acids from sources to sinks
   b   a tissue through which sucrose and amino acids are transported
   c   the collapse of leaves and shoots resulting from a loss of turgor in the cells
   d   a force that helps to hold water molecules together, allowing an uninterrupted column of
       water to move up xylem vessels

3   The list below includes some of the parts of a plant through which water moves as it passes from
    the soil into the air.

| xylem | stomata | root cortex cells |
| air spaces in leaf | root hairs | leaf mesophyll cells |

   a   Write these parts in the correct order, to describe the pathway of water through a plant.
   b   For each part in your list, state whether the water is in the form of a liquid or a gas as it
       passes through it.

4   The diagrams show a transverse section of a stem, and a transverse section of a root.

 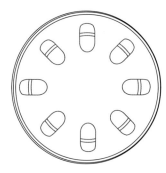

   a   Explain what is meant by the term transverse section.
   b   Make a copy of the diagram that shows a transverse section of a stem. Label the xylem tissue.
   c   Make a copy of the diagram that shows a transverse section of a root. Label the xylem tissue.
   d   On your two diagrams, label the position of the phloem tissue.

S 5   a   Using the term *water potential*, explain how water is absorbed into root hairs from the soil.   [3]
       A potometer is a piece of apparatus that is used to measure water uptake by plants.

       Most of the water taken up by plants replaces water lost in transpiration.

       A student used a potometer to investigate the effect of wind speed on the rate of water uptake by
       a leafy shoot. As the root absorbs water the air bubble moves upwards.

       The student's apparatus is shown in the diagram below.

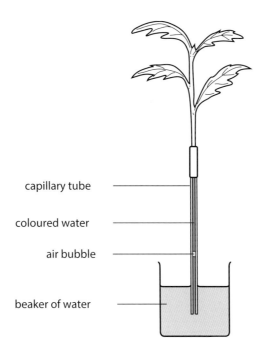

capillary tube

coloured water

air bubble

beaker of water

The student used a fan with five different settings and measured the wind speed. The results are shown in the table below.

Wind speed / metres per second	Distance travelled by the air bubble / mm	Time / minutes	Rate of water uptake / mm per minute
0	4	10	0.4
2	12	5	2.4
4	20	5	4.0
6	35	5	7.0
8	40	2	....

b   Calculate the rate of water uptake at the highest wind speed and write your answer in the table.   [1]

c   Describe the effect of increasing wind speed on the rate of water uptake. You may use figures from the table to support your answer.   [2]

d   State **two** environmental factors, **other than wind speed**, that the student should keep constant during the investigation.   [2]

[Adapted from Cambridge IGCSE® Biology 0610/31, Question 4, May/June 2009]

9 Transport in animals

In this chapter, you will find out about:

- ♦ double and single circulatory systems
- ♦ the structure and function of the heart
- ♦ how exercise affects the heart
- ♦ coronary heart disease
- ♦ blood vessels
- ♦ what blood contains, and its functions in the body
- Ⓢ ♦ the lymphatic system.

Why is blood red?

Your blood is red because it contains a red pigment (coloured substance) called haemoglobin. This pigment transports oxygen around your body, delivering it to every cell that needs it.

But haemoglobin is not the only pigment that animals use to transport oxygen. This means that many animals do not have red blood.

Squid and horseshoe crabs, for example, have blueblood. Their blood contains a blue pigment called haemocyanin. Whereas a haemoglobin molecule contains an iron atom at its centre, a haemocyanin molecule contains copper instead.

Other animals have a pigment called chlorocruorin in their blood. This substance is green when it is dilute, and red when concentrated. Chlorocruorin contains iron, like haemoglobin. It is found in some kinds of bristle worms that live in the sea.

Figure 9.1 Squid and cuttlefish have blue blood and three hearts.

9.1 Circulatory systems

The main transport system of all mammals, including humans, is the blood system, also known as the circulatory system. It is a network of tubes, called blood vessels. A pump, the heart, keeps blood flowing through the vessels. Valves in the heart and blood vessels make sure the blood flows in the right direction.

Figure **9.2** illustrates the general layout of the human blood system. The arrows show the direction of blood flow. If you follow the arrows, beginning at the lungs, you can see that blood flows into the left-hand side of the heart, and then out to the rest of the body. It is brought back to the right-hand side of the heart, before going back to the lungs again.

Oxygenating the blood

The blood in the left-hand side of the heart has come from the lungs. It contains oxygen, which was picked up by the capillaries surrounding the alveoli. It is called oxygenated blood.

This oxygenated blood is then sent around the body. Some of the oxygen in it is taken up by the body cells, which need oxygen for respiration (Chapter **11**). When this happens the blood becomes deoxygenated. The deoxygenated blood is brought back to the right-hand side of the heart. It then goes to the lungs, where it becomes oxygenated once more.

Double and single circulatory systems

The circulatory system shown in Figure **9.2** is a double circulatory system. This means that the blood passes through the heart twice on one complete circuit of the body. We can think of the circulatory system being made up of two parts – the blood vessels that take the blood to the lungs and back, called the pulmonary system, and the blood vessels that take the blood to the rest of the body and back, called the systemic system.

Double circulatory systems are found in all mammals, and also in birds and reptiles. However, fish have a circulatory system in which the blood passes through the heart only once on a complete circuit. This is called a single circulatory system, and is shown in Figure **9.3**.

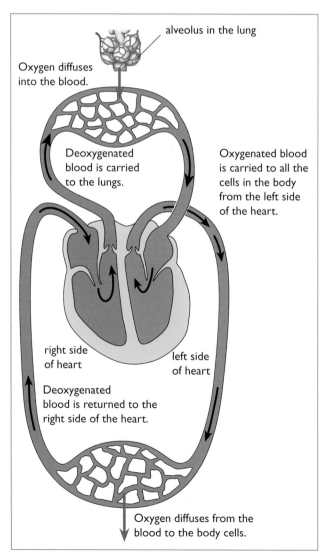

Figure 9.2 The general layout of the circulatory system of a human, as seen from the front.

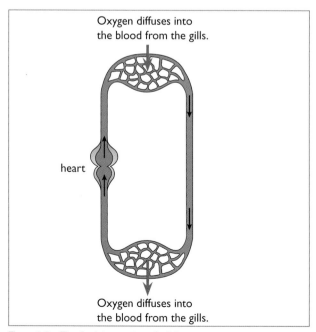

Figure 9.3 The circulatory system of a fish.

S Double circulatory systems have some advantages over single circulatory systems. When blood flows through the tiny blood vessels in a fish's gills, or a mammal's lungs, it loses a lot of the pressure that was given to it by the pumping of the heart. In a mammal, this low-pressure blood is delivered back to the heart, which raises its pressure again before sending it off to the rest of the body.

In a fish, though, the low-pressure blood just carries on around the fish's body. This means that blood travels much more slowly to a fish's body organs than it does in a mammal.

This is particularly important when you think about the delivery of oxygen for respiration. Any tissues that are metabolically very active need a lot of oxygen delivered to them as quickly as possible, and this delivery is much more effective in a mammal than in a fish.

9.2 The heart

The function of the heart is to pump blood around the body. It is made of a special type of muscle called cardiac muscle. This muscle contracts and relaxes regularly, throughout life.

Figure **9.4** is a section through a heart. It is divided into four chambers. The two upper chambers are called atria. The two lower chambers are ventricles. The chambers on the left-hand side are completely separated from the ones on the right-hand side by a septum.

If you look at Figures **9.2** and **9.4**, you will see that blood flows into the heart at the top, into the atria. Both of the atria receive blood. The left atrium receives blood from the pulmonary veins, which come from the lungs. The right atrium receives blood from the rest of the body, arriving through the venae cavae (singular: vena cava).

From the atria, the blood flows into the ventricles. The ventricles then pump it out of the heart. They do this by contracting the muscle in their walls. The strong cardiac muscle contracts with considerable force, squeezing inwards on the blood inside the heart and pushing it out. The blood in the left ventricle is pumped into the aorta, which takes the blood around the body. The right ventricle pumps blood into the pulmonary artery, which takes it to the lungs.

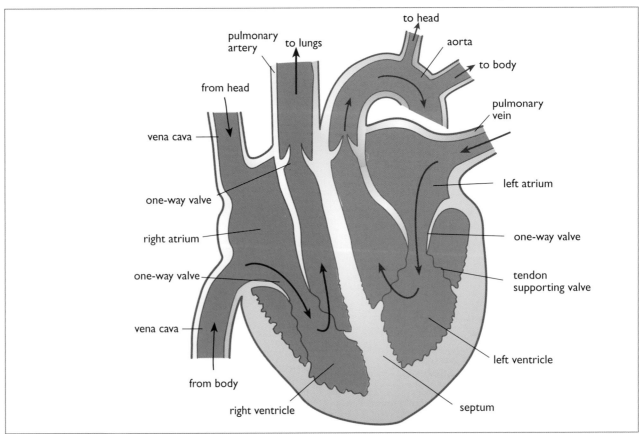

Figure 9.4 Vertical section through a human heart.

Ⓢ The function of the ventricles is quite different from the function of the atria. The atria simply receive blood, from either the lungs or the body, and supply it to the ventricles. The ventricles pump blood out of the heart and all around the body. To help them do this, the ventricles have much thicker, more muscular walls than the atria.

There is also a difference in the thickness of the walls of the right and left ventricles. The right ventricle pumps blood to the lungs, which are very close to the heart. The left ventricle, however, pumps blood all around the body. The left ventricle has an especially thick wall of muscle to enable it to do this. The blood flowing to the lungs in the pulmonary artery has a much lower pressure than the blood in the aorta.

Ⓢ **Activity 9.1**
Dissecting a heart

❓ **Questions**

9.1 Describe the human circulatory system, using the words **blood vessels**, **pump** and **valves**.
9.2 What is oxygenated blood?
9.3 Where does blood become oxygenated?
9.4 Which side of the heart contains oxygenated blood?
Ⓢ 9.5 Explain the difference between a double circulatory system and a single circulatory system.
9.6 What are the advantages of a double circulatory system?
9.7 Which parts of the heart receive blood from **a** the lungs, and **b** the body?
9.8 Where are the one-way valves found in the heart?
9.9 Which structure in the heart separates oxygenated blood from deoxygenated blood?
9.10 Which parts of the heart pump blood into **a** the pulmonary artery, and **b** the aorta?
Ⓢ 9.11 Why do the ventricles have thicker walls than the atria?
9.12 Why does the left ventricle have a thicker wall than the right ventricle?

Coronary arteries supply heart muscle.

In Figure **9.5**, you can see that there are blood vessels on the outside of the heart. They are called the coronary arteries. These vessels supply blood to the heart muscles.

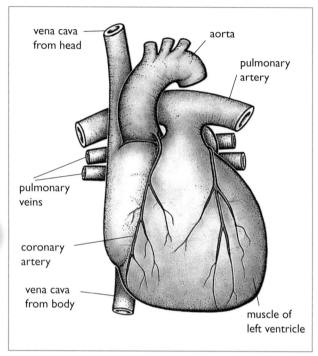

Figure 9.5 External appearance of a human heart.

It may seem odd that this is necessary, when the heart is full of blood. However, the muscles of the heart are so thick that the nutrients and oxygen in the blood inside the heart would not be able to diffuse to all the muscles quickly enough. The heart muscle needs a constant supply of nutrients and oxygen, so that it can keep contracting and relaxing. The coronary arteries supply this.

If a coronary artery gets blocked – for example, by a blood clot – the cardiac muscles run short of oxygen. They cannot respire, so they cannot obtain energy to allow them to contract. The heart therefore stops beating. This is called a heart attack or cardiac arrest.

Blockage of the coronary arteries is called coronary heart disease. It is a very common cause of illness and death, especially in developed countries. We know several factors that increase a person's risk of getting coronary heart disease (Figure **9.6**).

- **Smoking cigarettes**   Several components of cigarette smoke, including nicotine, cause damage to the circulatory system. Stopping smoking is the single most important thing a smoker can do in order to reduce their chances of getting coronary heart disease.
- **Diet**   There is evidence that a diet high in salt, saturated fats (fats from animals) or cholesterol increases the chances of getting coronary heart disease. To reduce the risk, it is good to eat a diet containing a very wide variety of foods, with not too many fats in it (though we do need some fat in the diet to stay healthy). Oils from plants and fish, on the other hand, can help to prevent heart disease.
- **Obesity**   Being very overweight increases the risk of coronary heart disease. Keeping your body weight at a suitable level, and taking plenty of exercise, helps to maintain the coronary arteries in a healthy condition.
- **Stress**   We all need some stress in our lives, or they would be very dull. However, unmanageable or long-term stress appears to increase the risk of developing heart disease. Avoiding severe or long-term stress is a good idea, if you can manage it. Otherwise, it is important to find ways to manage stress.
- **Genes**   Some people have genes that make it more likely they will get coronary heart disease. There is

not really anything you can do about this. However, if several people in your family have had problems with their hearts, then this could mean that you have these genes. In that case, it is important to try hard to reduce the other risk factors by having a healthy life-style.

Preventing CHD ⓢ

Coronary heart disease, often known as CHD, is the commonest cause of death in many countries. No-one can completely eliminate the risk of developing CHD, but there is a lot that can be done to reduce this risk.

The most obvious thing you can do is not to smoke cigarettes. Smoking greatly increases the chances of developing CHD, as well as many other unpleasant and dangerous health problems.

Taking care over your diet is also a good thing to do. A diet that is high in saturated fats (the kind that are found in foods originating from animals) is linked with an increase in the concentration of cholesterol in a person's blood, and this in turn increases the risk of CHD (Figure **9.7**). It's not too difficult to substitute plant oils for animal fats, and still be able to eat most of the things that you really like. Fast foods, though, are often high in animal fat, so these need to be eaten in moderation.

Regular exercise has a very beneficial effect on many

Smoking
Smokers are much more likely to die from a heart attack than non-smokers.

Blood cholesterol levels
There are two kinds of blood cholesterol – HDL and LDL. If you have a lot of LDL and only a little HDL, then you are more likely to develop CHD. This is partly affected by your genes, but also by your diet. Diets rich in animal fats can increase the LDL in your blood.

Age
The risk of developing CHD increases as you get older.

Stress
Some stress and excitement is good for you – for example, taking part in a competitive sport event, or challenging your brain with a difficult thinking task. But stress that gets out of hand is bad for your health, expecially if it goes on for a long time.

High blood pressure
High blood pressure can be caused by too much stress, a diet rich in animal fats or with too much salt, or by being overweight.

Gender
Men are more likely to develop CHD than women.

Figure 9.6   Life-style factors in CHD.

parts of the body, including the heart. Most people can find some kind of exercise that they enjoy. Exercise helps to keep you fit, prevents excessive weight gain and decreases blood pressure. It also has a 'feel-good' effect, by helping to clear your mind of things that may be worrying you, and causing the release of chemicals in the brain that increase feelings of well-being.

Many governments worldwide have run campaigns to try to encourage people to stop smoking, take more exercise and avoid diets high in animal fats. These have often been successful, and some countries have seen significant reductions in the incidence of CHD.

People who are thought to be at high risk of developing CHD – perhaps because they have high blood pressure, or are very overweight – may be prescribed a type of drug called statin. This drug helps to reduce cholesterol levels in the blood, and can be very beneficial. However, it can sometimes have some unpleasant side-effects, so most doctors will not prescribe it to people who can easily improve their health by changing their lifestyle a little.

Treating CHD

Once a person has developed CHD, there are various treatments that can help to control this disease, or even to cure it.

If a doctor diagnoses CHD, they will normally consider prescribing drugs for the patient. These include statins, and also other drugs that help to lower blood pressure, or to decrease the risk of blood clots forming inside blood vessels, such as aspirin. These drugs may need to be taken over a long period of time, unless the patient is able to improve their own health

through lifestyle changes.

If all else fails, then the patient may need to have surgery to try to correct the problem. A blocked or severely damaged coronary artery can be replaced with a length of blood vessel taken from another part of the body (Figure **9.8**). This is called a coronary bypass operation.

Another possibility is to insert a little mesh tube, called a stent, inside the artery to keep it open.

Yet another option is to use a tiny balloon. This is inserted into the collapsed artery, and then inflated using water. This pushes the artery open. The balloon is then removed. This process is called angioplasty.

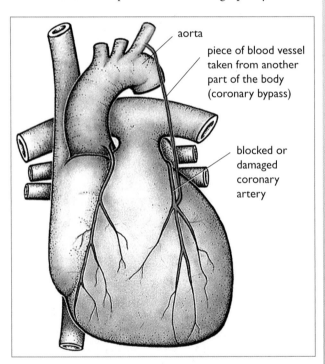

aorta

piece of blood vessel taken from another part of the body (coronary bypass)

blocked or damaged coronary artery

Figure 9.8 How a coronary bypass is constructed.

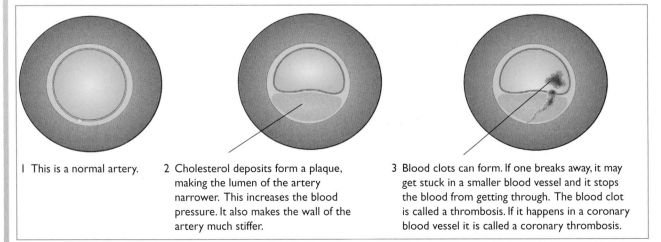

1 This is a normal artery.

2 Cholesterol deposits form a plaque, making the lumen of the artery narrower. This increases the blood pressure. It also makes the wall of the artery much stiffer.

3 Blood clots can form. If one breaks away, it may get stuck in a smaller blood vessel and it stops the blood from getting through. The blood clot is called a thrombosis. If it happens in a coronary blood vessel it is called a coronary thrombosis.

Figure 9.7 How coronary heart disease is caused.

S In really severe cases, even this may not be enough, and the patient may require a complete heart transplant. This is always tricky, because there are never enough organs available for all the patients that require them, and there is an ever present danger that the transplanted organ will be rejected by the recipient's immune system (page **133**). The recipient will need to take drugs to suppress the immune system for the rest of their life.

Heart beat

You may be able to feel your heart beating if you put your hand on your chest. Most people's hearts beat about 60 to 75 times a minute when they are resting. If you put your head against a friend's chest, or use a stethoscope, you can also the sounds of the valves closing with each heart beat. They sound rather like 'lub-dup'. Each complete 'lub-dup' represents one heart beat.

A good way to measure the rate of your heart beat is to take your pulse rate. A pulse is caused by the expansion and relaxation of an artery, caused by the heart pushing blood through it. Your pulse rate is therefore the same as your heart rate. You can find a pulse wherever there is an artery fairly near to the surface of the skin. Two suitable places are inside your wrist, and just to the side of the big tendons in your neck.

In a hospital, the activity of the heart can be recorded as an ECG. This stands for electrocardiograph. Little electrodes are stuck onto the person's body, and the electrical activity in the heart is recorded (Figure **9.9**). The activity is recorded as a kind of graph. An example of a normal ECG is shown in Figure **9.10**.

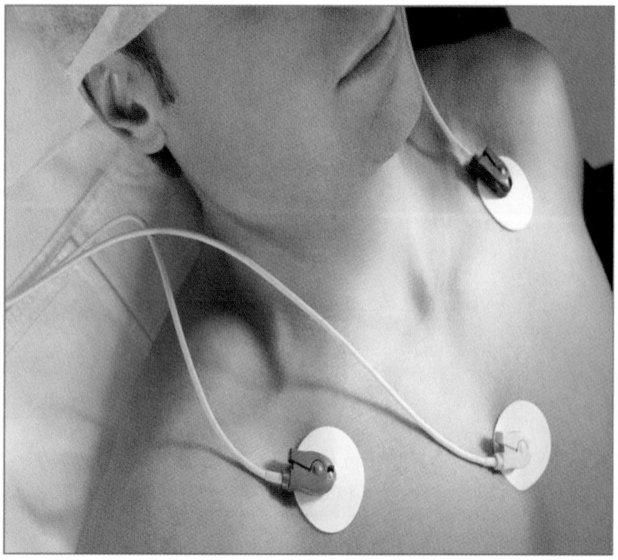

When a person exercises, their heart beats faster. This is because their muscles are using up oxygen more quickly in respiration, to supply the energy needed for movement. A faster heart rate means faster delivery of blood to the muscles, providing oxygen.

The rate at which the heart beats is controlled **S** by a patch of muscle in the right atrium called the pacemaker. The pacemaker sends electrical signals through the walls of the heart at regular intervals, which make the muscle contract. The pacemaker's rate, and therefore the rate of heart beat, changes according to the needs of the body. For example, during exercise, when extra oxygen is needed by the muscles, the brain sends impulses along nerves to the pacemaker, to make the heart beat faster.

The signal for this is an increase in the pH of the blood. During exercise, muscles respire more quickly than usual, in order to release the energy needed for movement. This increase in respiration rate means that more carbon dioxide is produced, and this dissolves in the blood. A weak acid is formed, lowering the pH of the blood. Receptor cells in the brain sense this drop in pH, and this triggers an increase in the frequency of the nerve impulse sent to the pacemaker.

Sometimes, the pacemaker stops working properly. An artificial pacemaker can then be placed in the person's heart. It produces an electrical impulse at a regular rate of about one impulse per second. Artificial pacemakers last for up to ten years before they have to be replaced.

Figure 9.9 A patient having an ECG test to check the functioning of his heart.

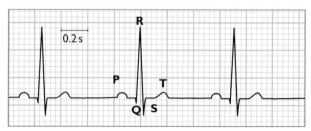

Figure 9.10 A normal ECG trace. The points labelled P, Q, R, S and T represent different stages of a heart beat.

Valves in the heart

The heart beats as the cardiac muscles in its walls contract and relax. When they contract, the heart becomes smaller, squeezing blood out. This is called systole. When they relax, the heart becomes larger, allowing blood to flow into the atria and ventricles. This is called diastole.

There is a valve between the left atrium and the left ventricle, and another between the right atrium and ventricle. These are called atrioventricular valves (Figure **9.11**).

The valve on the left-hand side of the heart is made of two parts and is called the bicuspid valve, or the mitral valve. The valve on the right-hand side has three parts, and is called the tricuspid valve.

The function of these valves is to stop blood flowing from the ventricles back to the atria. This is important, so that when the ventricles contract, the blood is pushed up into the arteries, not back into the atria. As the ventricles contract, the pressure of the blood pushes the valves upwards. The tendons attached to them stop them from going up too far.

Activity 9.2
To find the effect of exercise on the rate of heart beat

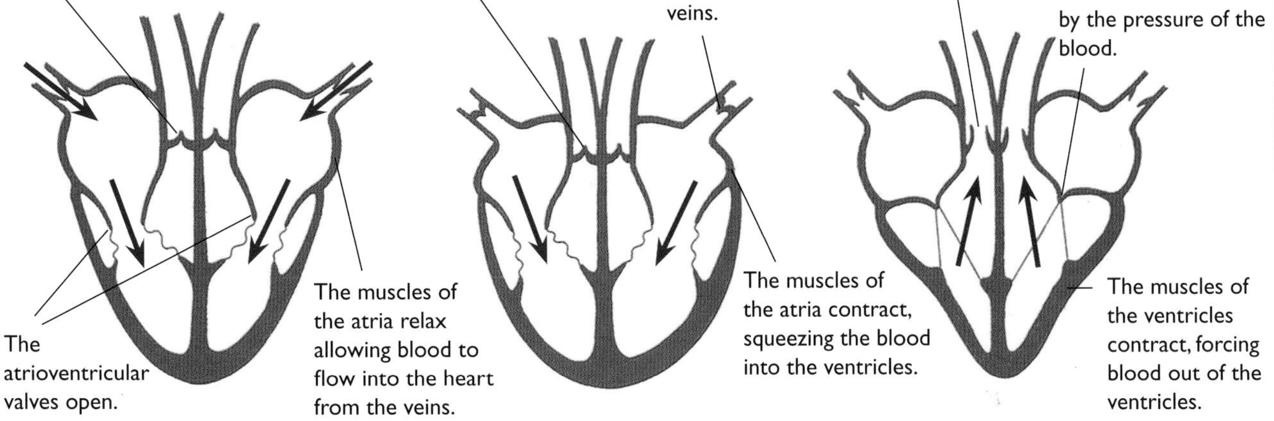

9.3 Blood vessels

There are three main kinds of blood vessels: arteries, capillaries and veins (Figure **9.12**). Arteries carry blood away from the heart. They divide again and again, and eventually form very tiny vessels called capillaries. The capillaries gradually join up with one another to form large vessels called veins. Veins carry blood towards the heart. These vessels are compared in Table **9.1**, page **116**.

Arteries   **S**

When blood flows out of the heart, it enters the arteries. The blood is then at very high pressure, because it has been forced out of the heart by the contraction of the muscular ventricles. Arteries therefore need very strong walls to withstand the high pressure of the blood flowing through them.

The blood does not flow smoothly through the arteries. It pulses through, as the ventricles contract and relax. The arteries have elastic tissue in their walls which can stretch and recoil with the force of the blood. This helps to make the flow of blood smoother. You can feel your arteries stretch and recoil when you feel your pulse in your wrist.

The blood pressure in the arteries of your arm can be measured using a sphygmomanometer (Figure **9.13**).

The semilunar valves shut, preventing blood from flowing into the ventricles.

The atrioventricular valves open.

The muscles of the atria relax allowing blood to flow into the heart from the veins.

The semilunar valves remain shut.

The muscles of the atria contract, squeezing the blood into the ventricles.

The valves in the veins are forced shut by the pressure of the blood, stopping the blood from flowing back into the veins.

The semilunar valves are forced open by the pressure of the blood.

The atrioventricular valves are forced shut by the pressure of the blood.

The muscles of the ventricles contract, forcing blood out of the ventricles.

Diastole: all muscles are relaxed. Blood flows into the heart.

Atrial systole: the muscles of the atria contract. The muscles of the ventricles remain relaxed. Blood is forced from the atria into the ventricles.

Ventricular systole: the muscles of the atria relax. The muscles of the ventricles contract. Blood is forced out of the ventricles into the arteries.

Figure 9.11 How the hearts pumps blood.

S Capillaries

The arteries gradually divide to form smaller and smaller vessels (Figures **9.14** and **9.15**). These are the capillaries. The capillaries are very small and penetrate to every part of the body. No cell is very far away from a capillary.

The function of the capillaries is to take nutrients, oxygen and other materials to all the cells in the body, and to take away their waste materials. To do this, their walls must be very thin so that substances can get in and out of them easily. The walls of the smallest capillaries are only one cell thick (Figure **9.12**).

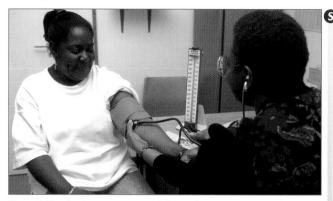

Figure 9.13 A sphygmomanometer being used to measure blood pressure.

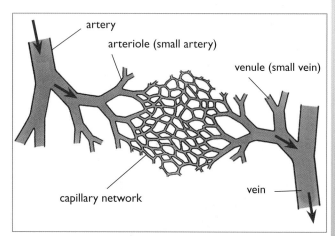

Figure 9.14 A capillary network.

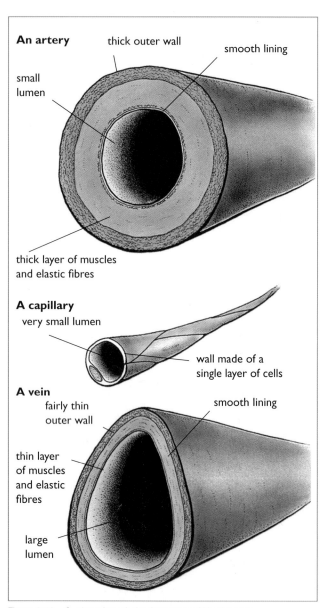

Figure 9.12 Sections through the three types of blood vessels.

Questions

9.13 List **three** ways in which the activity of the heart can be monitored.

9.14 Explain why your pulse rate is the same as your heart rate.

9.15 Look at Figure **9.10**.

  a How many heart beats are shown on the ECG trace?

  b Work out how long one heart beat lasts. (You need to measure between two identical points on two consecutive beats – for example between two Q points – and then use the scale to convert this to seconds.)

9.16 Why does your heart need to beat faster when you do exercise?

9.17 Where and what is the pacemaker?

9.18 Explain what makes your heart beat faster when you exercise.

9.19 Describe and explain the action of the atrioventricular valves during ventricular systole.

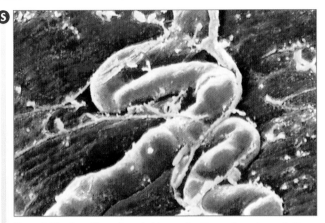

Figure 9.15   A capillary, shown in blue, snakes its way through muscle tissue (×600).

Veins

The capillaries gradually join up again to form veins. By the time the blood gets to the veins, it is at a much lower pressure than it was in the arteries. The blood flows more slowly and smoothly now. There is no need for veins to have such thick, strong, elastic walls.

If the veins were narrow, this would slow down the blood even more. To help keep the blood moving easily through them, the space inside the veins, called the lumen, is much wider than the lumen of the arteries.

Veins have valves in them to stop the blood flowing backwards (Figure 9.16). Valves are not needed in the arteries, because the force of the heart beat keeps blood moving forwards through them.

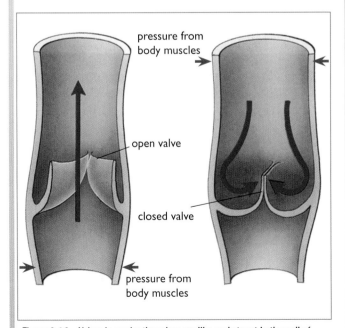

Figure 9.16   Valves in a vein: the valves are like pockets set in the wall of the vein.

Blood is also kept moving in the veins by the contraction of muscles around them (Figure 9.16). The large veins in your legs are squeezed by your leg muscles when you walk. This helps to push the blood back up to your heart. If a person is confined to bed for a long time, then there is a danger that the blood in these veins will not be kept moving. A clot may form in them, called a thrombosis. If the clot is carried to the lungs, it could get stuck in the arterioles. This is called a pulmonary embolism, and it may prevent the circulation reaching part of the lungs. In serious cases, this can cause death.

Naming blood vessels

Figures 9.17 and 9.18 illustrate the positions of the main arteries and veins in the body.

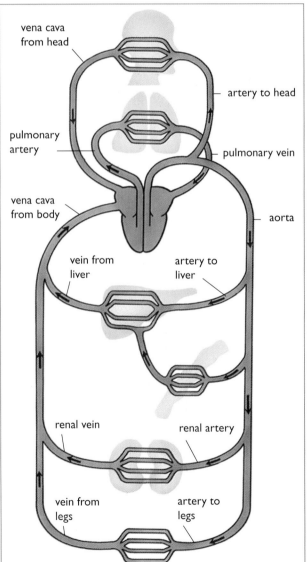

Figure 9.17   Plan of the main blood vessels in the human body.

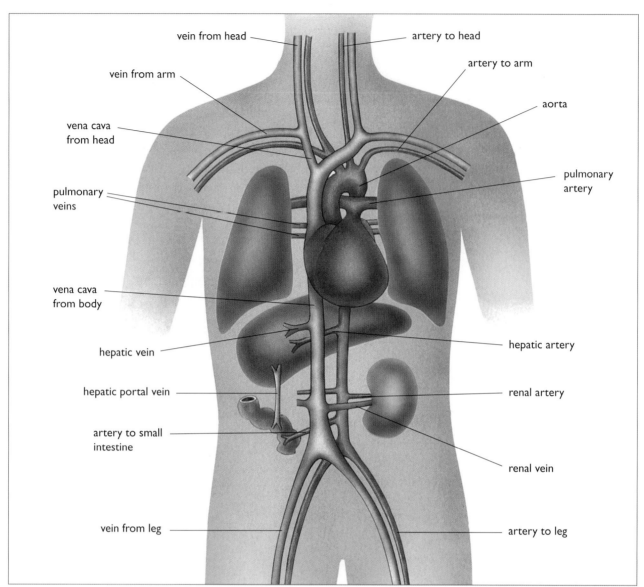

Figure 9.18   The main arteries and veins in the human body.

	Function	Structure of wall	Width of lumen	**S** How structure fits function
Arteries	carry blood away from the heart	thick and strong, containing muscles and elastic tissues	relatively narrow; it varies with heart beat, as it can stretch and recoil	strength and elasticity needed to withstand the pulsing of the blood as it is pumped through the heart
Capillaries	supply all cells with their requirements, and take away waste products	very thin, only one cell thick	very narrow, just wide enough for a red blood cell to pass through	no need for strong walls, as most of the blood pressure has been lost; thin walls and narrow lumen bring blood into close contact with body tissues
Veins	return blood to the heart	quite thin, containing far less muscle and elastic tissue than arteries	wide; contains valves	no need for strong walls, as most of the blood pressure has been lost; wide lumen offers less resistance to blood flow; valves prevent backflow

Table 9.1   Arteries, veins and capillaries.

Each organ of the body, except the lungs, is supplied with oxygenated blood from an artery. Deoxygenated blood is taken away by a vein. The artery and vein are named according to the organ with which they are connected. For example, the blood vessels of the kidneys are the **renal** artery and vein.

All arteries, other than the pulmonary artery, branch from the aorta. All the veins, except the pulmonary veins and hepatic portal vein, join up to one of the two venae cavae.

The liver has two blood vessels supplying it with blood. The first is the hepatic artery, which supplies oxygen. The second is the hepatic portal vein. This vein brings blood from the digestive system (Figure **9.17**), so that the liver can process the food which has been absorbed, before it travels to other parts of the body. All the blood leaves the liver in the hepatic vein.

9.4 Blood

The liquid part of blood is called **plasma**. Floating in the plasma are cells. Most of these are red blood cells. A much smaller number are white blood cells. There are also small fragments formed from special cells in the bone marrow, called **platelets** (Figures **9.19** and **9.20**).

Plasma is mostly water. Many substances are dissolved in it. Soluble nutrients such as glucose, amino acids, and mineral ions are carried in the plasma.

Plasma also transports hormones and carbon dioxide. More details about the substances carried in blood plasma are provided in Table **9.2**. The functions of components of blood are summarised in Table **9.3** (page **119**).

Red blood cells

Red blood cells are made in the bone marrow of some bones, including the ribs, vertebrae and some limb bones. They are produced at a very fast rate – about 9000 million per hour.

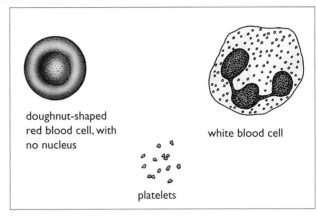

doughnut-shaped red blood cell, with no nucleus

white blood cell

platelets

Figure 9.19 Blood cells.

Red cells have to be made so quickly because they do not live for very long. Each red cell only lives for about four months. One reason for this is that they do not have a nucleus (Figure **9.19**).

Red cells are red because they contain the pigment haemoglobin. This carries oxygen. Haemoglobin is a protein, and contains iron. It is this iron that readily combines with oxygen where the gas is in good supply. It just as readily gives it up where the oxygen supply is low, as in active tissues.

The lack of a nucleus in a red blood cell means that there is more space for packing in millions of molecules of haemoglobin.

Another unusual feature of red blood cells is their shape. They are biconcave discs – like a flat disc that has been pinched in on both sides. This, together with their small size, gives them a relatively large surface area compared with their volume. This high surface area to volume ratio speeds up the rate at which oxygen can diffuse in and out of the red blood cell.

The small size of the red blood cell is also useful in enabling it to squeeze through even the tiniest capillaries. This means that oxygen can be taken very close to every cell in the body.

Questions

9.20   Which type of blood vessels carry blood **a** away from, and **b** towards the heart?

S 9.21   Why do arteries need strong walls?

9.22   Why do arteries have elastic walls?

9.23   What is the function of capillaries?

9.24   Why do veins have a large lumen? **S**

9.25   How is blood kept moving in the large veins of the legs?

9.26   What is unusual about the blood supply to the liver?

Component	Source	Destination	Notes
Water	Absorbed in small intestine and colon.	All cells.	Excess is removed by the kidneys.
Plasma proteins (including fibrinogen and antibodies)	Fibrinogen is made in the liver. Antibodies are made by lymphocytes.	Remain in the blood.	Fibrinogen helps in blood clotting. Antibodies kill invading pathogens.
Lipids including cholesterol and fatty acids	Absorbed in the ileum. Also derived from fat reserves in the body.	To the liver, for breakdown. To adipose tissue, for storage. To respiring cells, as an energy source.	Breakdown of fats yields energy – heart muscle depends largely on fatty acids for its energy supply. High cholesterol levels in the blood increase the risk of developing heart disease.
Carbohydrates, especially glucose	Absorbed in the ileum. Also produced by the breakdown of glycogen in the liver.	To all cells, for energy release by respiration.	Excess glucose is converted to glycogen and stored in the liver.
Excretory substances, e.g. urea	Produced by amino acid deamination in the liver.	To kidneys for excretion.	
Mineral ions, e.g. Na^+, Cl^-	Absorbed in the ileum and colon.	To all cells.	Excess ions are excreted by the kidneys.
Hormones	Secreted into the blood by endocrine glands.	To all parts of the body.	Hormones only affect their target cells. Hormones are broken down by the liver, and their remains are excreted by the kidneys.
Dissolved gases, e.g. carbon dioxide	Carbon dioxide is released by all cells as a waste product of respiration.	To the lungs for excretion.	Most carbon dioxide is carried as hydrogencarbonate ions (HCO_3^-) in the blood plasma.

Table 9.2 Some of the main components of blood plasma

White blood cells

White cells are easily recognised, because, unlike red blood cells they do have a nucleus, which is often quite large and lobed (Figures **9.19**, **9.20** and **9.21**). They can move around and can squeeze out through the walls of blood capillaries into all parts of the body. Their function is to fight **pathogens** (disease-causing bacteria and viruses), and to clear up any dead body cells. Some of them do this by taking in and digesting bacteria, in a process called phagocytosis. Others produce chemicals called antibodies.

There are many different kinds of white blood cells. They all have the function of destroying pathogens in your body, but they do it in different ways.

Ⓢ   **Phagocytes** are cells which can move around the body, engulfing and destroying pathogens (Figure **9.22**). They also destroy any of your own cells that are damaged or worn out. Phagocytes often have lobed nuclei. If you damage your skin, perhaps with a cut or graze,

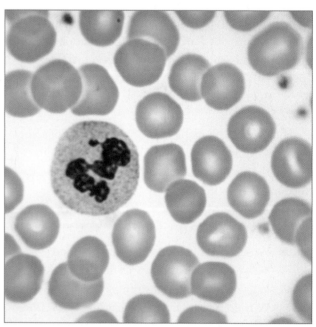

Figure 9.20   Blood seen through a microscope. The large cell is a white cell. The others are all red cells. There are also a few platelets (× 1700).

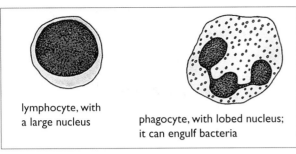

lymphocyte, with a large nucleus

phagocyte, with lobed nucleus; it can engulf bacteria

Figure 9.21 Two types of white blood cell.

(S) phagocytes will collect at the site of the damage, to engulf and digest any microorganisms which might possibly get in.

You can read more about antibodies in Chapter **10**.

Platelets

Platelets are small fragments of cells, with no nucleus. They are made in the red bone marrow, and they are involved in blood clotting.

(S) Blood clotting stops pathogens getting into the body through breaks in the skin. Normally, your skin provides a very effective barrier against the entry of bacteria and viruses. Blood clotting also prevents too much blood loss.

Key definition

pathogen – a disease-causing organism

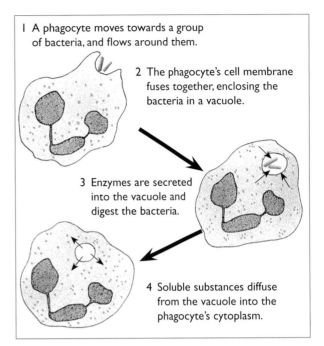

1 A phagocyte moves towards a group of bacteria, and flows around them.

2 The phagocyte's cell membrane fuses together, enclosing the bacteria in a vacuole.

3 Enzymes are secreted into the vacuole and digest the bacteria.

4 Soluble substances diffuse from the vacuole into the phagocyte's cytoplasm.

Figure 9.22 Phagocytosis.

Questions

9.27 List **five** substances that are transported in plasma.
9.28 What is the function of red blood cells?
9.29 What is unusual about the structure of red blood cells?
9.30 What is haemoglobin?
9.31 What are platelets?

Component	Structure	Functions
plasma	water, containing many substances in solution	1 liquid medium in which cells and platelets can float 2 transports CO_2 in solution 3 transports nutrients in solution 4 transports urea in solution 5 transports hormones in solution 6 transports heat 7 transports proteins, e.g. fibrinogen 8 transports antibodies
red cells	biconcave discs with no nucleus, containing haemoglobin	1 transport oxygen 2 transport small amount of CO_2
white cells	variable shapes, with nucleus	1 engulf and destroy pathogens (phagocytosis) 2 make antibodies
platelets	small fragments of cells, with no nucleus	help in blood clotting

Table 9.3 Components of blood.

Figure **9.23** shows how blood clotting happens. Platelets are very important in this process. Normally, blood vessel walls are very smooth. When a blood vessel is cut, the platelets bump into the rough edges of the cut, and react by releasing a chemical. The damaged tissues around the blood vessel also release chemicals.

In the blood plasma, there is a soluble protein called **fibrinogen**. The chemicals released by the platelets and the damaged tissues set off a chain of reactions, which cause the fibrinogen to change into **fibrin**.

Fibrin is insoluble. As its name suggests, it forms fibres. These form a mesh across the wound. Red blood cells and platelets get trapped in the tangle of fibrin fibres, forming a blood clot (Figures **9.24** and **9.25**.

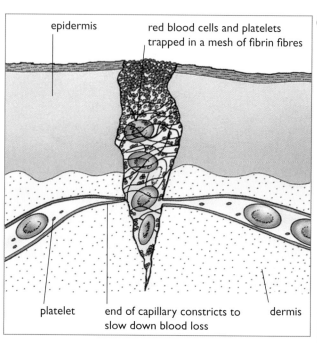

Figure 9.24   Vertical section through a blood clot.

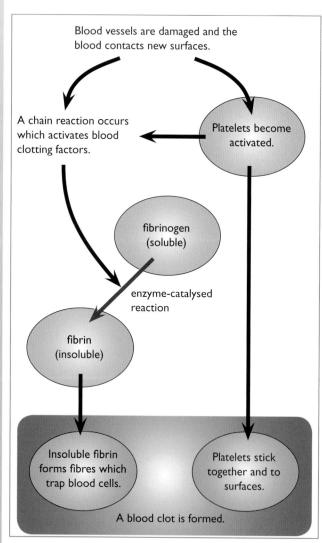

Figure 9.23   How blood clots.

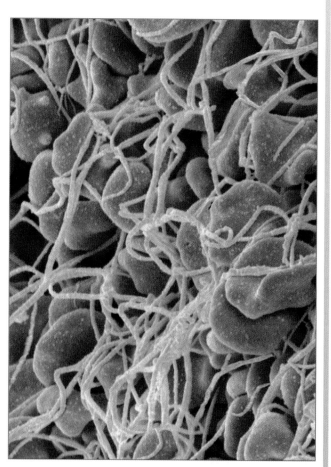

Figure 9.25   A scanning electron micrograph showing red cells tangled up in fibrin fibres (× 3600).

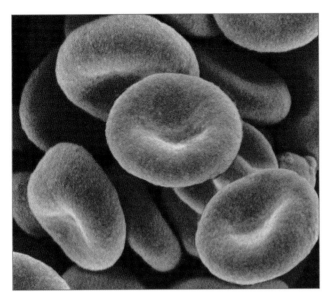

Figure 9.26 Scanning electron micrograph of red blood cells (× 4500).

Ⓢ Transport in the blood

Transport of oxygen

The main function of the blood is to transport substances from one part of the body to another. This is summarised in Table **9.2**.

In the lungs, oxygen diffuses from the alveoli into the blood (page **107**). We have seen that the doughnut shape of the red blood cells (Figure **9.19**) increases the surface area for diffusion, so that oxygen can diffuse into and out of the cells very rapidly. In the lungs, oxygen diffuses into the red blood cells, where it combines with haemoglobin (Hb) to form oxyhaemoglobin (oxyHb).

The blood is then taken to the heart in the pulmonary veins and pumped out of the heart in the aorta.

Arteries branch from the aorta to supply all parts of the body with oxygenated blood. When it reaches a tissue which needs oxygen, the oxyHb gives up its oxygen, to become Hb again.

Because capillaries are so narrow, the oxyHb in the red blood cells is taken very close to the tissues which need the oxygen. The oxygen only has a very short distance to diffuse. OxyHb is bright red, whereas Hb is purplish-red. The blood in arteries is therefore a brighter red colour than the blood in veins.

Transport of carbon dioxide

Carbon dioxide is made by all the cells in the body as they respire. The carbon dioxide diffuses through the walls of the capillaries into the blood.

Most of the carbon dioxide is carried by the blood plasma in the form of hydrogencarbonate ions, HCO^{3-}. A small amount is carried by Hb in the red cells.

Blood containing carbon dioxide is returned to the heart in the veins, and then to the lungs in the pulmonary arteries. The carbon dioxide diffuses out of the blood and is passed out of the body on expiration.

Transport of food materials

Digested food is absorbed in the ileum (page **85**). It includes nutrients such as amino acids, fatty acids and glycerol, monosaccharides (such as glucose), water, vitamins and minerals. These all dissolve in the plasma in the blood capillaries in the villi.

These capillaries join up to form the hepatic portal vein. This takes the dissolved nutrients to the liver. The liver processes each nutrient and returns some of it to the blood.

The nutrients are then carried, dissolved in the blood, to all parts of the body.

Transport of urea

Urea, a waste substance (page **154**), is made in the liver. It dissolves in the blood plasma, and is carried to the kidneys. The kidneys excrete it in the urine.

Transport of hormones

Hormones are made in endocrine glands (page **170**). The hormones dissolve in the blood plasma, and are transported all over the body.

Transport of heat

Some parts of the body, such as the muscles, make a great deal of heat. The blood transports the heat to all parts of the body. This helps to keep the rest of the body warm.

Transport of plasma proteins

Several different proteins are dissolved in plasma. They are called plasma proteins. Fibrinogen (page **118**) is an example of a plasma protein.

  Questions

9.32 Why is blood in arteries a brighter red than the blood in veins?

9.33 Which vessel transports digested food to the liver?

9.34 How is urea transported?

9.35 Outline **two** functions of blood other than transport.

⑤ 9.5 Lymph and tissue fluid

Capillaries leak. The cells in their walls do not fit together exactly, so there are small gaps between them. Plasma can therefore leak out from the blood.

White blood cells can also get through these gaps. They are able to move and can squeeze through, out of the capillaries. Red blood cells cannot get out. They are too large and cannot change their shape very much.

So plasma and white cells are continually leaking out of the blood capillaries. The fluid formed in this way is called tissue fluid. It surrounds all the cells in the body (Figure 9.27).

Functions of tissue fluid

Tissue fluid is very important. It supplies cells with all their requirements. These requirements, such as oxygen and nutrients, diffuse from the blood, through the tissue fluid, to the cells. Waste products, such as carbon dioxide, diffuse in the opposite direction.

The tissue fluid is the immediate environment of every cell in your body. It is easier for a cell to carry out its functions properly if its environment stays constant. For example, this means it should stay at the same temperature, and at the same osmotic concentration.

Several organs in the body work to keep the composition and temperature of the blood constant, and therefore the tissue fluid as well. This process is called homeostasis, and is described in Chapter 14.

Lymph

The plasma and white cells that leak out of the blood capillaries must eventually be returned to the blood. In the tissues, as well as blood capillaries, are other small vessels. They are lymphatic capillaries (Figure 9.27). The tissue fluid slowly drains into them. The fluid is now called lymph.

The lymphatic capillaries gradually join up to form larger lymphatic vessels (Figure 9.27). These carry the lymph to the subclavian veins which bring blood back from the arms (Figure 9.28). Here the lymph enters the blood again.

The lymphatic system has no pump to make the lymph flow. Lymph vessels do have valves in them, however, to make sure that movement is only in one direction. Lymph flows much more slowly than blood. Many of the larger lymph vessels run within or very close to muscles, and when the muscles contract they squeeze inwards on the lymph and force it to move along the vessels.

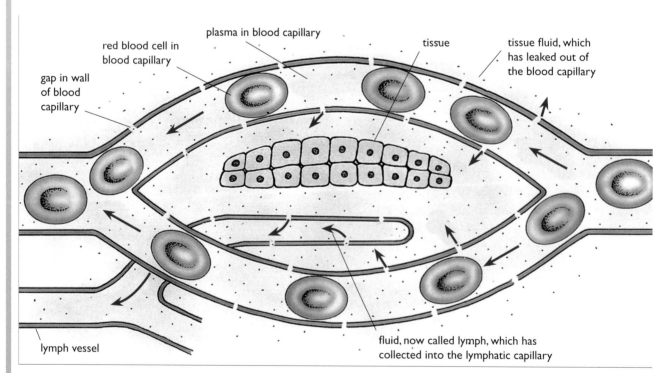

red blood cell in blood capillary

plasma in blood capillary

gap in wall of blood capillary

tissue

tissue fluid, which has leaked out of the blood capillary

lymph vessel

fluid, now called lymph, which has collected into the lymphatic capillary

Figure 9.27   Part of a capillary network, to show how tissue fluid and lymph are formed.

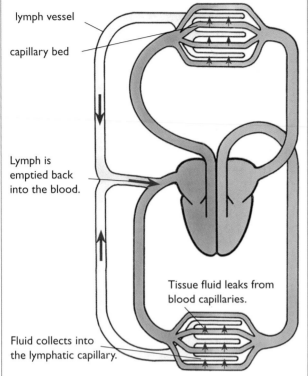

lymph vessel

capillary bed

Lymph is emptied back into the blood.

Tissue fluid leaks from blood capillaries.

Fluid collects into the lymphatic capillary.

Figure 9.28 The relationship between the blood circulation and the lymph circulation.

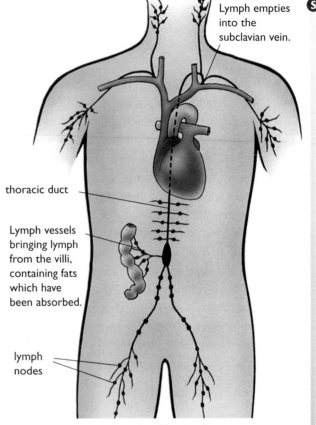

Lymph empties into the subclavian vein.

thoracic duct

Lymph vessels bringing lymph from the villi, containing fats which have been absorbed.

lymph nodes

Figure 9.29 The main lymph vessels and lymph nodes.

Lymph nodes

On its way from the tissues to the subclavian vein, lymph flows through several **lymph nodes**. Some of these are shown in Figure **9.29**.

Inside lymph nodes, new white blood cells are produced. Lymph nodes therefore contain large numbers of white cells. Most bacteria or toxins in the lymph can be destroyed by these cells.

Questions

9.36 What is tissue fluid?
9.37 Give **two** functions of tissue fluid.
9.38 What is lymph?
9.39 Why do lymphatic capillaries have valves in them?
9.40 Name **two** places where lymph nodes are found.
9.41 What happens inside lymph nodes?

Summary

You should know:

- ♦ the differences between double and single circulatory systems
- Ⓢ ♦ the differences between the structure of the heart and how it works
- ♦ reasons for the difference in thickness of the walls of the heart chambers
- ♦ the importance of the coronary arteries
- Ⓢ ♦ factors that increase the risk of developing coronary heart disease (CHD)
- ♦ how lifestyle can influence the risk of CHD
- ♦ what happens during one heart beat, including the roles of the valves
- Ⓢ ♦ how exercise affects heart rate
- ♦ the mechanism by which heart rate is changed during exercise
- Ⓢ ♦ about arteries, veins and capillaries
- ♦ how the structures of arteries, veins and capillaries help them to carry out their functions
- ♦ the names of the major blood vessels
- ♦ how to recognise red blood cells, white blood cells, platelets and plasma
- Ⓢ ♦ the functions of these components of blood
- ♦ about lymph and tissue fluid.

End-of-chapter questions

1   Using Figure **9.17** to help you, list in order the blood vessels and parts of the heart which:

  a   a glucose molecule would travel through on its way from your digestive system to a muscle in your leg

  b   a carbon dioxide molecule would travel through on its way from the leg muscle to your lungs.

2   Explain the difference between each of the following pairs.

  a   artery, vein
  b   deoxygenated blood, oxygenated blood
  c   atrium, ventricle
  d   red blood cell, white blood cell
  Ⓢ e   blood, lymph
  f   diastole, systole
  g   hepatic vein, hepatic portal vein

3   Identify the components of blood that have each of the following functions.

  a   transporting carbon dioxide
  b   destroying bacteria
  c   transporting urea
  d   transporting oxygen
  e   clotting
  f   transporting glucose

Ⓢ 4   Arteries, veins, capillaries, xylem vessels and phloem tubes are all tubes used for transporting substances in mammals and flowering plants. Describe how each of these tubes is adapted for its particular function.

5   The diagram shows two cells found in human blood.

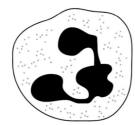 

a   The actual diameter of a red blood cell is 0.007 mm (7 μm) in diameter.
    Calculate the magnification of the diagram. Show your working.   [3]
b   Describe **three** differences between the structure of a red blood cell and a white blood cell.   [3]
c   i   State the function of a red blood cell.   [1]
    ii   Explain how the structure of a red blood cell helps it to carry out this function.   [3]

S 6   The diagram shows how the volume of the left ventricle changes over a time period of 1.3 seconds.

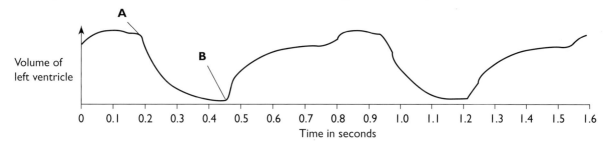

a   How many complete heart beats are shown in the diagram?   [1]
b   i   Use the graph to calculate how long one heart beat takes. Show your working.   [1]
    ii   Use your answer to **b i** to calculate the heart rate. Show your working.   [2]
c   Describe what is happening between points **A** and **B** on the graph.   [3]
d   Describe how the valves between the atria and ventricles help to ensure a one-way flow of blood
    through the heart.   [3]
e   Make a copy of the graph shown above. On your graph, sketch a line to show the volume of
    the right ventricle during this time period.   [2]

7 Heart surgeons may stop the heart beating during operations. While this happens, blood is pumped through a heart-lung machine that oxygenates the blood.
The diagram below shows a heart–lung machine in use.

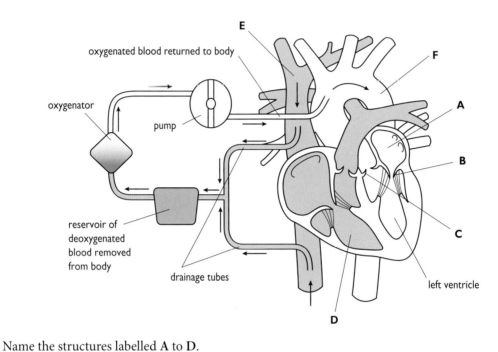

a Name the structures labelled **A** to **D**. [4]

b Name the blood vessels **E** and **F**. [2]

c The heart-lung machine is used so that surgeons can operate on the arteries supplying heart muscle. These arteries may be diseased. Name these arteries and explain how they may become diseased. [3]

d Suggest why a patient is put on a heart–lung machine during such an operation. [2]

Humans have a double circulation system. There is a low pressure circulation and a high pressure circulation.

e Explain how the structure of the heart enables it to pump blood into two circulations at different pressures. [4]

[Cambridge IGCSE® Paper 0610/32, Question 1, October/November 2011]

10 Pathogens and immunity

In this chapter, you will find out about:

♦ pathogens and transmissible diseases
♦ how pathogens are transmitted
♦ body defences against pathogens
Ⓢ ♦ the immune system.

Rabies

In March 2012, a British woman visited her family in India. While there, she was bitten by a dog. The bite wasn't a bad one, and she didn't bother to seek medical treatment. She soon forgot all about it.

Seven weeks later, when she was back at her home in Britain, she felt ill. She went to the Accident and Emergency department of a hospital near her home, but the doctors were unable to diagnose what was wrong with her, as her symptoms were quite mild at that point. She did not mention the dog bite. The doctors at the hospital had no reason to suspect rabies, which is almost unknown in Britain. Even a second visit failed to raise anyone's suspicions.

As her symptoms worsened, she visited her GP, who recognised that there might be a serious problem. She was sent to another hospital that specialises in the treatment of diseases that are generally found only in tropical countries. There, she was diagnosed with rabies. Despite receiving the best possible treatment, she died from the disease a few weeks later.

Rabies is a disease that is caused by a virus. The virus is passed to a person when they are bitten by an animal – often a dog, bat, skunk or raccoon – that has the virus in its saliva (Figure **10.1**). The virus enters the person's nervous system and eventually gets into the brain. The disease cannot be treated, so even if the woman had been correctly diagnosed on her first visit to the hospital, she could not have been saved. It can, however, be prevented by vaccination, but this has to be done well before the person is bitten. It's also possible to stop the disease developing with emergency treatment within 24 hours of being bitten. This involves giving the patient five doses of antibodies against the rabies virus, over a period of 30 days.

Figure 10.1   Skunks are one of several types of mammal that can carry the rabies virus.

10.1 Pathogens

A **pathogen** is a microorganism (a tiny organism that can only be seen with a microscope) that causes disease. Many diseases are caused by pathogens that get into our bodies and breed there. Table **10.1** shows the four kinds of microorganisms that can act as pathogens, and some of the diseases that they cause.

Group to which pathogen belongs	Examples of diseases which they cause
viruses	influenza, common cold, poliomyelitis, AIDS
bacteria	cholera, syphilis, whooping cough, tuberculosis, tetanus
protoctists	malaria, amoebic dysentery
fungi	athlete's foot, ringworm

Table 10.1   Types of pathogen.

Diseases that are caused by pathogens can usually be passed from one person to another. They are called **transmissible diseases**.

Once inside the body, some pathogens may damage our cells by living in them and using up their resources. Others cause harm to cells and body systems by producing waste products, called toxins, which spread around the body and cause symptoms such as high temperature and rashes and make you feel ill. Some toxins produced by pathogens – such as the one caused by the bacterium *Clostridium botulinum* – are among the most dangerous poisons in the world.

How pathogens enter the body

There are several ways in which pathogens can get into your body.

Direct contact

The passing of a pathogen to an uninfected person is called transmission. The entry of the pathogen into the body is known as infection. The person (or animal) in which the pathogen lives and breeds is said to be a host for that pathogen.

Some pathogens pass from one person to another when there is direct contact between an infected person and an uninfected one. Diseases transmitted like this are sometimes known as contagious diseases. For example, the virus that causes AIDS, called HIV (the human immunodeficiency virus) can be transmitted when an infected person's blood comes into contact with another person's blood. The fungus that causes the skin infection, athlete's foot, can be passed on by sharing a towel with an infected person.

Indirect transmission

Most pathogens are transmitted indirectly. Indirect methods of transmission include the following.

Through the respiratory passages

Cold and influenza viruses are carried in the air in tiny droplets of moisture. Every time someone with these illnesses speaks, coughs or sneezes, millions of viruses are propelled into the air (Figure **10.2**). If you breathe in the droplets, you may become infected. You can also pick up these viruses if you touch a surface on which they are present, and then put your hands to your face.

In food or water

Bacteria such as *Salmonella* can enter your alimentary canal with the food that you eat. If you eat a large number of these bacteria, you may get food poisoning. Fresh foods, such as fruit and vegetables, should be washed in clean water before you eat them. Cooking usually destroys bacteria, so eating recently cooked food is generally safe. Food bought from street stalls is safe if it is hot and has just been cooked, but you need to take care with anything that has been kept warm for a while, as this gives any bacteria on it a chance to breed. Many governments make sure that food sellers are checked regularly to make sure that they are using good hygiene, and that their food is safe to eat (Figure **10.3**).

Many pathogens, including the virus that causes poliomyelitis and the bacterium that causes cholera, are transmitted in water. If you swim in water that contains these pathogens, or drink water containing them, you run the risk of catching these diseases. These pathogens can also get onto your hands if you touch anything that contains them, and then be passed into your body when you eat food that you have touched, or touch your mouth with your fingers.

Keep your viruses to yourself!

Remember there may be cold or flu viruses on your hands, so keep them away from your face.

If possible, keep away from other people when you have a cold or flu.

Figure 10.2 How not to catch a cold or flu.

By vectors

A vector is an organism that carries a pathogen from one host to another. Dogs, skunks, raccoons and bats are vectors for the rabies virus, which is transmitted in their saliva when they bite. Anopheles mosquitoes are the vector for malaria. The female mosquitoes may have the protoctist pathogen *Plasmodium* in their saliva, which they inject into your blood when they bite (Figure **10.4**).

Key definition

transmissible disease – a disease in which the pathogen can be passed from one host to another

---

Figure 10.3 A public health inspection officer in Thailand, testing the hands of a food seller for pathogens.

Figure 10.4 A female Anopheles mosquito feeding on human blood.

10.2 Body defences

The human body has many natural defences against pathogens. Some of them prevent pathogens from getting to parts of the body where they could breed. Figure **10.5** shows some of these defences.

Mechanical barriers

These are structures that make it difficult for pathogens to get past them and into the body. For example, the nostrils contain hairs that help to trap dust that might be carrying pathogens. The skin has a thick outer layer of dead cells, containing a protein called keratin, that is very difficult to penetrate. Very few pathogens are able

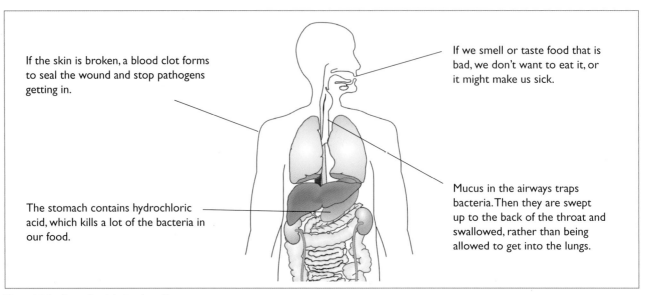

If the skin is broken, a blood clot forms to seal the wound and stop pathogens getting in.

If we smell or taste food that is bad, we don't want to eat it, or it might make us sick.

The stomach contains hydrochloric acid, which kills a lot of the bacteria in our food.

Mucus in the airways traps bacteria. Then they are swept up to the back of the throat and swallowed, rather than being allowed to get into the lungs.

Figure 10.5 Preventing infection by pathogens.

to infect undamaged skin. When the skin is cut, blood clots seal the wound, which not only prevents blood loss but also prevents pathogens from getting into the blood through the cut.

Chemical barriers

Many parts of the body – including the lining of the alimentary canal and the respiratory system – produce sticky mucus. This can trap pathogens. In the respiratory passages, cilia then sweep the mucus back up to the throat, where it can be swallowed.

In the stomach, hydrochloric acid is secreted. This strong acid kills many of the bacteria in the food that we eat, as well as those in swallowed mucus.

Pathogens that manage to get through all of these defences are usually destroyed by white blood cells. Some of these cells take in and digest the pathogens by phagocytosis (Figure 9.22 on page 119), while others produce chemicals called antibodies that incapacitate or directly kill the pathogens. Vaccination against a particular disease helps antibodies to be produced very quickly if a person is infected by the pathogen that causes it.

Food hygiene

Good food hygiene makes it much less likely that someone eating the food you have prepared will get ill. Most food poisoning is caused by bacteria, so understanding the conditions that bacteria need for growth and reproduction can help us to keep them under control.

A few simple rules can prevent you, or anyone else eating food you have prepared, from getting food poisoning.

1 Keep your own bacteria and viruses away from food. Always wash your hands before touching or eating food, or putting your hands into your mouth for any reason. Keep your hair out of food. People working in food preparation environments often wear uniforms that cover their clothes and hair (Figure 10.6). Never cough or sneeze over food.

Figure 10.6 Preparing food in a hospital kitchen.

2 Keep animals away from food. Animals are even more likely to have harmful bacteria on them than you are, so they should never be allowed to come into contact with food.

   Some are particularly dangerous. Houseflies usually have harmful bacteria on their feet, as they may have been walking on rubbish, faeces or dead animals. Moreover, when they feed they spit saliva onto the food (Figure 10.7). Rats and mice often carry pathogens. Covering food to keep flies and other animals from touching it is always a good idea.

3 Do not keep foods at room temperature for long periods. Figure 10.8 shows how bacterial growth and reproduction are affected by temperature. If there are even just a few harmful bacteria on food, these can reproduce and form large populations if the temperature is right for them. Keeping food in the fridge will slow down bacterial growth. Cooking it at a high temperature will kill most bacteria. If cooked food is reheated, it should be made really hot, not just warmed.

4 Keep raw meat away from other foods. Raw meat often contains bacteria. This is not a problem if the meat is to be cooked, as these bacteria will be killed. However, if the bacteria get onto other foods that might be eaten raw, then they might breed there. In any case, foods such as salads and vegetables that are to be eaten raw should be washed in clean water before eating, unless they have been packaged so that they cannot be contaminated with bacteria.

Personal hygiene

Personal hygiene means keeping your body clean. This can greatly reduce the risk of getting, or passing on, transmissible diseases. We have already seen how important this is when preparing or eating food.

   Human skin makes an oil that helps to keep it supple and waterproof. If the skin is not washed regularly, this oil can build up, as can dirt from things that we have touched (Figure 10.9).

   When we are hot, we produce sweat from sweat glands in the skin. The evaporation of water from the sweat helps us to keep our body temperature from rising too high.

Figure 10.7 This is a market stall in India. Houseflies are feeding on the balls of palm sugar (jaggery), and are probably leaving many bacteria on it.

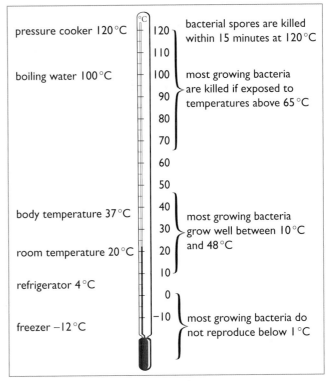

Figure 10.8 How temperature affects bacteria.

Questions

10.1 What is a pathogen?

10.2 List **three** diseases caused by pathogens.

10.3 Describe **three** ways in which pathogens can be transmitted from one person to another.

10.4 Outline **four** ways in which the body prevents pathogens from entering.

10.5 Suggest why the chef in Figure **10.6** is wearing **a** a hat and **b** simple white clothes.

Figure 10.9 Getting muddy is fun, but it is important to wash thoroughly afterwards.

Figure 10.10 Rats are attracted to rubbish. Rats and other animals, such as houseflies, may carry harmful bacteria from the rubbish to places where they can infect humans.

If oil, dirt and sweat are left on the skin for long, they provide breeding grounds for bacteria. These can produce substances that smell unpleasant. Washing regularly, using soap and shampoo to help to remove oils, prevents this from happening.

There are also millions of bacteria inside our mouths. Most of these are harmless and may even be beneficial to us. But some of them can cause bad breath and tooth decay. Brushing teeth twice a day, and perhaps also using a mouthwash, can keep these harmful bacteria under control.

Waste disposal

We produce an enormous amount of rubbish each year. Waste food, cardboard and paper packaging, bottles and cans, newspapers and magazines, plastic bags, old tyres – anything that we have finished with and no longer want to use – are all thrown away.

In many countries, this waste is collected up and taken to landfill sites. This is simply a place where there is space to put the rubbish. In some places, nothing is done to make the landfill site safe. All kinds of rubbish are just piled up. Animals such as houseflies, rats and stray dogs forage for food in the rubbish. (Figure **10.10**). Bacteria breed in the waste food. Dangerous chemicals seep out of the rubbish, polluting the ground and waterways. Landfill sites can be absolutely safe if they are properly managed. Figure **10.11** shows a well-designed landfill site. Only licenced operators are allowed to add material to the site, and the rubbish is checked as it is brought in, to make sure that nothing really dangerous is included. The rubbish is added in even layers, and is compacted (pressed down) to reduce the space it takes up.

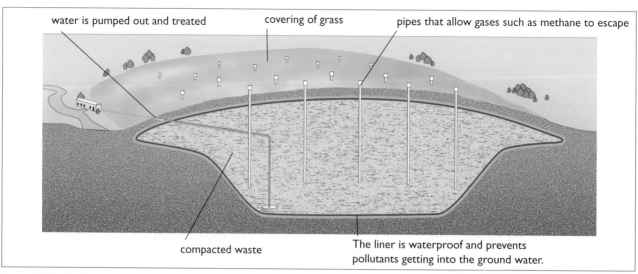

water is pumped out and treated — covering of grass — pipes that allow gases such as methane to escape

compacted waste

The liner is waterproof and prevents pollutants getting into the ground water.

Figure 10.11 A well-constructed landfill site.

Some of the rubbish in the landfill site is rotted by decomposers, especially bacteria. This produces a gas called methane, which is flammable and could cause explosions if it is allowed to build up. Placing pipes in the rubbish can allow the methane to escape harmlessly into the air. Better still, the methane can be collected and used as a fuel.

Eventually, when the landfill site is full, it can be covered over with soil and grass and trees allowed to grow.

Sewage treatment

Sewage is waste liquid that has come from houses, industry and other parts of villages, towns and cities. Some of it has just run off streets into drains when it rains. Some of it has come from toilets, bathrooms and kitchens in people's houses and offices. Some of it has come from factories. Sewage is mostly water, but also contains many other substances. These include urine and faeces, toilet paper, detergents, oil and many other chemicals.

Sewage should not be allowed to run into rivers or the sea before it has been treated. This is because it can harm people and the environment. Untreated sewage is called raw sewage.

Raw sewage contains many bacteria and other microorganisms, some of which are likely to be pathogens. People who come into contact with raw sewage, especially if it gets into their mouths, may get ill. Poliomyelitis and cholera are just two of the serious diseases that can be transmitted through water polluted with raw sewage.

 Questions

10.6 Explain why household waste should be kept covered.

10.7 Explain the importance of each of these features of a well-constructed landfill site.
  a The area is covered with a waterproof liner before waste is added.
  b As new waste is added, it is spread out and compacted.
  c The public are not allowed access to the site.
  d Pipes are inserted into the compacted waste.
  e When the site is full, it is covered with soil.

10.8 Why is raw sewage a health risk?

You can read about how sewage is treated on pages **309–310**.

10.3 The immune system Ⓢ

We have seen that one type of white blood cell, called lymphocytes, produce chemicals called antibodies. These chemicals can help to destroy pathogens.

Antibodies

In your body, you have thousands of different kinds of lymphocytes. Each kind is able to produce a different sort of antibody.

An antibody is a protein molecule with a particular shape. Rather like an enzyme molecule, this shape is just right to fit into another molecule. To destroy a particular pathogen, antibody molecules must be made which are just the right shape to fit into molecules on the outside of the pathogen. These pathogen molecules are called antigens.

When antibody molecules lock onto the pathogen, they kill the pathogen. There are several ways in which they do this. One way is simply to alert phagocytes to the presence of the pathogens, so that the phagocytes will come and destroy them. Or the antibodies may start off a series of reactions in the blood which produce enzymes to digest the pathogens.

Most of the time, most of your lymphocytes do not produce antibodies. It would be a waste of energy and materials if they did. Instead, each lymphocyte waits for a signal that a pathogen which can be destroyed by its particular antibody is in your body.

If a pathogen enters the body, it is likely to meet a large number of lymphocytes. One of these may recognise the pathogen as being something that its antibody can destroy. This lymphocyte will start to divide rapidly by mitosis, making a clone of lymphocytes just like itself. These lymphocytes then secrete their antibody, destroying the pathogen (Figure **10.12**).

This takes time. It may take a while for the 'right' lymphocyte to recognise the pathogen, and then a few days more for it to produce a big enough clone to make enough antibody to kill the pathogen. In the meantime, the pathogen breeds, making you ill. Eventually, however, the lymphocytes get the upper hand, and you get better.

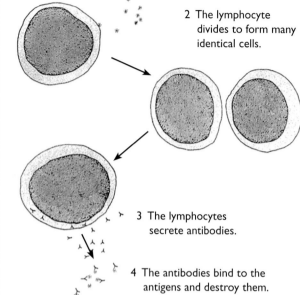

1 A lymphocyte comes into contact with antigens that fit the shape of the antibodies it can make.

2 The lymphocyte divides to form many identical cells.

3 The lymphocytes secrete antibodies.

4 The antibodies bind to the antigens and destroy them.

Figure 10.12 How lymphocytes respond to antigens.

Lymphocytes are a very important part of your immune system. The way in which they respond to pathogens, by producing antibodies, is called the immune response.

Memory cells

When a lymphocyte clones itself, not all of the cells make antibodies. Some of them simply remain in the blood and other parts of the body, living for a very long time. They are called memory cells.

If the same kind of pathogen gets into the body again, these memory cells will be ready and waiting for them. They will kill the pathogens before they have time to produce a large population and do any harm. The person has become immune to that type of pathogen.

Figure 10.13 shows how numbers of bacteria and antibodies in the body change after infection with a pathogen that your immune system has not met before, and when it infects you a second time.

Vaccination

In most countries, children are given vaccinations at various stages as they grow up. The vaccines immunise children against diseases caused by pathogens. Adults can also be given vaccinations if they are at risk of getting particular diseases.

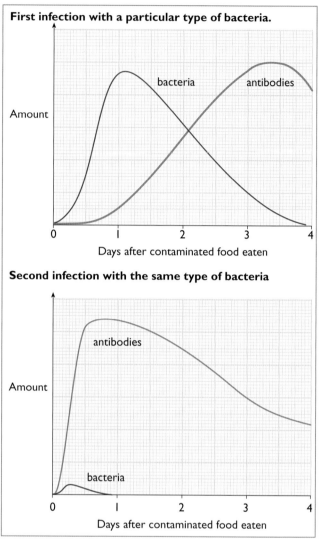

First infection with a particular type of bacteria.

Amount

Days after contaminated food eaten

Second infection with the same type of bacteria

Amount

Days after contaminated food eaten

Figure 10.13 Changes in amounts of antibodies and numbers of bacteria after a first and second infection.

❓ Questions

10.9 Explain why the number of antibodies does not begin to rise immediately after the first infection.

10.10 Describe and explain what happens to the number of bacteria the second time a person comes into contact with the bacteria.

10.11 Predict and explain what would happen if the person is infected with a different kind of bacterium, after an immune response like the one in Figure **10.13**.

S A vaccine contains weakened or dead viruses or bacteria that normally causes disease. These pathogens have the same antigens as the 'normal' ones, but they are not able to cause disease.

When these pathogens are introduced into the body, they are recognised by the lymphocytes that can make antibodies that will lock onto their antigens. These lymphocytes multiply and produce antibodies just as they would after a 'real' infection. They also make memory cells, which give long-term immunity. So, if the 'normal' viruses or bacteria get into the body one day, they will be attacked and destroyed immediately.

Active and passive immunity

A person has active immunity to a disease if they have made their own antibodies and memory cells that protect against it. These memory cells can last in the body for many years.

You can develop active immunity by:

♦ having the disease and getting over it
♦ being vaccinated with weakened pathogens

A person has passive immunity to a disease if they have been given antibodies that have been made by another organism (Figure **10.14**).

Babies get passive immunity by breast feeding. Breast milk contains antibodies from the mother, which are passed on to her baby. This is useful because a young baby's immune system is not well developed, and so the mother's antibodies can protect it against any diseases to which she is immune, for the first few months of its life.

Another way of getting passive immunity is to be injected with antibodies that have been made by another organism. For example, if a person is bitten by an animal that might have rabies, they can be given antibodies against the rabies virus. These can destroy the virus immediately, whereas waiting for the body to make its own antibodies will take too long and the person is unlikely to recover.

Active immunity can be very long-lasting. In some cases, it can last an entire lifetime. Passive immunity, however, only lasts for a short time. This is because the antibodies will eventually break down. No lymphocytes have been stimulated to make clones of themselves. The body has not made memory cells, so any infection will be treated as a first-time one.

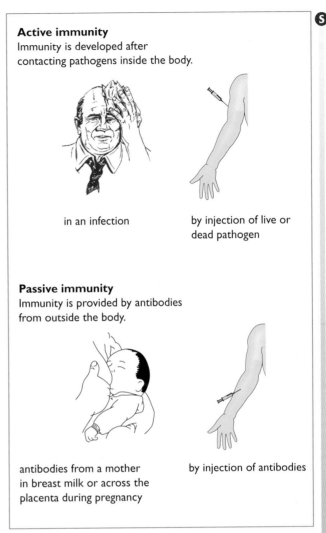

Active immunity
Immunity is developed after contacting pathogens inside the body.

in an infection

by injection of live or dead pathogen

Passive immunity
Immunity is provided by antibodies from outside the body.

antibodies from a mother in breast milk or across the placenta during pregnancy

by injection of antibodies

Figure 10.14 Methods of acquiring active and passive immunity.

Key definitions

active immunity – defence against a pathogen by antibody production in the body

passive immunity – short-term defence against a pathogen by antibodies acquired from another individual, such as from mother to infant

S Controlling disease by vaccination

Smallpox is a serious, often fatal, disease caused by a virus. It is transmitted by direct contact. If a person survives smallpox, they are often left with badly scarred skin, and may be made blind.

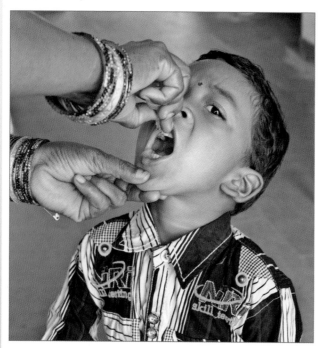

Figure 10.15 This Indian boy is being vaccinated against polio. The polio vaccine is unusual, because it can be given by mouth rather than having to be injected.

In 1956, the World Health Organization (WHO) began a campaign to try to completely eradicate smallpox. They wanted to make the smallpox virus extinct. They set up systems to get as many people as possible, all over the world, vaccinated against smallpox. The campaign was a success. More than 80% of people in the world who were at risk from the disease were vaccinated. The very last case of smallpox happened in 1977, in Somalia. By 1980, three years had gone by with no more cases, and the WHO were able to declare that smallpox had been eradicated.

Currently, attempts are being made to eradicate another very serious disease caused by a virus, poliomyelitis (polio for short) (Figure **10.15**). Polio leaves many people with permanent paralysis of parts of their body. Eradicating this virus is proving more problematical, as several countries are resisting efforts to vaccinate children. Polio is now very rare in most parts of the world, but cases are still occurring in Nigeria and Pakistan.

The control of many other serious infectious diseases relies on vaccination of children. For example, in most countries, children are vaccinated against measles, another disease caused by a virus. Measles is spread by airborne droplets. It causes a skin rash and fever,

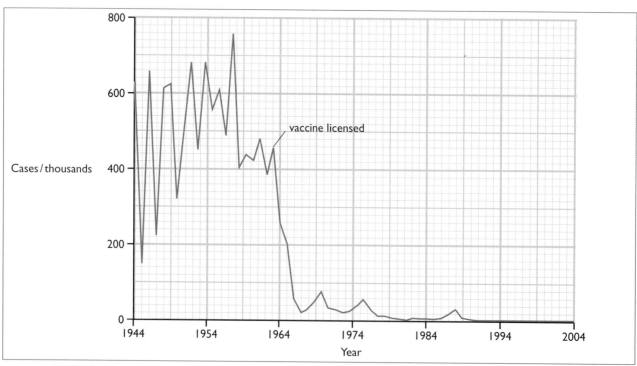

Figure 10.16 Number of cases of measles in the USA before and after vaccination was introduced.

and there can be very severe complications, such as blindness and brain damage.

Vaccinating children against measles protects not only the children that are vaccinated, but also those that are not (Figure **10.16**). This is because there are fewer places for the measles virus to breed – it can only do so if it enters the body of an unvaccinated person. However, this only works if at least 93% of children are vaccinated. If many parents decide not to have their children vaccinated, then outbreaks of measles can still occur. This happened in Swansea, in South Wales. Large numbers of parents did not allow their children to be vaccinated against measles in the late 1990s and the early years of the 21st century. In 2013, when these children were between 10 and 18 years old, a major epidemic of measles spread through the area.

Auto-immune diseases

Our immune system is very effective in protecting us against many different infectious diseases. But sometimes things go wrong, and it attacks parts of our bodies.

Lymphocytes normally respond only to 'foreign' cells that enter the body. They recognise our own cells as 'self', and do not produce antibodies against them. However, sometimes this system breaks down. Lymphocytes behave as though some of our own cells are 'foreign', and react to them as they would to an invasion of pathogens.

Diseases that result from this kind of malfunction of the immune system are called auto-immune diseases. One example is type 1 diabetes.

The pancreas is a gland that lies just beneath the stomach. As you have seen, it makes juices containing enzymes that help to digest food in the small intestine. But it has another function too – it makes hormones that help to control the concentration of glucose in the blood. You can read more about this in Chapter **14**.

One of the hormones produced by the pancreas is insulin. This hormone is made when blood glucose concentration rises above normal, and it brings about events that cause the concentration to fall. Insulin is made by a particular type of cell in the pancreas called beta cells.

In some people, the cells of their immune system attack the beta cells and destroy them. No-one understands exactly why this happens. It most commonly happens when a person is very young, so type 1 diabetes usually develops in children rather than in adults.

The loss of beta cells means that insulin is no longer produced, so blood glucose concentration is not controlled. This results in diabetes, in which blood glucose levels can fluctuate widely. The disease is very dangerous unless it is controlled. Most people with type 1 diabetes have to take insulin at regular intervals (Figure **10.17**), as well as taking great care over what they eat. This can keep blood glucose concentration within normal limits.

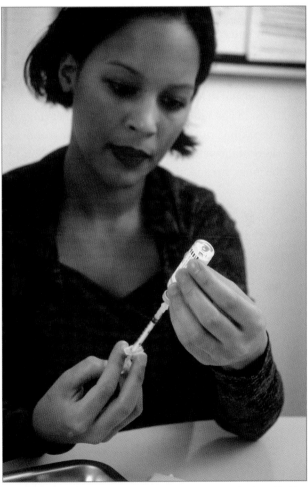

Figure 10.17 A woman with type 1 diabetes prepares to inject herself with insulin. Insulin cannot be taken by mouth, because it is a protein and would be digested by enzymes in the stomach.

Summary

You should know:

♦ about pathogens and transmissible diseases
♦ about indirect and direct methods by which pathogens can be transmitted
♦ how mechanical and chemical barriers prevent pathogens entering the body
♦ how food hygiene and personal hygiene can reduce the risk of infection
♦ the importance of hygienic waste disposal and sewage treatment
S ♦ about antibodies and what they do
♦ about vaccination (immunisation) and how it works
♦ about active and passive immunity
♦ how immunisation can control infectious diseases in the population
♦ how type 1 diabetes is caused.

End-of-chapter questions

1 Copy and complete these sentences.

A microorganism that can make a person ill is called a .... Some types of bacteria, ... , ... and .... are pathogens. Some pathogens can get into the body in food and drink. The stomach produces .... which helps to destroy these. The skin has a thick layer of .... that stops most pathogens getting into it. However, if the skin is cut, pathogens may enter the blood. Blood .... helps to prevent this. Many of the pathogens that are present in the air that we breathe in are prevented from reaching the lungs, because they are trapped by sticky .... in the respiratory passages.

S 2 Match each of the following terms with its description. You will need to use one of the terms twice.

active immunity   antibody   antigens   memory cell
passive immunity   lymphocyte   phagocyte

  a resistance to infection by a particular pathogen, obtained by having the disease or being injected with a weakened pathogen
  b resistance to infection by a particular pathogen, obtained by acquiring antibodies from another organism
  c chemicals on the outer surface of a pathogen that are recognised as foreign by lymphocytes
  d a type of white blood cell that ingests and digests bacteria
  e a type of white blood cell that produces antibodies
  f a long-lived cell produced by the division of activated lymphocytes
  g a long-lasting type of immunity
  h a protein produced by lymphocytes, which attaches to a specific antigen

3 An investigation was carried out into the changes in concentration of antibody molecules in the blood of two people. Person **R** was given passive immunity and person **S** was given active immunity. The concentration of antibody molecules in their blood is shown in the graph on the next page.

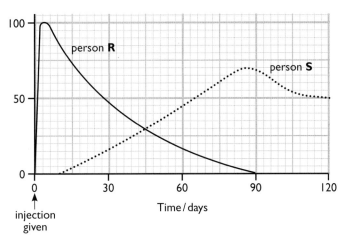

Concentration of antibody molecules in the blood / arbitrary units

Time / days

injection given

a   i   Define the term antibody.   [2]
    ii   Explain why the concentration of antibody molecules shown in the graph decreased
         to zero in person **R** by day 90.   [2]
    iii Explain why the concentration of antibody molecules shown in the graph for person **S**
         did not start to increase until 10 days after the injection.   [2]
b   Breast milk contains antibodies, which are absorbed by the baby. The antibodies give
    the baby immunity to the diseases to which the mother is immune.
    State the type of immunity that the baby has as a result of absorbing the mother's
    antibodies.   [2]

[Cambridge O Level Human Biology 5096/23, Question 5, May/June 2011]

4   These questions are about the graph in Figure **10.16** on page **136**.
    a   Describe the incidence of measles cases in the USA between 1944 and 1964.   [3]
    b   Suggest reasons for the patterns you have described in your answer to **a**.   [2]
    c   Describe the effect of the introduction of vaccination on the number of measles cases. [2]
    d   Explain why the vaccination of around 90% of a population can protect 100% of the
        population from an infectious disease.   [2]

5   a   Copy and complete the table to indicate the type of immunity – active or passive – that is
        obtained by each method.

Method	Type of immunity
having a disease and recovering from it	
feeding a baby on breast milk	
being injected with antibodies	
receiving a measles vaccination as a child	

[2]

    b   An aid worker is asked to travel immediately to a region where a disaster has taken place.
        There is a high risk of her being exposed to pathogens that could cause serious diseases.
        Her doctor recommends that she should have an injection of antibodies, rather than a
        vaccination of weakened pathogens, before she travels.
        Explain the reasons for this.   [4]

11 Respiration and gas exchange

In this chapter, you will find out about:

♦ why organisms need energy
♦ how respiration provides organisms with energy
♦ aerobic and anaerobic respiration
♦ gas exchange in humans
♦ the structure and function of the gas exchange system.

Breathing under water

If fish can breathe under water, why can't we?

Fish and humans, like almost all animals, need oxygen. We obtain our oxygen by breathing – that is, by drawing air into our lungs. This air contains oxygen, and some of the oxygen can diffuse into our blood from the lungs. Fish also obtain their oxygen by breathing, but in this case they draw water over their gills. The water contains dissolved oxygen, which diffuses into the blood in their gills.

Water contains much less oxygen than air does. Also, our breathing system cannot move water into and out of it. If we get water in our lungs, then it just stays there. We cannot get much oxygen out of the water, and we cannot move the water out to replace it with fresh water containing more oxygen, as we can with air.

So lungs are no use if you want to breathe under water. Some people can train themselves to stay under water for long periods of time, but they have to hold their breath all the time (Figure 11.1). A few species of mammals, such as whales and seals, are adapted to be able to dive to great depths, and stay under water for a long time, but they do not breathe while they are submerged. They have special mechanisms for taking large volumes of air into their lungs, and using up the oxygen gradually until they resurface.

To stay under water for long periods, we have to take air supplies with us. Scuba divers carry compressed air in tanks on their backs, and wear face masks that keep water away from their noses and mouths.

Figure 11.1   You have to hold your breath when you swim under water.

11.1 Respiration

Every living cell needs energy. In humans, our cells need energy for:

♦ contracting muscles, so that we can move parts of the body

♦ making protein molecules by linking together amino acids into long chains

♦ cell division, so that we can repair damaged tissues and can grow

♦ active transport, so that we can move substances across cell membranes up their concentration gradients

♦ transmitting nerve impulses, so that we can transfer information quickly from one part of the body to another

♦ producing heat inside the body, to keep the body temperature constant even if the environment is cold.

All of this energy comes from the food that we eat. The food is digested – that is, broken down into smaller molecules – which are absorbed from the intestine into the blood. The blood transports the nutrients to all the cells in the body. The cells take up the nutrients that they need.

The main nutrient used to provide energy in cells is glucose. Glucose contains a lot of chemical energy. In order to make use of this energy, cells have to break down the glucose molecules and release the energy from them. They do this in a series of metabolic reactions called respiration. Like all metabolic reactions, respiration involves the action of enzymes.

Aerobic respiration

Most of the time, our cells release energy from glucose by combining it with oxygen. This is called aerobic respiration.

This happens in a series of small steps, each one controlled by enzymes. We can summarise the reactions of aerobic respiration as an equation.

$$\text{glucose} + \text{oxygen} \longrightarrow \text{carbon dioxide} + \text{water}$$

The balanced equation is:

$$C_6H_{12}O_6 + 6O_2 \longrightarrow 6CO_2 + 6H_2O$$

Most of the steps in aerobic respiration take place inside mitochondria.

Anaerobic respiration

It is possible to release energy from sugar without using oxygen. It is not such an efficient process as aerobic respiration and not much energy is released per glucose molecule, but the process is used by some organisms. It is called anaerobic respiration ('an' means without). Yeast, a single-celled fungus, can respire anaerobically. It breaks down glucose to alcohol.

$$\text{glucose} \longrightarrow \text{alcohol} + \text{carbon dioxide}$$

$$C_6H_{12}O_6 \longrightarrow 2C_2H_5OH + 2CO_2$$

As in aerobic respiration, carbon dioxide is made. Plants can also respire anaerobically like this, but only for short periods of time.

Some of the cells in your body, particularly muscle cells, can respire anaerobically for a short time. They make lactic acid instead of alcohol and no carbon dioxide is produced. This happens when you do vigorous exercise, and your lungs and heart cannot supply oxygen to your muscles as quickly as they are using it.

$$\text{glucose} \longrightarrow \text{lactic acid}$$

Table 11.1 compares aerobic and anaerobic respiration.

Aerobic respiration	Anaerobic respiration
uses oxygen	does not use oxygen
no alcohol or lactic acid made	alcohol (in yeast and plants) or lactic acid (in animals) is made
large amount of energy released from each molecule of glucose	much less energy released from each molecule of glucose
carbon dioxide made	carbon dioxide is made by yeast and plants, but not by animals

Table 11.1   A comparison of aerobic and anaerobic respiration.

Activity 11.1
Investigating heat production by germinating peas

Key definition

aerobic respiration – the chemical reactions in cells that use oxygen to break down nutrient molecules to release energy

Key definition

anaerobic respiration – chemical reactions in cells that break down nutrient molecules to release energy, without using oxygen

Activity 11.2
To show the uptake of oxygen during aerobic respiration

Skills
AO3.1 Using techniques, apparatus and materials
AO3.2 Planning
AO3.3 Observing, measuring and recording
AO3.4 Interpreting and evaluating observations and data

Soda lime contains chemicals that absorb carbon dioxide. It's important not to let any animals touch the soda lime, as it could harm them.

Read through the instructions and construct a suitable results chart before you begin.

1   Set up both pieces of apparatus as shown in the diagrams. You could use any small living organisms, such as maggots (fly larvae) or germinating seeds, in apparatus **B**.

Make sure that the connections between the capillary tubes, rubber stoppers and the containers are completely airtight.

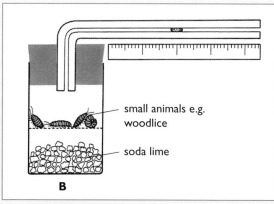

small animals e.g. woodlice

soda lime

B

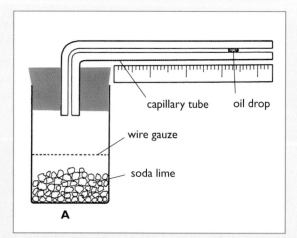

capillary tube   oil drop

wire gauze

soda lime

A

2   Dip the end of the capillary tube of each set of apparatus into oil. You should find that a small drop of oil goes into the capillary tube.

3   Record the initial position of the oil drop in each apparatus. Then continue to record this at regular intervals until you feel that you have enough readings.

4   Plot a line graph of your results for both sets of apparatus. Draw both lines on one set of axes.

❓ Questions

A1   When organisms respire, they take in oxygen and give out carbon dioxide. Explain what happened to the carbon dioxide that the organisms in apparatus **B** gave out.

A2   You should have found that the oil drop moved towards the container in apparatus **B**. Explain why this happened.

A3   Suggest why it is useful to set up apparatus **A**.

A4   Describe how you could modify this experiment to investigate the effect of temperature on the rate of germinating seeds. Remember to state clearly which variable you will change and how, and which variables you will keep constant. What do you predict that you will find? If possible, carry out your experiment.

Activity 11.3
Investigating the production of carbon dioxide by anaerobic respiration

Skills
AO3.1 Using techniques, apparatus and materials
AO3.2 Planning
AO3.3 Observing, measuring and recording
AO3.4 Interpreting and evaluating observations and data

1   Boil some water, to drive off any dissolved air.
2   Dissolve a small amount of sugar in the boiled water, and allow it to cool.
3   When it is cool, add yeast and stir with a glass rod.
4   Set up the apparatus as in the diagram. Add the liquid paraffin by trickling it gently down the side of the tube, using a pipette.
5   Set up an identical piece of apparatus, but use boiled yeast instead of living yeast.

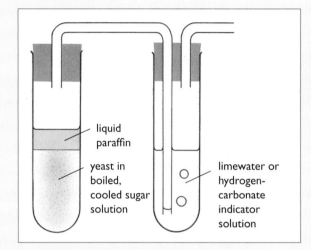

liquid paraffin

yeast in boiled, cooled sugar solution

limewater or hydrogen-carbonate indicator solution

6   Leave your apparatus in a warm place.
7   Observe what happens to the limewater after half an hour.

Questions

A1 Why is it important to boil the water?
A2 Why must the sugar solution be cooled before adding the yeast?
A3 What is the liquid paraffin for?
A4 What happened to the limewater or hydrogencarbonate indicator solution in each of your pieces of apparatus? What does this show?

A5 What new substance would you expect to find in the sugar solution containing living yeast at the end of the experiment?
A6 Describe a method you could use to compare the rate of carbon dioxide production by yeast using different kinds of sugar. Remember to describe the variables you will change, those you will control and how, and how you will collect, record and analyse your results.

Questions

11.1   What is the purpose of respiration?
11.2   What is the energy released by respiration used for?
11.3   What is anaerobic respiration?
11.4   Name an organism which can respire anaerobically.
11.5   List **three** ways in which anaerobic respiration in humans differs from aerobic respiration
11.6   List **two** ways in which anaerobic respiration in humans differs from anaerobic respiration in yeast.

Activity 11.4
Comparing the energy content of two kinds of food

11.2 Gas exchange in humans
Gas exchange surfaces

If you look back at the aerobic respiration equation on page **141**, you will see that two substances are needed. They are glucose and oxygen. The way in which cells obtain glucose is described in Chapters **6** and **7**. Animals get sugar from carbohydrates which they eat. Plants make theirs by photosynthesis.

Oxygen is obtained in a different way. Animals and plants get their oxygen directly from their surroundings. If you look again at the aerobic respiration equation you can see that carbon dioxide is made. This is a waste product and it must be removed from the organism. In organisms, there are special areas where the oxygen enters and carbon dioxide leaves. One gas is entering, and the other leaving, so these are surfaces for **gas exchange**. These surfaces have to be permeable. They have other characteristics which help the process to be quick and efficient.

1 They are thin to allow gases to diffuse across them quickly.
2 They are close to an efficient transport system to take gases to and from the exchange surface.
3 They have a large surface area, so that a lot of gas can diffuse across at the same time.
4 They have a good supply of oxygen (often brought by breathing movements).

The human breathing system

Figure **11.2** shows the structures which are involved in gas exchange in a human. The most important are the two lungs. Each lung is filled with many tiny air spaces called air sacs or **alveoli**. It is here that oxygen diffuses into the blood. Because they are so full of spaces, lungs feel very light and spongy to touch. The lungs are supplied with air through the windpipe or **trachea**.

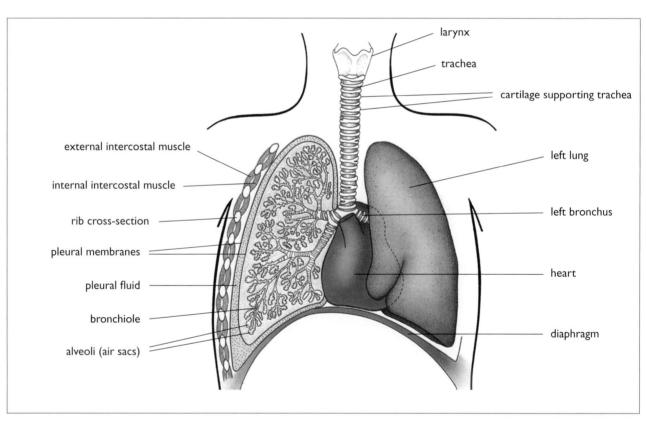

Figure 11.2 The human gas exchange system.

The pathway to the lungs

The nose and mouth

Air can enter the body through either the nose or mouth. The nose and mouth are separated by the palate (Figure **11.2**), so you can breathe through your nose even when you are eating.

S It is better to breathe through your nose, because the structure of the nose allows the air to become warm, moist and filtered before it gets to the lungs. Hairs in the nose trap dust particles in the air. Inside the nose are some thin bones called turbinal bones which are covered with a thin layer of cells. Some of these cells, called **goblet cells**, make a liquid containing water and mucus which evaporates into the air in the nose and moistens it (Figure **11.3**).

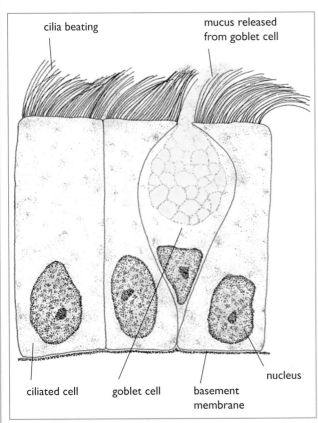

Figure 11.3 Part of the lining of the respiratory passages.

Other cells have very tiny hair-like projections called **cilia**. The cilia are always moving and bacteria or particles of dust get trapped in them and in the mucus. Cilia are found all along the trachea and bronchi, too. Here they waft the mucus, containing bacteria and dust, up to the back of the throat, so that it does not block up the lungs.

The trachea

From the nose or mouth, the air then passes into the windpipe or trachea. At the top of the trachea is a piece of cartilage called the epiglottis. This closes the trachea and stops food going down the trachea when you swallow. This is a reflex action that happens automatically when a bolus of food touches the soft palate.

Just below the epiglottis is the voice box or larynx. This contains the vocal cords. The vocal cords can be tightened by muscles so that they make sounds when air passes over them. The trachea has rings of cartilage around it which keep it open.

The bronchi

The trachea goes down through the neck and into the thorax. The thorax is the upper part of your body from the neck down to the bottom of the ribs and diaphragm. In the thorax, the trachea divides into two. The two branches are called the right and left **bronchi** (singular: **bronchus**). One bronchus goes to each lung and then branches out into smaller tubes called **bronchioles**.

The alveoli

At the end of each bronchiole are many tiny air sacs or alveoli (Figure **11.4**). This is where gas exchange takes place.

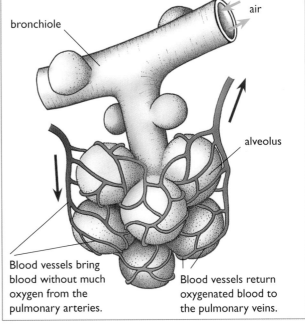

Figure 11.4 Alveoli.

Gas exchange in the lungs

The walls of the alveoli are the gas exchange surface. Tiny capillaries are closely wrapped around the outside of the alveoli (Figure 11.5). Oxygen diffuses across the walls of the alveoli into the blood (Figure 11.6). Carbon dioxide diffuses the other way.

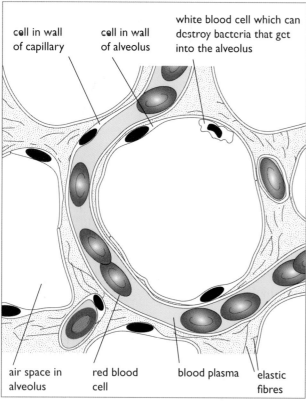

Figure 11.5 Section through part of the lung, magnified.

Labels: cell in wall of capillary; cell in wall of alveolus; white blood cell which can destroy bacteria that get into the alveolus; air space in alveolus; red blood cell; blood plasma; elastic fibres

The walls of the alveoli have several features which make them an efficient gas exchange surface.

♦ They are very thin. They are only one cell thick. The capillary walls are also only one cell thick. An oxygen molecule only has to diffuse across this small thickness to get into the blood.
♦ They have an excellent transport system. Blood is constantly pumped to the lungs along the pulmonary artery. This branches into thousands of capillaries which take blood to all parts of the lungs. Carbon dioxide in the blood can diffuse out into the air spaces in the alveoli and oxygen can diffuse into the blood. The blood is then taken back to the heart in the pulmonary vein, ready to be pumped to the rest of the body.

♦ They have a large surface area. In fact, the surface area is enormous. The total surface area of all the alveoli in your lungs is over 100 m².
♦ They have a good supply of oxygen. Your breathing movements keep your lungs well supplied with oxygen.

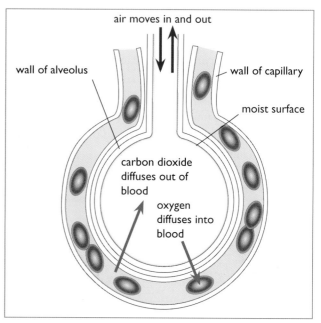

Figure 11.6 Gas exchange in an alveolus.

Labels: air moves in and out; wall of alveolus; wall of capillary; moist surface; carbon dioxide diffuses out of blood; oxygen diffuses into blood

❓ Questions

11.7 What is the function of the cilia in the respiratory passages? **S**
11.8 What is the larynx?
11.9 Where does gas exchange take place in a human?
11.10 How many cells does an oxygen molecule have to pass through, to get from an alveolus into the blood?

11.3 Breathing movements

To make air move in and out of the lungs, you must keep changing the volume of your thorax. First, you make it large so that air is sucked in. Then you make it smaller again so that air is squeezed out. This is called breathing.

Muscles in two parts of the body help you to breathe. **S** Some of them, called the intercostal muscles, are between the ribs (Figure 11.7). The others are in the diaphragm. The diaphragm is a large sheet of muscle and elastic tissue which stretches across your body, underneath the lungs and heart.

S Breathing in (inspiration)

When breathing in, the muscles of the diaphragm contract. This pulls the diaphragm downwards, which increases the volume in the thorax (Figure 11.8). At the same time, the external intercostal muscles contract. This pulls the rib cage upwards and outwards (Figure 11.9). This also increases the volume of the thorax.

As the volume of the thorax increases, the pressure inside it falls below atmospheric pressure. Extra space has been made and something must come in to fill it up. Air therefore rushes in along the trachea and bronchi into the lungs.

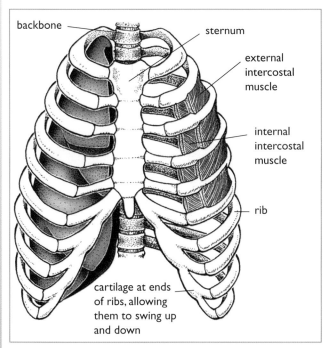

Figure 11.7 The rib cage and intercostal muscles.

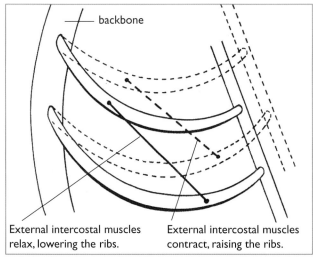

External intercostal muscles relax, lowering the ribs.

External intercostal muscles contract, raising the ribs.

Figure 11.9 How the external intercostal muscles raise the ribs.

Breathing out (expiration) S

When breathing out, the muscles of the diaphragm relax. The diaphragm springs back up into its domed shape because it is made of elastic tissue. This decreases the volume in the thorax. The external intercostal muscles also relax. The rib cage drops down again into its normal position. This also decreases the volume of the thorax (Figure 11.8).

Usually, relaxing the external intercostal muscles and the muscles of the diaphragm is all that is needed for breathing out. Sometimes, though, you breathe out more forcefully – when coughing, for example. Then the internal intercostal muscles contract strongly, making the rib cage drop down even further. The muscles of the abdomen wall also contract, helping to squeeze extra air out of the thorax.

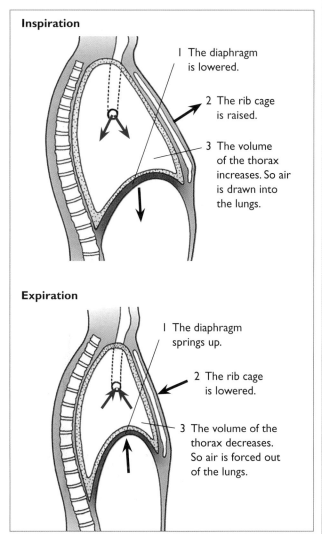

Inspiration

1 The diaphragm is lowered.

2 The rib cage is raised.

3 The volume of the thorax increases. So air is drawn into the lungs.

Expiration

1 The diaphragm springs up.

2 The rib cage is lowered.

3 The volume of the thorax decreases. So air is forced out of the lungs.

Figure 11.8 How the thorax changes shape during breathing.

Tables **11.2** and **11.3** compare the differences between respiration, gas exchange and breathing, and the composition of inspired and expired air.

S		
Respiration	a series of chemical reactions which happen in all living cells, in which food is broken down to release energy, usually by combining it with oxygen
Gas exchange	the exchange of gases across a respiratory surface; for example, oxygen is taken into the body, and carbon dioxide is removed from it; gas exchange also takes place during photosynthesis and respiration of plants
Breathing	muscular movements which keep the respiratory surface supplied with oxygen

Table 11.2 The differences between respiration, gas exchange and breathing.

Activity 11.5
Examining lungs

Activity 11.6
Modelling how the diaphragm helps with breathing

Activity 11.7
Gas exchange in small animals

	Inspired air	Expired air	S Reason for difference
Oxygen	21%	16%	Oxygen is absorbed across the gas exchange surface, then used by cells in respiration.
Carbon dioxide	0.04%	4%	Carbon dioxide is made inside respiring cells, and diffuses out across the gas exchange surface.
Argon and other noble gases	1%	1%	
Water content (humidity)	variable	always high	Gas exchange surfaces are made of living cells, so must be kept moist; some of this moisture evaporates into the air.
Temperature	variable	always warm	Air is warmed as it passes through the respiratory passages.

Table 11.3 A comparison of inspired and expired air.

Activity 11.8
Comparing the carbon dioxide content of inspired air and expired air

Skills
AO3.1 Using techniques, apparatus and materials
AO3.3 Observing, measuring and recording
AO3.4 Interpreting and evaluating observations and data

 The rubber tubing must be sterilised before you use it. Don't blow or suck hard when doing this experiment, just breathe gently.

You can use either limewater or hydrogencarbonate indicator solution for this experiment. Limewater changes from clear to cloudy when carbon dioxide dissolves in it. Hydrogencarbonate indicator solution changes from red to yellow.

1 Set up the apparatus as in the diagram.
2 Breathe in and out gently through the rubber tubing. Do not breathe too hard. Keep doing this until the liquid in one of the tubes changes colour.

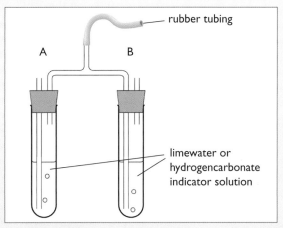

Activity 11.9
Investigating the effect of exercise on rate and depth of breathing

Questions

A1 In which tube did bubbles appear when you breathed out? Explain why.
A2 In which tube did bubbles appear when you breathed in? Explain why.
A3 What happened to the liquid in tube A?
A4 What happened to the liquid in tube B?
A5 What do your results tell you about the relative amounts of carbon dioxide in inspired air and expired air?

Exercise and breathing rate

All the cells in your body need oxygen for respiration and all of this oxygen is supplied by the lungs. The oxygen is carried by the blood to every part of the body.

Sometimes, cells may need a lot of oxygen very quickly. Imagine you are running in a race. The muscles in your legs are using up a lot of energy. The cells in the muscles will be combining oxygen with glucose as fast as they can, to release energy for muscle contraction.

A lot of oxygen is needed to work as hard as this. You breathe deeper and faster to get more oxygen into your blood. Your heart beats faster to get the oxygen to the leg muscles as quickly as possible.

But eventually a limit is reached. The heart and lungs cannot supply oxygen to the muscles any faster. But more energy is still needed for the race. How can that extra energy be found?

Extra energy can be produced by anaerobic respiration. Some glucose is broken down without combining it with oxygen.

$$\text{glucose} \longrightarrow \text{lactic acid} + \text{energy}$$

As explained on page 141, this does not release very much energy, but a little extra might make all the difference.

When you stop running, you will have quite a lot of lactic acid in your muscles and your blood. This lactic acid must be broken down by combining it with oxygen (aerobic respiration) in the liver. So, even though you do not need the energy any more, you go on breathing faster and more deeply, and your heart rate continues to be high. You are taking in and transporting extra oxygen to break down the lactic acid. The faster heart rate also helps to transport lactic acid as quickly as possible from the muscles to the liver.

While you were running, you built up an oxygen debt. You 'borrowed' some extra energy, without 'paying' for it with oxygen. Now, as the lactic acid is combined with oxygen, you are paying off the debt. Not until all the lactic acid has been used up, does your breathing rate and rate of heart beat return to normal (Figure 11.10).

The rate at which your breathing muscles work –

and therefore your breathing rate – is controlled by the brain. The brain constantly monitors the pH of the blood that flows through it. If there is a lot of carbon dioxide or lactic acid in the blood, this causes the pH to fall. When the brain senses this, it sends nerve impulses to the diaphragm and the intercostal muscles, stimulating them to contract harder and more often. The result is a faster breathing rate and deeper breaths.

Figure 11.10   These sprinters will pay back their oxygen debts after the race.

Summary

You should know:

- ♦ why humans and other organisms need energy
- ♦ about the release of energy from food in respiration
- ♦ the equation for aerobic respiration
- ♦ the equations for anaerobic respiration in yeast and in humans
- **S** ♦ how to investigate the uptake of oxygen by respiring organisms
- ♦ how to investigate the effect of temperature on the rate of respiration of germinating seeds
- ♦ the structure and functions of the organs of the human respiratory system
- **S** ♦ the features of the human gas exchange surface that adapt it for its function
- ♦ how goblet cells, mucus and ciliated cells help to protect the gas exchange surface from pathogens and particles
- ♦ how breathing is brought about by the intercostal muscles and diaphragm
- ♦ the differences between the composition of inspired air and expired air
- **S** ♦ the reasons for these differences
- ♦ why breathing rate and depth increases during exercise, and remains high for some time afterwards.

End-of-chapter questions

1 Which of these descriptions applies to aerobic respiration, which to anaerobic respiration and which to both?

    a   lactic acid or alcohol made
    b   energy released from glucose
    c   carbon dioxide made
    d   heat released

2   a   Explain the meaning of the term **gas exchange surface** in human lungs.
    b   List **three** features of gas exchange surfaces.
    c   Explain how each feature in your list helps gas exchange to happen efficiently.

3 Copy and complete this table to summarise what happens during breathing.

	Breathing in	Breathing out
External intercostal muscles		
Diaphragm muscles		
Volume of thorax		
Pressure in lungs		

4 Describe, in detail, the pathway of an oxygen molecule as it moves from the air outside your body, into your blood, and to a cell in a muscle in your arm. You could write your answer in words, or use a flow diagram, or perhaps a mixture of both. You will need to think about what you have learnt about the human transport system, as well as what you have learnt in this chapter.

5 A girl breathed into a machine that recorded the volume of the air that she breathed in and out. The results were recorded as a graph of volume against time. The diagrams show results obtained when she was resting and when she was exercising.

    a   Use the first graph to find how many breaths per minute the girl took while she was resting.   [1]

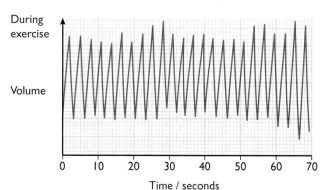

    b   Use the second graph to find how many breaths per minute the girl took while she was exercising.   [1]
    c   Use the first graph to find the volume of the first breath that she took while she was resting. (Remember to include the unit in your answer.)   [1]
    d   Use the second graph to find the volume of the second breath that she took while she was exercising.   [1]
    e   Explain how these changes in rate and depth of breathing helped the girl to do the exercise.   [4]
    f   Describe the mechanism that brought about these changes in rate and depth of breathing in the girl's body.   [4]

S 6 The graph shows how a student's breathing rate changed during and after exercise.

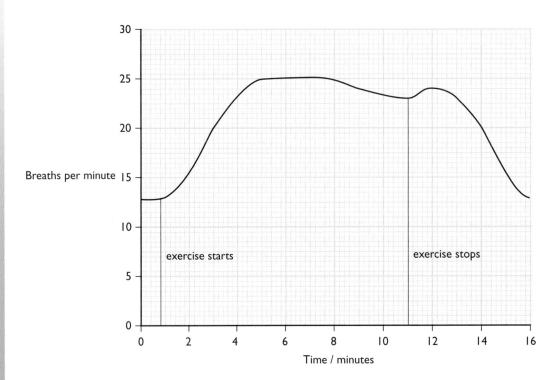

a Calculate the increase in the student's breathing rate from when he started to exercise, to its maximum rate. [2]

b Calculate how long it took, after he finished exercise, for his breathing rate to return to normal. [2]

c Explain why his breathing rate did not return to normal immediately after exercise stopped. [4]

d Describe and explain how you would expect the student's heart rate to change during the 16-minute period shown on the graph. [4]

12 Excretion

In this chapter, you will find out about:

♦ the excretory products that are formed in the body
♦ how the kidneys excrete urea
♦ why the volume and concentration of urine varies from day to day
S ♦ how urea is produced
♦ how the kidneys produce urine
♦ dialysis treatment for kidney failure.

Bird droppings

It's probable that, at some time in your life, a bird dropping has landed on you. You may not realise that white bird droppings are actually their urine, not faeces. Birds excrete urine in a semi-solid form rather than as a liquid, as we do (Figure **12.1**).

Think about how young birds develop. They grow inside a shelled egg. If they produced liquid urine, the egg would quickly become filled with it. Instead, they produce a concentrated, paste-like urine, which collects into one small area of the egg where it is kept

away from the growing bird. If you are ever able to watch a chick hatch from an egg, look for this little package of waste material that is left behind, inside the egg shell. The sack in which it is stored is called the allantois.

Reptiles, whose young also develop inside shelled eggs, also produce semi-solid urine in the same way as birds.

Another advantage of excreting semi-solid urine is that it wastes less water, which could be an advantage for adult birds that live in dry places. However, the body has to use more energy to make this semi-solid urine than it does to make liquid urine.

Clearly, the advantages for birds and reptiles outweigh this disadvantage, as they have been living successfully on Earth for more than 300 million years. Fossil dinosaur eggs show that they stored their waste in the same way that birds do today.

Figure 12.1 Baby birds produce their semi-solid waste in little packages, making it easy for the parents to tidy up the nest.

12.1 Excretory products

All living cells have a great many metabolic reactions going on inside them. The reactions of respiration (Chapter 11), for example, provide energy for the cell. Metabolic reactions often produce other substances as well, which the cells do not need. If allowed to remain in the cells, these substances may become poisonous or toxic.

Respiration, for example, produces not only energy, but also water and carbon dioxide. Animal cells need the energy, and may be able to make use of the water. They do not, however, need the carbon dioxide. The carbon dioxide is a waste product.

The carbon dioxide from respiration is excreted from the lungs, gills or other gas exchange surface (Figure 12.2). If it were allowed to remain in the body, it would be toxic to cells.

During daylight hours, plant cells can use the carbon dioxide that they produce in respiration for photosynthesis, so it is not a waste product for them at that time. However, at night, when they cannot photosynthesise but continue to respire, carbon dioxide is a waste product.

A waste product like carbon dioxide, which is made in a cell as a result of a metabolic reaction, is called an excretory product. The removal of excretory products is called excretion.

Key definition

excretion – the removal from organisms of the waste products of metabolism (chemical reactions in cells including respiration), toxic materials, and substances in excess of requirements

Egestion and excretion

Many animals have another kind of waste material to get rid of. Almost always, some of the food that an animal eats cannot be digested. Humans, for example, cannot digest cellulose in our food – it goes straight through the alimentary canal, and out of the anus in the faeces.

This cellulose is not an excretory product. It has never been involved in any metabolic reaction in the person's cells. It has not even been inside a cell – it has

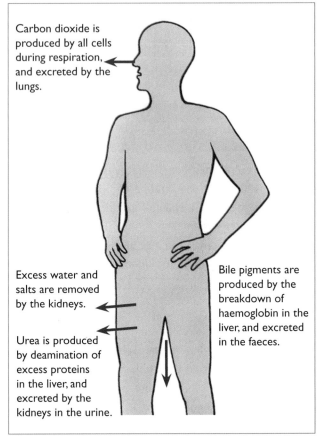

Figure 12.2 Excretory products of mammals.

Carbon dioxide is produced by all cells during respiration, and excreted by the lungs.

Excess water and salts are removed by the kidneys.

Urea is produced by deamination of excess proteins in the liver, and excreted by the kidneys in the urine.

Bile pigments are produced by the breakdown of haemoglobin in the liver, and excreted in the faeces.

simply passed, unchanged, through the digestive system. So getting rid of undigested cellulose in faeces is not excretion. It is called egestion.

12.2 Nitrogenous waste

Animals produce nitrogenous waste. This is formed from excess proteins and amino acids. Animals are not able to store these in their bodies, so any that are surplus to requirements are broken down to form a nitrogen-containing excretory product. In mammals, this substance is mainly urea. Urea is formed in the liver. Urea is a toxic substance and – as we shall see – is removed from the body by the kidneys.

When you eat proteins, digestive enzymes in your stomach, duodenum and ileum break them down into amino acids. The amino acids are absorbed into the blood capillaries in the villi in your ileum (page 86). The blood capillaries all join up to the hepatic portal vein, which takes the absorbed food to the liver.

The liver allows some of the amino acids to carry on, in the blood, to other parts of your body. But if you have

ⓢ eaten more than you need, then some of them must be got rid of.

It would be very wasteful to excrete the extra amino acids just as they are. They contain energy which, if it is not needed straight away, might be needed later.

So enzymes in the liver split up each amino acid molecule (Figure 12.3). The part containing the energy is kept, turned into carbohydrate and stored. The rest, which is the part that contains nitrogen, is turned into urea. This process is called **deamination**.

The urea dissolves in the blood plasma, and is taken to the kidneys to be excreted. A small amount is also excreted in sweat.

The liver has many other functions, as well as deamination. One of the more important ones is storage. Table **12.1** lists some of the functions.

❓ Questions

12.1 Name **two** excretory products of animals.

12.2 What processes produce these two products?

12.3 What happens to the excess protein you eat?

1	Converts excess amino acids into urea and carbohydrates, in a process called deamination.
2	Synthesises plasma proteins such as fibrinogen, from amino acids.
3	Controls the amount of glucose in the blood, with the aid of the hormones insulin and glucagon.
4	Stores carbohydrate as the polysaccharide glycogen.
5	Makes bile.
6	Breaks down old red blood cells, storing the iron and excreting the remains of the haemoglobin as bile pigments.
7	Breaks down harmful substances such as alcohol.
8	Stores vitamins A, B, D, E and K.
9	Stores potassium.
10	Makes cholesterol, which is needed to make and repair cell membranes.

Table 12.1   Some functions of the liver.

Key definition

deamination – the removal of the nitrogen-containing part of amino acids to form urea

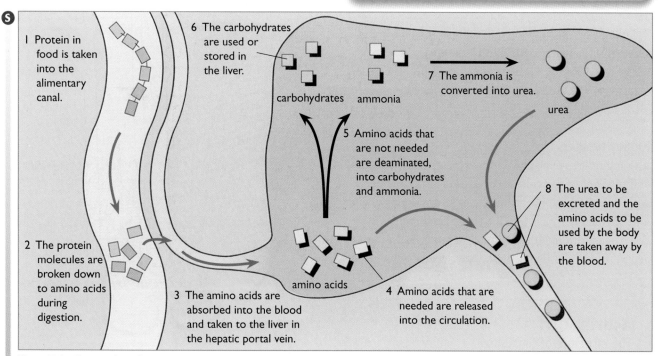

Figure 12.3   How urea is made.

ⓢ

1 Protein in food is taken into the alimentary canal.

2 The protein molecules are broken down to amino acids during digestion.

3 The amino acids are absorbed into the blood and taken to the liver in the hepatic portal vein.

amino acids

4 Amino acids that are needed are released into the circulation.

5 Amino acids that are not needed are deaminated, into carbohydrates and ammonia.

6 The carbohydrates are used or stored in the liver.

carbohydrates   ammonia

7 The ammonia is converted into urea.

urea

8 The urea to be excreted and the amino acids to be used by the body are taken away by the blood.

12.3 The human excretory system

The kidneys

Figure **12.4** illustrates the position of the two kidneys in the human body. They are at the back of the abdomen, behind the intestines.

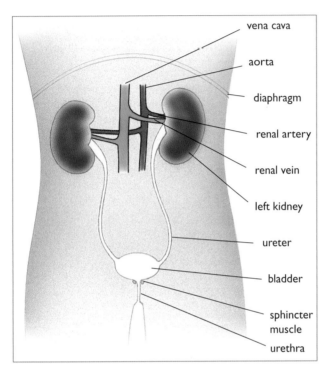

Figure 12.4 The human excretory system.

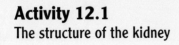

S Figure **12.5** illustrates a longitudinal section through a kidney. It has three main parts – the **cortex**, **medulla** and **pelvis**. Leading from the pelvis is a tube, called the **ureter**. The ureter carries urine that the kidney has made to the bladder.

Kidney tubules

Although they seem solid, kidneys are actually made up of thousands of tiny tubules, or **nephrons** (Figures **12.5** and **12.6**). Each tubule begins in the cortex, loops down into the medulla, back into the cortex, and then goes down again through the medulla to the pelvis. In the pelvis, the tubules join up with the ureter.

Activity 12.1
The structure of the kidney

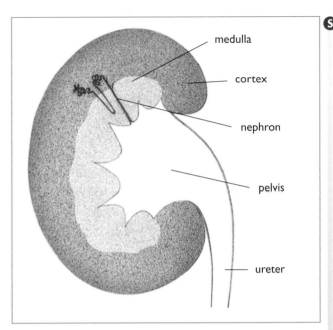

Figure 12.5 A longitudinal section through a kidney showing the position of one nephron (which is drawn much larger than its relative size).

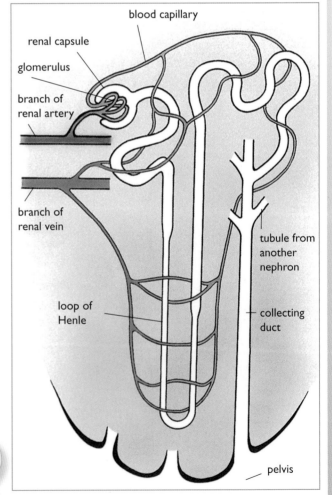

Figure 12.6 A nephron.

Urine formation

As blood passes through the kidneys, it is filtered. This removes most of the urea from it, and also excess water and salts. As this liquid moves through the kidneys, any glucose in it is reabsorbed back into the blood. Most of the water is also reabsorbed along with some of the salts.

The final liquid produced by the kidneys is a solution of urea and salts in water. It is called urine, and it flows out of the kidneys, along the ureters and into the bladder. It is stored in the bladder for a while, before being released from the body through the urethra.

The kidneys adjust the amount of urine that they produce, according to the needs of the body. If your body is short of water – perhaps because you have been doing exercise in the heat, and have lost a lot of water by sweating – then the kidneys produce small volumes of concentrated urine. If your body contains too much water – perhaps because you have been drinking a lot – then the kidneys produce large volumes of dilute urine, which helps to get rid of the excess water.

S Filtration

Blood is brought to the renal capsule in a branch of the renal artery. Small molecules, including water and most of the substances dissolved in it, are squeezed out of the blood into the renal capsule.

There are thousands of renal capsules in the cortex of each kidney. Each one is shaped like a cup. It has a tangle of blood capillaries, called a glomerulus, in the middle. The blood vessel bringing blood to each glomerulus is quite wide, but the one taking blood away is narrow. This means that the blood in the glomerulus cannot get away easily. Quite a high pressure builds up, squeezing the blood in the glomerulus against the capillary walls.

These walls have small holes in them. So do the walls of the renal capsules. Any molecules small enough to go through these holes will be squeezed through, into the space in the renal capsule (Figures 12.6 and 12.7).

Only small molecules can go through. These include water, salt, glucose and urea. Most protein molecules are too big, so they stay in the blood, along with the blood cells.

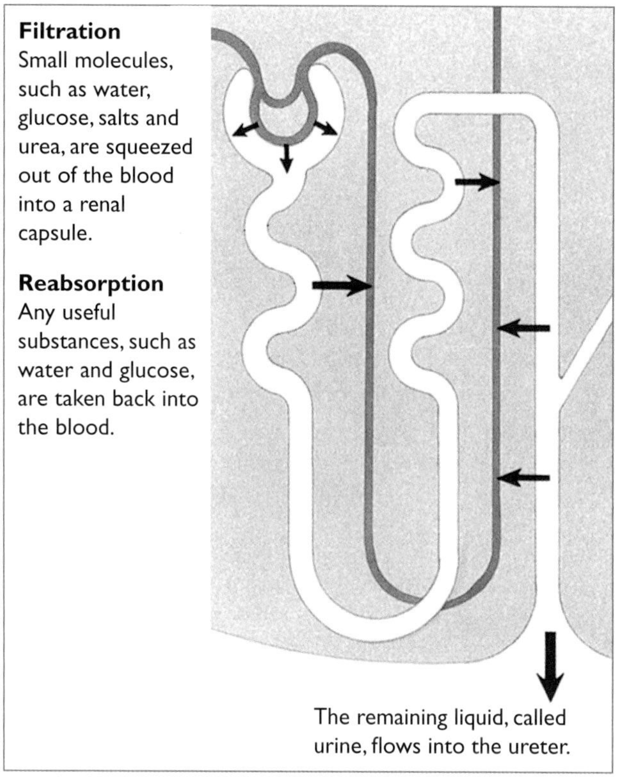

Filtration
Small molecules, such as water, glucose, salts and urea, are squeezed out of the blood into a renal capsule.

Reabsorption
Any useful substances, such as water and glucose, are taken back into the blood.

The remaining liquid, called urine, flows into the ureter.

Figure 12.7   How urine is made.

Reabsorption

The fluid in the renal capsule is a solution of glucose, salts and urea, dissolved in water. Some of the substances in this fluid are needed by the body. All of the glucose, some of the water and some of the salts need to be kept in the blood.

Wrapped around each kidney tubule are blood capillaries. Useful substances from the fluid in the kidney tubule are reabsorbed, and pass back into the blood in these capillaries.

The remaining fluid continues on its way along the tubule. By the time it gets to the collecting duct, it is mostly water, with urea and salts dissolved in it. It is called urine.

The kidneys are extremely efficient at reabsorbing water. Over 99% of the water entering the tubules is reabsorbed. In humans, the two kidneys filter about $170 \, dm^3$ of water per day, yet only about $1.5 \, dm^3$ of urine are produced in the same period.

The bladder

The urine from all the tubules in the kidneys flows into the ureters. The ureters take it to the bladder.

The bladder stores urine. It has stretchy walls, so that it can hold quite large quantities.

Leading out of the bladder is a tube called the urethra. There is a sphincter muscle at the top of the urethra, which is usually tightly closed. When the bladder is full, the sphincter muscle opens, so that the urine flows along the urethra and out of the body.

Adult mammals can consciously control this sphincter muscle. In young mammals, it opens automatically when the bladder gets full.

⑤ Kidney dialysis

Sometimes, a person's kidneys stop working properly. This might be because of an infection. Complete failure of the kidneys allows urea and other waste products to build up in the blood, and will cause death if not treated.

The best treatment is a kidney transplant, but this is not easy to arrange, because the 'tissue type' of the donor and the recipient must be a close match, or the recipient's immune system will reject the transplanted kidney. The donated kidney usually comes from a healthy person who has died suddenly – for example, in a car accident.

The usual treatment for a person with kidney failure is to have several sessions a week using a **dialysis** unit (Figure **12.8**), sometimes called a kidney machine. The person's blood flows through the machine and back into their body. Inside the machine, the blood is separated from a special fluid by a partially permeable membrane (like Visking tubing). This fluid contains water, glucose, salts and other substances that should be present in the blood.

As the patient's blood passes through the tubes, the substances in the fluid diffuse through the membrane, down their concentration gradients.

For example, there is no urea in the dialysis fluid, so urea diffuses out of the patient's blood and into the fluid. The amount of other substances in the blood can be regulated by controlling their concentrations in

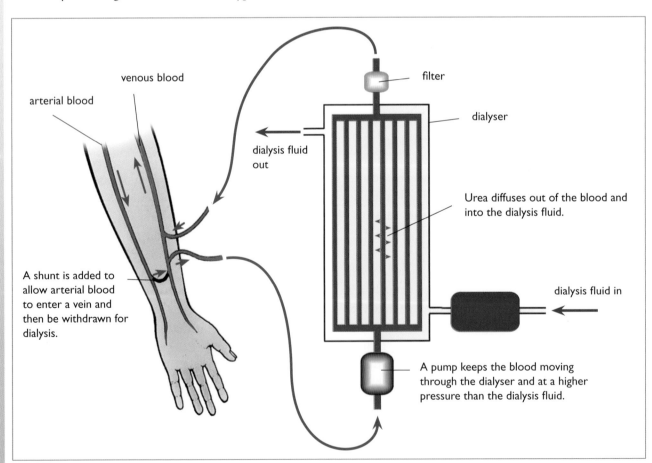

Figure 12.8   How kidney dialysis works.

the dialysis fluid. Proteins in the blood remain there, as their molecules are too big to pass through the membrane.

Patients need to be treated on a dialysis unit two or three times a week, and the treatment lasts for several hours.

Kidney transplants

Most people who have to use a dialysis machine would prefer to have to a kidney transplant. The person receiving the transplant is the recipient, and the person from whose body the organ was taken is the donor. Many people carry donor cards with them all the time, stating that they are happy for their organs to be used in a transplant operation. Organs for transplants must be removed quickly from a body and kept cold, so that they do not deteriorate. Sometimes, however, the donor may be alive. A person may donate a kidney to a brother or sister who needs one urgently. You can manage perfectly well with just one kidney.

Surgeons now have very few problems with transplant operations – they can almost always make an excellent job of removing the old organ and replacing it with a better one. The big problem comes afterwards. The recipient's immune system recognises the donor organ as being 'foreign', and attacks it. This is called rejection.

The recipient is given drugs called immunosuppressants which stop the white blood cells working efficiently, to decrease the chances of rejection.

The trouble with immunosuppressants is that they stop the immune system from doing its normal job, and so the person is more likely to suffer from all sorts of infectious diseases. The drugs have to be taken for the rest of the recipient's life.

The chances of rejection are reduced if the donor is a close relative of the recipient. Closely related people are more likely to have antigens on their cells which are similar to each other, so the recipient's immune system is less likely to react to the donated organ as if it were 'foreign'. If there is not a relative who can donate an organ, then a search may be made world-wide, looking for a potential donor with similar antigens to the recipient.

Questions

12.4 What is a kidney tubule?

12.5 Which blood vessels bring blood to the kidneys?

12.6 What is a glomerulus?

12.7 How is a high blood pressure built up in a glomerulus?

12.8 Why is this high blood pressure needed?

12.9 Name **two** substances found in the blood which you would not find in the fluid inside a renal capsule.

12.10 List **three** substances which are reabsorbed from the nephron into the blood.

12.11 What is urine?

Summary

You should know:

♦ what is meant by an excretory product
♦ the main excretory products of mammals, and the organs that excrete them
S ♦ how urea is formed by deamination in the liver
♦ the structure of a kidney
S ♦ the structure of a kidney tubule
♦ about filtration and reabsorption in a kidney tubule
♦ about kidney dialysis
♦ advantages and disadvantages of kidney dialysis and kidney transplants.

End-of-chapter questions

1   Copy and complete these sentences, using some of the words in the list. You may use each word once, more than once, or not at all.

absorption	amino acids	digestion	dioxide	fatty acids	ingestion
kidneys	liver	lungs	metabolism	monoxide	respiration
stomach	urea	urine	waste products		

Excretion involves the removal of .... of .... from the body. Carbon .... is produced by all cells during .... and is excreted by the .... Urea is produced in the .... from excess .... and is excreted by the .... , dissolved in water to form ....

2   Explain the difference between each of the following pairs of terms.

   a   ureter and urethra
   b   urine and urea
   c   excretion and egestion

⑤ 3   The diagram represents several different types of molecules in solution, separated by a membrane.

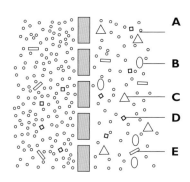

   a   State which letter represents a water molecule.   [1]
   b   State the type of membrane shown in the diagram.   [1]
   c   Explain the processes by which molecules move through the membrane.   [6]
   The diagram below shows what happens during filtration in the glomerulus of a kidney.

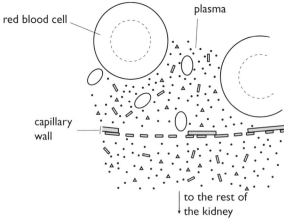

   d   Name the molecules that pass out of the blood plasma.   [4]
   e   Explain how filtration differs from the processes explained in c.   [3]
   f   Explain what happens to molecules in the filtrate before urine leaves the kidney.   [5]
   [Cambridge O Level Human Biology 5096/22, Question 1, October/November 2010]

13 Coordination and response

In this chapter, you will find out about:

- ◆ the human nervous system
- ◆ neurones and how they work
- ◆ reflex actions
- Ⓢ ◆ synapses
- ◆ the structure and function of the eye
- ◆ hormones, including adrenaline, insulin, oestrogen and testosterone
- ◆ how plants respond to stimuli.

Reaction times

Having a fast reaction time is important in many sports, but in a short sprint event it could make the difference between a gold medal and a silver one.

Sprint races are started with a gun. Because sound takes time to travel, it would not be fair for the starter to stand at one end of the starting line and simply fire the gun – the sound would take longer to reach the runner furthest away from him, so they would be at a significant disadvantage. Instead. the

firing of the gun is silent, and is transmitted as an electrical signal along wires (which you can see in Figure **13.1**) to individual speakers in each runner's starting blocks. Each runner should hear the sound of the gun at exactly the same moment.

In the 100 m final in the 2012 Olympics, Usain Bolt's reaction time between hearing the gun and pushing off from his blocks was 0.165 s. He won gold. The athletes who won silver and bronze medals – Yohan Blake and Justin Gatlin – had reaction times of 0.179 and 0.178 s respectively. However, these were not the fastest reaction times in that race; the fastest of all was that of Churandy Martina, which was only 0.139 s.

Most people's reaction times are longer than this, often around 0.2 s or more. Sprinters whose 'reaction time' is measured at less than 0.1 s are judged to have pushed off before the gun was fired – and disqualified.

Figure 13.1   Starting blocks have sensors that measure the time between the sound of the gun and the first push of the runner's feet against the block.

13.1 Coordination in animals

Changes in an organism's environment are called stimuli (singular: stimulus) and are sensed by specialised cells called receptors. The organism responds using effectors. Muscles are effectors, and may respond to a stimulus by contracting. Glands can also be effectors. For example, if you smell good food cooking, your salivary glands may respond by secreting saliva.

Animals need fast and efficient communication systems between their receptors and effectors. This is partly because most animals move in search of food. Many animals need to be able to respond very quickly to catch their food, or to avoid predators.

To make sure that the right effectors respond at the right time, there needs to be some kind of communication system between receptors and effectors. If you touch something hot, pain receptors on your fingertips send an impulse to your arm muscles to tell them to contract, pulling your hand away from the hot surface. The way in which receptors pick up stimuli, and then pass information on to effectors, is called coordination.

Most animals have two methods of sending information from receptors to effectors. The fastest is by means of nerves. The receptors and nerves make up the animal's nervous system. A slower method, but still a very important one, is by means of chemicals called hormones. Hormones are part of the endocrine system.

13.2 The human nervous system

The human nervous system is made of special cells called neurones. Figure 13.2 illustrates a particular type of neurone called a motor neurone.

Neurones contain the same basic parts as any animal cell. Each has a nucleus, cytoplasm, and a cell membrane. However, their structure is specially adapted to be able to carry messages very quickly.

To enable them to do this, they have long, thin fibres of cytoplasm stretching out from the cell body. The longest fibre in Figure 13.2 is called an axon. Axons can be more than a metre long. The shorter fibres are called dendrons or dendrites.

The dendrites pick up electrical signals from other neurones lying nearby. These signals are called nerve impulses. The signal passes to the cell body, then along the axon, which might pass it to another neurone.

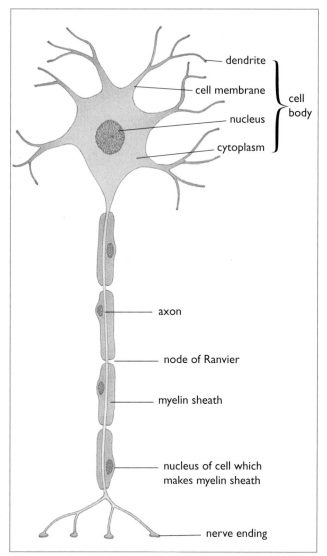

Figure 13.2 A human motor neurone.

Myelin

Some of the nerve fibres of active animals like mammals are wrapped in a layer of fat and protein called myelin. Every now and then, there are narrow gaps in the myelin sheath.

We have seen that the signals that neurones transmit are in the form of electrical impulses. Myelin insulates the nerve fibres, so that they can carry these impulses much faster. For example, a myelinated nerve fibre in a cat's body can carry impulses at up to 100 metres per second. A fibre without myelin can only carry impulses at about 5 metres per second.

The central nervous system

All mammals (and many other animals) have a **central nervous system** (CNS) and a **peripheral nervous system**. The CNS is made up of the brain and spinal cord (Figure **13.3**). The peripheral nervous system is made up of nerves and receptors.

Like the rest of the nervous system, the CNS is made up of neurones. Its role is to coordinate the messages travelling through the nervous system.

When a receptor detects a stimulus, it sends an electrical impulse to the brain or spinal cord. The brain or spinal cord receives the impulse, and sends an impulse on, along the appropriate nerve fibres, to the appropriate effector.

Reflex arcs

Figures **13.4** and **13.5** show how these impulses are sent. If your hand touches a hot plate, an impulse is picked up by a sensory receptor in your finger. It travels to the spinal cord along the axon from the receptor cell. This cell is called a sensory neurone, because it is carrying an impulse from a sensory receptor (Figure **13.6**).

In the spinal cord, the neurone passes an impulse on to several other neurones. Only one is shown in Figure **13.4**. These neurones are called relay neurones, because they relay the impulse on to other neurones. The relay neurones pass the impulse on to the brain. They also pass it on to an effector.

In this case, the effectors are the muscles in your arm. The impulse travels to the muscle along the axon of a

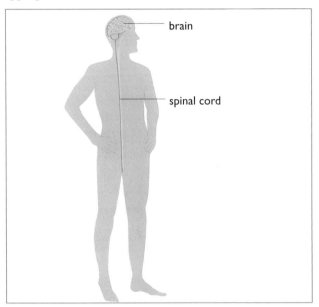

Figure 13.3　The human central nervous system.

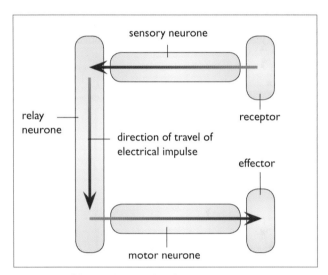

Figure 13.5　Schematic diagram of a reflex arc.

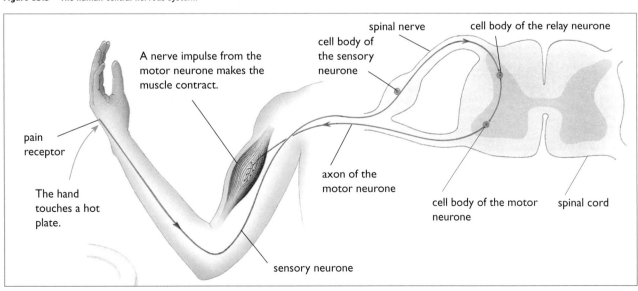

Figure 13.4　A reflex arc.

motor neurone. The muscle then contracts, so that your hand is pulled away.

This sort of reaction is called a reflex action. You do not need to think about it. Your brain is made aware of it, but you only consciously realise what is happening after the message has been sent on to your muscles.

Reflex actions are very useful, because the message gets from the receptor to the effector as quickly as possible. You do not waste time in thinking about what to do. The pathway along which the nerve impulse passes – the sensory neurone, relay neurones and motor neurone – is called a reflex arc. Figure 13.6 shows the structure of these three types of neurone.

Figure 13.7 shows a person's reflex actions being tested – you may have had this test yourself. Another reflex action is described on page 168.

Reflex actions are examples of involuntary actions. They are not under conscious control. Many of our actions, however, are voluntary. They happen because we decide to carry them out. For example, reading this book is a voluntary action.

❓ Questions

13.1 Give **two** examples of effectors.

13.2 What are the **two** main communication systems in an animal's body?

13.3 List **three** ways in which neurones are similar to other cells.

13.4 List **three** ways in which neurones are specialised to carry out their function of transmitting electrical impulses very quickly.

13.5 What is the function of the central nervous system?

13.6 Where are the cell bodies of each of these types of neurone found: **a** sensory neurone, **b** relay neurone, and **c** motor neurone?

13.7 What is the value of reflex actions?

13.8 Describe **two** reflex actions, other than the ones described on pages **164** and **168**.

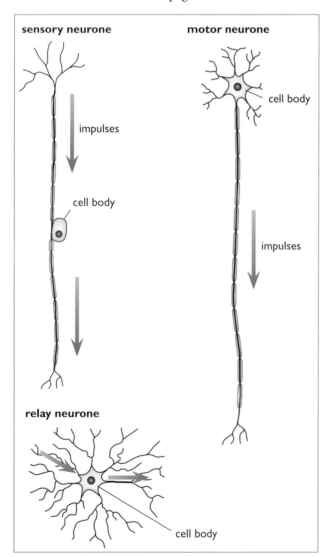

Figure 13.6 The structure of sensory, motor and relay neurones.

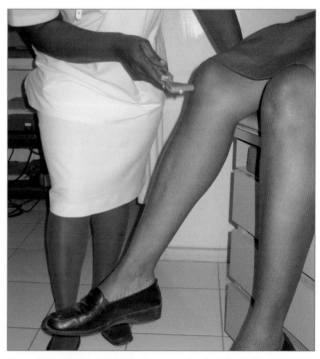

Figure 13.7 The knee jerk reflex is an example of a reflex action. A sharp tap just below the knee stimulates a receptor. This sends impulses along a sensory neurone into the spinal cord. The impulse then travels along a motor neurone to the thigh muscle, which quickly contracts and raises the lower leg.

Synapses

If you look carefully at Figure **13.5**, you will see that the three neurones involved in the reflex arc to not quite connect with each other. There is a small gap between each pair. These gaps are called synaptic clefts. The ends of the two neurones on either side of the cleft, plus the cleft itself, is called a synapse.

Figure **13.8** shows a synapse between a sensory neurone and a relay neurone in more detail. Inside the sensory neurone's axon are hundreds of tiny vacuoles, or vesicles. These each contain a chemical, called a transmitter substance or neurotransmitter.

S When an impulse arrives along the axon of the sensory neurone, it causes these vesicles to move to the cell membrane and empty their contents into the synaptic cleft. The neurotransmitter quickly diffuses across the tiny gap, and attaches to receptor molecules in the cell membrane of the relay neurone. This can happen because the shape of the neurotransmitter molecules is complementary to the shape of the receptor molecules.

The binding of the neurotransmitter with the receptors triggers a nerve impulse in the relay neurone. This impulse sweeps along the relay neurone, until it reaches the next synapse. Here, a similar process occurs to transmit the impulse to the motor neurone.

Synapses act like one-way valves. There is only neurotransmitter on one side of the synapse, so the impulses can only go across from that side. Synapses ensure that nerve impulses only travel in one direction.

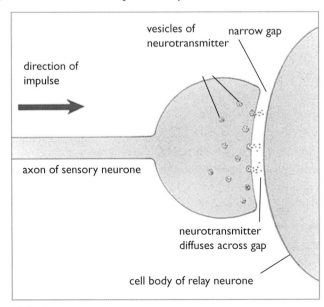

13.8 A synapse.

13.3 Receptors

Sense organs

The parts of an organism's body that detect stimuli, the receptors, may be specialised cells or just the endings of sensory neurones. In animals, the receptors are often part of a sense organ (Figure **13.9**). Your eye, for example, is a sense organ, and the rod and cone cells in the retina are receptors. They are sensitive to light.

Figure 13.9 Sense organs.

Key definitions

sense organs – groups of receptor cells responding to specific stimuli: light, sound, touch, temperature and chemicals

synapse – a junction between two nerve cells, consisting of a minute gap across which impulses pass by diffusion of a neurotransmitter

Activity 13.1
Measuring reaction time using a ruler

Activity 13.2
To measure mean reaction time

Skills
AO3.3 Observing, measuring and recording
AO3.4 Interpreting and evaluating observations and data

The time taken for a nerve impulse to travel from a receptor, through your CNS and back to an effector is very short. It can be measured, but only with special equipment. However, you can get a reasonable idea of the time it takes if you use a large number of people and work out an average time.

1 Get as many people as possible to stand in a circle, holding hands.

2 One person lets go of his or her neighbour with the left hand, and holds a stopwatch in it. When everyone is ready, this person simultaneously starts the stopwatch, and squeezes his or her neighbour's hand with the right hand.

3 As soon as each person's left hand is squeezed, he or she should squeeze his or her neighbour with the right hand. The message of squeezes goes all round the circle.

4 While the message is going round, the person with the stopwatch puts it into the right hand, and holds his or her neighbour's hand with the left hand. When the squeeze arrives, he or she should stop the watch.

5 Keep repeating this, until the message is going round as fast as possible. Record the time taken, and also the number of people in the circle.

6 Now try again, but this time make the message of squeezes go the other way around the circle.

Questions

A1 Using the fastest time you obtained, work out the mean time it took for one person to respond to the stimulus they received.

A2 Did people respond faster as the experiment went on? Why might this happen?

A3 Did the nerve impulse go as quickly when you changed direction? Explain your answer.

A4 If you have access to the Internet, find a site that allows you to measure your reaction time and try it out. Do you think the website gives you more reliable results than the 'circle' method? Compare the results you obtain, and discuss the advantages and disadvantages of each method.

The structure of the eye

Figure 13.10 shows the internal structure of the eye. The part of the eye that contains the receptor cells is the retina. This is the part which is actually sensitive to light. The rest of the eye simply helps to protect the retina, or to focus light onto it.

Each eye is set in a bony socket in the skull, called the orbit. Only the very front of the eye is not surrounded by bone (Figure 13.11).

The front of the eye is covered by a thin, transparent membrane called the conjunctiva, which helps to protect the parts behind it. The conjunctiva is always kept moist by a fluid made in the tear glands. This fluid contains an enzyme called lysozyme, which can kill bacteria.

The fluid is washed across your eye by your eyelids when you blink. The eyelids, eyebrows and eyelashes also help to stop dirt from landing on the surface of your eyes.

Even the part of the eye inside the orbit is protected. There is a very tough coat surrounding it called the sclera.

The retina

The retina is at the back of the eye. When light falls on a receptor cell in the retina, the cell sends an electrical impulse along the optic nerve to the brain. The brain sorts out all the impulses from each receptor cell, and builds up an image. Some of these receptor cells are sensitive to light of different colours, enabling us to see coloured images.

The closer together the receptor cells are, the clearer the image the brain will get. The part of the retina where the receptor cells are packed most closely together is called the fovea. This is the part of the retina where light is focused when you look straight at an object.

There are no receptor cells where the optic nerve leaves the retina. This part is called the blind spot. If light falls on this place, no impulses will be sent to the brain. Try Activity **13.2**.

Activity 13.3
Can you always see the image?

Hold this page about 45 cm from your face. Close the left eye, and look at the cross with your right eye. Gradually bring the page closer to you. What happens? Can you explain it?

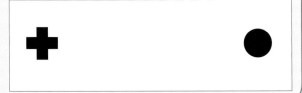

S Behind the retina is a black layer called the choroid. The choroid absorbs all the light after it has been through the retina, so it does not get scattered around the inside of the eye. The choroid is also rich in blood vessels which nourish the eye.

We have two kinds of receptor cells in the retina (Figure **13.12**). **Rod cells** are sensitive to quite dim light, but they do not respond to colour. **Cone cells** are able

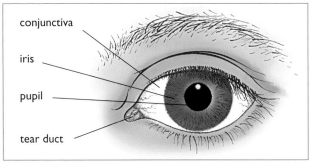

Figure 13.11 The eye from the front.

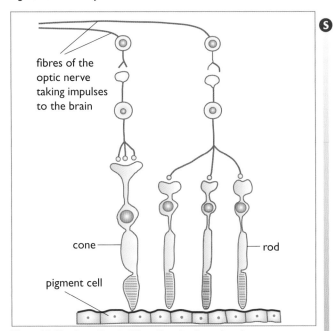

Figure 13.12 A small part of the retina, showing rods and a cone.

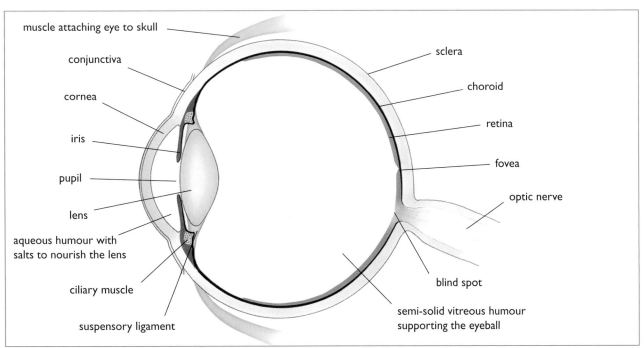

Figure 13.10 Section through a human eye (seen from above). (Note: you do not need to learn the labels for sclera, choroid, aqueous humour and vitreous humour but you may find these helpful if you do Activity 13.5.)

S to distinguish between the different colours of light, but they only function when the light is quite bright. We have three different kinds of cones, sensitive to red, green and blue light.

Rods therefore allow us to see in dim light but only in black and white, while cones give us colour vision.

The fovea contains almost entirely cones, packed tightly together. When we look directly at an object, we use our cones to produce a sharp image, in colour. Rods are found further out on the retina, and are less tightly packed. They show us a less detailed image.

The iris

In front of the lens is a circular piece of tissue called the iris. This is the coloured part of your eye. The iris contains pigments, which absorb light and stop it getting through to the retina.

In the middle of the iris is a gap called the pupil. The size of the pupil can be adjusted. The wider the pupil is, the more light can get through to the retina. In strong light, the iris closes in, and makes the pupil small. This stops too much light getting in and damaging the retina.

S To allow it to adjust the size of the pupil, the iris contains muscles. Circular muscles lie in circles around the pupil. When they contract, they make the pupil constrict, or get smaller. Radial muscles run outwards from the edge of the pupil. When they contract, they make the pupil dilate, or get larger (Figure **13.13**). This is called the iris reflex (or sometimes the pupil reflex).

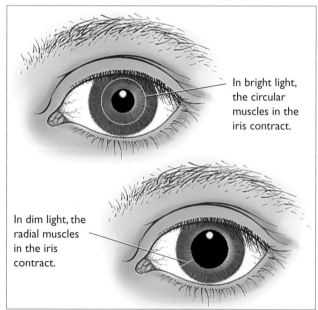

In bright light, the circular muscles in the iris contract.

In dim light, the radial muscles in the iris contract.

Figure 13.13 The iris reflex.

These responses of the iris are examples of a reflex action. Although the nerve impulses go into the brain, we do not need to think consciously about what to do. The response of the iris to light intensity (the stimulus) is fast and automatic. Like many reflex actions, this is very advantageous: it prevents damage to the retina that could be caused by very bright light falling onto it.

Activity 13.4
Looking at human eyes

Skills
AO3.3 Observing, measuring and recording
AO3.4 Interpreting and evaluating observations and data

It is best to perform this experiment with a partner, although it is possible to use a mirror and look at your own eyes.

1   First identify all the following structures: eyebrows; eyelashes; eyelids; conjunctiva; pupil; iris; cornea; sclera; small blood vessels; openings to tear ducts.
    Figure **13.11** will help you to do this.

2   Make a diagram of a front view of the eye and label each of these structures on it.

3   Use section **13.3** to find out the functions of each structure you have labelled. Write down these functions, as briefly as you can, next to each label or beneath your diagram.

4   Ask your partner to close his or her eyes, and cover them with something dark to cut out as much light as possible. (Alternatively, you may be able to darken the whole room.) After about 3 or 4 minutes, quickly remove the cover (or switch on the lights) and look at your partner's eyes as they adapt to the light. What happens? What is the purpose of this change?

S 5   Explain how this change is brought about.

Activity 13.5
Dissecting a sheep's eye

Focusing light

For the brain to see a clear image, there must be a clear image focused on the retina. Light rays must be bent, or refracted, so that they focus exactly onto the retina. The humours inside the eye are transparent and colourless so that light can pass through them easily.

The cornea is responsible for most of the bending of the light. The lens makes fine adjustments.

Figure **13.14** shows how the cornea and lens focus light onto the retina. The image on the retina is upside down. The brain interprets this so that you see it the right way up.

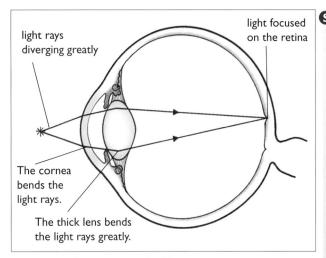

Figure **13.16**   Focusing on a nearby object.

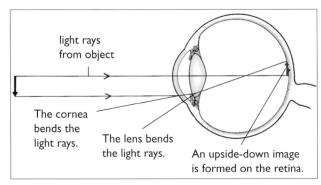

Figure **13.14**   How an image is focused onto the retina.

Ⓢ Adjusting the focus

Not all light rays need bending by the same amount to focus them onto the retina. Light rays coming from an object in the distance will be almost parallel to one another. They will not need much bending (Figure **13.15**).

Light rays coming from a nearby object are going away from one another, or diverging. They will need to be bent inwards quite strongly (Figure **13.16**).

The shape of the lens can be adjusted to bend light rays more, or less. The thicker the lens, the more it will bend the light rays. The thinner it is, the less it will bend them. This adjustment in the shape of the lens, to focus light coming from different distances, is called accommodation.

Figure **13.17** shows how the shape of the lens is changed. It is held in position by a ring of suspensory ligaments. The tension on the suspensory ligaments, and thus the shape of the lens, is altered by means of the ciliary muscle. When this muscle contracts, the suspensory ligaments are loosened. When it relaxes, they are pulled tight. When the suspensory ligaments are tight, the lens is pulled thin. When they are loosened, the lens gets thicker.

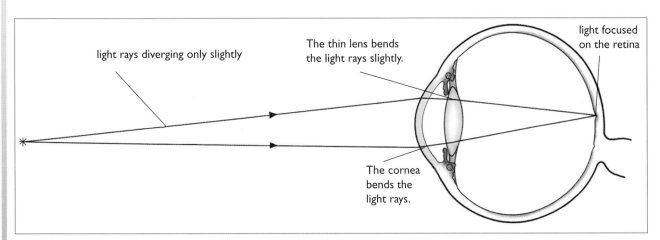

Figure **13.15**   Focusing on a distant object.

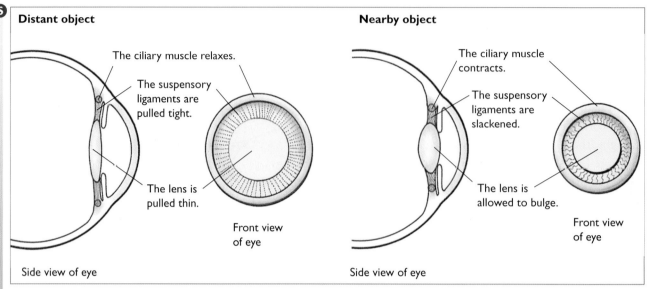

Distant object

The ciliary muscle relaxes.

The suspensory ligaments are pulled tight.

The lens is pulled thin.

Front view of eye

Side view of eye

Nearby object

The ciliary muscle contracts.

The suspensory ligaments are slackened.

The lens is allowed to bulge.

Front view of eye

Side view of eye

Figure 13.17 How the shape of the lens is changed.

Questions

13.9 What is a stimulus?

13.10 Name **two** parts of the body which contain receptors of chemical stimuli.

13.11 Which part of the eye contains cells which are sensitive to light?

13.12 Your brain can build up a very clear image when light is focused onto the fovea. Explain why it can do this.

13.13 If you look straight at an object when it is nearly dark, you may find it difficult to see it. It is easier to see if you look just to one side of it. Explain why this is.

13.14 What is the choroid, and what is its function?

13.15 List, in order, the parts of the eye through which light passes to reach the retina.

13.16 Name **two** parts of the eye which refract light rays.

Ⓢ 13.17 What is meant by accommodation?

13.18 a What do the ciliary muscles do when you are focusing on a nearby object?

    b What effect does this have on:

      i the suspensory ligaments?

      ii the lens?

13.4 The endocrine system

Endocrine glands

So far in this chapter, we have seen how nerves can carry electrical impulses very quickly from one part of an animal's body to another. But animals also use chemicals to transmit information from one part of the body to another.

The chemicals are called hormones. Hormones are made in special glands called endocrine glands. Figure **13.18** shows the positions of the most important endocrine glands in the human body. Table **13.1** summarises their functions.

Endocrine glands have a good blood supply. They have blood capillaries running right through them. When the endocrine gland makes a hormone, it releases it directly into the blood.

Other sorts of gland do not do this. The salivary glands, for example, do not secrete saliva into the blood. Saliva is secreted into the salivary duct, which carries it into the mouth. Endocrine glands do not have ducts, so they are sometimes called ductless glands.

Once the hormone is in the blood, it is carried to all parts of the body, dissolved in the plasma. Although the blood is carrying many hormones, each affects only certain parts of the body. These are called its target organs.

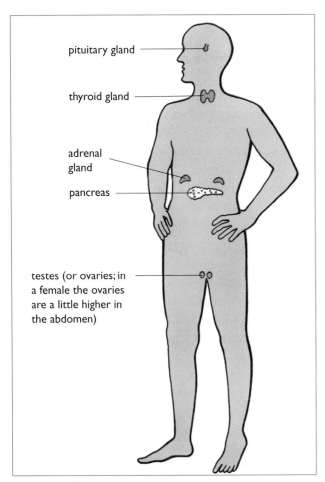

pituitary gland

thyroid gland

adrenal gland

pancreas

testes (or ovaries; in a female the ovaries are a little higher in the abdomen)

Figure 13.18 The main endocrine glands.

Adrenaline

There are two adrenal glands, one above each kidney. They make a hormone called **adrenaline**. When you are frightened, excited or keyed up, your brain sends impulses along a nerve to your adrenal glands. This makes them secrete adrenaline into the blood.

Adrenaline has several effects which are designed to help you to cope with danger known as the 'fight or flight' response. For example, it makes your heart beat faster, supplying oxygen to your brain and muscles more quickly. This gives them more energy for fighting or running away. It also increases breathing rate, so that more oxygen can enter the blood in the lungs.

Key definition

hormone – a chemical substance produced by a gland, carried by the blood, which alters the activity of one or more specific target organs

The blood vessels in your skin and digestive system contract so that they carry very little blood. This makes you go pale, and gives you 'butterflies in your stomach'. As much blood as possible is needed for your brain and muscles in the emergency. Adrenaline causes the pupils in the eye to widen. This allows more light into the eye, which might help you to see the danger more clearly.

Adrenaline also causes the liver to release glucose into the blood. This provides extra glucose for the muscles, so that they can release energy from it (by respiration) and use the energy for contracting.

Table **13.2** compares the nervous and endocrine systems.

Gland	Hormone that it secretes	Function of hormone
adrenal gland	adrenaline	prepares body for vigorous action
pancreas	insulin	reduces the concentration of glucose in the blood
testis	testosterone	causes the development of male secondary sexual characteristics
ovary	oestrogen	causes the development of female secondary sexual characteristics, and helps in the control of the menstrual cycle

Table 13.1 Some important endocrine glands and their functions.

Nervous system	Endocrine system
made up of neurones	made up of secretory cells
information transmitted in the form of electrical impulses	information transmitted in the form of chemicals called hormones
impulses transmitted along nerve fibres (axons and dendrons)	chemicals carried dissolved in the blood plasma
impulses travel very quickly	chemicals travel more slowly
effect of a nerve impulse usually only lasts for a very short time	effect of a hormone may last longer

Table 13.2 A comparison of the nervous and endocrine systems of a mammal.

Questions

13.19 Name **three** endocrine glands, and the hormone that each secretes.

13.20 How are hormones transported around the body?

13.21 Describe **two** situations in which adrenaline is likely to be secreted.

13.22 How does adrenaline help to prepare the body for action?

13.5 Coordination and response in plants

Like animals, plants are able to respond to their environment, although usually with much slower responses than those of animals.

In general, plants respond to stimuli by changing their rate or direction of growth. They may grow either towards or away from a stimulus. Growth towards a stimulus is said to be a positive response, and growth away from a stimulus is a negative response.

These responses are called **tropisms**. A tropism is a growth response by a plant, in which the direction of the growth is affected by the direction of the stimulus.

Two important stimuli for plants are light and gravity. Shoots normally grow towards light. Roots do not usually respond to light, but a few grow away from it.

Shoots tend to grow away from the pull of gravity, while roots normally grow towards it.

It is very important to the plant that its roots and shoots grow in appropriate directions. Shoots must grow upwards, away from gravity and towards the light, so that the leaves are held out into the sunlight. The more light they have, the better they can photosynthesise. Flowers, too, need to be held up in the air, where insects, birds or the wind can pollinate them.

Key definitions

gravitropism – a response in which a plant grows towards or away from gravity

phototropism – a response in which a plant grows towards or away from the direction from which light is coming

Roots, though, need to grow downwards, into the soil in order to anchor the plant in the soil, and to absorb water and minerals from between the soil particles.

Plant hormones

We have seen that for an organism to respond to a stimulus, there must be a receptor to pick up the stimulus, an effector to respond to it, and some kind of communication system in between. In mammals, the receptor is often part of a sense organ, and the effector is a muscle or gland. Information is sent between them along nerves, or sometimes by means of hormones.

Plants, however, do not have complex sense organs, muscles or nervous systems. So how do they manage to respond to stimuli like light and gravity?

Figure **13.19** shows an experiment that can be done to find out which part of a shoot picks up the stimulus of light shining onto it. The sensitive region is the tip of the shoot. This is where the receptor is.

The part of the shoot which responds to the stimulus is the part just below the tip. This is the effector.

These two parts of the shoot must be communicating with one another somehow. They do it by means of chemicals called plant hormones.

Auxin

One kind of plant hormone is called **auxin**. Auxin is being made all the time by the cells in the tip of a shoot. The auxin diffuses downwards from the tip, into the rest of the shoot.

Auxin makes the cells just behind the tip get longer. The more auxin there is, the faster they will grow. Without auxin, they will not grow (Figure **13.19**).

When light shines onto a shoot from all around, auxin is distributed evenly around the tip of the shoot. The cells all grow at about the same rate, so the shoot grows straight upwards. This is what normally happens in plants growing outside.

When, however, light shines onto a shoot from one side, the auxin at the tip concentrates on the shady side (Figure **13.20**). This makes the cells on the shady side grow faster than the ones on the bright side, so the shoot bends towards the light.

If the tip of the coleoptile is cut off and then replaced, the coleoptile will still grow towards the light.

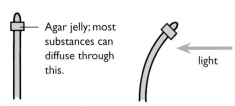

Agar jelly; most substances can diffuse through this.

light

If the tip is cut off and separated from the rest of the coleoptile by a piece of agar jelly, the coleoptile still grows towards the light.

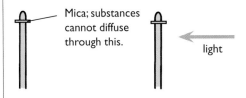

Mica; substances cannot diffuse through this.

light

But if a piece of mica separates the tip from the rest of the coleoptile, then it does not grow towards the light.
This suggests that the response to light is caused by a substance which is made in the tip, and diffuses down the coleoptile.

Figure 13.19 An experiment investigating the method by which shoots respond to light.

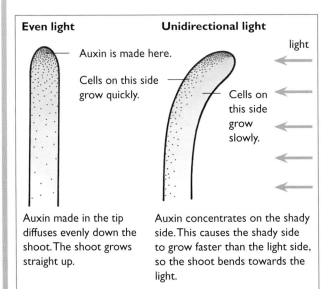

Even light	**Unidirectional light**

light

Auxin is made here.

Cells on this side grow quickly.

Cells on this side grow slowly.

Auxin made in the tip diffuses evenly down the shoot. The shoot grows straight up.

Auxin concentrates on the shady side. This causes the shady side to grow faster than the light side, so the shoot bends towards the light.

Figure 13.20 Auxin and phototropism.

If a potted *Coleus* plant is placed on its side in a dark room overnight, the shoot will bend upwards (Figure 13.21). Since there is no light, we can presume the result to be a response to gravity. (What other precaution should we take to be sure of this?)

With the stem in the horizontal position, auxin tends to collect on the lower side of the stem, causing faster growth there. Therefore, the stem curves upward.

In the same way, in the bean seedlings shown in Figure 13.22, auxin has built up on the lower surface of the root. The effect here, however, is the opposite to that in the *Coleus* shoot. This amount of auxin slows down the growth on this side, and so the radicle bends downwards.

before

after

Figure 13.21 The response to gravity in a *Coleus* shoot.

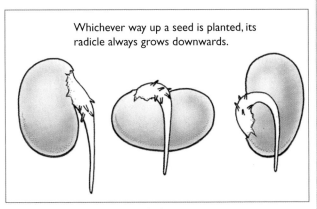

Whichever way up a seed is planted, its radicle always grows downwards.

Figure 13.22 The response to gravity in a root.

Activity 13.6
To find out how shoots respond to light

Skills
AO3.3 Observing, measuring and recording
AO3.4 Interpreting and evaluating observations and data

1   Label three Petri dishes **A**, **B** and **C**. Line each with moist cotton wool or filter paper, and put about six peas or beans in each.
2   Leave all three dishes in a warm place for a day or two, until the seeds begin to germinate. Check that they do not dry out.
3   Now put dish **A** into a light-proof box with a slit in one side, so that the seedlings get light from one side only.
4   Put dish **B** onto a clinostat (see diagram) in a light place. The clinostat will slowly turn the seedlings around, so that they get light from all sides equally. If you do not have a clinostat, arrange to turn the dish by hand three or four times per day to achieve a similar effect.
5   Put dish **C** into a completely light-proof box.
6   Leave all the dishes for a week, checking that they do not dry out.

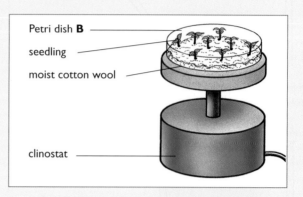

Petri dish **B**
seedling
moist cotton wool
clinostat

7   Make labelled drawings of one seedling from each dish.

❓ Questions

A1   How did the seedlings in **A** respond to light from one side? What is the name for this response?
A2   Why was dish **B** put onto a clinostat, and not simply left in a light place?
A3   Explain what happened to the seedlings in dish **C**.
A4   What was the control in this experiment?

Activity 13.7
To find out how roots respond to gravity

Skills
AO3.2 Planning
AO3.3 Observing, measuring and recording
AO3.4 Interpreting and evaluating observations and data
AO3.5 Evaluating methods

You are going to design this investigation yourself. You can use similar techniques to those in Activity 13.6. This is the hypothesis you are going to test:

Roots grow towards gravity.

When you have written your plan, get it checked by your teacher before you try to carry it out. Write it up in the usual way, including a discussion and evaluation.

Activity 13.8
To find out how auxin affects shoots

❓ Questions

13.23   What part of the shoot is sensitive to light?
13.24   What part of the shoot responds to light?
13.25   How do these parts communicate with each other? How is this like or unlike a similar system in a mammal?
13.26   How does the normal response of a shoot to light help the plant?
13.27   How does a root respond to gravity?
13.28   Describe **three** features of an etiolated plant.

Etiolation

Seedlings grown in the dark are very pale, tall and thin. In darkness, auxin is also distributed evenly around the tip, and the shoot grows rapidly upwards. But chloroplasts do not develop properly in darkness. Therefore plants without light become yellow and spindly. They grow very tall and thin, and have smaller leaves, which are often further apart than in a normal plant. Plants like this are said to be etiolated.

If these plants reach the light, chlorophyll will develop, and the plants will begin to grow normally. If they do not reach light, they will die because they cannot photosynthesise.

S Activity 13.9
To find out which part of a shoot is sensitive to light

Weedkillers

Many people use weedkillers in their gardens. Most weedkillers contain plant hormones. These hormones are often a type of auxin, usually a synthetic form (that is, it has been made in a factory and not extracted from plants) such as 2,4D. The weedkillers used to kill weeds in lawns are selective weedkillers. When they are sprayed onto the lawn, the weeds are affected by the auxin, but the grass is not (Figure **13.23**). The weeds respond by growing very fast. Then the weeds die, leaving more space, nutrients and water for the grass to grow. Farmers use similar weedkillers to kill weeds growing in cereal crops such as wheat, millet, maize or sorghum.

Figure 13.23   Spraying weedkiller on invasive weeds in a national park in Hawaii.

Summary

You should know:
- ♦ about the central and peripheral nervous system in humans
- ♦ about sensory, relay and motor neurones
- **S** ♦ about reflex arcs and reflex actions
- ♦ the structure and function of a synapse
- ♦ about voluntary and involuntary actions
- ♦ about sense organs and receptors
- **S** ♦ the structure and function of the eye
- ♦ how the eye adjusts the focusing of light
- ♦ how rods and cones provide night vision and colour vision
- ♦ about the pupil reflex
- ♦ about the endocrine system
- **S** ♦ the function of adrenaline
- ♦ how to compare control by hormones and the nervous system
- ♦ about tropisms in plants, and how to investigate gravitropism and phototropism
- ♦ how auxin is involved in gravitropism and phototropism.

End-of-chapter questions

1 Choose the term from the list that matches each of the descriptions. You may use each term once, more than once or not at all.

circular muscles	cones	conjunctiva	contraction	cornea
effector	lens	motor neurone	myelin sheath	radial muscles
receptor	relaxation	relay neurone	retina	rods
sensory neurone	suspensory ligaments	synaptic cleft		

 a a nerve cell that transmits impulses from the central nervous system to an effector
 b a cell that is sensitive to a stimulus
 c the part of the eye that refracts light rays most strongly
 d the part of the eye that contains receptor cells
 e a small gap between two neurones
 f the action of the ciliary muscle when the eye is focusing on a nearby object
 g the muscles in the iris that contract to reduce the amount of light entering the eye
 h cells that are sensitive to different colours of light

2 Explain the difference between each of the following pairs of terms.

 a cornea, conjunctiva
 b choroid, sclera
 c receptor, effector
 d sensory neurone, motor neurone
 e negative gravitropism, positive gravitropism

3 If you step on a sharp object, muscles in your leg will rapidly pull your foot away.

 a What is the correct term for this type of reaction?
 b Using each of the following words at least once, but not necessarily in this order, explain how this reaction is brought about.

effector	electrical impulse	motor neurone
receptor	relay neurone	sensory neurone

4 Identify the type of neurone – sensory, relay or motor – that matches each of these descriptions. For some descriptions, more than one type of neurone may match.

 a has its cell body in the central nervous system
 b carries nerve impulses away from a receptor
 c carries nerve impulses towards its cell body
 d carries nerve impulses away from its cell body
 e is entirely inside the central nervous system
 f can have an axon that is more than a metre long

⑤ 5 The diagram below shows a synapse.

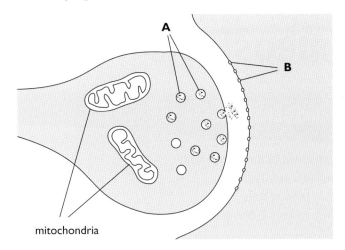

mitochondria

a   In which direction does this synapse allow a nerve impulse to travel? Explain your answer. [1]
b   Describe the roles of the parts labelled **A** and **B** in transmitting a nerve impulse from one
    neurone to the next. [5]
c   Suggest the role of the mitochondria shown in the diagram. [3]

6 The light sensitive cells in the eye are known as rods and cones.

The diagram shows drawings of a rod cell and a cone cell.

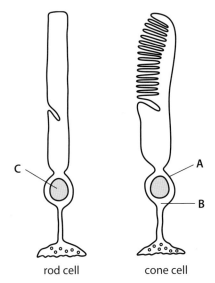

rod cell   cone cell

a   Name the structures labelled **A** to **C**. [3]
b   i   Name the tissue in the eye where rods and cones are found. [1]
    ii Name the parts of this tissue where there are
        cones but no rods [1]
        no cones or rods [1]
c   Describe how rods and cones function. [4]

[Cambridge IGCSE® Biology 0610/33, Question 2, May/June 2012]

14 Homeostasis

In this chapter, you will find out about:

♦ maintaining the internal environment of the human body
♦ how we keep our body temperature constant
(S) ♦ the role of negative feedback in homeostasis
♦ how the pancreas and liver help to keep blood glucose concentration steady.

Marine iguanas

Marine iguanas are reptiles – a type of lizard (Figure 14.1). They are found only in the remote Galapagos Islands in the Pacific Ocean.

These iguanas are almost the only reptiles that spend part of their time in the sea. They feed on seaweed, which most of them find on the rocks when the tide is out. But larger individuals need to find more food, and they dive into the sea in search of seaweed. They are able to go down to 25 m. The sea in this region is extremely cold, but the rocks on the shore get very hot during the day, when sunlight shines onto them.

Reptiles, unlike mammals, are not able to regulate their body temperature internally, and these lizards are no exception. When it enters the sea, an iguana's body temperature begins to fall, as heat is transferred from its body into the cold sea water. As its temperature drops, the metabolic reactions in the iguana's body slow down. This affects its activity – its movements get slower and slower as it gets colder, until eventually it is forced to leave the water and bask on the rocks to warm up again. This explains why these large individuals do most of their feeding round about midday, when the sun is at its hottest. At other times, they might not be able to get their body temperature back up again, and would stay cold and slow-moving for a long time after they have been in the sea.

Smaller marine iguanas do not feed like this. These smaller individuals feed only on the shore. Their small bodies have a larger surface area to volume ratio, so they lose heat faster. Submerged in cold sea water, they would cool down so fast that they would not have time to feed before they had to emerge and warm up again.

Figure 14.1 A large marine iguana basks on the rocks to raise its body temperature, after a long dive into the cold ocean.

14.1 Maintaining the internal environment

The environment (surroundings) of a living organism is always changing. Think about your own environment. The temperature of the air around you changes. For example, if you live in a temperate country, it might be −10 °C outside on a cold day in winter, and 23 °C indoors. If you live in the tropics, the outside temperature may be well over 40 °C.

The cells inside your body, however, do not have a changing environment. Your body keeps the environment inside you almost the same, all the time. In the tissue fluid surrounding your cells, the temperature and amount of water are kept almost constant. So is the concentration of glucose. Keeping this internal environment constant is called homeostasis.

Homeostasis is very important. It helps your cells to work as efficiently as possible. Keeping a constant temperature of around 37 °C helps enzymes to work at the optimum rate. Keeping a constant amount of water means that your cells are not damaged by absorbing or losing too much water by osmosis. Keeping a constant concentration of glucose means that there is always enough fuel for respiration.

In this chapter, you will see how homeostasis is carried out in humans. The nervous system and various endocrine glands are involved, as well as the skin, pancreas and liver.

14.2 Control of body temperature

Mammals and birds are endothermic

Some animals – including ourselves – are very good at controlling their body temperature. They can keep their temperature almost constant, even though the temperature of their environment changes. Animals that can do this are called endothermic animals. This term means that they get their heat energy from within themselves ('endo' means within). Mammals and birds are endothermic (Figure **14.2**). Animals that don't do this are called ectothermic.

Outside temperature 0 °C

At 0 °C, an ectothermic animal's metabolic rate slows down, because its body temperature is also 0 °C. The animal is inactive.

Outside temperature 20 °C

At 20 °C, an ectothermic animal's body temperature is 20 °C. Its metabolic rate speeds up, and it becomes active.

At 0 °C, an endothermic animal remains active. Its cells produce heat by breaking down food through respiration. Its body temperature stays high enough to keep its metabolism going.

At 20 °C, an endothermic animal is no more active than at 0 °C, because its body temperature does not change. It may even be less active, to avoid overheating.

Figure 14.2 Ectothermic and endothermic animals.

Being endothermic has great advantages. If the internal body temperature can be kept at around 37 °C, then enzymes can always work very efficiently, no matter what the outside temperature is. Metabolism can keep going, even when it is cold outside. In cold weather, or at night, an endothermic animal can be active when a ectothermic animal is too cold to move.

But there is a price to pay. The energy to keep warm has to come from somewhere. Endothermic animals get their heat energy from food, by respiration. Because of this, endothermic animals have to eat far more food than ectothermic ones.

The skin

One of the most important organs involved in temperature regulation in mammals is the skin. Figure **14.3** shows a section through human skin.

Key definition

homeostasis – the maintenance of a constant internal environment

Human skin is made up of two layers. The top layer is called the **epidermis**, and the lower layer is the dermis.

All the cells in the epidermis have been made in the layer of cells at the base of it. These cells are always dividing by a type of cell division called **mitosis** (page **232**). The new cells that are made gradually move towards the surface of the skin. As they go, they die, and fill up with a protein called keratin. The top layer of the skin is made up of these dead cells. It is called the cornified layer.

The cornified layer protects the softer, living cells underneath, because it is hard and waterproof. It is always being worn away, and replaced by cells from beneath. On the parts of the body which get most wear – for example, the soles of the feet – it grows thicker.

Some of the cells in the epidermis contain a dark brown pigment, called melanin. Melanin absorbs the harmful ultraviolet rays in sunlight, which would damage the living cells in the deeper layers of the skin.

Here and there, the epidermis is folded inwards, forming a hair follicle. A hair grows from each one. Hairs are made of keratin.

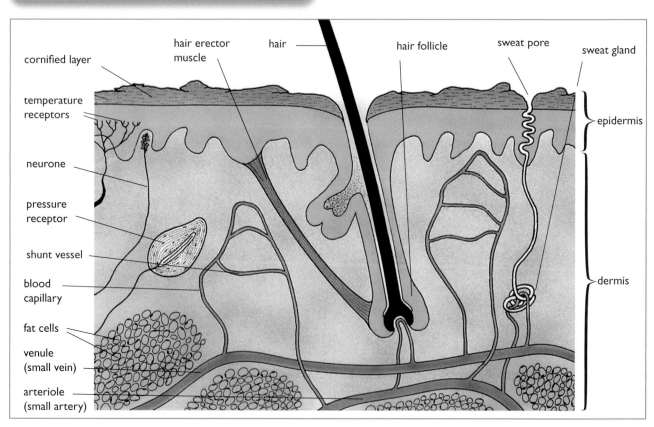

Figure 14.3 A section through human skin.

The dermis

Most of the dermis is made of connective tissue. This tissue contains elastic fibres and collagen fibres. As a person gets older, the fibres lose their elasticity, so the skin becomes loose and wrinkled.

The dermis also contains sweat glands. These secrete a liquid called sweat. Sweat is mostly water, with small amounts of salts and urea dissolved in it. It travels up the sweat ducts, and out onto the surface of the skin through the sweat pores. As we will see, sweat helps in temperature regulation.

The dermis contains blood vessels and nerve endings. These nerve endings are sensitive to touch, pain, pressure and temperature, so they help to keep you aware of changes in your environment.

Underneath the dermis is a layer of fat, called **adipose tissue**. This fatty tissue is made up of cells which contain large drops of oil. This layer helps to insulate your body against heat loss, and also acts as an energy reserve.

The hypothalamus

A part of the brain called the **hypothalamus** is at the centre of the control mechanism that keeps internal temperature constant. The hypothalamus coordinates the activities of the parts of the body that can bring about temperature changes.

The hypothalamus acts like a thermostat. It contains temperature receptors that sense the temperature of the blood running through it. If this is above or below 37 °C, then the hypothalamus sends electrical impulses, along nerves, to the parts of the body which have the function of regulating your body temperature.

When temperature falls

If your body temperature drops below 37 °C, nerve impulses from the hypothalamus cause the following things to happen (Figure **14.4**).

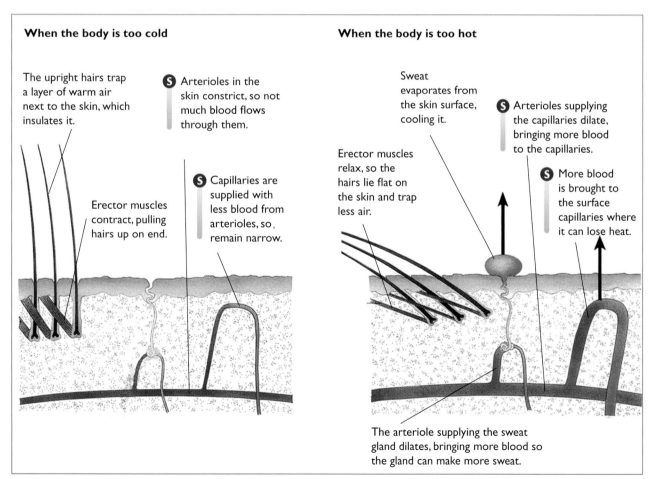

When the body is too cold

The upright hairs trap a layer of warm air next to the skin, which insulates it.

(S) Arterioles in the skin constrict, so not much blood flows through them.

Erector muscles contract, pulling hairs up on end.

(S) Capillaries are supplied with less blood from arterioles, so, remain narrow.

When the body is too hot

Sweat evaporates from the skin surface, cooling it.

Erector muscles relax, so the hairs lie flat on the skin and trap less air.

(S) Arterioles supplying the capillaries dilate, bringing more blood to the capillaries.

(S) More blood is brought to the surface capillaries where it can lose heat.

The arteriole supplying the sweat gland dilates, bringing more blood so the gland can make more sweat.

Figure 14.4 How skin helps with temperature regulation.

Muscles work

Muscles in some parts of the body contract and relax very quickly. This produces heat. It is called shivering. The heat generated in the muscles warms the blood as it flows through them. The blood distributes this heat all over the body.

Metabolism may increase

The speed of chemical reactions such as respiration may increase. This also releases more heat.

Hair stands up

The erector muscles in the skin contract, pulling the hairs up on end. In humans, this does not do anything very useful – it just produces 'goose pimples'. In a hairy animal though, like a cat, it traps a thicker layer of warm air next to the skin. This prevents the skin from losing more warmth. It acts as an insulator.

S Blood system conserves heat

The arterioles that supply the blood capillaries near to the surface of the skin become narrower, or constricted. This is called vasoconstriction. Only a very little blood can flow in them. The blood flows through shunt vessels and the deep-lying capillaries instead. Because these are deep under the skin, beneath the insulating fatty tissue, the blood does not lose so much heat to the air.

When temperature rises

Hair lies flat

The erector muscles in the skin relax, so that the hairs lie flat on the skin.

Blood system loses heat **S**

The arterioles supplying the capillaries near the surface of the skin get wider – they become dilated. This is called vasodilation. More blood therefore flows through them. Because a lot of blood is so near the surface of the skin, heat is readily lost from the blood into the air.

> **Study tip**
>
> The blood vessels do not move up and down through the skin. They just get wider and narrower.

Sweat

The sweat glands secrete sweat. The sweat lies on the surface of the hot skin. The water in it then evaporates, taking heat from the skin with it, thus cooling the body.

Negative feedback **S**

Figure 14.5 summarises the way in which the hypothalamus, skin and muscles work together to keep your internal body temperature within narrow set limits.

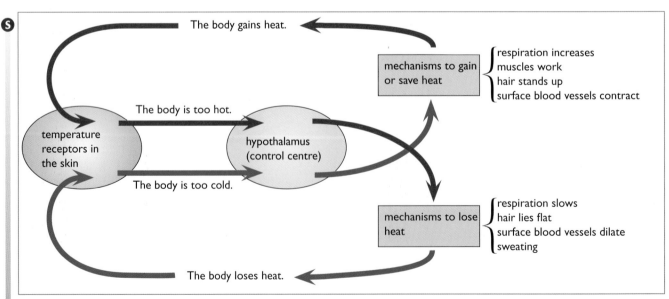

Figure 14.5 Maintaining body temperature in a steady state.

S We have seen that, when the temperature of your blood rises above the norm, the hypothalamus senses this. It responds by sending nerve impulses to your skin that bring about actions to help cool the blood. When the cooler blood reaches the hypothalamus, this responds by sending nerve impulses to your skin that bring about actions to help reduce the rate at which heat is lost from the blood. At the same time, the rate of heat production in the muscles is increased.

So, all the time, the hypothalamus is monitoring small changes in the temperature of your blood. As soon as this rises above normal, actions take place that help to reduce the temperature. Then, as soon as the hypothalamus senses the lowered temperature, it stops these actions taking place and starts off another set of actions that help to raise the blood temperature.

This process is called negative feedback. The term 'feedback' refers to the fact that, when the hypothalamus has made your skin take action to increase heat loss, information about the effects of these actions is 'fed back' to it, as it senses the drop in the blood temperature. It is called 'negative' because the information that the blood has cooled down *stops* the hypothalamus making your skin do these things.

Questions

14.1 Outline **two** advantages and **one** disadvantage of maintaining a constant internal body temperature.

14.2 Give **two** functions of the fatty tissue beneath the skin.

14.3 Explain how sweating helps to cool the body.

14.4 Name the organ which coordinates temperature regulation.

S 14.5 Explain what vasodilation is, and how it helps to cool the body.

14.6 Explain what is meant by negative feedback.

Activity 14.1
Experiment to investigate the effect of size on rate of cooling

Skills
AO3.3 Observing, measuring and recording
AO3.4 Interpreting and evaluating observations and data

Temperature regulation is an important part of homeostasis. We lose heat from our bodies to the air around us. Cells produce more heat to prevent the body temperature from dropping.

In this investigation, you will use containers of hot water to represent a human body. The experiment will test this hypothesis:

A large body cools more slowly than a small one.

1 Take two test tubes or other containers, identical except that one is large and one is small. You will also need two thermometers.

2 Read through what you are going to do. Draw a results chart in which you can write your results as you go along. Remember to put the units in your table headings.

3 Now collect some hot water. Pour water into each of your containers until they are almost full. Immediately take the temperature of each one and record your results for time 0.

4 Take readings every 2 minutes for at least 14 minutes.

5 Draw a line graph to display your results.

Questions

A1 a State **two** variables that are kept constant in this experiment.

  b Why is it important to keep these variables constant?

A2 a Calculate the number of °C by which the large container cooled during your experiment.

  b Calculate the number of °C by which the small container cooled during your experiment.

A3 Do your results support the hypothesis that you were testing? Explain your answer.

Activity 14.2
Investigating the effect of evaporation on the rate of cooling

❺ 14.3 Control of blood glucose concentration

The control of the concentration of glucose in the blood is a very important part of homeostasis. Cells need a steady supply of glucose to allow them to respire; without this, they cannot release the energy they need. Brain cells are especially dependent on glucose for respiration, and die quite quickly if they are deprived of it.

On the other hand, too much glucose in the blood is not good either, as it can cause water to move out of cells and into the blood by osmosis. This leaves the cells with too little water for them to carry out their normal metabolic processes.

The control of blood glucose concentration is carried out by the pancreas and the liver (Figure **14.6**).

The pancreas is two glands in one. Most of it is an ordinary gland with a duct. It makes pancreatic juice, which flows along the pancreatic duct into the duodenum (page **84**).

Scattered through the pancreas, however, are groups of cells called **islets of Langerhans**. These cells do not make pancreatic juice. They make two hormones called **insulin** and **glucagon**. These hormones help the liver to control the amount of glucose in the blood. Insulin has the effect of lowering blood glucose concentration, and glucagon does the opposite.

If you eat a meal which provides a lot of glucose, the concentration of glucose in the blood goes up. The islets of Langerhans detect this, and secrete insulin into the blood. When insulin reaches the liver, it causes the liver to absorb glucose from the blood. Some is used for respiration, but some is converted into the insoluble polysaccharide, **glycogen**. This is stored in the liver.

If the blood glucose concentration falls too low, the pancreas secretes glucagon. This causes liver cells to break down glycogen to glucose, and release it into the blood.

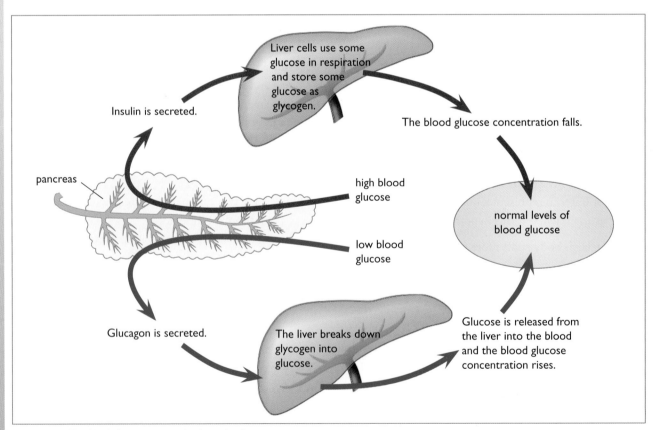

Figure 14.6 How blood glucose concentration is regulated.

Diabetes

When the control of blood glucose concentration does not work, a person is said to have diabetes.

One type of diabetes is caused by the death of the cells that secrete insulin. This is called **type 1 diabetes**. It is not certain exactly what causes this disease, but it is thought to result from the body's own immune system attacking and destroying the cells in the pancreas that secrete insulin. This type of diabetes usually develops when a person is a young child.

When a person eats a meal contain a lot of carbohydrate, the concentration of glucose in the blood increases. Normally, this would trigger the secretion of insulin from the pancreas, but in a person with type 1 diabetes this does not happen. The blood glucose concentration goes up, and stays up. This condition is called **hyperglycaemia**. It usually makes the person feel unwell – they may have a dry mouth, blurred vision and feel very thirsty. Their heart rate and breathing rate may increase.

On the other hand, not eating carbohydrate for a long time will cause the blood glucose concentration to drop very low. Because no insulin has been secreted, the liver has not built up stores of glycogen that can now be broken down to produce glucose. The person has **hypoglycaemia**. Cells do not have a supply of glucose to release energy by respiration, so the person feels very tired and may show confusion and irrational behaviour. Eventually, they can become unconscious. People with diabetes usually become very good at recognising when this series of events is beginning, and know that they need to eat something sweet to get their blood glucose concentration up towards normal.

Having blood glucose concentrations that swing very high and very low can, over long periods of time, do damage to numerous body organs. It is important that a person with type 1 diabetes tries to keep their blood glucose concentration within reasonably normal limits.

Most people with diabetes get into the habit of checking their blood glucose concentration regularly, using a simple sensor (Figure **14.7**). They can also test their urine for glucose, using a simple dipstick (Figure **14.8**). Urine should not contain any glucose, but if a person's blood glucose concentration rises very high, then the kidneys are not able to reabsorb it all from the filtrate in the nephron, and some remains in the urine that is excreted.

Eating little and often, and particularly avoiding large amounts of carbohydrate, can help to stop blood glucose concentration fluctuating too widely. People with type 1 diabetes also need to inject themselves with insulin to reduce blood glucose concentration.

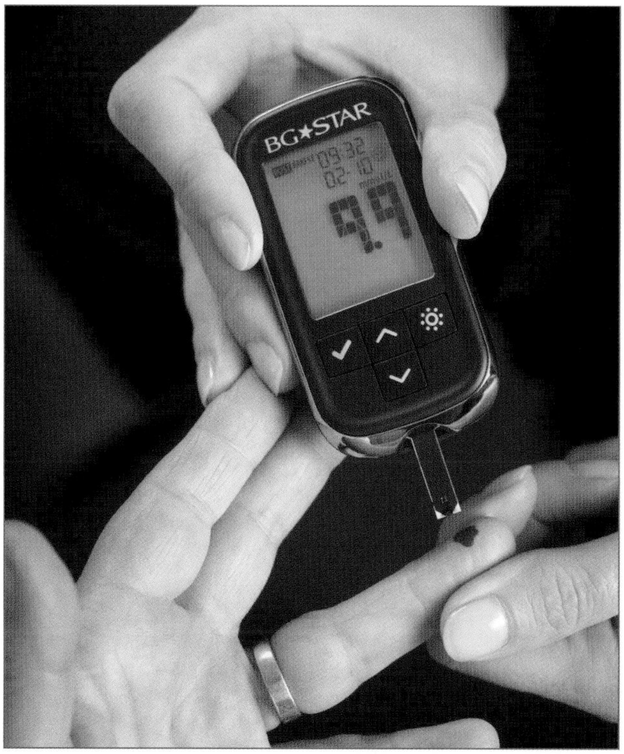

Figure 14.7 This blood sugar monitoring device quickly measures the concentration of glucose in a tiny drop of blood.

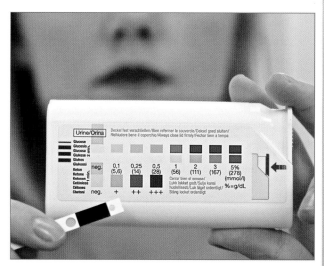

Figure 14.8 Disposable test sticks can be used to test urine for the presence of glucose. Normally, there should be no glucose present in urine – as is indicated by the result on this stick.

Summary

You should know:

- ♦ what homeostasis is and why it is important
- ♦ the advantages of controlling body temperature
- ♦ the structure of the skin
- ⓢ ♦ how the brain (hypothalamus), skin and muscles help to control body temperature
- ♦ the role of negative feedback mechanisms in homeostasis
- ♦ the roles of the liver and pancreas in keeping blood glucose concentration within narrow limits
- ♦ the symptoms and treatment of type 1 diabetes.

End-of-chapter questions

1 Explain the difference between each of the following pairs of terms.

    a endothermic, ectothermic

    b dermis, epidermis

ⓢ   **c** vasoconstriction, vasodilation

    d glycogen, glucagon

2 Each of these sentences contains incorrect information. Identify what is wrong, and then write a sentence that provides correct information.

    a Homeostasis means keeping your body temperature constant.

    b When we are cold, our hairs stand on end, which keeps us warm.

    c The fatty layer under the skin stops cold air getting into the body.

    d When we are too hot, our sweat glands secrete a cold liquid that cools us down.

ⓢ   **e** When you are too hot, your blood capillaries move closer to the skin surface.

    f Insulin is an enzyme that changes glucose to glycogen.

3 When a person is submerged in cold water, their body temperature can drop very quickly. This is because heat is transferred quickly, by conduction, from the warm body into the cold water. An experiment was carried out to see if it is better to stay still if you fall into cold water, or to try to swim.

    • Two men sat for 30 minutes, in air at a temperature of 15 °C.

    • They then got into a swimming pool, where the water was also at a temperature of 15 °C.

    • Person **A** swam for the next 30 minutes. Person **B** lay still in the water.

The body temperatures of both men were measured at 10 minute intervals throughout the experiment. The results are shown in the graph on the next page.

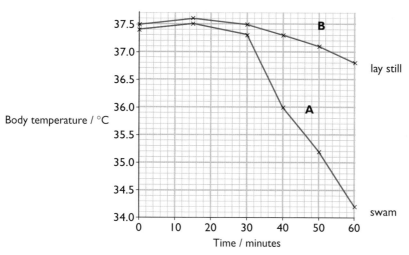

a State the body temperature of each man at the start of the experiment. [2]

b Explain why their body temperatures remained roughly constant for the first 30 minutes of the experiment. [4]

c Explain why the body temperatures of both men dropped between 30 minutes and 60 minutes. [2]

d Suggest why person **A**'s temperature dropped faster than person **B**'s temperature during this time period. (This is a difficult question! You may find thinking about exchange surfaces is helpful.) [3]

S 4 a Explain why body cells need a constant supply of glucose. [3]

b In healthy humans, the blood normally contains about 90 mg of glucose per 100 cm³ of blood. Name the gland that secretes the hormones that help to keep this concentration fairly constant. [1]

c The graph below shows the changes in concentration of blood glucose after a meal containing starch.

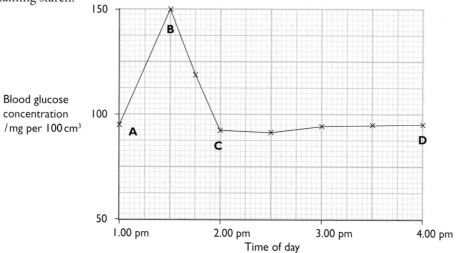

i Explain why the concentration of glucose in the blood rises between **A** and **B**. [3]

ii Explain why the concentration of glucose in the blood falls between **B** and **C**. [3]

d The graph shows that the blood glucose concentration remains fairly constant between **C** and **D**. Explain the role of negative feedback in keeping blood glucose level constant. [3]

e i Make a copy of the graph. On your graph, sketch a curve to show how you would expect the blood glucose concentration of a person with type 1 diabetes to change, if they ate the same meal at the same time. [2]

ii Explain your answer to **e i**. [3]

15 Drugs

In this chapter, you will find out about:

♦ the meaning of the term drug
♦ antibiotics
♦ misused drugs, including heroin, alcohol, anabolic steroids and nicotine.

Arms race

You have probably never heard of the drug carbapenem. This drug is an antibiotic – a substance that is used to kill bacteria that are causing infections in a person's body. The reason that the name of this antibiotic is not well known is because it a 'last resort' antibiotic. It is only used when bacteria cannot be killed by any other antibiotics.

The more that a particular antibiotic is used, the more risk there is that some populations of bacteria will develop resistance to it. This means that antibiotics that were once very effective at curing bacterial infections may no longer work. Doctors therefore try to keep some antibiotics 'in reserve'. If these drugs are hardly ever used, then the chances

that any bacteria will develop resistance is much smaller. Then, when the drug is really needed, it is there to be used as an effective weapon.

Some of the people who are most vulnerable to infections by bacteria are those who are already ill, and are in hospital receiving long-term care (Figure 15.1). One group of bacteria that can cause serious infections in such people are called enterobacteria. Until recently, these infections could be treated using carbapenem.

But, in 2001, in a hospital in North Carolina in the USA, several patients with enterobacteria infections who were treated with carbapenem did not recover. The bacteria that were making them ill were resistant to carbapenem. Since then, these carbapenem-resistant bacteria have been found in other parts of the USA, and also as far away as Australia. Up to 50% of patients with these infections can die from them.

Hospitals are now trying other antibiotics to treat these infections. But it is a constant battle. The more we use antibiotics, the more bacteria become resistant to them. We have to keep finding new antibiotics, to keep one step ahead of the bacteria.

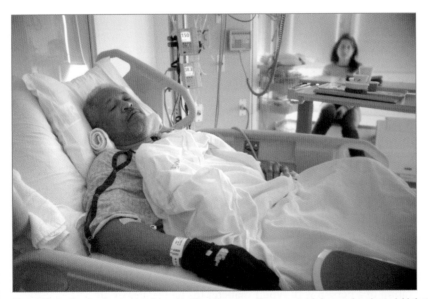

Figure 15.1 People who are already weak with an illness are the most at risk from serious bacterial infections.

15.1 What is a drug?

People have always used drugs. Long ago, people discovered that some plants could help to cure diseases or to heal wounds. They also used substances obtained from plants and animals to change their perception of the world around them, inducing hallucinations and feelings of contentment or excitement. Today, many of the drugs we use still come from plants.

Without drugs, many people would live much shorter lives, or suffer greater pain. Drugs used in medical care, or to relieve mild pain, are very helpful to us. However, some people misuse drugs, so that they cause harm to themselves and to others around them.

Key definition

drug – any substance taken into the body that modifies or affects chemical reactions in the body

15.2 Medicinal drugs

Antibiotics

Sometimes, a person's body needs help in its fight against a bacterial infection. Until 1944, there was little help that could be given. People died from diseases which we now think quite harmless, such as infected cuts.

Then a discovery was made which has had a tremendous effect on our ability to treat diseases. Antibiotics were discovered.

Antibiotics are substances which kill bacteria, but do not harm other living cells. Most of them are made by fungi. It is thought that the fungi make antibiotics to kill bacteria living near them – bacteria and fungi are both decomposers, so they might compete for food. We use the chemical warfare system of the fungus to wage our own war against bacteria.

The first antibiotic to be discovered was penicillin. It is made by the fungus *Penicillium*, which you might sometimes see growing on decaying fruit. The way in which penicillin is made is described on page 284. Penicillin kills bacteria by stopping them making their cell walls. Since the introduction of penicillin, many more antibiotics have been found (Figure 15.2).

We have to go on trying to find more and more antibiotics, because bacteria evolve to become resistant to them, as described in Chapter 19. The more we use antibiotics, the more selection pressure we put on bacteria to evolve resistance (Figure 15.3). People did not realise this when antibiotics were first discovered, and used them for all sorts of diseases where they did not help at all, such as diseases caused by viruses. Now doctors are much more careful about the amounts of antibiotics which they prescribe. We should only use antibiotics when they are really needed – then there is more chance that they will work when we need them to.

Many antibiotics kill bacteria by damaging their cell walls. Viruses do not have cell walls, so they are unharmed by antibiotics.

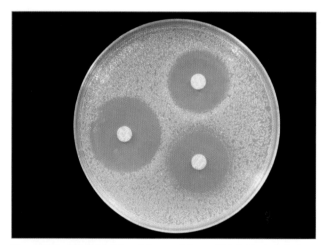

Figure 15.2 This Petri dish contains agar jelly on which the bacteria that cause typhoid fever are growing. The three white circles are little discs of filter paper soaked in different antibiotics. You can see how the bacteria are unable to grow close to the discs, showing that these antibiotics are effective against the bacteria.

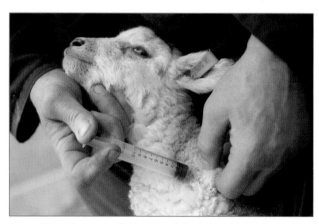

Figure 15.3 Many farm animals are regularly given antibiotics. Unnecessary treatments should be avoided, to reduce the risk of resistant populations of bacteria arising.

15.3 Misuse of drugs

Heroin

Opium poppies produce a substance called opium, which contains a number of different chemicals. Some of these, especially morphine and codeine, are used in medicine for the relief of pain. Opium is also the raw material from which heroin is produced, which is also used in medicine.

Heroin can be addictive. An addictive drug is one which causes a person to become dependent on it – they are not able to stop taking it without suffering severe psychological and physical symptoms.

Heroin is a powerful **depressant**. This means that it slows down many functions of the brain. It reduces pain, and slows down breathing. It also slows down the functions of the hypothalamus. When a person takes heroin, it produces a feeling of euphoria – that is, they feel intensely happy. However, in many people it can rapidly become addictive. They feel so ill when they do not take it that they will do anything to obtain more. As their bodies become more tolerant of the drug, they need to take more and more of it in order to obtain any feelings of pleasure.

Not everyone who takes heroin becomes addicted to it, but many do. Addiction can develop very rapidly, so that a person who has taken it for only one or two weeks may find that they cannot give it up.

A person who has become addicted to heroin may lose any ability to be a part of normal society. He or she may think only of how they will get their next dose. They may not be able to hold down a job, and therefore become unable to earn money, so many heroin addicts turn to crime in order to obtain money to buy their drug. They are not able to help and support their family.

Some people take heroin by injecting it into their veins. This can be dangerous as the needles used for injection are often not sterile, and pathogens such as the hepatitis virus can be introduced into the body. The sharing of needles by heroin addicts has been a major method by which HIV has spread from one person to another.

It is possible for a heroin addict to win the battle against his or her addiction, but it needs a great deal of will-power and much help from others. The withdrawal symptoms that an addict suffers after a few hours without the drug can be extremely unpleasant, and even life threatening.

In the brain, there are many different neurotransmitters that transfer nerve impulses across synapses from one neurone to another. We have seen that there are receptors on the cell surface membrane of the second neurone, which have a shape into which the neurotransmitter molecules precisely fit.

One group of these neurotransmitters is called endorphins. Endorphins help to reduce sensations of pain, affect mood and reduce sensations of hunger and thirst. One situation in which endorphins are produced is when we do exercise – this is why exercise often has a 'feel-good' effect.

When it enters the brain, heroin is metabolised to morphine. Morphine molecules fit into some of the endorphin receptors. This is why heroin makes people feel good. Unfortunately, taking heroin can reduce the production of natural endorphins, and also affect the brain's production of other important neurotransmitters. Users often find that they have to keep taking more and more heroin to get the same effect and, if they stop using it, will suffer extremely unpleasant withdrawal symptoms.

Alcohol

Alcohol is a very commonly used drug in many different countries. People often drink alcoholic drinks because they enjoy the effect that alcohol has on the brain. Alcohol can make people feel more relaxed and release their inhibitions, making it easier for them to enjoy themselves and to mix and interact with other people.

Alcohol is quickly absorbed through the wall of the stomach, and carried all over the body in the blood. It is eventually broken down by the liver, but this takes quite a long time.

Drinking fairly small quantities of alcohol is not dangerous, but alcohol does have many effects on the body which can be very dangerous if care is not taken.

♦ **Alcohol lengthens reaction time.**
   Alcohol is a depressant, which means that even small amounts of alcohol slow down the actions of parts of the brain, so alcohol lengthens the time you take to respond to a stimulus. This can mean the difference between life and death – often someone else's death – if the affected person is driving a car. A very high

proportion of road accidents involve people who have recently drunk alcohol – either drivers or pedestrians (Figure 15.4). Most countries in which drinking alcohol is allowed have legal limits on blood alcohol level when you drive. However, we now know that even very small quantities of alcohol increase the risk of an accident, so the only safe rule is not to drink alcohol at all if you drive.

Figure 15.4 Many road accidents would not happen if no-one drank alcohol before driving.

- **Alcohol can increase aggression in some people.**
  Different people react differently to alcohol. In some people, it increases their feelings of aggression, and releases their inhibitions so that they are more likely to be violent or commit other crimes. They may be violent towards members of their family. Research has shown that at least 50% of violence in the home in many countries is related to drunkenness, and that alcohol has played a part in the criminal behaviour of around 60% of people in prison in western countries.
- **Large intakes of alcohol can kill.**
  Every year, people die as a direct result of drinking a lot of alcohol over a short period of time. Alcohol is a poison. Large intakes of alcohol can result in unconsciousness, coma and even death. Sometimes, death is caused by a person vomiting when unconscious, and then suffocating because their airways are blocked by vomit.

Alcoholism

Alcoholism is a disease in which a person cannot manage without alcohol. The cause of the disease is not fully understood. Although it is obvious that you cannot become an alcoholic if you never drink alcohol, many people regularly drink large quantities of alcohol, but do not become alcoholics. Probably, there are many factors which decide whether or not a person becomes alcoholic. They may include a person's genes, their personality, and the amount of stress in their lives.

An alcoholic needs to drink quite large quantities of alcohol regularly. This causes many parts of the body to be damaged, because alcohol is poisonous to cells. The liver is often damaged, because it is the liver which has the job of breaking down drugs such as alcohol in the body. One form of liver disease resulting from alcohol damage is cirrhosis, where fibres grow in the liver (Figure 15.5). This can be fatal.

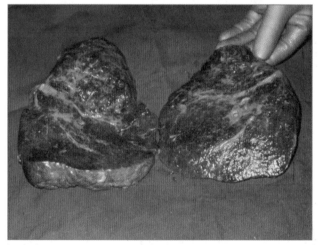

Figure 15.5 This was a person's liver. She was a heavy drinker, and you can see that there are fibres and dark areas in her liver. This is cirrhosis.

Excessive alcohol drinking also damages the brain. Over a long period of time, it can cause loss of memory and confusion. One way in which the damage is done is that alcohol in the body fluids draws water out of cells by osmosis. When this happens to brain cells, they shrink, and may be irreversibly damaged. This osmotic effect is made worse because alcohol inhibits the release of a hormone which stops the kidneys from allowing too much water to leave the body in the urine. So drinking alcohol causes a lot of dilute urine to be produced, resulting in low levels of water in the blood.

Anabolic steroids

Some hormones belong to a class of chemicals called steroids. Steroid hormones include the reproductive hormones testosterone, oestrogen and progesterone.

Many steroid hormones stimulate metabolic reactions in body cells that build up large molecules from small ones. These reactions are called anabolic reactions. Steroid hormones that stimulate these reactions are called anabolic steroids.

One type of reaction that is stimulated by anabolic steroids is the synthesis of proteins from amino acids. Testosterone, for example, causes more proteins to be made in muscles, so that muscles become larger and stronger.

You can see that this could help someone to compete successfully in some kinds of sport. Athletes and others have taken anabolic steroids to increase their muscle size and strength. These hormones can help athletes to train harder and for longer periods of time. They also increase aggression, which could give someone an edge in competition.

The use of anabolic steroids in sport is banned. Apart from giving someone an unfair advantage, taking anabolic steroids carries a serious health risk. For example, these substances decrease the ability of the immune system to destroy pathogens, and they can damage the liver.

In most sports there is a testing regime that checks for the presence of anabolic steroids in a person's blood or urine (Figure 15.6). The tests can be done at any time, not just when a person is competing. This is because drugs such as anabolic steroids can have effects that last

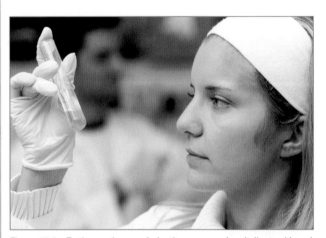

Figure 15.6 Testing a urine sample for the presence of anabolic steroids and their break-down products.

long after the time when the drugs are still present in the body. In the past, athletes may have 'got away' with cheating by stopping taking the drugs several weeks before their competition took place. Now they know that a tester can turn up at any time, without notice.

15.4 Tobacco smoking

Everyone knows that smoking damages your health, but still people do it. Figure 15.7 shows smoking rates in some countries.

Figure 15.8 shows the main components of tobacco smoke. There are, in fact, many more substances in tobacco smoke, and researchers are still finding out more about them, and the damage that each of them can do to the smoker's health.

One public health concern is that these dangers exist for both smokers and non-smokers. The possible damage is just as real for non-smokers who are in a smokers' environment. They breathe in smoke from burning cigarettes, and from smoke exhaled by smokers. This is termed passive smoking. In many countries, smoking is now banned in all public places. It is also very strongly recommended that parents do not smoke anywhere near their children.

Nicotine affects the brain. It is a stimulant, which means it makes a person feel more alert. Nicotine is an addictive drug. This is why smokers often find it extremely difficult to give up.

Nicotine damages the circulatory system, making blood vessels get narrower. This can increase blood pressure, leading to hypertension. Smokers have a much greater chance of developing coronary heart disease than non-smokers.

Tar contains many different chemicals, some of which are carcinogens – that is, they can cause cancer. The chemicals can affect the behaviour of some of the cells in the respiratory passages and the lungs, causing them to divide uncontrollably. The cells divide over and over again, forming a lump or tumour. If this tumour is malignant, this is cancer. Cells may break away from the first tumour and spread to other parts of the body, where new tumours will grow. Almost everyone who gets lung cancer is a smoker, or has lived or worked in an environment where they have been breathing in other people's cigarette smoke. Smoking cigarettes increases the risk of developing many different kinds of cancer. All forms of cancer are more common in smokers than in non-smokers.

Carbon monoxide is a poisonous gas which affects the blood. The carbon monoxide diffuses from the lungs into the blood, and combines with haemoglobin inside the red blood cells. This means that less oxygen can be carried. The body cells are therefore deprived of oxygen. This is not good for anyone, but it is especially harmful for a baby growing in its mother's uterus. When the mother smokes, the baby gets all the harmful chemicals in its blood. The carbon monoxide can prevent it from growing properly.

Smoke particles are little particles of carbon and other materials that are present in cigarette smoke. They get trapped inside the lungs. White blood cells try to remove them, and secrete chemicals that are intended to get rid of these invading particles. Unfortunately, the chemicals secreted by the white blood cells can do serious damage to the lungs themselves, resulting in chronic obstructive pulmonary disease (COPD). The delicate walls of the alveoli tend to break down (Figure 15.9). There is therefore less surface area across which gas exchange can take place. The person is said to have emphysema. They find it difficult to get enough oxygen into their blood. A person with emphysema may not be able to do anything at all active, and eventually

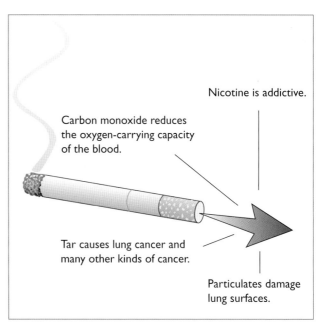

Nicotine is addictive.

Carbon monoxide reduces the oxygen-carrying capacity of the blood.

Tar causes lung cancer and many other kinds of cancer.

Particulates damage lung surfaces.

Figure 15.8 Some of the substances in tobacco smoke.

they may not even have the energy to walk.

Several of the chemicals in cigarette smoke harm the cells lining the respiratory passages. You may remember that these cells clean the air as it passes through, stopping bacteria and dust particles from getting down to the lungs (page 145). Figure 15.10 shows how smoking affects this cleaning mechanism.

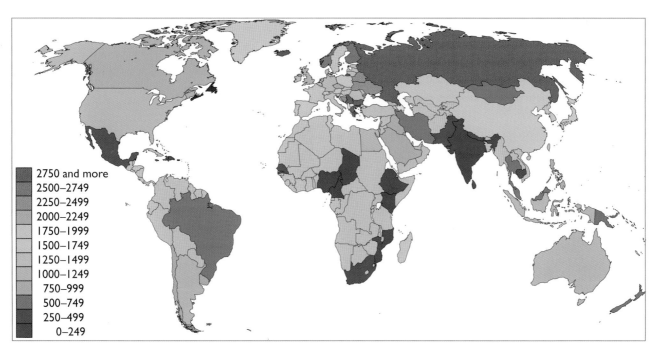

2750 and more
2500–2749
2250–2499
2000–2249
1750–1999
1500–1749
1250–1499
1000–1249
750–999
500–749
250–499
0–249

Figure 15.7 The map shows the mean number of cigarettes smoked per person, per year.

S Smoking and heart disease

Smoking increases the risk of developing high blood pressure. As the blood passes through the lungs, it absorbs many substances from cigarette smoke. Some of these make the walls of the arteries get thicker and harder. The walls cannot stretch and recoil as easily as the blood surges through them. Smoking also makes it more likely that a blood clot will form inside blood vessels, including the coronary arteries that supply the wall of the heart with oxygenated blood.

Smoking and lung cancer

It was in the 1950s that people first began to realise that there was a link between smoking cigarettes and getting lung cancer. The person at the forefront of this new understanding was a medical researcher called Richard Doll (Figure 15.11).

At that time, doctors were becoming concerned about the rapid rise of lung cancer in the British population. No-one knew why this was happening. Richard Doll interviewed lung cancer patients in 20 hospitals in London, trying to find out if they had anything in common. His initial theory was that this was something to do with the new substance, tarmac, that was being used to build roads. However, it rapidly became clear to him that all of these people were smokers. Very quickly, he himself stopped smoking.

Doll published the results of his research in a journal in 1950, but it was many years before everyone was prepared to accept the link between smoking and lung cancer. The difficulty was that you could not really do a controlled experiment on it. Instead, researchers had

Normal airway

Cilia beat and sweep mucus up to the mouth.

Airway of a smoker

There are fewer cilia and those that remain work less well.

Goblet cells work faster than usual, producing extra mucus.

Mucus trickles down to the lungs and stays there.

The mucus provides a good place for bacteria to live. The bacteria can cause chronic (long-term) infections in the lungs and bronchi. Mucus in the lungs makes it difficult for oxygen and carbon dioxide to diffuse between the alveoli and the blood.

Figure 15.10   How smoking damages the respiratory system.

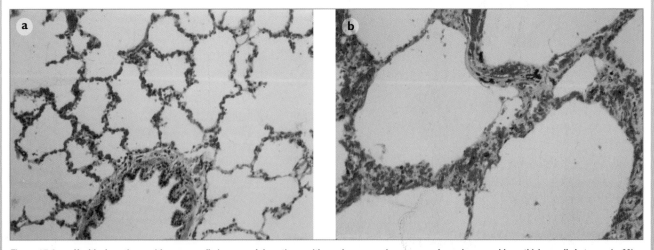

Figure 15.9   a Healthy lung tissue with many small air spaces, **b** lung tissue with emphysema – air spaces are fewer, larger and have thicker walls between (× 60).

to rely on looking for a correlation between these two factors. The graphs in Figure 15.12 show that there is a correlation between the number of cigarettes smoked per year and the number of deaths from lung cancer.

For many years, tobacco companies tried to play down this link. They suggested many other possible reasons for the correlation, because they did not want people to stop smoking. However, much research has now been done on the effects of smoking on health, and we now understand how smoking – both passive and active – can cause lung and other cancers.

For example, we know that tar contains chemicals that affect the DNA in cell nuclei. These chemicals can damage the normal control mechanisms of a cell, so that it begins to divide over and over again. This is how cancer begins. Chemicals that can cause this to happen are called carcinogens. Tar in cigarette smoke contains many different carcinogens.

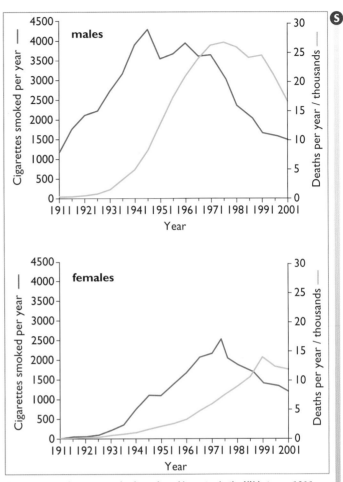

Figure 15.12   Lung cancer deaths and smoking rates in the UK between 1911 and 2001.

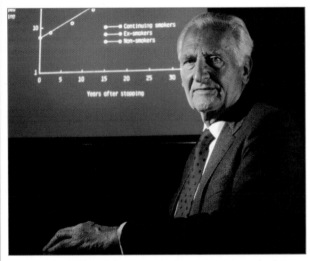

Figure 15.11   Richard Doll, who was the first person to recognise that smoking causes lung cancer.

Summary

You should know:
- ♦ what is meant by the term drug
- ♦ about antibiotics, and why we need to limit their use
- ♦ the effects of the abuse of heroin
- ♦ the effects of excessive consumption of alcohol
- ♦ how tobacco smoking affects the gas exchange system and the circulatory system
- ♦ the evidence for the link between smoking and lung cancer
- ♦ about the misuse of anabolic steroids to improve sporting performance.

End-of-chapter questions

1 Explain the difference between each of the following pairs of terms.

    a   stimulant, depressant, **b** carbon dioxide, carbon monoxide, **c** cirrhosis, COPD, **d** tar, nicotine

2 Suggest explanations for each of the following statements.

    a   Antibiotics cannot be used to treat influenza.
    b   People who smoke cigarettes usually find it very difficult to give up.
    c   Heroin users have a high risk of getting HIV/AIDS.
    d   Passive smoking can cause lung cancer.

Ⓢ 3 This question is about the graphs in Figure **15.12**.

    a   Describe how
        i   the number of cigarettes smoked per year by males changed between 1911 and 2001
        ii   the number of deaths from lung cancer per year in males changed between 1911 and 2001.   **[4]**
    b   Discuss the extent to which the graph for males provides evidence that smoking cigarettes
        causes lung cancer.   **[5]**
    c   If the graph for females is also considered, does this strengthen or weaken this evidence?
        Explain your answer.   **[3]**

4 Information was collected about the relative death rates of men in different categories. The men were divided into categories according to whether they smoked or not, and if they did smoke, at what age they started. The data are shown in the bar chart below.

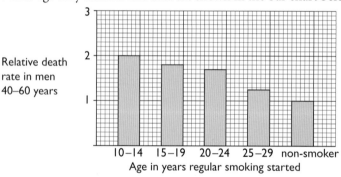

The men in the study were also divided into categories according to the number of cigarettes smoked per day. These data are shown in the table below.

Number of cigarettes smoked each day	Relative death rates in men 40–60 yrs
0	1.0
1–9	1.6
10–19	2.0
20–29	2.2
30–39	2.4

    a   Using the data in the table, draw a bar chart similar to one shown above.   **[4]**
    b   Using the information in the above graph and the graph you drew, state **three** different conclusions
        about the connection between cigarette smoking and risk of dying between ages 40–60 years.   **[3]**

16 Reproduction in plants

In this chapter, you will find out about:

♦ the differences between asexual and sexual reproduction
♦ the structure and functions of the parts of a flower
♦ pollination and fertilisation in flowers
♦ conditions that affect germination of seeds.

Bananas

Bananas are one of the world's favourite fruits. Wild banana plants grow in Asia, and it is thought that people first began to grow them as crops in New Guinea, about 10 000 years ago. The fruits of wild banana plants contain seeds. Reproducing by producing seeds is a type of sexual reproduction. The new plants that grow from the seeds are all a little bit different from each other. One of the advantages of this is that, if a new disease strikes, then at least some of the individual plants are likely to have resistance to it and will survive.

However, modern banana cultivars have been bred to be seedless. The only way of propagating the plants is to dig up suckers that grow from a mature plant, and plant them so that they will grow into new plants. A sucker is a stem, with roots, that grows out of the parent plant. Suckers are produced by asexual reproduction, and they have exactly the same genes as their parent.

One particularly popular variety of banana is called Cavendish. Because they are always propagated asexually, all Cavendish banana plants are genetically identical to one another. And this could mean that, before long, there will no longer be any Cavendish bananas. Every Cavendish banana plant is susceptible to a fungal disease called Panama disease (Figure **16.1**). This fungus cannot be killed with fungicides. As the disease spreads across the world, scientists and breeders are working hard to try to produce new varieties of banana to replace Cavendish.

Figure 16.1   These banana plants in South Africa are being killed by Panama disease.

16.1 Asexual reproduction

Reproduction is one of the fundamental characteristics of all living things. Each kind of organism has its own particular method of reproducing, but all of these methods fit into one of two categories – asexual reproduction or sexual reproduction.

In reproduction, each new organism obtains a set of chromosomes from its parent or parents. Chromosomes are long threads of DNA found in the nucleus of a cell, and they contain sets of instructions known as genes. As you will find out in Chapter 18, these genes vary slightly from one another in different individuals.

Asexual reproduction involves just one parent. Some of the parent organism's cells divide by a kind of cell division called mitosis (page 232). This cell division produces new cells that contain exactly the same genes as the parent cell, and so they are said to be genetically identical. They grow into new organisms, which are all genetically identical to each other and to their single parent.

An example of asexual reproduction

Many plants are able to reproduce asexually, and gardeners and farmers make use of this. Asexual reproduction can quickly and efficiently produce many new plants, all genetically identical to one another. This is advantageous to the grower if the original plant had exactly the characteristics that are wanted, such as large and attractive flowers, or good flavour, or high yield.

Potatoes, for example, reproduce using stem tubers (Figure 16.2). Some of the plant's stems grow normally, above ground, producing leaves, which photosynthesise. Other stems grow under the soil. Swellings called tubers form on them. Sucrose is transported from the leaves into these underground stem tubers, where it is converted into starch and stored. The tubers grow larger and larger. Each plant can produce many stem tubers.

❓ Questions

16.1 Explain why offspring produced by asexual reproduction are genetically identical to each other.

16.2 Explain why a gardener might choose to propagate a plant asexually.

16.3 What is a stem tuber?

The tubers are harvested, to be used as food. Some of them, however, are saved to produce next year's crop. These tubers are planted underground, where they grow shoots and roots to form a new plant. Because each potato plant produces many tubers, one plant can give rise to many new ones. To get more plants, tubers can be cut into several pieces. As long as each piece has a bud on it, it can grow into a complete new plant.

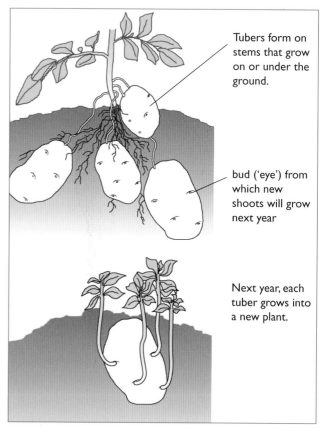

Tubers form on stems that grow on or under the ground.

bud ('eye') from which new shoots will grow next year

Next year, each tuber grows into a new plant.

Figure 16.2 Tuber formation in potatoes.

16.2 Sexual reproduction

In sexual reproduction, the parent organism produces sex cells called gametes. Eggs and sperm are examples of gametes. Two of these gametes join and their nuclei fuse together. This is called fertilisation. The new cell which is formed by fertilisation is called a zygote. The zygote divides again and again, and eventually grows into a new organism.

The zygote contains chromosomes from both its parents. It can have any combination of their genes. Sexual reproduction therefore produces offspring that are genetically different from each other and from their parents.

Gametes

Gametes are different from ordinary cells, because they contain only half as many chromosomes as usual. This is so that when two of them fuse together, the zygote they form will have the correct number of chromosomes.

Humans, for example, have 46 chromosomes in each of their body cells. But human egg and sperm cells only have 23 chromosomes each. When an egg and sperm fuse together at fertilisation, the zygote which is formed will therefore have 46 chromosomes, the normal number (Figure **16.3**).

The 46 chromosomes in an ordinary human cell are of 23 different kinds. There are two of each kind. This is because there are two sets of chromosomes in the cell. One set came from the father, and one set from the mother. A cell which has the full number of chromosomes, with two complete sets, is called a diploid cell.

An egg or sperm, though, only has 23 chromosomes – a single set. It is called a haploid cell. Gametes are always haploid. When two gametes fuse together, they form a diploid zygote.

The same is true for plants. For example, the cells of a eucalyptus tree have 22 chromosomes. Their male and female gametes each have 11 chromosomes. When these fuse together they produce a zygote, inside a seed, that has 22 chromosomes.

Gametes are made by ordinary cells dividing. For example, human sperm are made when cells in a testis divide. The gametes inside pollen grains are made when cells in anthers divide.

Because gametes need to have only half as many chromosomes as their parent cell, division by mitosis will not do. When gametes are being made, cells divide in a different way, called meiosis. This process is described in Chapter **18**.

In flowering plants and animals, meiosis only happens when gametes are being made. Meiosis produces new cells with only half as many chromosomes as the parent cell.

Key definitions

sexual reproduction – a process involving the fusion of the nuclei of two gametes to form a zygote and the production of offspring that are genetically different from each other

asexual reproduction – a process resulting in the production of genetically identical offspring from one parent

fertilisation – the fusion of gamete nuclei

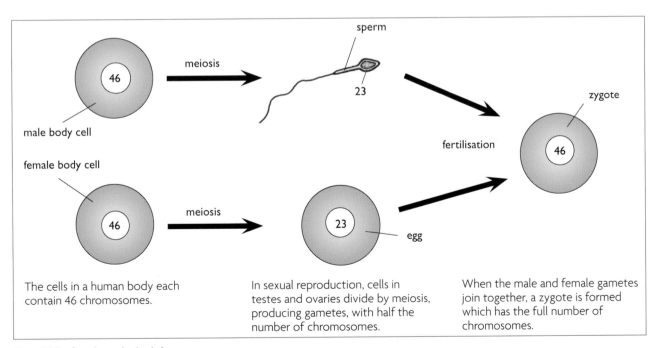

The cells in a human body each contain 46 chromosomes.

In sexual reproduction, cells in testes and ovaries divide by meiosis, producing gametes, with half the number of chromosomes.

When the male and female gametes join together, a zygote is formed which has the full number of chromosomes.

Figure 16.3 Sexual reproduction in humans.

Male gametes and female gametes

In many organisms, there are two different kinds of gamete. One kind is quite large, and does not move much. This is called the female gamete. In humans, the female gamete is the egg. In flowering plants the female gamete is a nucleus inside the ovule (Figures 16.4 and 16.6).

The other sort of gamete is smaller, and usually moves actively in search of the female gamete. This is called the male gamete. In humans, the male gamete is the sperm. In flowering plants, the male gamete is found inside the pollen grain. It does not move by itself, but is carried to the female gamete by a pollen tube (Figure 16.12, page 205).

Often, one organism can only produce one kind of gamete. Its sex is either male or female, depending on what kind of gamete it makes. All mammals, for example, are either male or female.

Sometimes, though, an organism can produce both sorts of gamete. Earthworms and slugs, for example, can produce both eggs and sperm. An organism which produces both male and female gametes is a hermaphrodite. Many flowering plants are also hermaphrodites.

Questions

16.4 What is a gamete?
16.5 What is a zygote?
16.6 Why do gametes contain only half the normal number of chromosomes?
16.7 What is meant by a diploid cell?
16.8 Name one part of your body where you have diploid cells.
16.9 What is meant by a haploid cell?
16.10 Give one example of a haploid cell.
16.11 When do cells divide by meiosis?
16.12 What is the purpose of meiosis?

16.3 Sexual reproduction in flowering plants

Flowers

Many flowering plants can reproduce in more than one way. Often, they can reproduce asexually and also sexually, by means of flowers.

The function of a flower is to make gametes, and to ensure that fertilisation will take place. Figure 16.4 illustrates the structure of an insect-pollinated flower.

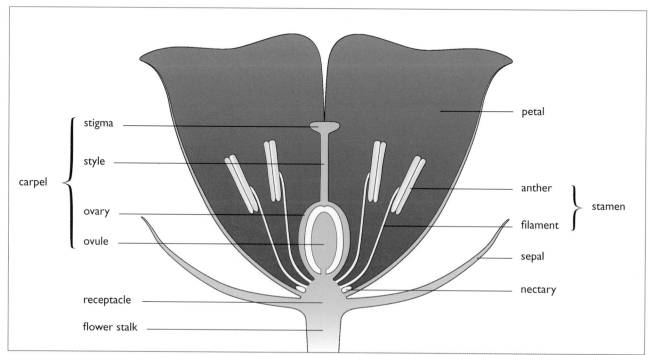

Figure 16.4   A generalised flower.

Figure **16.5** shows flowers of *Eucryphia* which makes both male and female gametes, so it is a hermaphroditic flower. Most, but not all, flowers are hermaphrodites.

On the outside of the flower are the sepals. The sepals protect the flower while it is a bud. Sepals are normally green.

Just inside the sepals are the petals. These are often brightly coloured. The petals attract insects to the flower. The petals of some flowers have lines running from top to bottom. These lines are called guide-lines, because they guide insects to the base of the petal. Here, there is a gland called a nectary. The nectary makes a sugary liquid called nectar, which insects feed on.

Inside the petals are the stamens. These are the male parts of the flower. Each stamen is made up of a long filament, with an anther at the top. The anthers contain pollen grains, which contain the male gametes.

The female part of the flower is in the centre. It consists of one or more carpels. A carpel contains an ovary. Inside the ovary are many ovules, which contain the female gametes. At the top of the ovary is the style, with a stigma at the tip. The function of the stigma is to catch pollen grains.

Figure 16.5 *Eucryphia* flowers.

The female parts of different kinds of flower vary. One of the differences is the arrangement of the ovules in the ovary. Figure **16.6** shows one arrangement.

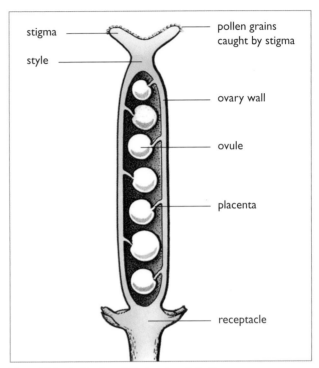

Figure 16.6 Section through the female part of a flower.

Pollen grains and ovules

The male gametes are inside the pollen grains, which are made in the anthers.

Figure **16.7a** illustrates a young anther, as it looks before the flower bud opens. You can see in Figure **16.7b** that the anther has four spaces or pollen sacs inside it. Some of the cells around the edge of the pollen sacs divide by meiosis to make pollen grains. When the flower bud opens, the anthers split open (Figure **16.7c**). Now the pollen is on the outside of the anther.

The pollen looks like a fine powder. It is often yellow. Under the microscope, you can see the shape of individual grains (Figure **16.8**). Pollen grains from different kinds of flower have different shapes. Each grain is surrounded by a hard coat, so that it can survive in difficult conditions if necessary. The coat protects the male gametes that are inside the grains, as the pollen is carried from one flower to another.

The female gametes are inside the ovules, in the **S** ovary. They have also been made by meiosis. Each ovule contains a nucleus. Fertilisation happens when a pollen grain nucleus fuses with an ovule nucleus.

Pollination

For fertilisation to take place, the male gametes must travel to the female gametes. The first stage of this journey is for pollen to be taken from the anther where it was made, to a stigma. This is called pollination.

Pollination is often carried out by insects (Figure **16.9**). Insects such as honey bees come to the flowers, attracted by their colour and strong sweet scent. The bee follows the guide-lines to the nectaries, brushing past the anthers as it goes. Some of the pollen sticks to its body.

The bee then goes to another flower, looking for more nectar. Some of the pollen it picked up at the first flower sticks onto the stigma of the second flower when the bee brushes past it. The stigma is sticky, and many pollen grains get stuck on it. If the second flower is from the same species of plant as the first, pollination has taken place.

Key definition

pollination – the transfer of pollen grains from the male part of the plant (anther of stamen) to the female part of the plant (stigma)

Figure 16.8   These pollen grains from a daisy flower are sticking to the surface of a petal. The electron micrograph is magnified about ×800.

Figure 16.9   The bee has come to the flower to collect nectar. Pollen gets stuck to its body, and the bee will then carry this to the next flower it visits.

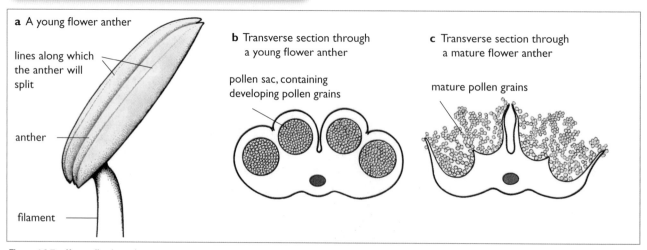

a A young flower anther

lines along which the anther will split

anther

filament

b Transverse section through a young flower anther

pollen sac, containing developing pollen grains

c Transverse section through a mature flower anther

mature pollen grains

Figure 16.7   How pollen is made.

Activity 16.1
Investigating the structure of a flower

Skills
AO3.3 Observing, measuring and recording
AO3.4 Interpreting and evaluating observations and data

 Take care with the sharp knife blade.

During this investigation, make large, labelled drawings of the structures that you observe.

1   Take an open, fresh-looking flower. Can you suggest two ways in which the flower advertises itself to insects?

2   Gently remove the sepals from the outside of the flower. Look at the sepals on a flower bud, near the top of the stem. What is the function of the sepals?

3   Now remove the petals from your flower. Make a labelled drawing of one of them, to show the markings. What is the function of these markings?

4   Find the stamens. If you have a young flower, there will be pollen on the anthers at the top of the stamens. Dust some onto a microscope slide, and look at it under a microscope. Draw a few pollen grains.

5   Now remove the stamens. What do you think is the function of the filaments?

6   Using a hand lens, try to find the nectaries at the bottom of the flower. What is their function?

7   The carpel is now all that is left of the flower. Find an ovary, style and stigma. Look at the stigma under a binocular microscope or a lens. What is its function, and how is it adapted to perform it?

8   Using a sharp blade, make a clean cut lengthways through the ovary, style and stigma. You have made a longitudinal section. Find the ovules inside the ovary. How big are they? What colour are they? About how many are there?

Activity 16.2
Pollination

Skills
AO3.2 Planning
AO3.3 Observing, measuring and recording
AO3.4 Interpreting and evaluating observations and data

You are going to design and carry out an investigation to test this hypothesis:

Bees visit yellow flowers more often than flowers of other colours.

You will need to carry out this investigation outdoors. It will be much easier to control variables if you make artificial flowers rather than using real ones. You can make them using coloured plastic to make 'petals', surrounding a central area where you can put a little pot of sugar solution. You will need to do your experiment on a sunny day, when there are plenty of bees flying.

Remember to think about controlling variables. Think carefully about exactly how you will count the bee visits, how you will record them and how you will display your results.

Write a simple conclusion from your results, and then discuss the results in the light of what you know about pollination. (You might also be interested in finding out about how bees see colour.) Evaluate your experiment, and suggest improvements you could make.

⑤ Self- and cross-pollination

Sometimes, pollen is carried to the stigma of the same flower, or to another flower on the same plant. This is called self-pollination.

If pollen is taken to a flower on a different plant of the same species, this is called cross-pollination. If pollen lands on the stigma of a different species of plant, the pollen grain usually dies.

Wind-pollination

In some plants, it is the wind which carries the pollen between flowers. Figure **16.10** shows a grass flower, which is an example of a wind-pollinated flower. Figure **16.11** shows pollen grains from a grass flower.

Table **16.1** compares insect-pollinated and wind-pollinated flowers.

Figure 16.11   Grass pollen (magnified ×35 000).

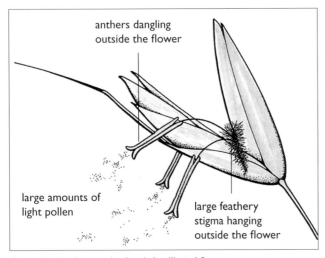

Figure 16.10   An example of a wind-pollinated flower.

Key definitions

self-pollination – the transfer of pollen grains ⑤
from the anther of a flower to the stigma of the
same flower, or a different flower on the same
plant

cross-pollination – the transfer of pollen grains
from the anther of a flower to the stigma of a
flower on a different plant of the same species

Insect-pollinated	Wind-pollinated
large, conspicuous petals, often with guide-lines	small, inconspicuous petals, or no petals at all
often strongly scented	no scent
often have nectaries at the base of petals	no nectaries
anthers inside flower, where insect has to brush past them to reach nectar	anthers dangling outside the flower, where they catch the wind
stigma inside flower, where insect has to brush past it to reach nectar	stigmas large and feathery and dangling outside the flower, where pollen in the air may land on it
sticky or spiky pollen grains, which stick to insects	smooth, light pollen, which can be blown in the wind
quite large quantities of pollen made, because some will be eaten or will be delivered to the wrong kind of flower	very large quantities of pollen made, because most will be blown away and lost

Table 16.1   A comparison between insect-pollinated and wind-pollinated flowers.

Fertilisation

After pollination, the male gamete inside the pollen grain on the stigma still has not reached the female gamete. The female gamete is inside the ovule, and the ovule is inside the ovary.

If it has landed on the right kind of stigma, the pollen grain begins to grow a tube. You can try growing some pollen tubes, in Activity **16.3**. The pollen tube grows down through the style and the ovary, towards the ovule (Figure **16.12**). It secretes enzymes to digest a pathway through the style.

The ovule is surrounded by several layers of cells called the integuments. At one end, there is a small hole in the integuments, called the **micropyle**. The pollen tube grows through the micropyle, into the ovule.

The pollen nucleus (male gamete) travels along the pollen tube, and into the ovule. It fuses with the ovule nucleus (female gamete). Fertilisation has now taken place. One pollen grain can only fertilise one ovule. If there are many ovules in the ovary, then many pollen grains will be needed to fertilise them all.

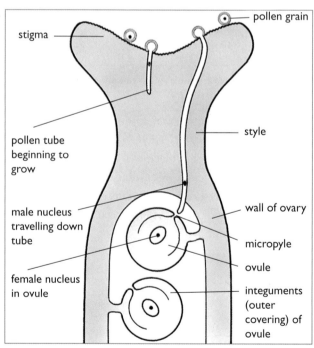

Figure 16.12 Fertilisation in a flower.

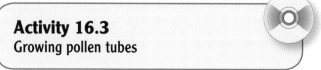

Activity 16.3
Growing pollen tubes

Seeds

Once the ovules have been fertilised, many of the parts of the flower are not needed any more. The sepals, petals and stamens have all done their job. They wither, and fall off.

Inside the ovary, the ovules start to grow. Each ovule now contains a **zygote**, which was formed at fertilisation. The zygote divides by mitosis to form an **embryo** plant.

The ovule is now called a **seed**. The integuments of the ovule become hard and dry, to form the testa of the seed. Water is withdrawn from the seed, so that it becomes dormant.

The embryo consists of a **radicle**, which will grow into a root, and a **plumule**, which will grow into a shoot (Figure **16.13**).

The seed also contains food for the embryo. In a bean seed, the food is stored in two cream-coloured **cotyledons**. These contain starch and protein. The cotyledons also contain enzymes. Surrounding the cotyledons is a tough, protective covering called the testa. The testa stops the embryo from being damaged and it prevents bacteria and fungi from entering the seed. The testa has a tiny hole in it – the micropyle. When a seed has been separated from the plant, near the micropyle there is a scar, the **hilum**, where the seed was joined to the pod (ovary).

The ovary also grows. It is now called a **fruit**.

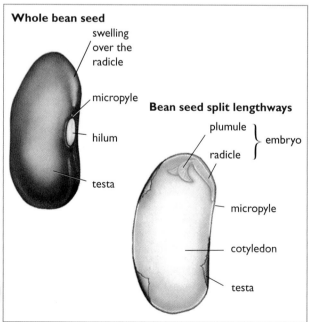

Figure 16.13 Structure of a bean seed.

Questions

16.13 What is the function of a flower?
16.14 In which part of a flower are male gametes made?
16.15 In which part of a flower are female gametes made?
16.16 What is pollination?
16.17 Why do wind-pollinated flowers usually produce more pollen than insect-pollinated ones?
16.18 After pollination, how does the male gamete reach the ovule?
16.19 What is a micropyle?
16.20 What happens to each of the following once a flower's female gametes have been fertilised?
    a   petals
    b   stamens
    c   zygote
    d   ovule
    e   integuments of the ovules
    f   ovary

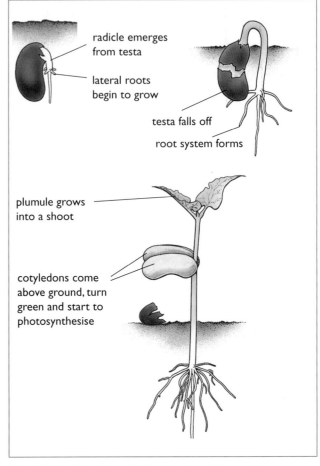

Figure 16.14   Stages in germination of one type of bean seed.

Seed germination

A seed contains hardly any water. When it was formed on the plant, the water in it was drawn out, so that it became dehydrated. Without water, almost no metabolic reactions can go on inside it. The seed is inactive or dormant. This is very useful, because it means that the seed can survive harsh conditions, such as cold or drought, which would kill a growing plant.

A seed must be in certain conditions before it will begin to germinate. You can find out what they are if you do Activity 16.4.

When a seed germinates, it first takes up water through the micropyle. As the water goes into the cotyledons, they swell. Eventually, they burst the testa (Figure 16.14).

Once there is sufficient water, the enzymes in the cotyledons become active. Amylase begins to break down the stored starch molecules to maltose. Proteases break down the protein molecules to amino acids.

Maltose and amino acids are soluble, so they dissolve in the water. They diffuse to the embryo plant, which uses these foods for growth.

Questions

16.21 What do the cotyledons of a bean seed contain?
16.22 What does dormant mean?
16.23 What is the advantage of seed dormancy?

16.24 What activates the enzymes in the cotyledons of a germinating seed?
16.25 What do the enzymes do?

Activity 16.4
To find the conditions necessary for the germination of tomato seeds

Skills
AO3.2 Planning
AO3.3 Observing, measuring and recording
AO3.4 Interpreting and evaluating observations and data

5 Construct a results table and begin to fill it in to show what conditions the seeds in each tube have.

6 Leave your seeds for a day or so. Then complete your results table to show which seeds have germinated.

 Pyrogallol is very caustic. Your teacher will handle it for you. You should not use it yourself.

1 Set up five tubes as shown in the diagram. Pyrogallol absorbs oxygen.

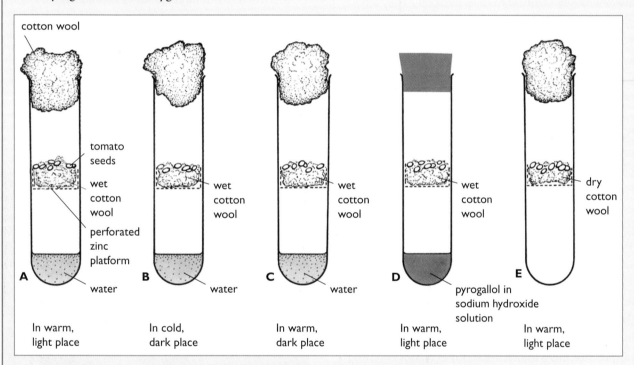

cotton wool

A — tomato seeds / wet cotton wool / perforated zinc platform / water
In warm, light place

B — wet cotton wool / water
In cold, dark place

C — wet cotton wool / water
In warm, dark place

D — wet cotton wool / pyrogallol in sodium hydroxide solution
In warm, light place

E — dry cotton wool
In warm, light place

2 Put tubes A, D and E in a warm place in the laboratory, in the light.

3 Put tube B in a refrigerator.

4 Put tube C in a warm, dark cupboard.

 **Questions**

A1 What three conditions do tomato seeds need for germination?

A2 Explain why each of these conditions is needed for successful germination.

Activity 16.5
To find the effect of storage time on the germination rate of seeds

ⓢ 16.4 Comparing sexual and asexual reproduction

Many plants can reproduce in two ways – asexually and sexually. Which is better?

In asexual reproduction, some of the parent's cells divide by mitosis. This makes new cells that are genetically identical to the parent cell. They are clones. Asexual reproduction does not produce genetic variation.

But in sexual reproduction, some of the parent's cells divide by meiosis. The new cells that are made are called gametes, and they have only half as many chromosomes as the parent cell. When two sets of chromosomes in the two gametes combine at fertilisation, a new combination of genes is produced. So sexual reproduction produces offspring that are genetically different from their parents.

Is it useful or not to have genetic variation among offspring? This depends on the circumstances.

Sometimes, it is a good thing not to have any variation. If a plant, for example, is growing well in a particular place, then it must be well adapted to its environment. If its offspring all inherit the same genes, then they will be equally well adapted and are likely to grow well. This is especially true if there is plenty of space for them in that area. However, if it is getting crowded, then it may not be a good thing for the parent to produce new offspring that grow all around it.

Another advantage of asexual reproduction is that a single organism can reproduce on its own. It does not need to wait to be pollinated, or to find a mate. This can be good if there are not many of those organisms around – perhaps there is only a single one growing in an isolated place. In that case, asexual reproduction is definitely the best option. Do remember, though, that even a single plant may be able to reproduce sexually, by using self-pollination.

However, if the plant is not doing very well in its environment, or if a new disease has come along to which it is not resistant, then it could be an advantage for its offspring to be genetically different from it. There is a good chance that at least some of the offspring may be better adapted to that environment, or be resistant to that disease.

In flowering plants, sexual reproduction produces seeds, which are likely to be dispersed over a wide area. This spreads the offspring far away from the parents, so that they are less likely to compete with them. It also allows them to colonise new areas.

You will find out more about variation, and its importance for evolution, in Chapter **19**.

Farmers and other commercial plant growers also make use of these two possible methods of propagating their plants. For example, if a rose grower wants to produce many more rose plants that will have flowers exactly the same as the parent plant, they will use asexual reproduction (Figure **16.15**). But if they want to

Figure 16.15   All the roses in each row are genetically identical to each other – they have been produced using asexual reproduction. The different varieties of roses have been produced using sexual reproduction.

❓ Questions

16.26 Do you think that cross-pollination is likely to result in more or less variation amongst the offspring than self-pollination? Explain your answer.

16.27 Suggest some advantages and disadvantages of self-pollination to a species of plant.

S produce a new variety of rose, they will breed together two different rose plants, using sexual reproduction. They can then grow the seeds that are produced, each of which will grow into a plant that isn't quite the same as any of the others. With luck, one of these might prove to be a commercial success.

We have seen that, if growers rely on producing new plants by asexual reproduction over long periods of time, they run the risk of all their plants becoming vulnerable to attack by a pest or disease. This has happened with some varieties of bananas. Breeders are now going back to wild banana plants, and trying new breeding programmes, using sexual reproduction, to try to produce new varieties to replace the old ones.

Summary

You should know:
♦   the differences between asexual reproduction and sexual reproduction
♦   the names of the parts of a flower, and what each part does
♦   how insect pollination and wind pollination take place
♦   differences between insect-pollinated and wind-pollinated flowers
♦   how fertilisation happens in a flower
S ♦   how to investigate the environmental conditions that seeds need to make them germinate
♦   the advantages and disadvantages to a plant species of reproducing asexually or sexually
♦   the advantages and disadvantages to farmers and other plant growers of making their plants reproduce asexually or sexually.

End-of-chapter questions

1   Match each of these words with its definition.

fertilisation	gamete	meiosis	mitosis
pollination	seed	zygote	

   a   a sex cell; it can be male or female
   b   a cell formed by the fusion of the nuclei of two gametes
   c   a type of cell division used in growth and asexual reproduction, which produces new cells genetically identical to the parent cell
   d   the transfer of pollen from an anther to a stigma
   e   an ovule after fertilisation
   f   the fusion of the nuclei of two gametes

2 Construct a two-column table, with the headings Asexual reproduction and Sexual reproduction.

Write each of these statements in the correct column.

- only one parent involved
- one or two parents involved
- involves gametes
- involves fertilisation
- zygote formed
- all offspring genetically identical
- genetic variation among offspring

3 a A student investigated the conditions needed for the germination of mustard seeds.
The diagram below shows the apparatus at the start of his experiment.
Tubes **A** to **D** were placed in the laboratory at room temperature. Tube **E** was placed in a freezer at −4 °C.

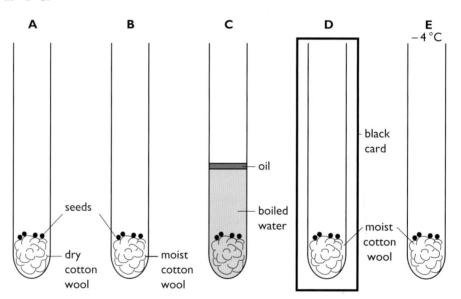

i Which **one** of these factors should the student have kept the same for all of the tubes? Choose from the list: age of seeds, amount of water, temperature. [1]

ii After three days, the seeds in tubes **B** and **D** had germinated.
The seeds in all the other tubes had not germinated.
Use these results to deduce the conditions needed for the germination of mustard seeds. [3]

b In a tropical rainforest, the trees often grow very closely together, which reduces the amount of light reaching the forest floor.
The seeds of many species of rainforest trees will not germinate unless they get plenty of light.

i Suggest why this is an advantage to the seedlings. [1]

ii In a separate experiment the student used seeds of rainforest trees.
State the tube in the diagram above in which the result would differ from those he obtained for mustard seeds. [1]

[Cambridge IGCSE® Combined Science 0653/22, Question 4, May/June 2010]

4 The diagram below shows a banana plant producing suckers.

a Name the type of reproduction that is shown in the diagram. [1]

b Describe **two** advantages to the growers of banana plants of using this type of reproduction to propagate their plants. [2]

c Banana plants can be killed by fungal diseases, such as black sigatoka and Panama disease. Explain why a population of bananas produced by the method shown in the diagram could all be wiped out by the same disease. [2]

5 The diagram below shows two types of primrose flower.

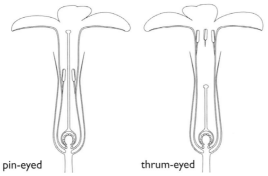

pin-eyed   thrum-eyed

These types of flower are often found growing close together. Any one primrose plant, however, only has one type of flower.

a Describe the difference in the arrangement of the anthers and stigmas in the pin-eyed and thrum-eyed primrose. [2]

b Primroses are pollinated by insects, which reach into the bottom of the flower to get nectar. Which part of the insect's body would pick up pollen in **i** a pin-eyed primrose and [1]
ii a thrum-eyed primrose? [1]

c Which part of the insect's body would touch the stigma in **i** a pin-eyed primrose and [1]
ii a thrum-eyed primrose? [1]

d Explain how this will help to ensure that cross-pollination takes place. [3]

e Self-pollination does sometimes occur in primroses. Would you expect it to occur more often in pin-eyed or thrum-eyed primroses? Explain your answer. [2]

f Explain the advantages of cross-pollination to a plant species. [2]

17 Reproduction in humans

In this chapter, you will find out about:

♦ the structure and functions of the male and female human reproductive systems
♦ fertilisation and development of the embryo
♦ the roles of the placenta
♦ ante-natal care and birth
♦ the menstrual cycle
♦ oestrogen, progesterone and testosterone
♦ methods of birth control
♦ some sexually transmitted infections.

The homunculus theory

In 1654, a Dutch scientist, Anton van Leeuwenhoek, looked down his microscope at a sample of semen (Figure 17.1). He was the first person to see sperm. However, he was too embarrassed to talk about his findings until a student, Johan Ham, spoke to him in 1677, about what he himself had seen when studying semen under the microscope. He said that he could see small animals with tails.

Leeuwenhoek gradually overcame his reluctance to talk about his findings, and shared them with other scientists. As more and more people continued these studies, various theories emerged about how human life began. One suggestion was that these 'small animals with tails' each contained a tiny human being – a homunculus. Indeed, in 1695 Nicholas Hartsoecker, a Dutch physicist, made a drawing of what he thought one might look like, though he made it clear that he never actually saw one through his microscope (Figure 17.2).

At this time, no-one understood that an egg was also involved in creating a new life. This caused difficulties in explaining why children resembled both their father and their mother. One idea was the little developing homunculus gradually absorbed characteristics of its mother as it developed inside her uterus.

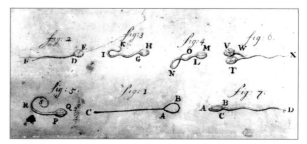

Figure 17.1 Leeuwenhoek's drawing of sperm.

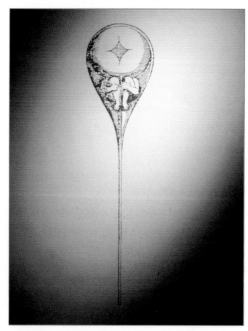

Figure 17.2 Nicholas Hartsoecker's drawing of a homunculus inside a sperm.

17.1 Human reproductive organs

Humans, like all mammals, reproduce sexually. A new life begins when a male gamete fuses with a female one, forming a zygote. This is how you and every other human being was formed.

The female reproductive organs.

Figure **17.3** shows the reproductive organs of a woman. The female gametes, called eggs, are made in the two **ovaries**. Leading away from the ovaries are the **oviducts**, sometimes called Fallopian tubes. They do not connect directly to the ovaries, but have a funnel-shaped opening just a short distance away.

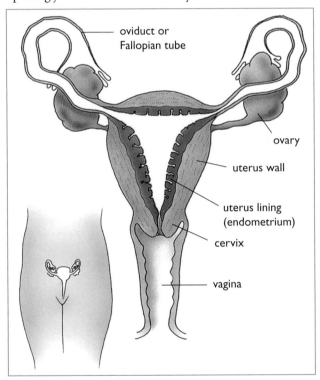

Figure 17.3 The female reproductive organs.

The two oviducts lead to the womb or **uterus**. This has very thick walls, made of muscle. It is quite small – only about the size of a clenched fist – but it can stretch a great deal when a woman is pregnant.

At the base of the uterus is a narrow opening, guarded by muscles. This is the neck of the uterus, or cervix. It leads to the vagina, which opens to the outside.

The opening from the bladder, called the urethra, runs in front of the vagina, while the rectum is just behind it. The three tubes open quite separately to the outside.

The male reproductive organs

Figure **17.4** and **17.5** shows the reproductive organs of a man. The male gametes, called spermatozoa or **sperm**, are made in two **testes** (singular: **testis**). These are outside the body, in two sacs of skin called the scrotum.

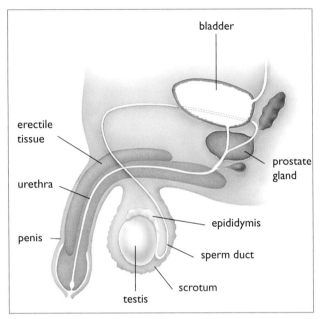

Figure 17.4 Side view of the male reproductive organs.

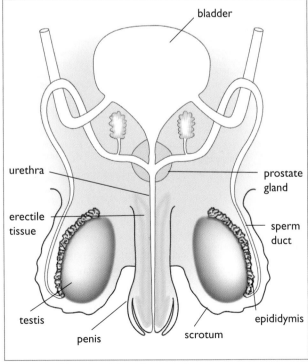

Figure 17.5 Front view of the male reproductive organs.

The sperm are carried away from each testis in a tube called the sperm duct. The sperm ducts from the testes join up with the urethra just below the bladder. The urethra continues downwards and opens at the tip of the penis. The urethra can carry both urine and sperm at different times.

Where the sperm ducts join the urethra, there is a gland called the prostate gland. This makes a fluid which the sperm swim in.

Egg production

Eggs begin to be formed inside a girl's ovaries before she is born. At birth, she will already have thousands of partly developed eggs inside her ovaries.

When she reaches puberty (page 221), some of these eggs will begin to mature. Usually, only one develops at a time. When it is mature (Figure 17.6), an egg cell bursts out of the ovary and into the funnel at the end of the oviduct. This is called ovulation. In humans, it happens once a month.

Sperm production

Figure 17.7 shows a section through a testis. It contains thousands of very narrow, coiled tubes or tubules. These are where the sperm are made. Sperm develop from cells in the walls of the tubules, which divide by meiosis. Sperm are made continually from puberty onwards. Figure 17.8 shows the structure of a sperm.

Sperm production is very sensitive to heat. If they get too hot, the cells in the tubules will not develop into sperm. This is why the testes are outside the body, where they are cooler than they would be inside.

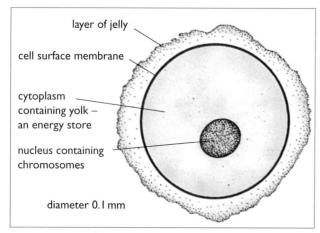

Figure 17.6   A human egg cell.

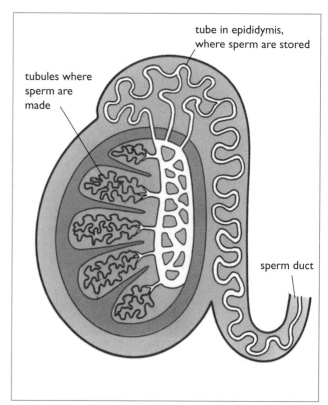

Figure 17.7   Section through a testis.

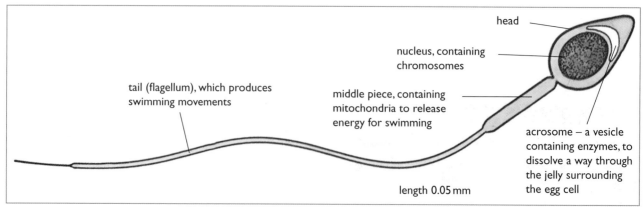

Figure 17.8   A human sperm.

17.2 Fertilisation and development

After ovulation, the egg is caught in the funnel of the oviduct. The funnel is lined with cilia which beat rhythmically, wafting the egg into the entrance of the oviduct.

Very slowly, the egg travels towards the uterus. Cilia lining the oviduct help to sweep it along. Muscles in the wall of the oviduct also help to move it, by peristalsis. (Figure 7.16 on page 83 shows peristalsis in the alimentary canal.)

If the egg is not fertilised by a sperm within 8–24 hours after ovulation, it will die. By this time, it has only travelled a short way along the oviduct. So a sperm must reach an egg while it is quite near the top of the oviduct if fertilisation is to be successful.

When the man is sexually excited, blood is pumped into spaces inside the penis, so that it becomes erect. To bring the sperm as close as possible to the egg, the man's penis is placed inside the vagina of the woman. This is called sexual intercourse.

Sperm are pushed out of the penis into the vagina. This happens when muscles in the walls of the tubes containing the sperm contract rhythmically. The wave of contraction begins in the testes, travels along the sperm ducts, and into the penis. The sperm are squeezed along, out of the man's urethra and into the woman's vagina. This is called ejaculation.

The fluid containing the sperm is called semen. Ejaculation deposits the semen at the top of the vagina, near the cervix.

The sperm are still quite a long way from the egg. They swim, using their tails, up through the cervix, through the uterus, and into the oviduct (Figure 17.9 and Figure 17.10).

Sperm can only swim at a rate of about 4 mm per minute, so it takes quite a while for them to get as far as the oviducts. Many will never get there at all. But one ejaculation deposits about a million sperm in the vagina, so there is a good chance that some of them will reach the egg.

One sperm enters the egg. Only the head of the sperm goes in; the tail is left outside. The nucleus of the sperm fuses with the nucleus of the egg. This is fertilisation (Figure 17.11).

As soon as the successful sperm enters the egg, the egg membrane becomes impenetrable, so that no other sperm can get in. The unsuccessful sperm will all die.

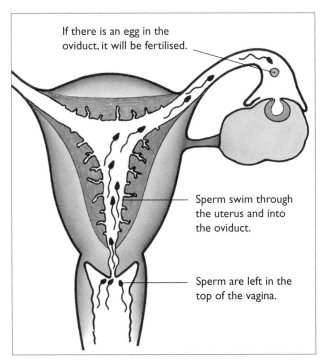

If there is an egg in the oviduct, it will be fertilised.

Sperm swim through the uterus and into the oviduct.

Sperm are left in the top of the vagina.

Figure 17.10 How sperm get to the egg (sperm and egg are drawn to different scales).

Figure 17.9 This sperm cell is swimming over the surfaces of the ciliated cells in the oviduct.

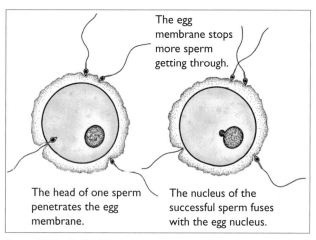

Figure 17.11 Fertilisation.

The egg membrane stops more sperm getting through.

The head of one sperm penetrates the egg membrane.

The nucleus of the successful sperm fuses with the egg nucleus.

Implantation

When the sperm nucleus and the egg nucleus have fused together, they form a zygote. The zygote continues to move slowly down the oviduct. As it goes, it divides by mitosis. After several hours, it has formed a ball of cells. This is called an **embryo**. The embryo obtains food from the yolk of the egg.

It takes several hours for the embryo to reach the uterus, and by this time it is a ball of 16 or 32 cells. The uterus has a thin, spongy lining, and the embryo sinks into it. This is called **implantation** (Figure 17.12).

The placenta and amnion

The cells in the embryo, now buried in the soft wall of the uterus, continue to divide. As the embryo grows, a **placenta** also grows, which connects it to the wall of the uterus (Figure 17.13). The placenta is soft and dark red, and has finger-like projections called villi. The villi fit closely into the uterus wall. The placenta is where substances are exchanged between the mother's blood and the embryo's blood. It is the embryo's life support system.

After eleven weeks, the embryo has developed into a **fetus**. The placenta is joined to the fetus by the **umbilical cord**. Inside the cord are two arteries and a vein. The arteries take blood from the fetus into the placenta, and the vein returns the blood to the fetus.

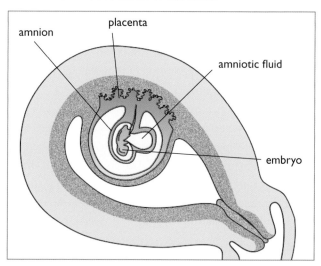

amnion
placenta
amniotic fluid
embryo

Figure 17.13 A developing embryo inside the uterus.

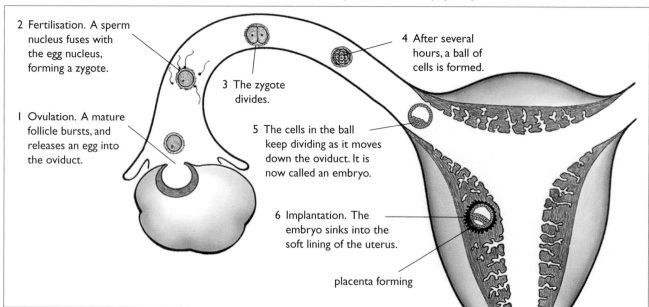

2 Fertilisation. A sperm nucleus fuses with the egg nucleus, forming a zygote.

3 The zygote divides.

4 After several hours, a ball of cells is formed.

1 Ovulation. A mature follicle bursts, and releases an egg into the oviduct.

5 The cells in the ball keep dividing as it moves down the oviduct. It is now called an embryo.

6 Implantation. The embryo sinks into the soft lining of the uterus.

placenta forming

Figure 17.12 Stages leading to implantation.

ⓢ In the placenta are capillaries filled with the fetus's blood (Figure **17.14**). In the wall of the uterus are large spaces filled with the mother's blood. The fetus's and mother's blood do not mix. They are separated by the wall of the placenta. But they are brought very close together, because the wall of the placenta is very thin.

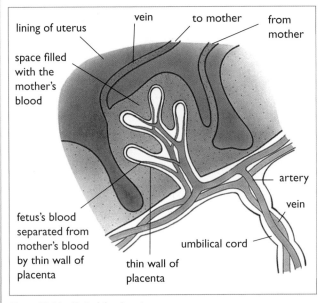

Figure 17.14   Part of the placenta.

Oxygen and food materials in the mother's blood diffuse across the placenta into the fetus's blood, and are then carried along the umbilical cord to the fetus. Carbon dioxide and waste materials diffuse the other way, and are carried away in the mother's blood. As the fetus grows, the placenta grows too. By the time the baby is born, the placenta will be a flat disc, about 12 cm in diameter, and 3 cm thick.

The fetus is surrounded by a strong membrane, called the amnion. This makes a liquid called amniotic fluid. This fluid helps to support the embryo, and to protect it.

Development of the embryo and fetus

When it first sinks into the lining of the uterus, the tiny embryo is just a simple ball of cells. All of these cells look identical to each other at this stage. They continue to divide, moving into position to start to form the organs of the new individual. The cells now begin to develop into different types, specialised for different functions. Some will become skin cells, some will be muscle cells, some will be blood cells and so on. The little ball of cells gradually becomes more and more complex.

By 6 weeks after fertilisation (Figure **17.15**), all the major organs are beginning to grow. By 8 weeks, the tiny embryo – still only about 1.5 cm long – has muscles and is starting to move. By 10 or 11 weeks, all of the organs are in place, and the embryo is now called a fetus.

From now on, the fetus grows steadily, until about 38 weeks after fertilisation, when it is ready to be born (Figure **17.16**).

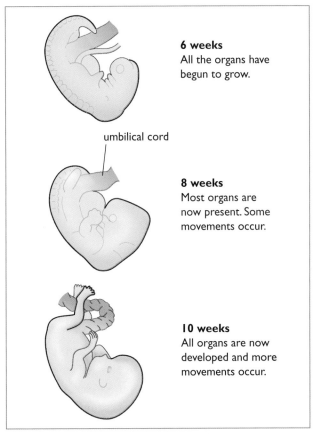

6 weeks
All the organs have begun to grow.

umbilical cord

8 weeks
Most organs are now present. Some movements occur.

10 weeks
All organs are now developed and more movements occur.

Figure 17.15   Stages in the development of an embryo.

❓ Questions

17.1   What is the name for the narrow opening between the uterus and the vagina?

17.2   Where is the prostate gland, and what is its function?

17.3   Explain how ovulation happens.

17.4   Where are sperm made?

17.5   How does an egg travel along the oviduct?

17.6   Where does fertilisation take place?

17.7   Compare the size, structure and ability to move of a sperm and an egg. **ⓢ**

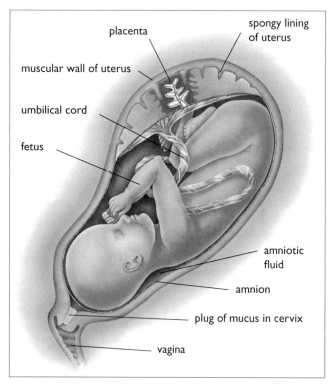

Figure 17.16   Side view of fetus in the uterus just before birth.

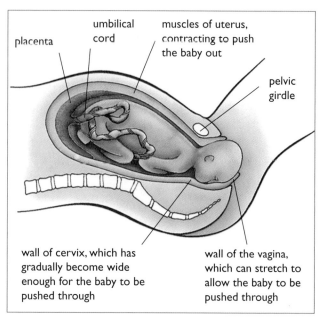

Figure 17.17   Birth.

Birth

A few weeks before birth, the fetus usually turns over in the uterus, so that it is lying head downwards. Its head lies just over the opening of the cervix.

Birth begins when the strong muscles in the wall of the uterus start to contract. This is called labour. To begin with, the contractions of the muscles slowly stretch the opening of the cervix. The amniotic sac usually breaks at this stage.

After several hours, the cervix is wide enough for the head of the baby to pass through. Now, the muscles start to push the baby down through the cervix and the vagina (Figure 17.17). This part of the birth happens quite quickly.

The baby is still attached to the uterus by the umbilical cord and the placenta. Now that it is in the open air, the baby can breathe for itself, so the placenta is no longer needed. The placenta falls away from the wall of the uterus, and passes out through the vagina. It is called the afterbirth.

The umbilical cord is cut, and clamped just above the point where it joins the baby. This is completely painless, because there are no nerves in the cord. The stump of the cord forms the baby's navel.

The contractions of the muscles of the uterus are painful. They feel rather like cramp. The mother can help herself a lot by preparing her body with exercises before labour begins, by breathing in a special way during labour, and she can also be given pain-killing drugs if she needs them.

Ante-natal care

When a woman is pregnant, she should take extra care of her health, both for her own benefit and that of her baby. This is sometimes called ante-natal care, meaning 'before birth'.

She should ensure that her diet contains plenty of calcium, to help to form the growing fetus's bones. She also needs extra iron, because her body will produce a lot of extra blood to help to carry oxygen and nutrients to the placenta, and her growing baby is also forming blood. Iron is needed to make the haemoglobin in the red blood cells. She may also need a little extra carbohydrate, because she needs extra energy to help to move her heavier body around, and extra protein, to help to form her growing fetus's new cells.

She should continue to take exercise. Most people consider that steady, gentle exercise is best, such as swimming or walking. She may also be given special exercises to do which will help her to stay fit during pregnancy, and also allow her to take an active part when she is giving birth.

S We have seen that many useful substances cross the placenta from the mother's blood to the fetus's blood. Unfortunately, harmful substances can cross, too. For example, if the mother smokes, nicotine and carbon monoxide can enter the baby's blood, and this can cause the baby to grow more slowly and be born smaller than if the mother was a non-smoker. A woman should never smoke during pregnancy. She also needs to take care not to drink too much alcohol, or to take any drug without advice from her doctor.

The mother also needs to avoid some illnesses. Rubella is caused by a virus, producing a rash and a fever. If the rubella virus crosses the placenta, it can cause serious harm to the fetus, who may be born deaf or with other disabilities. In many countries, teenage girls are offered vaccination against rubella.

Caring for a young baby

Although it has been developing for nine months, a human baby is very helpless when it is born. Usually, both parents help to care for it.

During pregnancy, the glands in the mother's breasts will have become larger. Soon after the birth of the baby, they begin to make milk. This is called lactation. Lactation happens in all mammals, but not in other animals.

Milk contains all the nutrients that the baby needs (Figure 17.18). It also contains antibodies (page **133**) which will help the baby to resist infection.

As well as being fed, the baby needs to be kept warm. Because it is so small, a baby has a large surface area in relation to its volume, so it loses heat very quickly.

It is extremely important that a young baby is cared for emotionally, as well as physically. Babies need a lot of close contact with their parents.

Most mammals care for their young by feeding them and keeping them warm. In humans, parental care also involves teaching the baby and young child how to look after itself, and how to live in society. This continues into its 'teens' – a much longer time than for any other animal.

S Breast-feeding and bottle feeding

Most people consider that feeding a baby on breast milk is much better than bottle-feeding. Formula milk is

Figure 17.18 Many mothers choose to breast-feed their babies.

bought as powder that is mixed with boiled (sterilised) **S** water. The baby then sucks this milk from a bottle.

This can make life easier for the mother, because she can hand over the feeding of her baby to someone else. It can also help the father to bond with the baby, if he helps to feed it.

However, formula milk is much more expensive than breast milk, which is free! And, unless the equipment used for making up the formula milk is kept clean, it is easy for bacteria to get into the milk and make the baby ill.

Another advantage of breast milk is that it contains antibodies from the mother, which help the baby to fight off infectious diseases. Breast-feeding also helps a close relationship to develop between the mother and her baby, which is beneficial to both of them.

The composition of breast milk changes as the baby grows, so that the nutrients it contains are exactly right for the different stages of its development.

17.8 What is implantation?

17.9 What is a fetus?

17.10 How is the fetus connected to the placenta?

17.11 List **two** substances which pass from the mother's blood into the fetus's blood.

17.12 Describe what happens to each of the following during the birth of a baby: **a** muscles in the uterus wall, **b** the cervix and **c** the placenta.

S 17.13 Describe the advantages and disadvantages of breast-feeding and bottle-feeding.

17.3 The menstrual cycle

Usually, one egg is released into the oviduct every month in an adult woman. Before the egg cell is released, the lining of the uterus becomes thick and spongy, to prepare itself for a fertilised egg cell. It is full of tiny blood vessels, ready to supply the embryo with food and oxygen if it should arrive.

If the egg cell is not fertilised, it is dead by the time it reaches the uterus. It does not sink into the spongy wall, but continues onwards, down through the vagina. As the spongy lining is not needed now, it gradually disintegrates. It, too, is slowly lost through the vagina. This is called **menstruation**, or a period. It usually lasts for about five days. After menstruation, the lining of the uterus builds up again, so that it will be ready to receive the next egg, if it is fertilised.

Figure **17.19** shows what happens during the human menstrual cycle.

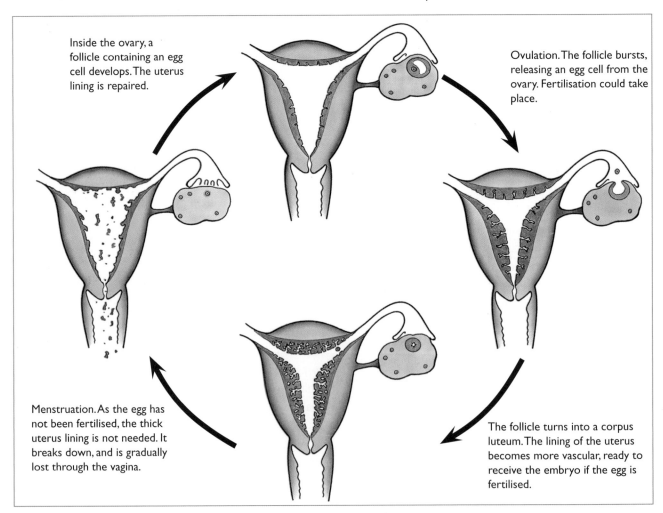

Inside the ovary, a follicle containing an egg cell develops. The uterus lining is repaired.

Ovulation. The follicle bursts, releasing an egg cell from the ovary. Fertilisation could take place.

Menstruation. As the egg has not been fertilised, the thick uterus lining is not needed. It breaks down, and is gradually lost through the vagina.

The follicle turns into a corpus luteum. The lining of the uterus becomes more vascular, ready to receive the embryo if the egg is fertilised.

Figure 17.19 The menstrual cycle.

Puberty

The time when a person approaches sexual maturity is called adolescence. Sperm production begins in a boy, and ovulation in a girl.

During adolescence, the secondary sexual characteristics develop. In boys, these include growth of facial and pubic hair, breaking of the voice, and muscular development. In girls, pubic hair begins to grow, the breasts develop, and the pelvic girdle becomes broader.

These changes are brought about by hormones. The male hormone is **testosterone**. It is produced in the testes. The female hormone is **oestrogen**. It is produced in the ovaries.

The point at which sexual maturity is reached is called **puberty**. This is often several years earlier for girls than for boys. At puberty, a person is still not completely adult, because emotional development is not complete.

Ⓢ Hormonal control of the menstrual cycle

Oestrogen is not the only female sex hormone. The ovaries also produce a hormone called **progesterone** during certain stages of the menstrual cycle, and during pregnancy. The secretion of these hormones is controlled by two other hormones secreted by the pituitary gland in the head, called LH and FSH (Figure 17.20).

Whereas male mammals make sperm all the time, females only produce eggs at certain times. We have seen that, in humans, ovulation happens once a month. Ovulation is part of the menstrual cycle.

First, a **follicle** develops inside an ovary. The development of the follicle is stimulated by FSH. The developing follicle secretes oestrogen, and the concentration of oestrogen in the blood steadily increases. The oestrogen makes the lining of the uterus grow thick and spongy. Throughout this time, the pituitary gland secretes LH and FSH. These two hormones stimulate the follicle to keep on secreting oestrogen.

When the follicle is fully developed, there is a surge in the production of LH. This causes ovulation to take place. The now empty follicle stops secreting oestrogen. It becomes a **corpus luteum**. The corpus luteum starts to secrete another hormone – progesterone. Levels of FSH and LH fall.

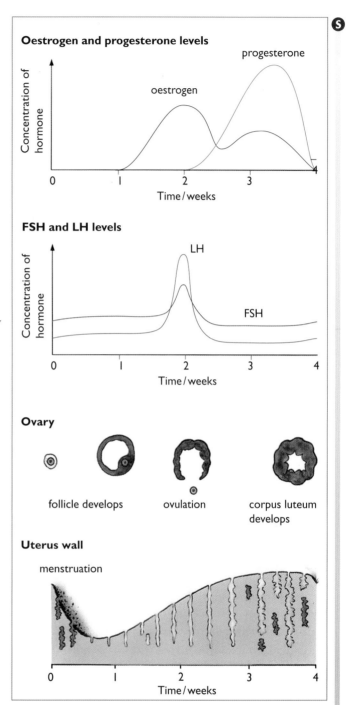

Figure 17.20   Hormones and the menstrual cycle.

Progesterone keeps the uterus lining thick, spongy, and well supplied with blood, in case the egg is fertilised. If it is not fertilised, then the corpus luteum gradually disappears. Progesterone is not secreted any more, and so the lining of the uterus breaks down. Menstruation happens. A new follicle starts to develop in the ovary, and the cycle begins again.

But if the egg is fertilised, the corpus luteum does not degenerate so quickly. It carries on secreting progesterone until the embryo sinks into the uterus wall, and a placenta develops. Then the placenta secretes progesterone, and carries on secreting it all through the pregnancy. The progesterone maintains the uterus lining, so that menstruation does not happen during the pregnancy.

❓ Questions

17.14 Why does the uterus wall become thick and spongy before ovulation?

17.15 What happens if the egg is not fertilised?

17.16 What is meant by **a** adolescence, and **b** puberty?

17.17 What is testosterone?

17.18 List **two** effects of testosterone.

17.4 Birth control

Birth control can help couples to have no more children than they want. Birth control is important in keeping family sizes small, and in limiting the increase in the human population. Careful and responsible use of birth control methods means no unwanted children are born.

Natural methods

Natural methods of birth control involve the couple avoiding sexual intercourse completely (abstinence) or ensuring that they do not have sexual intercourse when the woman has an egg in her oviducts. This is a risky method, and only works for women who have very regular and predictable menstrual cycles. However, it is useful for couples who do not wish to use other birth control methods for religious or other reasons.

Figure **17.21** shows how a woman can work out the 'safe period', when an egg is least likely to be in her oviducts. She needs to keep a careful record of her body temperature. You can see from the graph that temperature rises slightly around the time of ovulation. In addition, a woman can check the mucus that is produced in her vagina. This becomes more liquid and slippery around the time of ovulation.

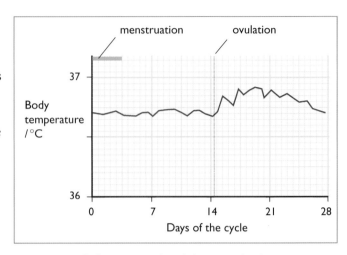

Figure 17.21 Body temperature through the menstrual cycle.

If the woman has a regular cycle, then she can use this to predict when ovulation will take place. She should then avoid sexual intercourse on the three or four days either side of this date. However, few women have completely regular cycles, and this makes this method of birth control unreliable.

Chemical methods

Chemicals called spermicides can be used to kill sperm when they enter the vagina. They are best used in combination with another method. For example, spermicides may be inserted into the vagina with a diaphragm, or cap (see below).

Another type of chemical birth control is the use of sex hormones to disrupt the menstrual cycle. A woman can take the contraceptive pill, which stops eggs being produced in her ovaries. The pill contains progesterone and oestrogen. She may have to take a pill each day, or she may be given a long-lasting injection of contraceptive hormones.

An IUD (intra-uterine device) is a device that is placed inside the uterus (and therefore has to be fitted by a doctor). Some types of IUD contain copper. A similar device, called an IUS, slowly releases hormones that prevent implantation. This interferes with the ability of sperm to find and fertilise an egg, and also prevents the implantation and development of any egg that does get fertilised.

Mechanical methods

Some birth control methods work by putting a barrier between the eggs and sperm. The most widely used mechanical method of birth control is a condom – a thin sheath that is placed over the man's erect penis and that stops any sperm getting into the woman's vagina. This also has the advantage that it stops any pathogens passing between the couple, so it is good protection against the transmission of diseases such as gonorrhoea or HIV/AIDS (pages **225–226**). Women can use a female version of a condom, called a femidom, which is placed inside the vagina and works in a similar way.

An alternative method for a woman is to use a diaphragm, sometimes called a cap. This is a circular, slightly domed piece of rubber which is inserted into the vagina and which covers the cervix, stopping sperm getting past it and into the uterus. To make absolutely sure that none can squeeze past, it is a good idea to use a spermicide cream as well.

Surgical methods

These tend to be most suitable for couples who already have as many children as they want. The operation for a man is called a vasectomy. It is a quick and simple operation, usually done under local anaesthetic. The operation for a woman usually involves a short stay in hospital, and a general anaesthetic. Figure **17.22** shows what the operations entail.

The various methods of birth control, and their advantages and disadvantages, are summarised in Table **17.1**.

Increasing fertility

Whereas many couples want to use birth control methods to limit the number of children that they have, others have the opposite problem – they are not able to have children. The problem that is causing the couple's infertility may be in the man or in the woman. For example, the man may not be producing healthy sperm. If this is the case, then the couple may decide that they will have a baby using sperm from another man. Sperm from a donor is collected in a clinic, and can be stored at a low temperature for many months or even years. The woman can then attend the clinic, and some of the sperm can be placed into her vagina. This is called artificial insemination (AI).

This may be a real help to a couple, as it allows them to have a child that they could not otherwise have. However, they need to think very carefully about this before they go ahead, and make sure that they are both happy with the idea. The man has to be able to accept that the child they have is not biologically his. Problems can also be caused when the child grows up and wants to know who his or her biological father is. It can be very difficult for a young person not to know this, so some people think that the identity of the sperm donor should be given to the child. Others, however, think this may cause more problems than it solves, because

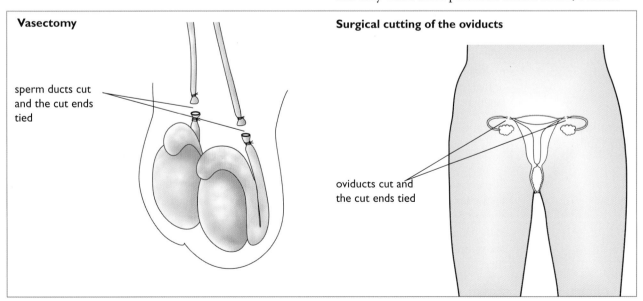

Figure 17.22 Surgical methods of birth control.

one sperm donor could end up being the father of many children. Indeed, fewer people would be likely to become sperm donors in many countries if this information was freely available.

Another way in which an infertile couple can be helped is using fertility drugs. This method is used when the woman is not producing enough eggs. She is given hormones, including FSH, that cause her to produce eggs. Sometimes, these are simply allowed to be released into the oviducts in the normal way. Sometimes, they are removed from her ovaries just before they are due to be released, and placed in a warm liquid in a Petri

dish. Some of her partner's sperm are then added, and fertilisation takes place in the dish. This is called *in vitro* fertilisation or IVF ('*in vitro*' means 'in glass') (Figure 17.23). Two or three of the resulting zygotes are then placed into her uterus, where they develop in the usual way.

This method is quite expensive, and some people think that it should not be freely available to anyone who wants it. Others think that the inability to have children can be so devastating to a couple that they should receive the treatment free of charge. The treatment is not always successful, and may have to

Method	How it works	Advantages and disadvantages
Condom (mechanical)	The condom is placed over the erect penis. It traps semen as it is released, stopping it from entering the vagina.	This is a very safe method of contraception if used correctly, but care must be taken that no semen is allowed to escape before it is put on or after it is removed. It can also help to prevent the transfer of infection, such as gonorrhoea and HIV, from one partner to another.
Diaphragm, or cap (mechanical)	The diaphragm is a circular sheet of rubber, which is placed over the cervix, at the top of the vagina. Spermicidal (sperm-killing) cream is first applied round its edges. Sperm deposited in the vagina cannot get past the diaphragm into the uterus.	This is an effective method, if used and fitted correctly. Fitting must be done by a doctor, but after that a woman can put her own diaphragm in and take it out as needed.
The pill or oral contraceptive (chemical)	The pill contains the female sex hormones oestrogen and progesterone. One pill is taken every day. The hormones are like those that are made when a woman is pregnant, and stop egg production.	This is a very effective method, so long as the pills are taken at the right time. However, some women do experience unpleasant side-effects, and it is important that women on the pill have regular check-ups with their doctor.
Sterilisation (surgical)	In a man, the sperm ducts are cut or tied, stopping sperm from travelling from the testes to the penis. In a woman, the oviducts are cut or tied, stopping eggs from travelling down the oviducts.	An extremely sure method of contraception, with no side-effects. However, the tubes often cannot be re-opened if the person later decides that they do want to have children, so it is not a method for young people.
Spermicides (chemical)	Spermicidal cream in the vagina kills sperm.	This is quite easy to use. It is only effective, however, if used in combination with another method, such as the diaphragm.
Natural	The woman keeps a careful record of her menstrual cycle over several months, so that she can predict roughly when an egg is likely to be present in her oviducts. She must avoid sexual intercourse for several days around this time.	This is a very unsafe method, because it is never possible to be 100% certain when ovulation is going to happen. Nevertheless, it is used by many people who do not want to use one of the other contraceptive methods.

Table 17.1 Some methods of birth control.

S be repeated many times before a woman becomes pregnant. Another problem is that, while usually only one of the embryos develops, sometimes two or three do, so that the couple might have twins or triplets when they really only wanted one child.

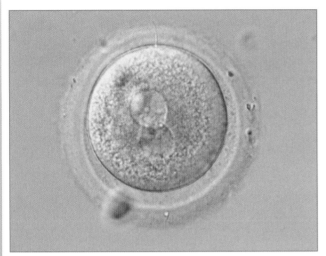

Figure 17.23 This egg is about to be fertilised during IVF. You can just make out the two nuclei – one from the sperm and one from the egg – beginning to fuse together.

17.5 Sexually transmitted infections

Sexually transmitted infections are caused by bacteria or viruses that can be passed from one person to another during sexual intercourse. By far the most important of these infections is HIV/AIDS.

The disease AIDS, or acquired immune deficiency syndrome, is caused by HIV. HIV stands for human immunodeficiency virus. Figure **17.24** shows this virus.

S HIV infects lymphocytes, and in particular a type called T cells. Over a long period of time, HIV slowly destroys T cells. Several years after infection with the virus, the numbers of certain kinds of T cells are so low that they are unable to fight against other pathogens effectively. Because HIV attacks the very cells which would normally kill viruses – the T cells – it is very difficult for someone's own immune system to protect them against HIV.

Key definition

sexually transmitted infection – an infection that is transmitted via body fluids through sexual contact

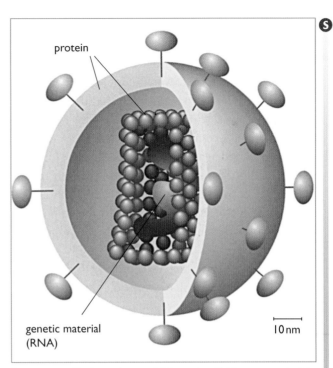

Figure 17.24 The human immunodeficiency virus, HIV. A nanometre (nm) is 1×10^{-9} m, so this virus is very, very small.

About ten years after initial infection with HIV, a person is likely to develop symptoms of AIDS unless they are given effective treatment. They become very vulnerable to other infections, such as pneumonia. They may develop cancer, because one function of the immune system is to destroy body cells which may be beginning to produce cancers. Brain cells are also quite often damaged by HIV. A person with AIDS usually dies from a collection of several illnesses.

There is still no cure for AIDS, though drugs can greatly increase the life expectancy of a person infected with HIV. Researchers are always trying to develop new drugs, which will kill the virus without damaging the person's own cells. As yet, no vaccine has been produced either, despite large amounts of money being spent on research.

Preventing HIV transmission

The virus that causes AIDS cannot live outside the human body. In fact, it is an especially fragile virus – much less tough than the cold virus, for example. You can only become infected with HIV through direct contact of your body fluids with those of someone with the virus. This can be in one of the following ways.

Through sexual intercourse

HIV can live in the fluid inside the vagina, rectum and urethra. During sexual intercourse, fluids from one partner come into contact with fluids of the other. It is very easy for the virus to be passed on in this way.

The more sexual partners a person has, the higher the chance of them becoming infected with HIV. In some parts of the world, where it is common practice for men to have many different sexual partners, extremely high percentages of people have developed AIDS. This is so in some parts of Africa and Asia, and also amongst some homosexual communities in parts of Europe and the USA.

The best way of avoiding AIDS is never to have more than one sexual partner. If everyone did that, then AIDS would immediately stop spreading. Using condoms is a good way of lowering the chances of the virus passing from one person to another during sexual intercourse – though it does not rule it out.

Through blood contact

Many cases of AIDS have been caused by HIV being transferred from one person's blood to another. In the 1970s and 1980s, when AIDS first appeared, and before anyone knew what was causing it, blood containing HIV was used in transfusions. People being given the transfusions were infected with HIV, and later developed AIDS. Now all blood used in transfusions in most countries is screened for HIV before it is used.

Blood can also be transferred from one person to another if they share hypodermic needles. This most commonly happens in people who inject drugs, such as heroin. Many drug users have died from AIDS. It is essential that any hypodermic needle used for injection is sterile.

People who have to deal with accidents, such as police and paramedics, must always be on their guard against HIV if there is blood around. They often wear protective clothing, just in case a bleeding accident victim is infected with HIV.

However, in general, there is no danger of anyone becoming infected with HIV from contact with someone with AIDS. You can quite safely talk to the person, shake hands with them, drink from cups which they have used and so on. In fact, there is far more danger to the person who has AIDS from such contacts, because they are so vulnerable to any bacterium or virus which they might catch from you.

Summary

You should know:

- ◆ the structure and functions of the male and female reproductive organs
- ◆ how and where fertilisation takes place
- ◆ how the structures of sperm and egg cells are adapted to their functions
- ◆ about implantation, the amnion and the placenta
- ◆ about the development and growth of an embryo and fetus
- Ⓢ ◆ about ante-natal care and birth
- ◆ advantages of breast-feeding or bottle-feeding
- ◆ about the menstrual cycle
- Ⓢ ◆ how hormones control the menstrual cycle
- ◆ about methods of birth control
- Ⓢ ◆ about using hormones to help conception, including AI and IVF
- ◆ about HIV/AIDS as an example of a sexually transmitted infection
- Ⓢ ◆ how HIV affects the immune system.

End-of-chapter questions

1 Copy and complete these sentences about the male reproductive system. You can use each of the words in the list once, more than once or not at all.

oestrogen   oviducts   primary   progesterone
prostate   secondary   sperm   sperm ducts
testes   testosterone   ureter   urethra

Sperm are made in the .... and can travel along the .... and then the .... to the outside world. The .... gland adds fluid to the sperm.

The testes make a hormone called .... This causes .... production to begin, and also causes the development of .... sexual characteristics.

2 Write the name of the parts of the female reproductive system that match each description.

   a   the place where an egg is fertilised
   b   the organ where eggs are made
   c   the organ in which an embryo develops
   d   a ring of muscle at the base of the uterus

3 The diagram shows a fetus developing in the uterus.

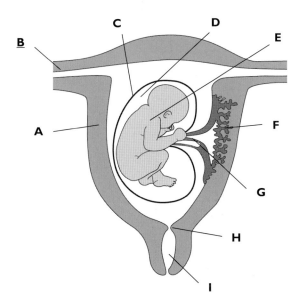

   a   Name each of the parts labelled **A** to **I**.
   b   Describe the function of part **C**.
   c   Outline the function of part **F**.

4 a The diagram below shows two gametes: a sperm cell and an egg cell.

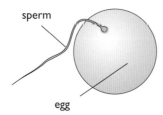

    i   State **one** way in which both of these cells differ from other cells of the body. [1]

    ii Suggest an advantage of the egg cell being larger than the sperm cell. [1]

    iii A fertilised egg divides into a ball of cells and becomes attached to the lining of the uterus.
        Explain why it is important that this ball of cells soon becomes attached to the lining of the uterus. [4]

  b The diagram below shows a developing fetus inside its mother's body.

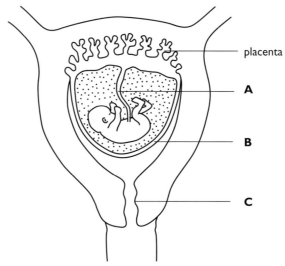

    i   Identify the parts labelled **A**, **B** and **C**. [3]

    ii State what causes blood to flow along **A**. [1]

    iii State a function of the fluid inside structure **B**. [1]

    iv State **two** substances which pass from the mother to the fetus, and **two** waste substances which pass from the fetus to the mother. [4]

S c The placenta acts as a barrier keeping the blood of the mother and the fetus separate.

    i   Suggest why the blood of the mother is separated from the blood of the fetus. [2]

    ii Despite the barrier between the maternal and fetal blood systems, some harmful chemical substances may pass from the mother to the fetus.
        Suggest **one** example. [1]

  d After it is born, the baby's main source of food is milk.
    Give **two** advantages of feeding a baby on breast milk rather than using milk prepared from milk powder. [2]

[Cambridge O level Human Biology 5096/21, Question 1, October/November 2011]

5 The diagram shows a human sperm.

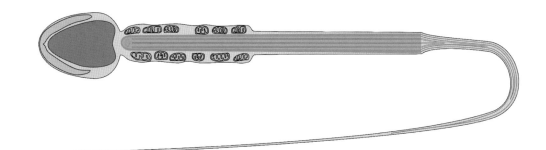

a Make a copy of the diagram. On your diagram label the following parts:

cell membrane   cytoplasm   nucleus

mitochondrion   flagellum   acrosome   [3]

b With reference to your diagram, explain how the structure of a sperm adapts it for its function. [4]

c Describe how a human egg cell is adapted for its function. [3]

6 The graph shows the number of people in the Caribbean who were known to be infected with HIV, who had AIDS and who died from AIDS, between 1982 and 2008.

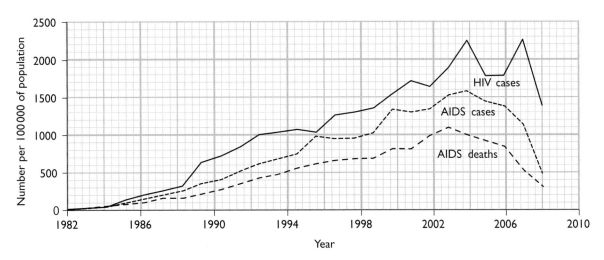

a With reference to the graph, describe the changes in the number of people infected with HIV between 1982 and 2008. [3]

b Suggest why the actual number of people infected with HIV may be greater than the numbers shown on the graph. [2]

c Explain how infection with HIV leads to the symptoms of AIDS. [5]

d Suggest the reasons for the shape of the graphs between 2004 and 2008. [4]

18 Inheritance

In this chapter, you will find out about:

♦ chromosomes and genes

Ⓢ ♦ the structure and function of DNA

♦ cell division by mitosis

♦ cell division by meiosis

♦ how to use genetic diagrams to predict and explain the features of the offspring of two parents.

Breeding chinchillas

Davide breeds chinchillas. These small rodents, with extremely soft and thick fur, originate from the Andes mountains in South America. They make good pets.

Davide wants to produce some unusual types of chinchillas, as these are worth more when he sells them.

All the chinchillas that he has are the normal, grey colour. He decides he would like to breed some charcoal-coloured ones, so he buys a male chinchilla with charcoal (very dark grey) fur. He breeds this with one of his grey females. To his disappointment, all the offspring are grey (Figure **18.1**).

Davide reads up about the genetics of chinchilla fur colour. He finds that, although all of the offspring of the grey and charcoal chinchilla parents are grey, in fact they are carrying a 'hidden' gene for charcoal fur. To get more charcoal chinchillas, his best bet is to breed these offspring with their father. He tries this, and is successful – half of the offspring of this cross have grey fur, and half have charcoal fur.

Figure 18.1   A cross between a normal, grey chinchilla and a charcoal chinchilla is likely to produce grey offspring.

18.1 Chromosomes

In the nucleus of every cell there are a number of long threads called chromosomes.

Most of the time, the chromosomes are too thin to be seen except with an electron microscope. But when a cell is dividing, they get shorter and fatter so they can be seen with a light microscope. Figure 18.2 shows human chromosomes seen with a powerful electron microscope.

Each chromosome contains one very long molecule of DNA. The DNA molecule carries a code that instructs the cell about which kinds of proteins it should make. Each chromosome carries instructions for making many different proteins. A part of a DNA molecule coding for one protein is called a gene.

It is the genes on your chromosomes which determine all sorts of things about you – what colour your eyes or hair are, whether you have a snub nose or a straight one, and whether you have a genetic disease such as cystic fibrosis. You inherited these genes from your parents.

Each species of organism has its own number and variety of genes. This is what makes their body chemistry, their appearance and their behaviour different from those of other organisms.

Humans have a large number of genes. You have 46 chromosomes inside each of your cells, all with many genes on them. Every cell in your body has an exact copy of all your genes. But, unless you are an identical twin, there is no-one else in the world with exactly the same combination of genes that you have. Your genes make you unique.

18.2 Cell division

You began your life as a single cell – a zygote – formed by the fusion of an egg cell and a sperm cell. The nuclei of each of these gametes contained a single complete set of 23 chromosomes. When they fused together, they produced a zygote with 46 chromosomes.

A cell with a single set of choromosomes, such as a gamete, is said to be haploid. The nucleus of the zygote contained two sets of chromosomes. It was a diploid cell.

Figures 18.3 and 18.4 show the chromosomes in a cell of a man and of a woman. They have been arranged in order, largest first. You can see that there are two chromosomes of each kind, because they are from diploid cells. In each pair, one is from the person's mother and the other from their father. The two chromosomes of a pair are called homologous chromosomes.

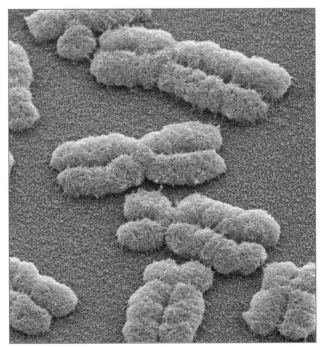

Figure 18.2   A scanning electron micrograph of human chromosomes. You can see that each one is made of two identical chromatids, linked at a point called the centromere.

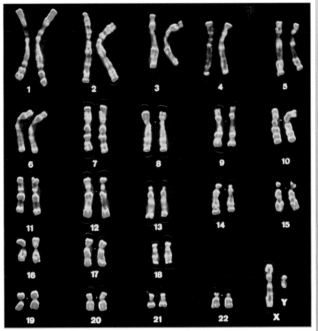

Figure 18.3   Chromosomes of a man, arranged in order.

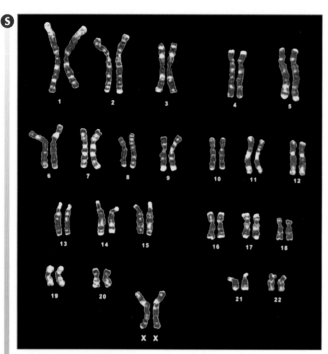

Figure 18.4 Chromosomes of a woman, arranged in order.

Mitosis is the way in which any cell – plant or animal – divides when an organism is growing, or repairing a damaged part of its body. It produces new cells to replace damaged ones. For example, if you cut yourself, new skin cells will be made by mitosis to help to heal the wound.

Mitosis is also used in asexual reproduction. You have seen, for example, how a potato plant can reproduce by growing stem tubers which eventually produce new plants (page **198**). All the cells in the new tubers are produced by mitosis, so they are all genetically identical.

Just before mitosis takes place, the chromosomes in the parent cell are copied. Each copy remains attached to the original one, so each chromosome is made up of two identical threads joined together (Figure **18.5**). The two threads are called chromatids, and the point where they are held together is called the centromere.

Key definitions

chromosome – a thread-like structure of DNA, carrying genetic information in the form of genes
gene – a length of DNA that codes for a protein.
inheritance – the transmission of genetic information from generation to generation
ⓢ haploid nucleus – a nucleus containing a single set of unpaired chromosomes (e.g. in sperm and egg cells)
diploid nucleus – a nucleus containing two sets of chromosomes (e.g. in body cells)

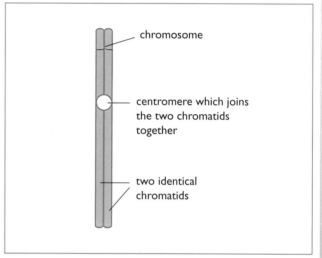

Figure 18.5 A chromosome just before division.

- chromosome
- centromere which joins the two chromatids together
- two identical chromatids

Figure **18.6** shows what happens when a cell with four chromosomes (two sets of two) divides by mitosis. Two new cells are formed, each with one copy of each of the four chromosomes. As the new cells grow, they make new copies of each chromosome, ready to divide again.

Mitosis

Soon after the zygote was formed, it began to divide over and over again, producing a ball of cells that eventually grew into you. Each time a cell divided, the two new cells produced were provided with a perfect copy of the two sets of chromosomes in the original zygote. The new cells produced were all genetically identical.

This type of cell division, which produces genetically identical cells, is called **mitosis**.

Key definition

mitosis – nuclear division giving rise to genetically identical cells

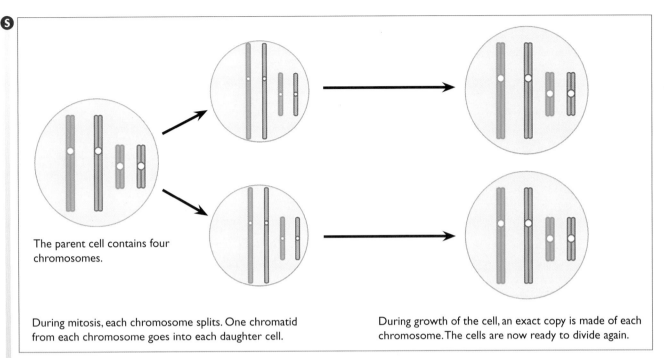

The parent cell contains four chromosomes.

During mitosis, each chromosome splits. One chromatid from each chromosome goes into each daughter cell.

During growth of the cell, an exact copy is made of each chromosome. The cells are now ready to divide again.

Figure 18.6 Chromosomes during the life of a cell dividing by mitosis.

Meiosis

On page **199**, we saw that gametes have only half the number of chromosomes of a normal body cell. They have one set of chromosomes instead of two. This is so that when they fuse together, the zygote formed has two sets.

Human gametes are formed by the division of cells in the ovaries and testes. The cells divide by a special type of cell division called meiosis. Meiosis shares out the chromosomes so that each new cell gets just one of each type.

Figure 18.7 summarises what happens during meiosis.

You may remember that one of each pair of homologous chromosomes came from the person's mother, and one from their father. During meiosis, the new cells get a mixture of these. So a sperm cell could contain a chromosome 1 from the man's father and a chromosome 2 from his mother, and so on. There are all sorts of different possible combinations. This is one of the reasons why gametes are genetically different from the parent cell. Meiosis produces genetic variation.

Stem cells

Shortly after a zygote is formed, it begins to divide by mitosis. Over the next few hours and days, the cells divide over and over again. Each division is done by mitosis, so every new cell is genetically identical.

However, as the embryo develops, the cells begin to take on different roles. This is called differentiation. Some of them will become skin cells, others muscle cells, others goblet cells or white blood cells. How does this happen?

Every cell in your body has the same genes. But in each cell, only a particular set of these genes is 'switched on', or expressed. The cells in your hair follicles, for example, are the only ones that actually express the gene for hair colour. This gene is present in all your other cells, but it is not expressed. So differentiation involves switching particular sets of genes on or off.

Key definition

meiosis – nuclear division giving rise to cells that are genetically different

meiosis – reduction division in which the chromosome number is halved from diploid to haploid, resulting in genetically different cells

First division – meiosis I

The parent cell contains four chromosomes.

Homologous chromosomes pair together. Crossing over takes place.

Homologous chromosomes separate. One from each pair goes into each daugher cell.

Second division – meiosis II

Each chromosome separates into two chromatids. One chromatid of each kind goes into each daughter cell.

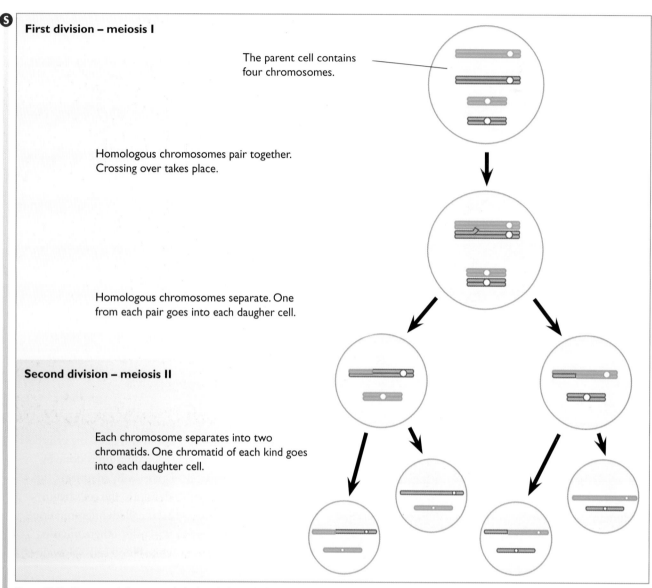

Figure 18.7 Summary of chromosome behaviour during meiosis.

The cells in the very early embryo, before they start to become different kinds of cells, are called **embryonic stem cells**. Embryonic stem cells are able to produce every kind of specialised cell in the body. But once a cell has differentiated into a particular type of cell, then it cannot change its role. A muscle cell, for example, cannot divide and produce liver cells or skin cells.

By the time you have become an adult, most cells have differentiated. But some stem cells still remain. They are called **adult stem cells**. Like embryonic stem cells, these are able to divide to produce different types of specialised cell. But the range of different cells they can produce is limited. For example, you have stem cells in your bone marrow that can divide to produce red blood cells, platelets and the different types of white blood cell. But they cannot produce nerve cells, liver cells or any other kind of specialised cell.

Medical researchers are very interested in finding out more about stem cells. It is likely that we will be able to use them to help to cure diseases that are caused by some of our cells failing to work properly. For example, we have seen that type 1 diabetes is caused by the loss of the pancreatic cells that secrete insulin. If we could use stem cells to replace these, then it might be possible to cure this kind of diabetes.

18.3 Inheritance

We have seen that chromosomes each contain many genes. We think there are about 20 000 human genes, carried on our two sets of 23 chromosomes.

Because you have two complete sets of chromosomes in each of your cells, you have two complete sets of genes. Each chromosome in a homologous pair contains genes for the same characteristic in the same positions (Figure **18.8**).This is true for all animals and most plants. Let us look at one kind of gene to see how it behaves, and how it is inherited.

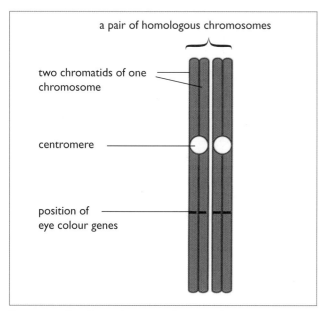

Figure 18.8   Homologous chromosomes have genes for the same characteristic in the same position.

Genes and alleles

In chinchillas, genes determine the colour of the fur. The genes are sets of instructions for producing the proteins that cause different fur colours.

There are several different forms of the fur colour gene. The different forms are called **alleles**. We can refer to these alleles using letters as symbols.

For example, we can call the allele that gives grey fur **G**, and the allele that gives charcoal fur **g**.

Key definition

allele – any of two or more alternative forms of a gene

In each cell in a chinchilla's body, there are two genes giving instructions about which kind of fur colour protein to make. This means that there are three possible combinations of alleles. A chinchilla might have two **G** alleles, **GG**. It might have one of each, **Gg**. Or it might have two g alleles, **gg** (Figure **18.9**).

If the two alleles for this gene in your cells are the same – that is, **GG** or **gg**– the chinchilla is said to be **homozygous**. If the two alleles are different – that is, **Gg** – then it is **heterozygous**.

Key definitions

homozygous – having two identical alleles of a particular gene (e.g. **GG** or **gg**). Two identical homozygous individuals that breed together will be pure-breeding

heterozygous – having two different alleles of a particular gene (e.g. **Gg**), not pure-breeding

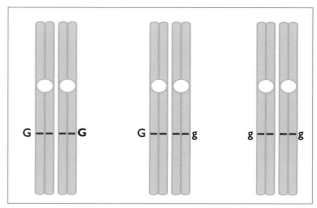

Figure 18.9   Genotypes for the fur colour gene in chinchillas.

Genotype and phenotype

The genes that that a chinchilla has are its **genotype**. Its genotype for fur colour could be **GG**, **Gg** or **gg**.

If its genotype is **GG**, then it has grey fur. If its genotype is **gg** it has charcoal fur. If its genotype is **Gg** it has grey fur.

The features the chinchilla has are called its **phenotype**. This can include what it looks like – for example, the colour of its fur – as well as things which we cannot actually see, such as what kind of protein it has in its cell membranes.

You can see that, in this example, the chinchilla's phenotype for colour depends entirely on its genotype. This is not always true. Sometimes, other things, such as what it eats, can affect its phenotype. However, for the moment, we will only consider the effect that genotype has on phenotype, and not worry about effects which the environment might have.

Key definitions

genotype – the genetic makeup of an organism in terms of the alleles present (e.g. **Tt** or **GG**)

phenotype – the features of an organism

Dominant and recessive alleles

We have seen that there are three different possible genotypes for chinchilla fur colour, but only two phenotypes. We can summarise this as follows:

genotype	phenotype
GG	grey
Gg	grey
gg	charcoal

This happens because the allele **G** is dominant to the allele **g**. A dominant allele has just as much effect on phenotype when there is only one of it as when there are two of it. A chinchilla that is homozygous for a dominant allele has the same phenotype as a chinchilla that is heterozygous. A heterozygous chinchilla is said to be a carrier of the charcoal colour, because it has the allele for it but does not have charcoal fur.

The allele g is recessive. A recessive allele only affects the phenotype when there is no dominant allele present. Only chinchillas with the genotype **gg** – homozygous recessive – have charcoal fur.

Key definitions

dominant – an allele that is expressed if it is present (e.g. **G**)

recessive – an allele that is only expressed when there is no dominant allele of the gene present (e.g. **g**)

Codominance

Sometimes, neither of a pair of alleles is completely dominant or completely recessive. Instead of one of them completely hiding the effect of the other in a heterozygote, they both have an effect on the phenotype. This is called codominance (Figure **18.10**).

Imagine a kind of flower which has two alleles for flower colour. The allele C^W produces white flowers, while the allele C^R produces red ones. If these alleles show codominance, then the genotypes and phenotypes are:

genotype	phenotype
C^WC^W	white flowers
C^WC^R	pink flowers
C^RC^R	red flowers

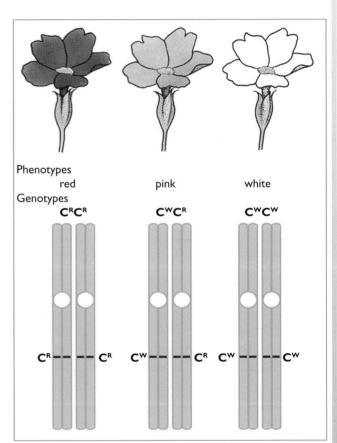

Figure 18.10 Codominance.

The inheritance of the ABO blood group antigens in humans is another example of codominance. There are three alleles of the gene governing this instead of the usual two. Alleles I^A and I^B are codominant, but both are dominant to I^o. A person with the genotype $I^A I^B$ has the blood type AB, in which characteristics of both A and B

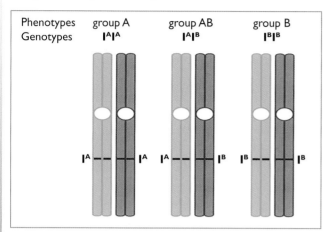

Figure 18.11 Codominance in human blood groups.

Alleles in gametes

Each gamete has only one of each kind of chromosome instead of two, as in the body cells. So, for example, human egg and sperm cells have 23 chromosomes, not 46 as in other cells. These cells, therefore, only carry *one* of each pair of alleles of all the genes.

Imagine a male chinchilla that has the genotype **Gg**. It is a carrier for charcoal fur. In its testes, sperm are made by meiosis. Each sperm cell gets either a **G** allele or **g** allele. Half of his sperm cells have the genotype **G** and half have the genotype **g**.

Genes and fertilisation

If this heterozygous chinchilla is crosssed with a female with charcoal fur (genotype **gg**), will their offspring have charcoal fur?

The eggs that are made in the female's ovaries are also made by meiosis. She can only make one kind of egg. All of the eggs will carry a **g** allele.

When the chinchillas mate, hundreds of thousands of sperm will begin a journey towards the egg. About half of them will carry a **G** allele, and half will carry a **g** allele. If there is an egg in the female's oviduct, it will probably be fertilised. There is an equal chance of either kind of sperm getting there first.

If a sperm carrying a **G** allele wins the race, then the zygote will have a **G** allele from its father and a **g** allele from its mother. Its genotype will be **Gg**. When the baby chinchilla is born, it will have the genotype **Gg**.

But if a sperm carrying a **g** allele manages to fertilise the egg, then the baby will have the genotype **gg**, like its mother (Figure **18.12**).

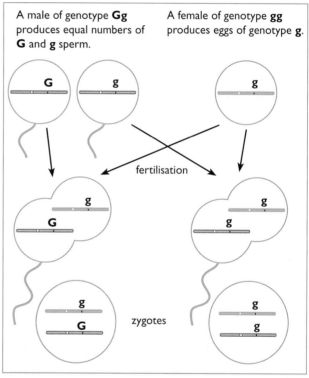

Figure 18.12 Fertilisation between a heterozygous grey chinchilla and a chinchilla with charcoal fur.

 Questions

18.1 What are chromosomes made of?

18.2 What are homologous chromosomes?

18.3 What are alleles?

18.4 a The allele for brown eyes is dominant to the allele for blue eyes. Write down suitable symbols for these alleles.

b What is the phenotype of a person who is heterozygous for this characteristic?

18.5 What is codominance? **S**

18.6 Alleles of the gene for the ABO blood group antigens in humans show two unusual characteristics. What are these?

18.7 Figure **18.11** shows three possible genotypes for blood group. Write down all the other possible genotypes, and the phenotype that is associated with each one.

Genetic diagrams

There is a standard way of writing out all this information. It is called a **genetic diagram**.

First, write down the phenotypes and genotypes of the parents. Next, write down the different types of gametes they can make, like this.

Parents' phenotypes	grey	charcoal
Parents' genotypes	**Gg**	**gg**
Gametes	Ⓖ or Ⓖ	Ⓖ

The next step is to write down what might happen during fertilisation. Either kind of sperm might fuse with an egg.

Offspring genotypes and phenotypes

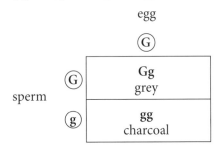

To finish your summary of the genetic cross, write out in words what you would expect the offspring from this cross to be.

So we would expect approximately half of the offspring to be heterozygous with grey fur, and half to be homozygous, with charcoal fur. Another way of putting this is to say that the expected ratio of grey fur to charcoal fur would be 1:1.

Another cross

What happens if both parents are heterozygous?

Parents' phenotypes	grey	grey
Parents' genotypes	**Gg**	**Gg**
Gametes	Ⓖ or Ⓖ	Ⓖ or Ⓖ

Offspring genotypes and phenotypes

eggs

	Ⓖ	Ⓖ
Ⓖ	**GG** grey	**Gg** grey
Ⓖ	**Gg** grey	**gg** charcoal

(sperm)

About one quarter of the offspring would be expected to have charcoal fur, and three quarters would have grey fur.

This example illustrates the inheritance of one pair only of contrasting characteristics. This is known as monohybrid inheritance.

Probabilities in genetics

In the last example, there were four possible offspring genotypes at the end of the cross. This does not mean that the two chinchillas will have four offspring. It simply means that each time they have offspring, these are the possible genotypes that they might have (Figure **18.13**).

Figure 18.13   Genetic diagrams do not tell us how many offspring there will be – just the probabilities of any one offspring having a particular feature.

For any one offspring, there is a 1 in 4 chance that its genotype will be **GG**, and a 1 in 4 chance that its genotype will be **gg**. There is a 2 in 4, or rather 1 in 2, chance that its genotype will be **Gg**.

However, as you know, probabilities do not always work out. If you toss a coin up four times you might expect it to turn up heads twice and tails twice. But does it always do this? Try it and see.

With small numbers like this, probabilities do not always match reality. If you had the patience to toss your coin up a few thousand times, though, you will almost certainly find that you get much more nearly equal numbers of heads and tails.

The same thing applies in genetics. The offspring genotypes which you work out are only probabilities. With small numbers, they are unlikely to work out exactly. With very large numbers of offspring from one cross, they are more likely to be accurate.

So, if the parent chinchillas in the last example had eight offspring, we might expect six of them to be grey and two to be charcoal. But we should not be too surprised if they have three offspring with charcoal fur.

Ⓢ Test crosses

An organism that shows a dominant characteristic could have either of two possible genotypes. It could be homozygous for the dominant allele, or it could be heterozygous. For example, a grey chinchilla could have the genotype **GG** or **Gg**.

We can find out the genotype of an individual with the dominant phenotype for a particular gene by crossing it with one known to have the homozygous recessive genotype for the same gene. This is called a test cross.

For example, if we know that the allele for tallness is dominant to the allele for dwarfness in a certain species of pea, then the genotype of any tall plant could be determined by crossing it with a dwarf plant. If any of the offspring are dwarf, then this must mean that the tall parent had an allele for dwarfness. It must have been heterozygous. Try this out for yourself, using a genetic diagram.

If none of the offspring are dwarf, this almost certainly means that the tall parent was homozygous for the tallness allele. However, unless there are large numbers of offspring, this could also happen if the tall parent is heterozygous but, just by chance, none of its gametes carrying the recessive allele were successful in fertilisation.

Pure breeding

Some populations of animals or plants always have offspring just like themselves. For example, a rabbit breeder might have a strain of rabbits which all have brown coats. If he or she interbreeds them with one another, all the offspring always have brown coats as well. The breeder has a pure-breeding strain of brown rabbits. Pure-breeding strains are always homozygous for the pure-breeding characteristics.

The offspring of two different pure-breeding (homozygous) strains are sometimes called the first filial generation, or F1 generation. They are always heterozygous.

Sex determination

The last pairs of chromosomes in Figures **18.3** and **18.4** are responsible for determining what sex a person will be. They are called the sex chromosomes (Figure **18.14**). A woman's chromosomes are both alike and are called X chromosomes. She has the genotype **XX**. A man, though, only has one X chromosome. The other, smaller one is a Y chromosome. He has the genotype **XY**.

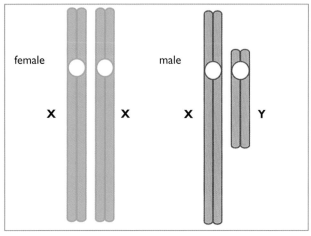

female   male

Figure 18.14   The sex chromosomes.

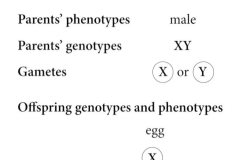

Parents' phenotypes	male	female
Parents' genotypes	XY	XX
Gametes	X or Y	X

Offspring genotypes and phenotypes

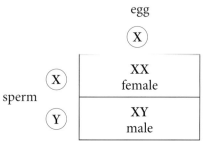

egg

	X
X	XX female
Y	XY male

sperm

You can work out sex inheritance in just the same way as for any other characteristic, but using the letter symbols to describe whole chromosomes, rather than individual alleles.

So each time a child is conceived, there is a 1:1 chance of it being either sex.

❓ Questions

18.8 If a normal human cell has 46 chromosomes, how many chromosomes are there in a human sperm cell?

18.9 Using the symbols **N** for normal wings, and **n** for vestigial wings, write down the following:
   a the genotype of a fly which is heterozygous for this characteristic.
   b the possible genotypes of its gametes.

18.10 Using a complete genetic diagram, work out what kind of offspring would be produced if the heterozygous fly in question **18.9** mated with one which was homozygous for normal wings.

18.11 In humans, the allele for red hair, **b**, is recessive to the allele for brown hair, **B**. A man and his wife both have brown hair. They have five children, three of whom have red hair, while two have brown hair. Explain how this may happen, using a genetic diagram to explain your answer.

S 18.12 In Dalmatian dogs, the allele for black spots is dominant to the allele for liver spots. If a breeder has a black-spotted dog, how can he or she find out whether it is homozygous or heterozygous for this characteristic? Use genetic diagrams to explain your answer.

18.13 A man of blood type A married a woman of blood type B. They had three children, of blood types O, B and AB, respectively. What are the genotypes of the parents and children? Use genetic diagrams to explain your answer. **S**

18.14 The pedigree diagram shows the known blood groups in three generations of a family. Squares represent males and circles represent females. What are the genotypes of **1** and **3**? What is the blood group of **2**?

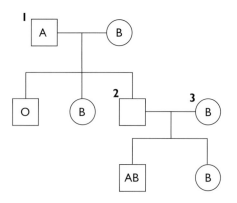

Activity 18.1
'Breeding' beads

Skills
AO3.3 Observing, measuring and recording
AO3.4 Interpreting and evaluating observations and data

In this investigation, you will use two containers of beads. Each container represents a parent. The beads represent the gametes they make. The colour of a bead represents the genotype of the gamete. For example, a red bead might represent a gamete with genotype **A**, for 'tongue rolling'. A yellow bead might represent a gamete with the genotype **a**, for 'non-tongue rolling'.

1 Put 100 red beads into the first beaker. These represent the gametes of a person who is homozygous for 'tongue rolling', **AA**.
2 Put 50 red beads and 50 yellow beads into the second beaker. These represent the gametes of a heterozygous person with the genotype **Aa**.
3 Close your eyes, and pick out one bead from the first beaker, and one from the second. Write down the genotype of the 'offspring' they produce. Put the two beads back.
4 Repeat step **3** 100 times.
5 Now try a different cross – for example, **Aa** crossed with **Aa**.

❓ Questions

A1 In the first cross, what kinds of offspring were produced, and in what ratios?
A2 Is this what you would have expected? Explain your answer.
A3 Why must you close your eyes when choosing the beads?
A4 Why must you put the beads back into the beakers after they have 'mated'?

ⓢ Sex linkage

The X and Y chromosomes do not only determine sex. They have other genes on them as well.

We have seen that, for most chromosomes, we have two copies of each one – a homologous pair. They contain the same genes in the same positions. This means that we have two copies of each gene.

But this isn't true for the sex chromosomes. The Y chromosome is tiny, and only has a few genes (Figure **18.15**). The X chromosome is much larger, and has many more genes. This means that, for most of the genes on the X chromosome, we have only one copy. There is no second copy on the Y chromosome.

There are also a few genes on the Y chromosome that are not found on the X chromosome. This means that a woman never has a copy of these genes, and a man has only one copy.

Genes that are found only on the non-homologous parts of the X or Y chromosomes are called **sex-linked genes**.

One of these sex-linked genes controls the production of the three different kinds of cone cells in the retina. A recessive allele of this gene, **b**, results in

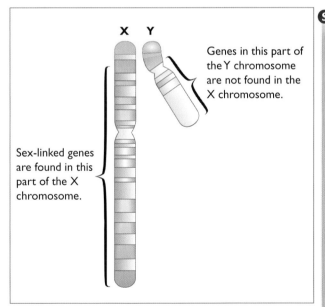

Figure 18.15 Genes on the X and Y chromosomes.

only two types of cone cell being made. A person who is homozygous for this allele cannot tell the difference between red and green. They are said to be red–green colour-blind. This condition is much more common in men than in women.

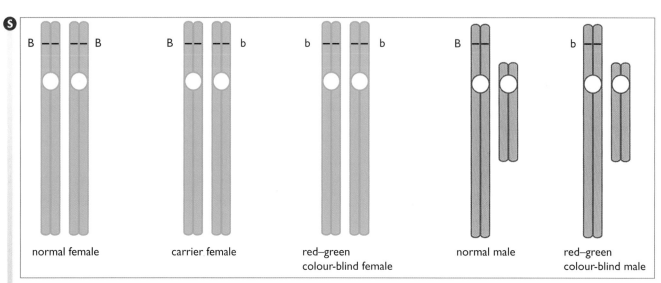

Figure 18.16 Red–green colour-blindness genotypes and phenotypes.

Figure 18.16 shows the various genotypes and phenotypes for this sex-linked condition. You can see that there are three possible genotypes that a woman might have, but only two possible genotypes for a man.

When we write genotypes involving sex-linked genes, we need to show the chromosome as well as the allele. So the five possible genotypes and their phenotypes for red–green colour-blindness are:

genotype	phenotype
$X^B X^B$	woman with normal vision
$X^B X^b$	woman with normal vision (who is a carrier)
$X^b X^b$	woman with red–green colour blindness
$X^B Y$	man with normal vision
$X^b Y$	man with red–green colour blindness

Inheritance of sex-linked characteristics

We can use a genetic diagram to show how sex-linked genes are inherited. For example, what might happen if a woman who is a carrier for red–green colour blindness marries a man with normal vision?

Parents' phenotypes   normal man   carrier woman

Parents' genotypes $X^B Y$ $X^B X^b$

Gametes X^B or Y X^B or X^b

Offspring genotypes and phenotypes

	eggs	
	X^B	X^b
sperm X^B	$X^B X^B$ normal female	$X^B X^b$ normal female (carrier)
Y	$X^B Y$ normal male	$X^b Y$ red–green colour-blind male

This genetic diagram predicts that about half of their male children will be red–green colour-blind. All of the female children will have normal vision.

Key definition

sex-linked characteristic – a characteristic in which the gene responsible is located on a sex chromosome, which makes it more common in one sex than in the other.

Questions

(S) **18.15** **a** A man who is red–green colour-blind marries a woman with normal vision. They have three sons and two daughters. One of the sons is red–green colour-blind. All the other children have normal colour vision. Draw a genetic diagram to suggest an explanation for this.

b What is the chance that the couple's next child will be a colour-blind boy?

18.4 DNA and protein synthesis

Chromosomes are made of DNA. In Chapter 4, we saw that a DNA molecule is made up of two long strands of molecules called nucleotides. There are four different nucleotides, each containing a different base – A, C, T or G. You can see a diagram showing the structure of DNA on page **47**.

We have also seen that protein molecules are made up of long chains of amino acids (page 45). There are 20 different amino acids. The sequence of these amino acids in a protein molecule determines the final shape of the molecule. This shape affects how the protein works.

DNA contains a code that determines exactly what sequence of amino acids a cell should string together when it makes a particular protein. This is how genes affect an organism's features. A gene – a length of DNA coding for a particular protein – determines what protein will be made, and the protein affects a feature of the organism. Many proteins do this by acting as enzymes – enzymes determine the metabolic reactions that take place, and therefore the substances that are made through these reactions (Figure **18.17**). Other proteins have different functions, such as antibodies and receptors for neurotransmitters.

The genetic code

DNA has only four bases, but proteins have 20 different amino acids. This means that the four DNA 'letters' have to be combined to make different 'words', each one signifying a particular amino acid.

The DNA bases are 'read' in sets of three, called triplets. For example, the sequence CCG in a DNA molecule stands for the amino acid glycine. CAG stands for valine. So the base sequence: CCG CAG tells the cell: Join a valine amino acid to a glycine amino acid.

Protein synthesis

DNA is found in the nucleus. Protein synthesis happens on the ribosomes, in the cytoplasm. To carry information from the DNA to the ribosome, a messenger molecule called messenger RNA (mRNA) is used (Figure **18.18**).

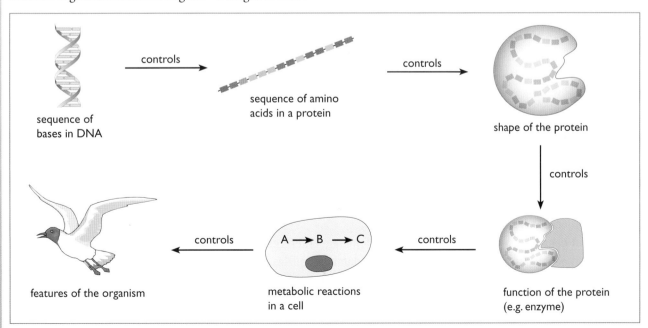

Figure 18.17 How DNA affects an organism's characteristics.

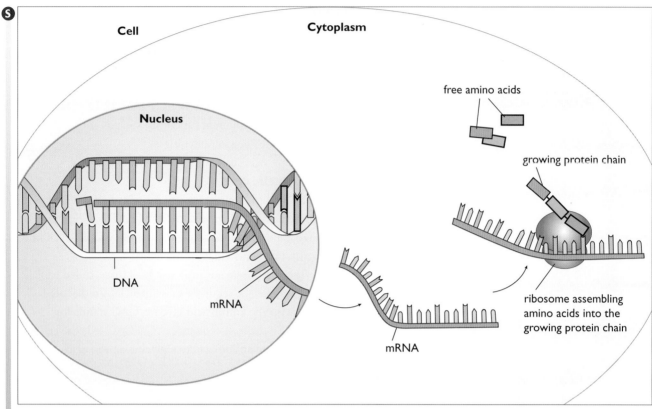

Figure 18.18 Proteins are made by linking together amino acids, in the sequence determined by an mRNA molecule.

When a protein is to be made, an mRNA molecule is made in the nucleus, copying the base sequence from the appropriate length of DNA. The mRNA then moves out from the nucleus into the cytoplasm, and attaches to a ribosome.

If you have been eating a good diet, then the cytoplasm in your cells will contain plenty of all the 20 different amino acids. As the long, thin mRNA molecule passes through it, the ribosome links amino acids together in exactly the right order to make the desired protein, following the code contained on the mRNA molecule.

Summary

You should know:

- ◆ about chromosomes and genes
- ◆ how and why cells divide by mitosis
- Ⓢ ◆ how and why cells divide by meiosis
- ◆ about haploid and diploid nuclei
- ◆ about embryonic and adult stem cells
- ◆ about genotypes and phenotypes involving dominant and recessive alleles
- Ⓢ ◆ about genotypes and phenotypes involving codominant alleles and sex-linked genes
- ◆ how to use genetic diagrams to predict or explain the results of crosses
- Ⓢ ◆ how DNA controls protein synthesis.

End-of-chapter questions

1 In guinea pigs, the allele for smooth fur is dominant to the allele for rough fur.

    a   Suggest suitable symbols for these two alleles.
    b   Write down the three possible genotypes for these alleles.
    c   Write down the phenotype that each of these genotypes will produce.

2 In a species of plant, flower colour can be red or white. Heterozygous plants have red flowers.

    a   Choose suitable symbols for the alleles of the flower colour gene.
    b   Which allele is dominant, and which is recessive? Explain how you worked this out.
    c   Write down all the possible genotypes for flower colour in this plant, and the phenotypes they will produce.

3 Explain the difference between each of the following pairs of terms:

    a   gene, allele
    b   dominant, recessive
    c   homozygous, heterozygous
    d   genotype, phenotype
S   e   mitosis, meiosis
    f   haploid, diploid
    g   base sequence, amino acid sequence
    h   DNA, RNA

4 The leaves of tomato plants can have leaves with smooth or indented edges. The allele for indented edges is dominant, and the allele for smooth edges is recessive.

    a   Write down the genotypes of a homozygous smooth plant and a homozygous indented plant.   [2]
    b   A pure-breeding (homozygous) smooth plant was crossed with a homozygous indented plant. All of the offspring had indented leaves.
        Construct a complete genetic diagram to explain how this happened.   [4]
    c   Several of these indented offspring were crossed together. There were 302 plants with indented leaves and 99 with smooth leaves.
        Construct a complete genetic diagram to explain this result.   [5]

S 5 A breeder has several black rabbits and white rabbits. He knows that black fur in rabbits is caused by a dominant allele, **B**. White fur is caused by the recessive allele **a**.

    Explain what the breeder can do to determine the genotype of one of his black rabbits.

    Use genetic diagrams as part of your answer.   [6]

6   A breed of domestic chickens can have black, grey or white feathers. These colours are produced by two alleles, C^B and C^W.

   a   Write down the genotypes that produce black, grey and white feathers.   [2]
   b   Explain why the alleles are written in this way, rather than as a capital letter for one allele and a small letter for the other.   [2]
   c   A cockerel with grey feathers was mated with a hen with white feathers.
       Draw a complete genetic diagram to predict the ratio of the different colours of chicks that will be produced.   [5]

Ⓢ 7   The diagram shows a pedigree chart for a family in which some of the members are red–green colour-blind.

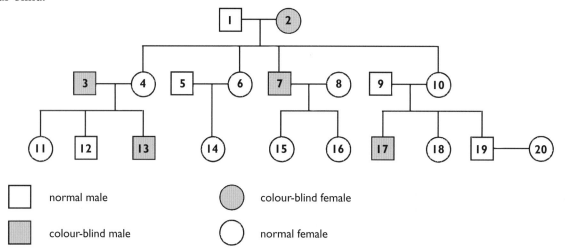

   a   Explain how the pedigree supports the idea that red–green colour blindness is a sex-linked characteristic.   [2]
   b   Using the symbols X^B for the allele for normal vision, and X^b for the allele for colour blindness, state the genotypes of each of the following individuals. If there is more than one possible genotype, write down both of them.
          2, 3, 11, 13, 19   [5]
   c   If individuals 3 and 4 have another son, what is the probability that he will be colour-blind? Use a genetic diagram to explain your answer.   [5]
   d   Explain why a colour-blind man cannot pass on this condition to his son.   [2]

8   Two women gave birth in the same hospital on the same afternoon. Their babies were taken away, and then brought back to them one hour later. One of the women was worried that she had been given the wrong baby. She asked for blood tests to be carried out. The hospital found that she was group A and her husband was group O. The other mother was group AB and her husband was group A. The woman with blood group A had been given the baby with blood group O. The woman with group AB was given the baby with blood group B. Use genetic diagrams to determine whether the women had been given the right babies.   [8]

19 Variation and natural selection

In this chapter, you will find out about:

♦ continuous and discontinuous variation
♦ mutation and what causes it
S ♦ sickle cell anaemia
♦ adaptation to the environment
♦ natural selection
♦ selective breeding.

Confusing butterflies

The two butterflies in Figure **19.1** look very different. Most people would assume they belong to two different species. But that is not the case. Both butterflies belong to the species *Papilio polytes*, the common mormon butterfly.

This species of butterfly is found in many different countries in Asia. The males always look the same – like the one on the left. Some of the females look just like the male. But some – such as the one shown on the right – have very different wing shapes and colours.

The butterfly on the right is called the *stichius* form of the common mormon. This form is found only where another butterfly, the common rose swallowtail, is found. The common rose swallowtail is poisonous, so predators quickly learn to avoid catching it. The common mormon is not poisonous. By pretending to be a common rose swallowtail, the female butterflies are much less likely to be eaten.

This pretence is called mimicry. It only works if there are large numbers of the genuinely poisonous butterfly, and much smaller numbers of the non-poisonous one – otherwise, predators would not learn to avoid them.

Figure 19.1 Variations in colour and shape in the common mormon butterfly.

19.1 Variation

You have only to look around a group of people to see that they are different from one another. Some of the more obvious differences are in height or hair type. We also vary in intelligence, blood groups, whether we can roll our tongues or not, and many other ways. Differences between the features of different individuals are called phenotypic variation.

There are two basic kinds of **variation**. One kind is **discontinuous variation**. Blood groups are an example of discontinuous variation. Everyone fits into one of four definite categories – each of us has group A, B, AB or O. There are no in-between categories.

The other kind is **continuous variation**. Height is an example of continuous variation. There are no definite heights that a person must be. People vary in height, between the lowest and highest extremes.

You can try measuring and recording discontinuous and continuous variation in Activity **19.1**. Your results for continuous variation will probably look similar to Figure **19.2**. This is called a **normal distribution**. Most people come in the middle of the range, with fewer at the lower or upper ends. Human height (Figure **19.3**) shows a normal distribution.

By describing variation as continuous or discontinuous, we can begin to explain *how* organisms vary. But the *cause* of the variation is another question altogether.

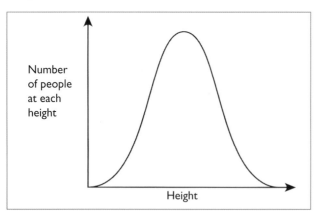

Figure 19.2   A normal distribution curve. This is a graph that shows the numbers of people of different heights.

Key definition

variation – differences between individuals of the same species

Figure 19.3   Human height shows continuous variation. What characteristic here shows discontinuous variation?

Genetic variation

One reason for the differences between individuals is that their genotypes are different. This is called genetic variation. Blood groups, for example, are controlled by genes. There are also genes for hair colour, eye colour, height and many other characteristics (Figure **19.4**).

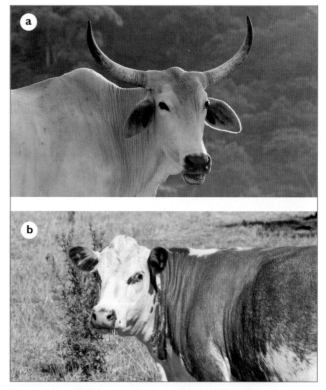

Figure 19.4   **a** The presence of horns in cattle is controlled by a dominant allele of a gene. **b** Polled (hornless) cattle have two copies of the recessive allele of this gene.

Environmental variation

Another important reason for variation is the difference between the environments of individuals. Pine trees possess genes that enable them to grow to a height of about 30 m. But if a pine tree is grown in a very small pot, and has its roots regularly pruned, it will be permanently stunted (Figure **19.5**). The tree's genotype gives it the potential to grow tall, but it will not realise this potential unless its roots are given plenty of space and it is allowed to grow freely.

In general, discontinuous variation is caused by genes alone. Continuous variation is often influenced by both genes and the environment.

Causes of genetic variation

There are several ways in which genetic variation is produced.

Mutation

Sometimes, a gene may suddenly change. This is called mutation. Mutation is how new alleles are formed. Mutations are the only source of brand-new characteristics in the gene pool. So mutations are really the source of all genetic variation.

Another type of mutation affects whole chromosomes. For example, when eggs are being made by meiosis in a woman's ovaries, the chromosome 21s sometimes do not separate from one another. One of the daughter cells therefore gets two chromosome 21s and the other one gets none. The cell with none dies. The other one may survive, and eventually be fertilised by a sperm. The zygote from this fertilisation will have three copies of chromosome 21. The child that grows from the zygote has Down's syndrome.

❓ Questions

19.1 Decide whether each of these features shows continuous variation or discontinuous variation.
  a   blood group in humans
  b   foot size in humans
  c   leaf length in a species of tree
  d   presence of horns in cattle

Ⓢ 19.2 For each of the examples in **a** to **d** above, suggest whether the variation is caused by genes alone, or by both genes and environment.

Variation caused by the environment is not inherited. A cutting from a bonsai pine tree would grow into a full size tree, if given sufficient space.

bonsai

A bonsai pine tree is dwarfed by being grown in a very small pot, and continually pruned.

A dwarf pony, such as a Shetland pony, is small because of its genes. The offspring of Shetland ponies are small like their parents, no matter how well they are fed and cared for.

Figure 19.5   The inheritance of variation.

Children with Down's have characteristic facial features and are usually very happy and friendly people. However, they often have heart problems and other physical and physiological difficulties.

Mutations often happen for no apparent reason. However, we do know of many factors which make mutation more likely. One of the most important of these is ionising radiation. Radiation can damage the bases in DNA molecules. If this happens in the ovaries or testes, then the altered DNA may be passed on to the offspring.

Many different chemicals are known to increase the risk of a mutation happening. The heavy metals lead and mercury and their compounds can interfere with the process in which DNA is copied. If this process goes wrong, the daughter cells will get faulty DNA when the cell divides. Chemicals which can cause mutations are called mutagens.

Ⓢ Meiosis

During sexual reproduction, gametes are formed by meiosis. In meiosis, homologous chromosomes exchange genes, and separate from one another, so the gametes which are formed are not all exactly the same.

Fertilisation

Any two gametes of opposite types can fuse together at fertilisation, so there are many possible combinations of genes which may be produced in the zygote. In an organism with a large number of genes the possibility of two offspring having identical genotypes is so small that it can be considered almost impossible.

19.2 Adaptive features

Every organism has features that help it to survive in its environment. Sometimes these are very obvious. All fish, for example, have gills that allow them to obtain oxygen under water. Different species of fish have adaptations that help them to survive in different environments (Figure **19.6**). For example, fish that live on sand in shallow water may have very flat, sand-coloured bodies, so that they are camouflaged from predators. Predatory fish that live in the open ocean have streamlined bodies for fast swimming, and teeth that they use to kill their prey.

Activity 19.1
Measuring variation

Skills
AO3.3 Observing, measuring and recording
AO3.4 Interpreting and evaluating observations and data

1 Make a survey of at least 30 people, to find out whether or not they can roll their tongue. Record your results.
2 Measure the length of the third finger of the left hand of 30 people. Take the measurement from the knuckle to the finger tip, not including the nail.
3 Divide the finger lengths into suitable categories, and record the numbers in each category, like this.

Length / cm	Number of measurements
8.0–8.4	2
8.5–8.9	4

4 Draw a histogram of your results.

❓ Questions
A1 Which characteristic shows continuous variation, and which shows discontinuous variation?
A2 Your histogram may be a similar shape to the curve in Figure **19.2**. This is called a normal distribution. The category, or class, which has the largest number of individuals in it is called the modal class. What is the modal class for finger length in your results?
A3 The mean finger length is the total of all the finger lengths, divided by the number of people in your sample. What is the mean finger length of the sample?

Key definitions

mutation – genetic change
Ⓢ gene mutation – a change in the base sequence of DNA

Figure 19.6 The pygmy seahorse, *Hippocampus bargibanti*, is adapted to be perfectly camouflaged among the seaweed in which it lives.

An animal or plant that is well adapted to its environment is much more likely to survive than one that is not. A pygmy seahorse that was bright blue instead of yellow would not be camouflaged, and would probably be killed and eaten by a predator long before it reached adulthood. Only well adapted individuals have a good chance of living long enough to reproduce.

S Biologists often use the word **fitness** to describe how well adapted an organism is. (This has nothing doing to being fit, in the sense of being able to do exercise.) The greater the organism's fitness, the greater its chance of surviving to adulthood and reproducing.

Xerophytes

Plants that live in deserts can easily run short of water, especially if the temperatures are hot. Desert plants, such as succulents (Figure **19.7**) and cacti (Figure **19.8**), must be well adapted to survive in these difficult conditions. Plants that are adapted to live in places where water is in short supply are called **xerophytes**.

Key definitions

adaptive feature – an inherited feature that helps an organism to survive and reproduce in its environment *or*

S the inherited functional features of an organism that increase its fitness

fitness – the probability of an organism surviving and reproducing in the environment in which it is found

 Question

19.3 The photograph shows a small mammal called a tarsier. Tarsiers feed on insects, which they hunt at night.

How is the tarsier adapted for survival in its environment?

Figure 19.7 *Pachypodium*, a succulent living in Madagascar.

Figure 19.8 *Ferocactus* – a plant adapted to live in deserts.

All xerophytes have adaptations that help them to survive in these difficult environment.

Closing stomata

Plants lose most water through their stomata. If they close their stomata, then transpiration will slow right down. Figure **19.9** shows how they do this.

However, if its stomata are closed, then the plant cannot photosynthesise, because carbon dioxide cannot diffuse into the leaf. Stomata close when it is very hot and dry, or when they could not photosynthesise anyway, such as at night.

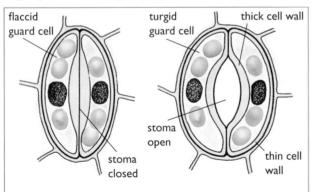

When a plant is short of water, the guard cells become flaccid, closing the stomata.

When a plant has plenty of water, the guard cells become turgid. The cell wall on the inner surface is very thick, so it cannot stretch as much as the outer surface. So as the guard cells swell up, they curve away from each other, opening the stoma.

Figure 19.9 How stomata open and close.

Waxy cuticle

The leaves of desert plants are often covered with a waxy cuticle, made by the cells in the epidermis. The wax makes the leaf waterproof.

Hairy leaves

Some plants have hairs on their leaves. These hairs trap a layer of moist air next to the leaf.

Stomata on underside of leaves

In most leaves, there are more stomata on the lower surface than on the upper surface. The lower surface is usually cooler than the upper one, so less water will evaporate. In desert plants, there may be fewer stomata than usual, and they may be sunk into deep pits in the leaf.

Cutting down on the surface area

The smaller the surface area of the leaf, the less water will evaporate from it. Plants like cacti (Figure **19.8**) have leaves with a small surface area, to help them to conserve water. However, this slows down photosynthesis, because it means less light and carbon dioxide can be absorbed.

Having deep or spreading roots

Desert plants may have to seek water very deep down in the soil, or across a wide area. They usually have either very deep roots, or roots that spread a long way sideways from where the plant is growing.

In fact, many plants – even those that do not live in deserts – have at least some of these adaptations. For example, a plant growing in your garden may have to cope with hot, dry conditions at least some of the time. Most plants have stomata only on the undersides of their leaves, which close when the need arises. Most of them have waxy cuticles on their leaves, to cut down water loss. Desert plants, though, show these adaptations to a much greater extent.

Hydrophytes

Plant that live in very wet places, including those that live in water, are called **hydrophytes**. These plants have no problem of water shortage. They do not need adaptations to conserve water, as desert plants do.

The water hyacinth, *Eichhornia crassipes*, is an example of a plant adapted to live in water (Figure **9.10**). The roots of water hyacinths do not attach to the bed of the river or pond where they grow, but just float freely in the water. The stems and leaf stalks have hollow spaces in them, filled with air, which help them to float on

S the top of the water where they can get plenty of light for photosynthesis.

Water hyacinth leaves have stomata on both surfaces, not just on the underside as in most plants. This allows them to absorb carbon dioxide from the air, for photosynthesis. The cuticle on the upper and lower surfaces of the leaves is much thinner than in plants that don't live in water. There is no need for a thick cuticle, because there is no need to prevent water loss.

Figure 19.10 These big clumps of water hyacinth are floating freely in the water. Water hyacinth has become a very serious weed in many parts of the world, clogging up waterways and preventing light, oxygen and carbon dioxide reaching other plants growing in the water.

19.3 Selection

Over the many millions of years that living things have existed, there have been gradual changes in organisms and populations. Fossils tell us that many animals and plants that once lived no longer exist.

In the 19th century, several ideas were put forward to suggest how this might have happened. By far the most important was suggested by Charles Darwin (Figure **19.11**). He put forward his theory in a book called *On the Origin of Species*, which was published in 1859.

Darwin's theory of how evolution could have happened may be summarised like this.

Variation

Most populations of organisms contain individuals which vary slightly from one to another. Some slight variations may better adapt some organisms to their environment than others.

Over-production

Most organisms produce more young than will survive to adulthood.

Figure 19.11 A portrait of Charles Darwin at the age of 72.

Struggle for existence

Because populations do not generally increase rapidly in size, there must therefore be considerable competition for survival between the organisms.

Survival of the fittest

Only the organisms which are really well adapted to their environment will survive (Figures **19.12** and **19.13**).

Advantageous characteristics passed on to offspring

Only these well-adapted organisms will survive and be able to reproduce successfully, and will pass on the alleles that produce advantageous characteristics to their offspring.

Gradual change

In this way, over a period of time, the population will lose all the poorly adapted individuals. The population will gradually become better adapted to its environment.

The theory is often called the theory of natural selection, because it suggests that the best-adapted organisms are selected to pass on their characteristics to the next generation. We can describe evolution as the change in adaptive features over time, as the result of natural selection.

> ## Key definition
>
> S **process of adaptation** – the process resulting from natural selection, by which populations become more suited to their environment over many generations

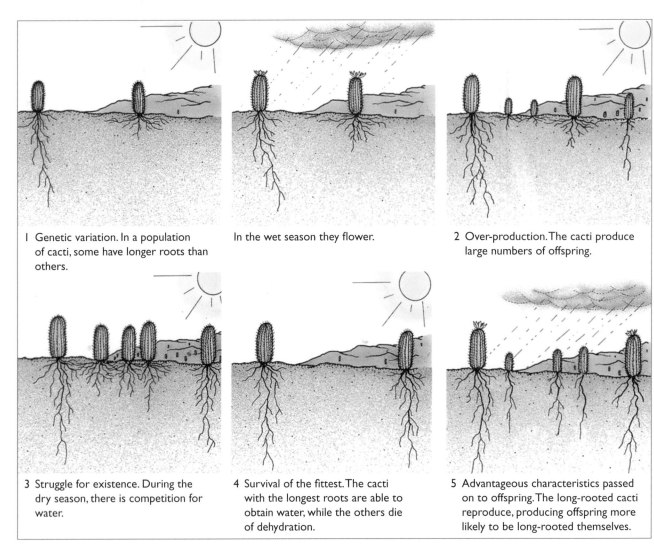

1 Genetic variation. In a population of cacti, some have longer roots than others.

In the wet season they flower.

2 Over-production. The cacti produce large numbers of offspring.

3 Struggle for existence. During the dry season, there is competition for water.

4 Survival of the fittest. The cacti with the longest roots are able to obtain water, while the others die of dehydration.

5 Advantageous characteristics passed on to offspring. The long-rooted cacti reproduce, producing offspring more likely to be long-rooted themselves.

Figure 19.12 An example of how natural selection might occur.

Figure 19.13 When large numbers of organisms, such as these wildebeest of East African plains, live together, there is competition for food, and the weaker ones are likely to be killed by predators. Individuals best adapted to their environment survive and reproduce.

Darwin proposed his theory before anyone understood how characteristics were inherited. Now that we know something about genetics, his theory can be stated slightly differently. We can say that natural selection results in the genes producing advantageous phenotypes being passed on to the next generation more frequently than the genes which produce less advantageous phenotypes.

⑤ An example of natural selection

Darwin's theory of natural selection provides a good explanation for our observations of the many types of animals and plants. For example, it can help us to understand some changes that have taken place in a species of moth in Britain and Ireland.

The peppered moth, *Biston betularia*, lives in most parts of Great Britain and Ireland. It flies by night, and spends the daytime resting on tree trunks. It has speckled wings, which camouflage it very effectively on lichen-covered tree trunks (Figure **19.14**).

People have collected moths for many years, so we know that up until 1849, all the peppered moths in collections were speckled. But in 1849, a black or melanic form of the moth was caught near Manchester. By 1900, 98% of the moths near Manchester were black.

The distribution of the black and speckled forms in 1958 is shown in Figure **19.15**.

How can we explain the sudden rise in numbers of the dark moths, and their distribution today?

We know that the black colour of the moth is caused by a single dominant allele of a gene. The mutation from a normal to a black allele happens fairly often, so it is reasonable to assume that there have always been a few black moths around, as well as pale speckled ones.

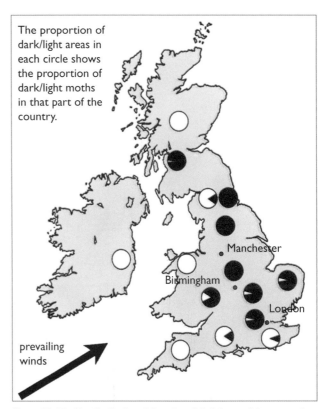

The proportion of dark/light areas in each circle shows the proportion of dark/light moths in that part of the country.

prevailing winds

Figure 19.15 The distribution of the pale and dark forms of the peppered moth, *Biston betularia*, in 1958. Since then, the number of dark moths has dramatically decreased, because now there is much less air pollution.

Figure 19.14 Peppered moths. **a** Lichen-covered bark hides a speckled moth perfectly. **b** Dark moths are better camouflaged on lichen-free trees.

Up until the beginning of the Industrial Revolution, the pale moths had the advantage, as they were better camouflaged on the lichen-covered tree trunks.

But in the middle of the 19th century, some areas became polluted by smoke. Because the prevailing winds in Britain blow from the west, the worst affected areas were to the east of industrial cities like Manchester and Birmingham. The polluted air prevented lichens from growing. Dark moths were better camouflaged than pale moths on trees with no lichens on them.

Proof that the dark moths do have an advantage in polluted areas has been supplied by several investigations. Figure **19.16** summarises one of them.

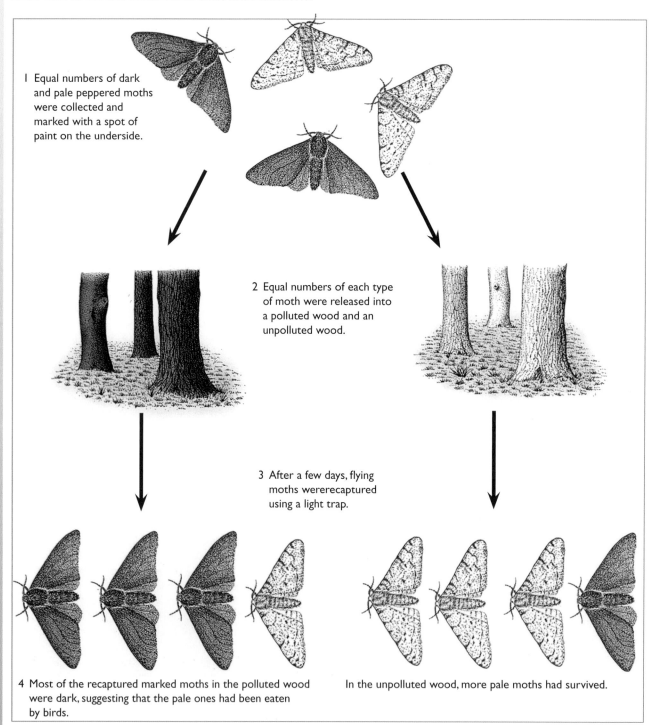

1 Equal numbers of dark and pale peppered moths were collected and marked with a spot of paint on the underside.

2 Equal numbers of each type of moth were released into a polluted wood and an unpolluted wood.

3 After a few days, flying moths wererecaptured using a light trap.

4 Most of the recaptured marked moths in the polluted wood were dark, suggesting that the pale ones had been eaten by birds.

In the unpolluted wood, more pale moths had survived.

Figure 19.16 An investigation to measure the survival of dark and pale peppered moths in polluted and unpolluted environments.

The factor which confers an advantage on the dark moths, and a disadvantage on the pale moths in polluted areas, is predation by birds. This is called a selection pressure, because it 'selects' the dark moths for survival. In unpolluted areas, the pale moths are more likely to survive.

Antibiotic resistance in bacteria

Another example of evolution by natural selection can be seen in the way that bacteria may become resistant to antibiotics, such as penicillin. Penicillin works by stopping bacteria from forming cell walls. When a person infected with bacteria is treated with penicillin, the bacteria are unable to grow new cell walls, and they burst open.

However, the population of bacteria in the person's body may be several million. The chances of any one of them mutating to a form which is not affected by penicillin is quite low, but because there are so many bacteria, it could well happen. If it does, the mutant bacterium will have a tremendous advantage. It will be able to go on reproducing while all the others cannot. Soon, its descendants may form a huge population of penicillin-resistant bacteria (Figure **19.17**).

This does, in fact, happen quite frequently. This is one reason why there are so many different antibiotics available – if some bacteria become resistant to one, they may be treated with another.

The more we use an antibiotic, the more we are exerting a selection pressure which favours the resistant forms. If antibiotics are used too often, we may end up with resistant strains of bacteria that are very difficult to control. A form of the bacterium *Staphyloccus aureus* has become resistant to several different antibiotics, and is known as MRSA. This can cause infections that are very difficult to treat.

Stabilising selection

Natural selection does not always produce change. Natural selection ensures that the organisms which are best adapted to their environment will survive. Change will only occur if the environment changes, or if a new mutation appears which adapts the organism better to the existing environment.

For example, in the south-west of Britain, the environment of the peppered moth has never changed very much. The air has not become polluted, so lichens have continued to grow on trees. The best camouflaged moths have always been the pale ones. So selection has always favoured the pale moths in this part of Britain. Any mutant dark moths which do appear are at a disadvantage, and are unlikely to survive.

Most of the time, natural selection tends to keep populations very much the same from generation to generation. It is sometimes called stabilising selection. If an organism is well adapted to its environment, and if that environment stays the same, then the organism will not evolve. Coelacanths, for example, have remained virtually unchanged for 350 million years. They live deep in the Indian Ocean, which is a very stable environment (Figure **19.18**).

Figure 19.18   Coelacanths, which live deep in the Indian Ocean, have existed almost unchanged for 350 million years. Humans have existed for only about 4 million years.

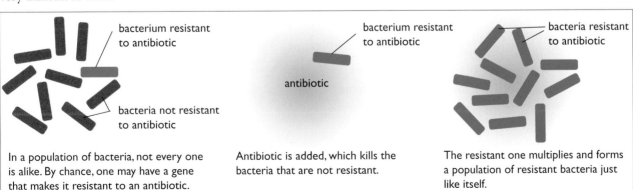

bacterium resistant to antibiotic

bacteria not resistant to antibiotic

bacterium resistant to antibiotic

antibiotic

bacteria resistant to antibiotic

In a population of bacteria, not every one is alike. By chance, one may have a gene that makes it resistant to an antibiotic.

Antibiotic is added, which kills the bacteria that are not resistant.

The resistant one multiplies and forms a population of resistant bacteria just like itself.

Figure 19.17   How resistance to antibiotics increases in a population of bacteria.

S Sickle cell anaemia

A genetic disease called sickle cell anaemia is a good example of how natural selection can work in humans.

Some people have a mutation in the gene that codes for the production of haemoglobin. The normal allele, **Hb^A**, codes for normal haemoglobin. The mutant allele, **Hb^S**, codes for an allele that produces a faulty type of haemoglobin. This allele has a tiny difference in the DNA base sequence. This changes the amino acid sequence in the haemoglobin, preventing the haemoglobin working as it should.

This faulty haemoglobin has a tendency to produce fibres inside red blood cells when oxygen concentration is low. The red blood cells get pulled into a 'sickle' shape and get stuck in blood capillaries.

When this happens, the person is said to be suffering a sickle cell crisis. The blockages in the blood vessels stop blood flowing to some parts of the body, and they cause pain. The pain can last for a few hours, or for more than a week.

Even when they are not having a sickle cell crisis, a person with sickle cell anaemia may feel tired and short of breath, because their faulty haemoglobin does not deliver oxygen to their cells efficiently. This means that the cells cannot carry out as much respiration to release energy for body activities.

If a person with sickle cell anaemia has frequent crises, then damage will be done to many different organs, including the kidneys, liver, eyes and heart. With good hospital treatment, many people with sickle cell anaemia will live into their 80s. Without treatment, however, many will die earlier than people who do not have this disease.

The two alleles are codominant. A person with genotype **Hb^AHb^A** has normal haemoglobin, a person with genotype **Hb^AHb^S** has a mix of normal and sickle cell haemoglobin, and a person with genotype **Hb^SHb^S** has all sickle cell haemoglobin. Heterozygous people don't usually show any symptoms.

If sickle cell anaemia is such a dangerous disease, then why has natural selection not removed it from the human population? The answer lies with another disease – malaria.

Malaria is a serious disease caused by a single-celled parasite that is injected into the blood when an infected mosquito bites. Millions of people are killed by this disease each year, most of them children. A person who lives in a part of the world where malaria is present, and who has some resistance to the disease, will be at an advantage compared with others who are susceptible. S

Malaria is common in many parts of the world where the sickle cell allele is present in the population (Figure **19.19**). In the past, people homozygous for the sickle cell allele often died early from sickle cell disease. People homozygous for the normal allele often died early from malaria. Those, however, who were heterozygous (with one **Hb^S** allele and one **Hb^A** allele) were more resistant to malaria than those with all normal haemoglobin. In parts of the world where malaria was present, people with the heterozygous genotype were most likely to survive until they were old enough to reproduce.

Therefore, in each generation, the people most likely to reproduce were heterozygous people. Some of the children of heterozygous parents will also be heterozygous, but some will be homozygous dominant and some homozygous recessive. This continued for generation after generation.

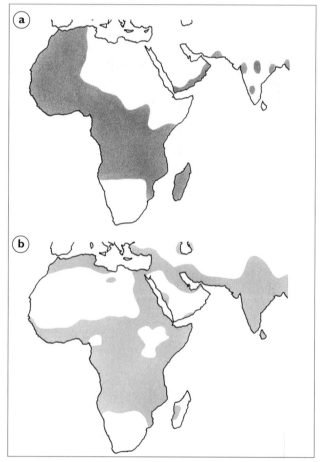

Figure 19.19   The distribution of **a** the sickle cell allele and **b** malaria.

Selective breeding

Humans can also bring about changes in living organisms, by selecting certain individuals for breeding. Figures **19.20** and **19.21** show examples of the results of this kind of selection. For example, from the varied individuals amongst a herd of cattle, the breeder chooses the ones with the characteristics he or she wants to appear in the next generation. He or she then allows these individuals, and not the others, to breed. If this selection process is repeated over many generations, these characteristics will become the most common ones in the population.

Figure 19.21   **a** White Park cattle, like these in England, are a very old breed. They are thought to be quite similar to original wild cattle. **b** Friesian cattle have been bred for high milk yield.

Figure 19.20   Wild and cultivated apples.

S This process is called **artificial selection**. It has been going on for thousands of years, ever since humans first began to cultivate plants and to domesticate animals. It works in just the same way as natural selection. Individuals with 'advantageous' characteristics breed, while those with 'disadvantageous' ones do not.

However, what humans think are desirable characteristics would often not be at all advantageous to the plant or animal if it was living in the wild. Modern varieties of cattle, for example, selected over hundreds of years for high milk yield or fast meat production, would stand little chance of surviving for long in the wild.

Some farmers are now beginning to think differently **S** about the characteristics they want in their animals and plants. Instead of enormous yields as their first priority, they are now looking for varieties which can grow well with less fertiliser or pesticides in the case of food plants, and with less expensive housing and feeding in the case of animals. Luckily, many of the older breeds, which had these characteristics, have been conserved, and can now be used to breed new varieties with 'easy-care' characteristics.

S 19.4 Using the six points listed on page 253, explain why the proportion of dark peppered moths near Manchester in Britain increased at the end of the 19th century.

19.5 Why is it unwise to use antibiotics unnecessarily?

19.6 What is meant by stabilising selection? Give one example.

19.7 Draw a genetic diagram to show how two heterozygous parents can have a child with sickle cell anaemia.

19.8 Imagine you are a farmer with a herd of dairy cattle. You want to build up a herd with a very high production of milk. You have access to sperm samples from bulls, for each of which there are records of the milk production of his offspring. What will you do?

19.9 Wheat is attacked by many different pests, including a fungus called yellow rust. **S**

a Describe how you could use artificial selection to produce a new variety of wheat which is naturally resistant to yellow rust.

b How could the growing of resistant varieties reduce pollution?

c When resistant varieties of wheat are produced, it is found that after a few years they are infected by yellow rust again. Explain how this might happen.

Summary

You should know:
- ♦ about continuous and discontinuous variation, and what causes them
- ♦ about mutation
- **S** ♦ how organisms are adapted to their environments
- ♦ what is meant by fitness
- **S** ♦ how natural selection happens
- ♦ how antibiotic-resistant strains of bacteria develop
- ♦ about sickle cell anaemia and the reasons for its distribution
- ♦ about selective breeding.

End-of-chapter questions

1 Copy and complete the following sentences, using words from the list. You may use each word once, more than once or not at all.

| adapted | continuous | discontinuous | environment | genes | genus |
| matched | mutation | selection | sex | species | |

Variation can be defined as differences between individuals of the same .... Sometimes, the differences are clear-cut, and each individual fits into one a small number of defined categories. This is called .... variation. This kind of variation is caused by the organisms' .... In other cases, the differences have no definite categories. This is called .... variation.

Cell division by mitosis does not usually produce variation, unless there is a change in the DNA, called .... Most mutations are harmful, because they make an organism less well .... to its environment.

2 Distinguish between each of these pairs of terms.

    a genetic variation, environmental variation

    b continuous variation, discontinuous variation

(S)   **c** natural selection, artificial selection

(S) 3 Suggest explanations for each of the following.

    a A population of organisms that can reproduce sexually often becomes adapted to a new environment more quickly than a population that can only reproduce asexually.

    b Changes in the characteristics of a species may continue to happen even after it has become well adapted to its environment.

4 There is variation in the way in which human ear lobes are naturally joined to the head. The diagram below shows the two versions.

attached

free

    a Feel your own ear lobes and record whether you have attached or free ear lobes. [1]
    The results of a survey of the ear lobes of some students are shown in the table below.

Age / years	Number of students with free ear lobes		Number of students with attached ear lobes	
	male	female	male	female
12	11	12	4	2
13	9	14	3	5
14	10	8	4	3
15	13	10	2	5
total	43	44	13	15

    b **i** What can you conclude from these results? [2]

        ii Calculate the approximate ratio of free to attached ear lobes in this group. [2]

       iii Explain how this ratio might help in understanding the way in which the attachment of ear lobes is inherited. [2]

[Cambridge O Level Biology Paper 5090/62, Question 2, May/June 2010]

⑤ 5 Reed warblers are small birds that migrate over long distances between western Africa and northern Europe.

The photograph below shows a reed warbler, *Acrocephalus scirpaceus*.

a State three characteristic features of birds that are visible in the photograph. [3]

A study was carried out in Sweden into the effects of natural selection on wing length in reed warblers.

The wings of young reed warblers reach their maximum length a few days after leaving the nest.

At this age the wing length in millimetres of each bird was recorded. Each bird was identified by putting a small ring around one of its legs.

When the birds were caught in net traps as adults, the information on the rings was used to identify specific birds and their ages.

The length of time between ringing and trapping was recorded for each bird that was identified before it was released.

The mean age at trapping was calculated for birds with each wing length.

The results are shown in the table opposite.

Wing length at ringing / mm	Number of birds trapped	Mean age at trapping / days
63 or less	24	253
64	72	256
65	130	297
66	183	346
67	167	349
68	106	270
69	66	237
70 or more	23	199
	total = 771	

b i   Explain why wing length is an example of continuous variation.   [2]

   ii   Suggest a feature of reed warblers, **other than wing length**, that shows
      continuous variation.   [1]

c   The researchers concluded that reed warblers with a wing length of 66–67 mm had the
   best chance of survival.

   i   Describe the evidence from the table that supports this conclusion.   [4]

   ii   The researchers also suggested that more evidence was needed to make
      this conclusion.
      Suggest what other evidence would show that birds with wings 66–67 mm in length
      have the best chance of survival.   [3]

d   Scientists have discovered that genes are responsible for wing length in reed warblers.
   The most common length of wing has been 66–67 mm for many generations of
   these birds.
   Explain how natural selection may be responsible for maintaining the mean wing length
   of reed warblers at 66–67 mm.   [4]

[Adaptd from Cambridge IGCSE® Biology 0610/32, Question 5, October/November 2011]

20 Organisms and their environment

In this chapter, you will find out about:

- ♦ food chains and webs
- Ⓢ♦ efficiency of energy transfer in food chains
- ♦ pyramids of numbers
- Ⓢ♦ pyramids of biomass
- ♦ the carbon cycle and the water cycle
- Ⓢ♦ the nitrogen cycle
- ♦ populations and the factors that affect them.

A fossil food chain

About 250 million years ago, there was a huge supercontinent on Earth, called Pangaea. The centre of this enormous landmass was so far from the sea that rain rarely fell. Later, as the plates that make up the Earth's crust drifted apart, Pangaea broke up. Some of the central areas became what is now Russia.

We know something about the animals that lived in this area at that time, because we have found their fossils. We know that there were herbivores that ate vegetation, and carnivores that fed on the herbivores. We can work this out from their skeletons and teeth. For example, if an animal has broad, flat teeth with ridges on them, this suggests it was adapted to feed on plants. If its teeth were pointed and sharp, this suggests it killed and ate other animals.

It's difficult, though, to be certain exactly what any one species ate, so we can only guess at what food chains and food webs might have existed 250 million years ago in this part of the world. One strong possibility is that a carnivore called *Inostrancevia* preyed on a herbivore called *Scutosaurus* (Figure **20.1**). Fossils of both of these dinosaurs are found in similar areas, and date from the same time. But we can only guess that these two species were part of the same food chain.

Figure 20.1 It is possible that the predator *Inostrancevia* killed and ate the well-armoured herbivore *Scutosaurus*.

20.1 Ecology

One very important way of studying living things is to study them where they live. Animals and plants do not live in complete isolation. They are affected by their surroundings, or environment. Their environment is also affected by them. The study of the interaction between living organisms and their environment is called ecology.

There are many words used in ecology with which it is useful to be familiar.

The area where an organism lives is called its habitat. The habitat of a tadpole might be a pond. There will probably be many tadpoles in the pond, forming a population of tadpoles. A population is a group of organisms of the same species, living in the same area at the same time.

But tadpoles will not be the only organisms living in the pond. There will be many other kinds of animals and plants making up the pond community. A community is all the organisms, of all the different species, living in the same habitat.

The living organisms in the pond, the water in it, the stones and the mud at the bottom, make up an ecosystem. An ecosystem consists of a community and its environment (Figure 20.2).

Within the ecosystem, each living organism has its own life to live and role to play. The way in which an organism lives its life in an ecosystem is called its niche. Tadpoles, for example, eat algae and other weeds in the pond; they disturb pebbles and mud at the bottom of shallow areas in the pond; they excrete ammonia into the water; they breathe in oxygen from the water, and breathe out carbon dioxide. All these things, and many others, help to describe the tadpoles' role, or niche, in the ecosystem.

Key definitions

population – a group of organisms of one species, living in the same area at the same time

S ecosystem – a unit containing all of the organisms and their environment, interacting together, in a given area e.g. decomposing log or a lake

community – all of the populations of different species in an ecosystem

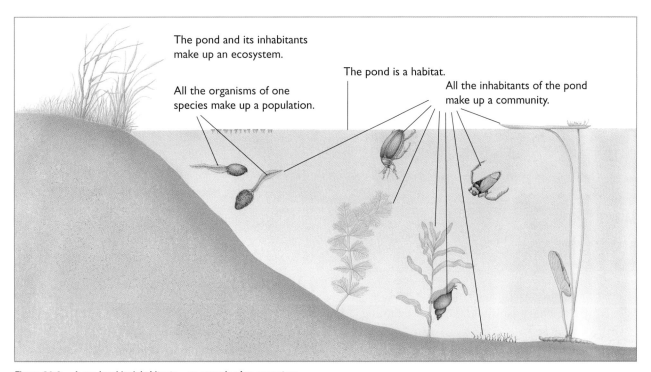

The pond and its inhabitants make up an ecosystem.

All the organisms of one species make up a population.

The pond is a habitat.

All the inhabitants of the pond make up a community.

Figure 20.2   A pond and its inhabitants – an example of an ecosystem.

20.2 Energy flow

All living organisms need energy. They get energy from food, by respiration. All the energy in an ecosystem originates from the Sun. Some of the energy in sunlight is captured by plants, and used to make food – glucose, starch and other organic substances such as fats and proteins. These contain some of the energy from the sunlight. When the plant needs energy, it breaks down some of this food by respiration.

Animals get their food, and therefore their energy, by ingesting (eating) plants, or by eating animals which have eaten plants.

The sequence by which energy, in the form of chemical energy in food, passes from a plant to an animal and then to other animals, is called a food chain. Figure 20.3 shows one example of a food chain.

Many different food chains link to form a food web. Figure 20.4 shows an example of a food web.

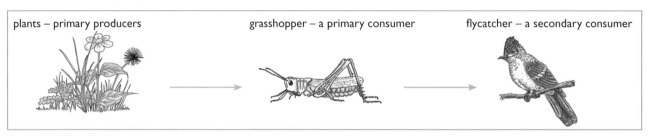

Figure 20.3   A food chain.

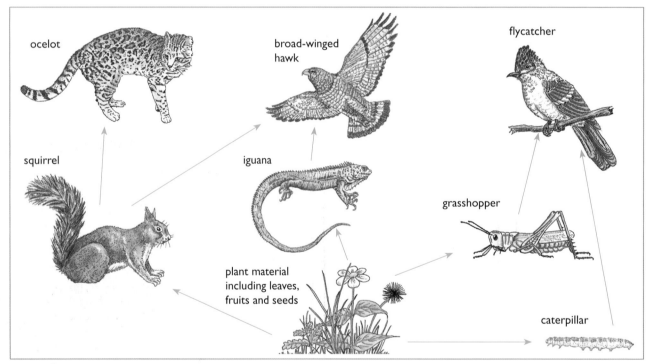

Figure 20.4   A food web.

❓ Questions

20.1   What is ecology?

20.2   What is a population?

20.3   Give **two** examples of an ecosystem, other than a pond.

Producers and consumers

Every food chain begins with green plants because only they can capture the energy from sunlight. They are called producers, because they produce food.

Animals are consumers. An animal which eats plants is a primary consumer, because it is the first consumer in a food chain. An animal which eats that animal is a secondary consumer, and so on along the chain. Primary consumers are also called herbivores, and higher level consumers are carnivores.

If we count the numbers of organisms at different positions in a food chain, we usually find that there are more plants than animals, and more herbivores than carnivores. We can show this by drawing a kind of graph called a pyramid of numbers (Figure 20.5). In the pyramid, the size of each block represents the number of organisms at that step in the food chain.

Ⓢ Energy losses

As energy is passed along a food chain, some of it is lost to the environment. This happens in many ways.

♦ When an organism uses food for respiration, some of the energy released from the food is lost as heat energy to the environment.

♦ When one organism eats another, it rarely eats absolutely all of it. For example, the grasshopper in the food chain in Figure 20.3 may eat almost all of the parts of the plant above ground, but it will not eat the roots. So not all of the energy in the plant is transferred to the grasshoppers.

♦ When an animal eats another organism as food, enzymes in its digestive system break down most of the large food molecules, so that they can be absorbed. But not all of the food molecules are digested and absorbed, and the ones that are not are eventually lost from the body in the faeces. These faeces contain energy that is lost from this food chain.

This means that, the further you go along a food chain, the less energy is available for each successive group of organisms (Figure 20.6). The plants get a lot of energy from the Sun, but only a fraction of this energy is absorbed by the grasshoppers, and only a fraction of that is absorbed by the flycatchers. This explains why predators are usually much rarer than herbivores, and why there are usually many more plants than animals in an ecosystem.

Trophic levels

In Figure 20.5, the number of organisms in the food chain is shown as a pyramid. Each level in the pyramid is called a trophic level ('trophic' means feeding).

The pyramid is this shape because there is less energy available as you go up the trophic levels, so there are fewer organisms at each level. This loss of energy limits the length of food chains. They rarely have more than five trophic levels, as there is not enough energy left to support a sixth.

Many organisms feed at more than one trophic level. You, for example, are a primary consumer when you eat vegetables, a secondary consumer when you eat meat or drink milk, and a tertiary consumer when you eat a predatory fish such as a salmon.

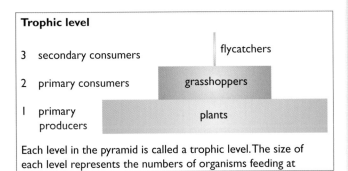

Figure 20.5   A pyramid of numbers.

Trophic level

3   secondary consumers — flycatchers

2   primary consumers — grasshoppers

1   primary producers — plants

Each level in the pyramid is called a trophic level. The size of each level represents the numbers of organisms feeding at

Key definitions

producer – an organism that makes its own organic nutrients, usually using energy from sunlight, through photosynthesis

consumer – an organism that gets its energy by feeding on other organisms

herbivore – an animal that gets its energy by eating plants

carnivore – an animal that gets its energy by eating other animals

trophic level – the position of an organism in a Ⓢ food chain, food web or pyramid of biomass or numbers

Figure 20.6   Energy losses in a food chain.

Activity 20.1
Studying an ecosystem

Skills
AO3.3 Observing, measuring and recording
AO3.4 Interpreting and evaluating observations and data

In this activity, you will try to work out some food chains in an ecosystem. Remember that you must disturb the ecosystem as little as possible. Do not take plants or animals away from the ecosystem unless your teacher tells you that you can do this. If you have a digital camera, take photographs of the organisms rather than collecting them.

1   Search the area thoroughly and try to identify all the types of plants in the area. If you cannot identify a plant, and there appears to be a lot of it, then collect samples of leaves and flowers to take back to your laboratory, where you can spend longer trying to find out what it is. Better still, take photographs of the plant so that you do not need to take samples from it.

2   Try to identify any small animals you see. Where possible, take photographs of each kind of animal.

3   Make notes about the large animals in the area, such as the types of bird present and what they are feeding on.

4   In the laboratory, with your teacher's assistance, try to identify all the organisms you found.

5   Use books or the Internet to find out what some of the animals feed on.

6   Construct a food web for this ecosystem.

S Pyramids of biomass

Figure 20.7 shows a differently shaped pyramid of numbers. The pyramid is this shape because of the sizes (biomass) of the organisms in the food chain. Although there is only a single tree, it is huge compared with the caterpillars which feed on it.

If you make the areas of the blocks represent the mass of the organisms, instead of their numbers, then the pyramid becomes the right shape again. It is called a **pyramid of biomass** (Figure 20.8), and gives a much better idea of the actual quantity of animal or plant material at each trophic level.

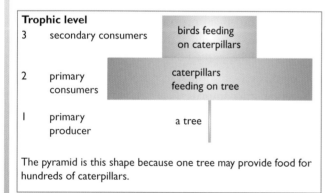

The pyramid is this shape because one tree may provide food for hundreds of caterpillars.

Figure 20.7   An inverted pyramid of numbers.

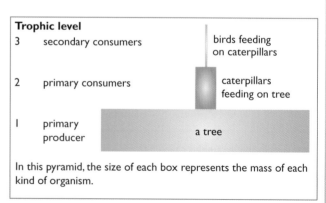

In this pyramid, the size of each box represents the mass of each kind of organism.

Figure 20.8   A pyramid of biomass.

Energy efficiency

Understanding how energy is passed along a food chain can be useful in agriculture. We can eat a wide variety of foods, and can feed at several different trophic levels. Which is the most efficient sort of food for a farmer to grow, and for us to eat?

The nearer to the beginning of the food chain we feed, the more energy there is available for us. This is why our staple foods, such as wheat, rice and potatoes, are plants.

When we eat meat, eggs or cheese, or drink milk, we are feeding further along the food chain. There is less energy available for us from the original energy provided by the Sun. It would be more efficient in principle to eat the grass in a field, rather than to let cattle eat it, and then to eat them.

In fact, however, although there is far more energy in the grass than in the cattle, it is not available to us. We simply cannot digest the cellulose in grass, so we cannot release the energy from it. The cattle can; they turn the energy in cellulose into energy in protein and fat, which we can digest.

However, there are many plant products which we can eat. Soya beans, for example, yield a large amount of protein, much more efficiently and cheaply than cattle or other animals. A change towards vegetarianism would enable more food to be produced on the Earth, if the right crops were chosen.

Questions

20.4 Where does all the energy in living organisms originate from?

20.5 Write down a food chain **a** which ends with humans, **b** is in the sea, and **c** that has five links in it.

20.6 Why are green plants called producers?

20.7 Why are there rarely more than five links in a food chain?

Activity 20.2
Investigating the food preferences of slugs

Skills
AO3.3 Observing, measuring and recording
AO3.4 Interpreting and evaluating observations and data

1 Collect 12 slugs or other small herbivores of the same species.

2 Collect leaves from four different kinds of plant growing in the same area.

3 Identify the plants and call them A, B, C and D.

4 Place pairs of undamaged leaves into six jars as follows:

A and B   B and C   A and C
B and D   A and D   C and D

Make sure that you label the jars.

5 To each jar add two animals and put the lid on.

6 On the next day, remove the animals and examine the leaves.

7 Draw up a suitable results table. For each leaf record the amount eaten as follows:

No damage	0
Leaf nibbled	1
Less than half eaten	2
More than half eaten	3
Leaf completely eaten	4

8 For each type of leaf, add the scores. Construct a histogram or pie chart to show the results.

Questions

A1 Which kind of plant did your animals prefer?

A2 Can you suggest why your animals preferred this kind of plant?

A3 Why must undamaged leaves be used in the experiment?

A4 Why were the leaves used in pairs rather than one at a time?

A5 Do you think that it would have been better to give the animals all the leaves at one time?

20.3 Nutrient cycles

Decomposers

One very important group of organisms which is easy to overlook when you are studying an ecosystem, is the **decomposers**. They feed on waste material from animals and plants, and on their dead bodies. Many fungi and bacteria are decomposers.

Decomposers are extremely important, because they help to release substances from dead organisms, so that they can be used again by living ones. Two of these substances are carbon and nitrogen.

The carbon cycle

Carbon is a very important component of living things, because it is an essential part of carbohydrates, fats and proteins.

Figure **20.9** shows how carbon circulates through an ecosystem. The air contains about 0.04% carbon dioxide. When plants photosynthesise, carbon atoms from carbon dioxide become part of glucose or starch molecules in the plant.

Some of the glucose is then broken down by the plant in respiration. The carbon in the glucose becomes part of a carbon dioxide molecule again, and is released back into the air.

Some of the carbon in the plant will be eaten by animals. The animals respire, releasing some of it back into the air as carbon dioxide.

When the plant or animal dies, decomposers will feed on them. The carbon becomes part of the decomposers' bodies. When they respire, they release carbon dioxide into the air again.

The ways in which human activities such as deforestation and burning fossil fuels, can affect the carbon cycle are described on pages 299–301.

> ## Key definition
>
> **S** **decomposer** – an organism that gets its energy from dead or waste organic matter

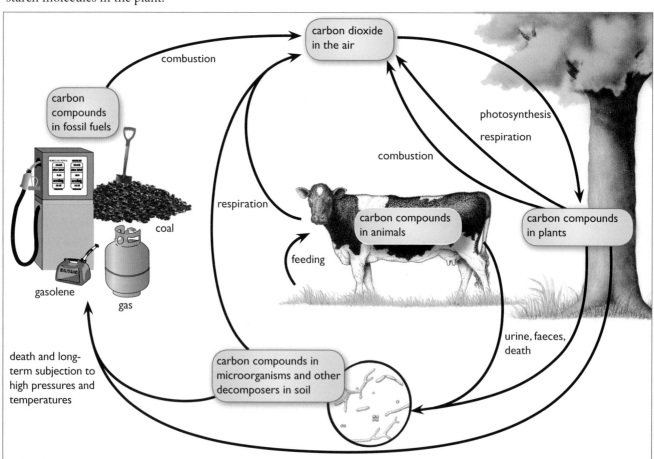

Figure 20.9 The carbon cycle.

⑤ The nitrogen cycle

Living things need nitrogen to make proteins. There is plenty of nitrogen around. The air is about 78% nitrogen gas. Molecules of nitrogen gas, N_2, are made of two nitrogen atoms joined together. These molecules are very inert, which means that they will not readily react with other substances.

So, although the air is full of nitrogen, it is in such an unreactive form that plants and animals cannot use it at all. It must first be changed into a more reactive form, such as ammonia (NH_3) or nitrates (NO_3^-).

Changing nitrogen gas into a more reactive form is called **nitrogen fixation** (Figure **20.10**). There are several ways that it can happen.

Lightning

Lightning makes some of the nitrogen gas in the air combine with oxygen, forming nitrogen oxides. They dissolve in rain, and are washed into the soil, where they form nitrates.

Artificial fertilisers

Nitrogen and hydrogen can be made to react in an industrial chemical process, forming ammonia. The ammonia is used to make ammonium compounds and nitrates, which are sold as fertilisers.

Nitrogen-fixing bacteria

These bacteria live in the soil, or in root nodules (small swellings) on plants like peas, beans and clover. One kind is called *Rhizobium* ('rhizo' means root, 'bium' means living). (Note that you do not need to remember this name.) They use nitrogen gas from the air spaces in the soil, and combine it with other substances to make ammonium ions and other compounds.

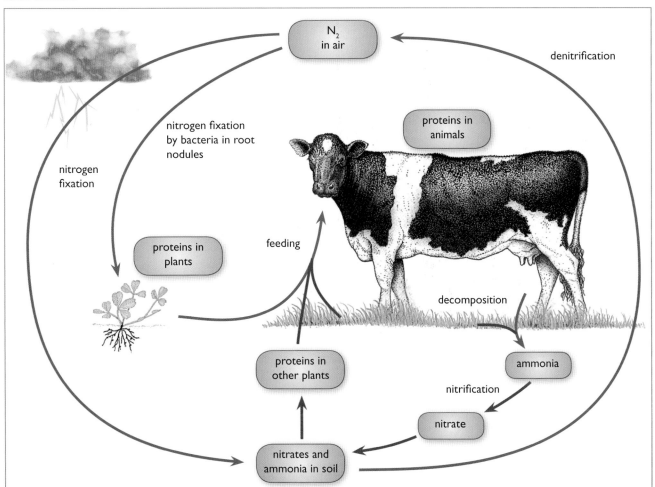

Figure 20.10   The nitrogen cycle.

S Once the nitrogen has been fixed, it can be used to make proteins. Animals eat the plants, so animals get their nitrogen in the form of proteins.

When an animal or plant dies, bacteria and fungi decompose the body. The protein, containing nitrogen, is broken down to ammonium ions and this is released. Another group of bacteria, called **nitrifying bacteria**, turn these ions into nitrates, which plants can use again.

Nitrogen is also returned to the soil when animals excrete nitrogenous waste material, which they have produced by deamination of excess amino acids (page **155**). It may be in the form of ammonia or urea. Again, nitrifying bacteria will convert it to nitrates.

A third group of bacteria complete the nitrogen cycle. They are called **denitrifying bacteria**, because they undo the work done by nitrifying bacteria. They turn nitrates and ammonia in the soil into nitrogen gas, which goes into the atmosphere.

The water cycle

Figure **20.11** shows how water cycles between living organisms and their environment. Living things, especially trees, play a very important role in this cycle. When precipitation occurs, the tree roots absorb water from the soil. The water travels up through xylem vessels into the leaves, where some of it evaporates and diffuses out of the stomata as water vapour (Figure **8.11**, page **98**).

20.4 Population size

We have seen that a population is all the individuals of a particular species that live together in a habitat. In this section, we will look at how and why population sizes change, and begin to consider the implication of Earth's rapidly increasing human population.

Most populations tend to stay roughly the same size over a period of time. They may go up and down (fluctuate) but the average population will probably

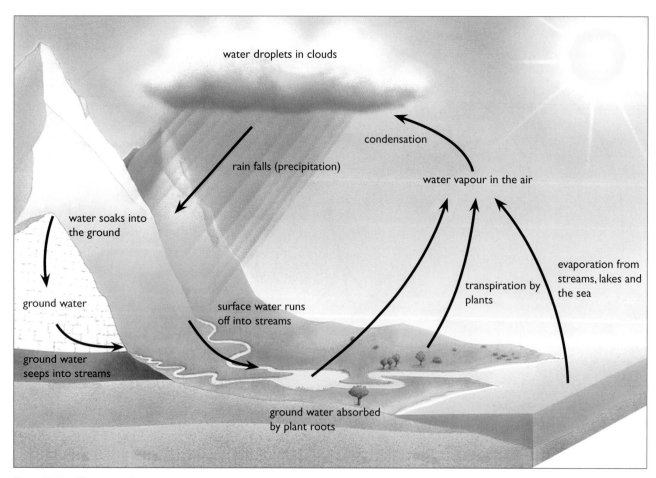

Figure 20.11 The water cycle.

stay the same over a number of years. The population of greenfly in a garden, for example, might be much greater one year than the next. But their numbers will almost certainly be back to normal in a year or so. Over many years, the sizes of most populations tend to remain at around the same level.

Yet if all the offspring of one female greenfly survived and reproduced, she could be the ancestor of 600 000 000 000 greenfly in just one year. Why doesn't the greenfly population shoot upwards like this? Why isn't the world overrun with greenfly?

The answers to those questions are of great importance to human beings, because our own population is doing just that; it is shooting upwards at an alarming rate. Every hour, there are more than 9000 extra people in the world. We need to understand why this is happening, and what is likely to happen next. Can we slow down the increase? What happens if we don't?

Birth rate and death rate

The size of a population depends on how many individuals leave the population, and how many enter it.

Individuals leave a population when they die, or when they migrate to another population. Individuals enter a population when they are born, or when they migrate into the population from elsewhere. Usually, births and deaths are more important in determining population sizes than immigration and emigration.

A population increases if new individuals are born faster than the old ones die – that is, when the birth rate is greater than the death rate. If birth rate is less than death rate, then the population will decrease. If birth rate and death rate are equal, the population will stay the same size.

This explains why we are not knee-deep in greenfly. Although the greenfly population's birth rate is enormous, the death rate is also enormous. Greenfly are eaten by ladybirds and birds, and sprayed with pesticides by gardeners and farmers. Over a period of time, the greenfly's birth and death rates stay about the same, so the population doesn't change very much.

Factors affecting population growth

By looking at changes in population sizes in other organisms, we can learn quite a lot about our own. Many experiments on population sizes have been done on organisms like bacteria and yeast, because they

reproduce quickly and are easy to grow. Figure **20.12** shows the results of an experiment in which a few yeast cells are put into a container of nutrient broth. The cells feed on the broth, grow and reproduce. The numbers of yeast cells are counted every few hours.

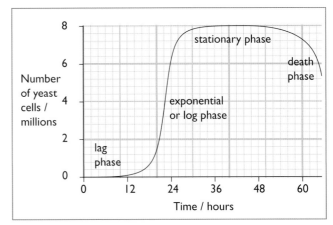

Figure 20.12 The growth of a population of yeast.

At the beginning of the experiment, the population only grows quite slowly, because there are not many cells there to reproduce. They also need time to adjust to the new conditions. This is called the **lag phase**.

But once they get going, growth is very rapid. Each cell divides to form 2, then 4, then 8, then 16. There is nothing to hold them back except the time it takes to grow and divide. This is called the **log phase**, or **exponential phase**.

As the population gets larger, the individual cells can no longer reproduce as fast, and begin to die off more rapidly. This may be because there is not enough food left for them all, or it might be that they have made so much alcohol that they are poisoning themselves. The cells are now dying off as fast as new ones are being produced, so the population stops growing and levels off. This is called the **stationary phase**.

Eventually, the death rate exceeds the birth rate, so the number of living yeast cells in the population starts to fall. This is called the **death phase**.

This curve is sometimes called a sigmoid growth curve. 'Sigma' is the old Greek letter s, so 'sigmoid' means S-shaped.

Although the experiment with the yeast is done in artificial conditions, a similar pattern is found in the growth of populations of many species in the wild. If a few individuals get into a new environment, then their

S population curve may be very like the one for yeast cells in broth. The population increases quickly at first, and then levels off.

The levelling off is always caused by some kind of environmental factor. In the case of the yeast, the factor may be food supply. Other populations may be limited by disease, or the number of nest sites, or the number of predators, for example. The factor that stops the population from getting any larger is called a limiting factor.

It is usually very difficult to find out which environmental factors are controlling the size of a population. Almost always, many different factors will interact. A population of rabbits, for example, might be affected by the number of foxes and other predators, the amount of food available, the amount of space for burrows, and the amount of infection by the virus which causes myxomatosis.

Figure 20.13 shows an example of how the size of population of a **predator** may be affected by its prey. This information comes from the number of skins which were sold by fur traders in Northern Canada to the Hudson Bay Company, between 1845 and 1925. Snowshoe hares and northern lynxes were both trapped for their fur, and the numbers caught probably give a very good idea of their population sizes.

Snowshoe hare populations tend to vary from year to year. No-one is quite sure why this happens, but it may be related to their food supply. Whenever the snowshoe hare population rises, the lynx population also rises shortly afterwards, as the lynxes now have more food. A drop in the snowshoe hare population is rapidly followed by a drop in the lynx population.

The numbers tend to go up and down, or oscillate, but the average population sizes stay roughly the same over many years.

Age pyramids

When scientists begin to study a population, they want to know whether the population is growing or shrinking. This can be done by counting the population over many years, or by measuring its birth rate and death rate. But often it is much easier just to count the numbers of individuals in various age groups at one point in time, and to draw an age pyramid.

Figure 20.14 shows two examples of age pyramids. The area of each box represents the numbers of individuals in that age group.

Figure 20.14a is a bottom-heavy pyramid, because there are far more young individuals than old ones. This indicates that birth rate is greater than death rate, so this population is increasing.

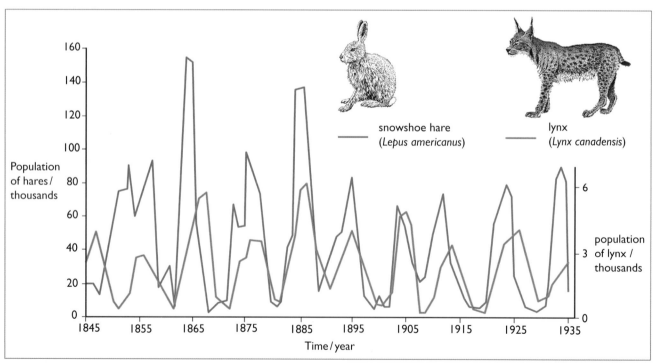

Figure 20.13 Variations in snowshoe hare and lynx populations in northern Canada.

Figure **20.14b** shows a much more even spread of ages. Birth rate and death rate are probably about the same. This population will remain about the same size.

If an age pyramid is drawn for the human population on Earth, it is bottom-heavy, like Figure **20.14a**. Age pyramids for many of the world's developing countries are also this shape, showing that their populations are increasing. But an age pyramid for a European country such as France looks more like Figure **20.14b**. The human population in France is staying about the same.

The human population

Figure **20.15** shows how the human population of the world has changed since about 3000 BC. For most of that time, human populations have been kept in check by a combination of disease, famine and war. Nevertheless, there has still been a steady increase.

Twice there have been definite 'spurts' in this growth. The first was around 8000 BC, not shown on the graph, when people in the Middle East began to farm, instead of just hunting and finding food. The second began around 300 years ago, and is still happening now. In 2012, the world's population reached 7 billion.

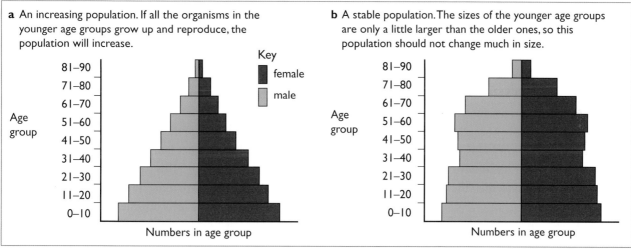

a An increasing population. If all the organisms in the younger age groups grow up and reproduce, the population will increase.

b A stable population. The sizes of the younger age groups are only a little larger than the older ones, so this population should not change much in size.

Figure 20.14 Age pyramids.

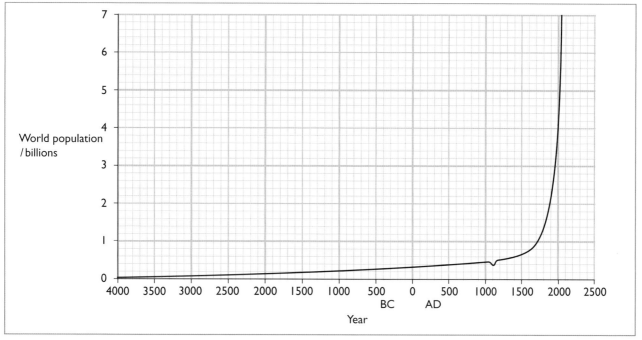

Figure 20.15 The growth of the human population on Earth.

There are two main reasons for this recent growth spurt. The first is the reduction of disease. Improvements in water supply, sewage treatment, hygienic food handling and general standards of cleanliness have virtually wiped out many diseases in countries such as the USA and most European countries – for example typhoid and dysentery. Immunisation against diseases such as polio has made these very rare indeed. Smallpox has been totally eradicated. And the discovery of antibiotics has now made it possible to treat most diseases caused by bacteria.

Secondly, there has been an increase in food supply. More and more land has been brought under cultivation. Moreover, agriculture has become more efficient, so that in many parts of the world each hectare of land is now producing more food than ever before.

Birth rate and death rate

The human population has increased dramatically because the death rate has been brought down. More and more people are now living long enough to reproduce. If the birth rate doesn't drop by the same amount as the death rate, then the world population will continue to increase.

In developed countries, the dramatic fall in the death rate began in about 1700. To begin with, the birth rate stayed high, so the population grew rapidly. But since 1800, there has been a marked drop in birth rate. In 1870, for example, the 'average' British family was 6.6 children, but by 1977 it was only 1.8. In Britain, birth rate and death rate are now about equal.

However, in many developing countries, the fall in the death rate only began about 50 years ago. As yet, the birth rates have not dropped, and so the populations are rising rapidly.

The human population could be brought back under control in two ways – increasing the death rate or decreasing the birth rate. There is no question as to which of these is the best.

In the developed countries, the single largest factor which brought down the birth rate was the introduction of contraceptive techniques. Considerable efforts are being made to introduce these to people in the developing countries, with some success. But many people are suspicious of contraceptive methods, or barred from using them by their religion, or simply want to have large families. It looks as though the population will go on rising for some time.

If we do not control the overall human birth rate, then it may happen that famine, war or disease will increase the death rate. This cannot be the best thing for the human race. We must do our best to stabilise the world population at a level at which everyone has a fair chance of a long, healthy life.

There are hopeful signs. Birth rates are steadily falling, and the rate of increase in the world population is predicted to slow and perhaps even start to fall later in this century.

Summary

You should know:

- ♦ how food chains and food webs describe energy flow between living organisms
- ♦ about pyramids of numbers
- (S) ♦ how energy is lost in the transfer between trophic levels
- ♦ about pyramids of biomass
- ♦ about the carbon cycle
- (S) ♦ about the nitrogen cycle
- ♦ about the water cycle
- ♦ about populations, and the factors that affect the rate of their growth
- ♦ how to interpret age pyramids
- (S) ♦ the different phases of a population growth curve, and the effect of limiting factors
- ♦ the reasons for the increase in size of the human population.

End-of-chapter questions

1   **a**   Why do living organisms need carbon?
      b   Explain how carbon atoms become part of a plant.
      c   What happens to some of these carbon atoms when a plant respires?
      d   Explain the role of decomposers in the carbon cycle.

2   Explain the difference between each of the following pairs, giving examples where you can:

      a   producer, consumer,
      b   primary consumer, secondary consumer,
      c   community, population,
      d   food chain, food web,
      e   pyramid of biomass, pyramid of numbers.

S 3   **a**   Why do living organisms need nitrogen?
      b   Explain why plants and animals cannot use the nitrogen in the air
      c   What is nitrogen fixation?
      d   Where do nitrogen-fixing bacteria live?
      e   Explain how animals obtain nitrogen.
      f   What do nitrifying bacteria do?
      g   Which type of bacteria return nitrogen to the air?

4   **a**   In what form do each of the following obtain their nitrogen?
         i a green plant
         ii nitrogen-fixing bacteria
         iii a mammal
      b   In the sea, the main nitrogen-fixing organisms are blue–green algae, which float near the top of the water in the plankton. Construct a diagram or chart similar to Figure **20.10**, showing how nitrogen is circulated amongst marine organisms.

5   The graph below shows population changes over one summer, for two insects. One is a type of greenfly, and the other is a ladybird which feeds on it.

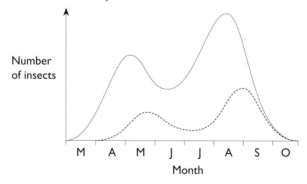

      a   Which curve represents the ladybird population, and which the greenfly population?
      b   Give a reason for your answer to part **a**.
      c   Explain why the two curves are similar.
      d   Why do the two curves rise and fall at slightly different times?

6 The diagram below shows what happens to energy as it passes through an herbivorous mammal (a wildebeest).

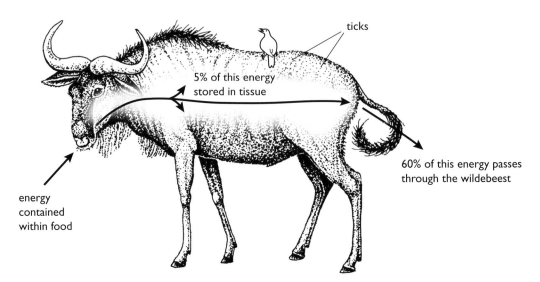

ticks

5% of this energy stored in tissue

60% of this energy passes through the wildebeest

energy contained within food

a i   State the source of the energy in the food eaten by the wildebeest.   [1]
   ii State the form in which the energy is present in the carbohydrate eaten by the wildebeest.   [1]
b i   Name the process that makes the remaining 35% of the energy in the food available
        to the wildebeest.   [1]
   ii State **three** ways in which the energy may be used within the wildebeest.   [3]
The bird on the wildebeest's back is an oxpecker that feeds both on blood-sucking parasites (ticks)
living on the wildebeest, and on blood from the wildebeest's wounds.
c i   Draw a food web to show the feeding relationships of the organisms in the diagram.   [1]
   ii Explain why there must always be fewer oxpeckers than ticks in this food web.   [3]
[Adapted from Cambridge O Level Biology 5090/21, Question 1, May/June 2010]

Ⓢ 7 a   List four chemical elements that are found in proteins.   [4]
       The photograph below shows some root nodules from a pea plant, which is a type of legume.

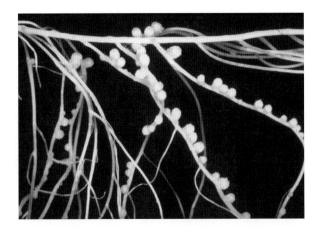

b Nodules like those in the photograph develop on the roots of pea plants and other legumes when the soil is lacking in nitrate ions.
Explain what happens inside the nodule to help legume plants grow in soils lacking nitrate ions. [3]

c After the peas have been harvested, the plants are ploughed back into the soil.
Describe what happens in the soil to convert dead plant material into nitrate ions that plants can absorb. [6]

d Nutrients in the soil can act as a limiting factor for crop growth.
List three **other** factors that may limit the growth of a crop plant. [3]

e The soya bean aphid is an insect pest of soya bean plants in North America. The aphids can show an exponential growth rate where populations can double in two to three days under favourable conditions.
The diagram below shows the growth of soya bean aphids in a field in North America during the growing season.

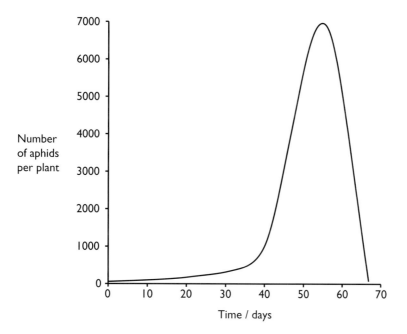

Suggest why the population of aphids did not increase rapidly until about day 40. [3]

[Cambridge IGCSE® Biology 0610/32, Question 6, October/November 2009]

21 Biotechnology

In this chapter, you will find out about:

- ◆ why bacteria are used in biotechnology and genetic engineering
- ◆ how yeast is used to make ethanol and bread
- ◆ the uses of pectinase and other enzymes in industry and the home
- **S** ◆ how penicillin is made
- ◆ genetic engineering, and some of the ways it is useful to us.

Enzymes to treat disease

Gaucher disease is a rare inherited illness caused by a recessive allele of a gene that affects how the body deals with fat molecules. The normal allele causes the production of an enzyme that helps in fat metabolism. This is missing in people with Gaucher disease. As a result, a fatty substance called glucocerebroside builds up in several body organs, including the spleen and liver (Figure **21.1**). There are several types of the disease, but all of them can cause severe damage to various organs.

Researchers thought that if they could replace the missing enzyme, they might be able to improve the health of at least some of the people who have this disease. In the 1970s, a method was found to extract this enzyme from human placentas. The results were encouraging, but with only very small supplies of the enzyme it was never going to be possible to treat many people.

In the 1980s, scientists found a way to make the enzyme using genetic engineering. Now larger quantities of it were available, and it was much cheaper. The enzyme could also be made in a slightly modified form, which made it work better. Today, some patients with Gaucher disease are given regular doses of the enzyme. This does not cure the disease, but in some people it does help to reduce their symptoms, and improves the quality and length of their lives.

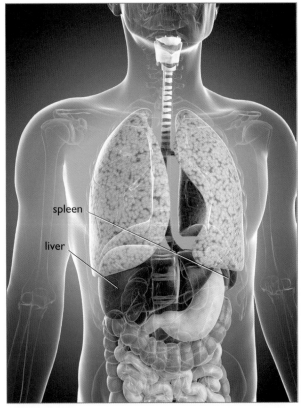

Figure 21.1 This diagram shows the position of the liver and the spleen, which become enlarged in people with Gaucher disease.

21.1 What is biotechnology?

Biotechnology involves using living organisms to carry out processes that make substances that we want. Usually, the term is used only when microorganisms are involved, or when plants or animals are used to produce something other than food.

We have been using microorganisms to make various products for us for thousands of years. Yeast has been used to make bread and alcohol. Bacteria have been used to make yoghurt and cheese. Of course, people did not know that these microorganisms were involved in the processes they used.

Today, we still use microorganisms to make these foods, but we now also use them to make many other substances, such as enzymes. And, in the 1970s, a new branch of biotechnology began, when scientists first found out how to take a gene from one organism and put it into a different one. This is called genetic engineering, and it has opened up entirely new possibilities for using microorganisms and other organisms.

Using microorganisms

Biotechnology and genetic engineering often make use of microorganisms, such as bacteria and microscopic fungi. There are several reasons for this.

♦ Bacteria and fungi are very small, and are easy to grow in a laboratory. They do not take up a lot of space. They reproduce very quickly. They are able to make a huge range of different chemical substances.

S ♦ No one minds what is done to bacteria and fungi. There are no ethical issues like those that might arise if we used animals.

♦ Although bacterial cells are very different from animal and plant cells, in fact we all share the same kind of genetic material – DNA. The genetic code is the same for bacteria as it is for humans and all other organisms. So we can take a gene from a human cell and place it into a bacterial cell, and it will work to produce the human protein.

♦ As well as their 'main' DNA – their 'chromosome' – bacteria also have little loops of DNA called plasmids. These are quite easy to transfer from one cell to another. We can use plasmids for moving genes from one organism's cells to another.

21.2 Using yeast

Yeast is a single-celled fungus. Figures **21.2** and **21.3** show yeast cells.

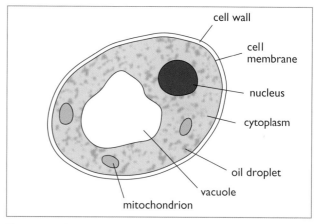

Figure 21.2 A yeast cell.

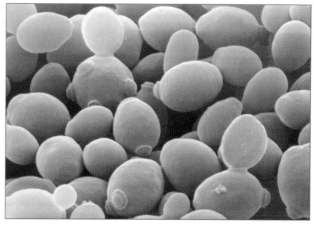

Figure 21.3 Yeast cells seen with a scanning electron microscope. You can see little buds growing from some of the cells – this is the way that yeast reproduces.

Yeast is able to respire anaerobically. When it does so, it produces ethanol and carbon dioxide.

glucose ⟶ ethanol + carbon dioxide

This process is also called **fermentation**.

Making biofuels

In chapter **22**, you will see that we need to reduce our use of fossil fuels. One alternative is to use plants to provide sugars, which yeast can then break down to form ethanol. The ethanol – sometimes called bioethanol – can then be used as a fuel.

Maize is one of the crops that is used in this process. It is first treated with amylase enzymes, which break down stored starch to glucose. Yeast is then added, and allowed to use the glucose in anaerobic respiration. The ethanol that is produced can then be extracted from the mixture by distillation.

Although alcohol burns well, it does not contain as much energy per litre as fossil fuels. It is therefore normally mixed with gasoline (petrol) to make a fuel that is used in vehicle engines (Figure 21.4).

Figure 21.4 This fuel station in Brazil sells fuel containing bioethanol.

The main advantage of using a biofuel like this is that it is a sustainable resource. We can keep growing more maize to make more fuel. It also helps to reduce the amount of carbon dioxide that we add to the atmosphere. Although carbon dioxide is produced when the biofuel is burnt, the plants that were grown to make the fuel took carbon dioxide from the air when they made the sugars and starch by photosynthesis. When we burn fossil fuels, however, we are releasing carbon dioxide into the air that has been stored in the Earth for millions of years.

However, there are arguments against growing crops to make biofuels. These crops take up land that could otherwise be used to grow food for people. Using large quantities of maize and other crops to make biofuels puts up their price, making it more expensive for people to buy food.

Making bread

Bread is made from flour, which is made by grinding the grains (seeds) of cereal crops. Most bread is made from wheat flour.

Flour contains a lot of starch, and also protein – especially a protein called gluten. To make bread, the flour is mixed with water and yeast to make dough (Figure 21.5).

Amylase enzymes break down some of the starch in the dough to make maltose and glucose, which the yeast can use in anaerobic respiration. It produces bubbles of carbon dioxide. These get trapped in the dough. Gluten makes the dough stretchy, so the carbon dioxide bubbles cause the dough to rise.

Figure 21.5 Making bread dough in a bakery in Iran.

Anaerobic respiration also makes alcohol, but this is all broken down when the bread is baked. Baking also kills the yeast.

❓ Questions

21.1 List **three** reasons why microorganisms, rather than animals, are often used in biotechnology.

21.2 Which product of anaerobic respiration is used to make biofuels?

21.3 Which product of anaerobic respiration is important in bread-making?

21.3 Making use of enzymes

Many different enzymes are used in industry. Most of them are obtained from microorganisms.

The microorganisms are grown inside large vessels called fermenters. Inside the fermenter, the microorganisms are provided with everything they need to grow and reproduce. This generally includes oxygen, a supply of a nutrients, a suitable pH and a suitable temperature. The microorganisms make the enzymes and release them into the liquid in which they are growing. The liquid can then be collected from the fermenter, and the enzymes purified before use.

Biological washing powders

Biological washing powders contain enzymes, as well as detergents. The detergents help greasy dirt to mix with water, so that it can be washed away. The enzymes help to break down other kinds of substances which can stain clothes. They are especially good at removing dirt which contains coloured substances from animals or plants, like blood or egg stains.

Some of the enzymes are proteases, which catalyse the breakdown of protein molecules. This helps with the removal of stains caused by proteins, such as blood stains. Blood contains the red protein haemoglobin. The proteases in biological washing powders break the haemoglobin molecules into smaller molecules, which are not coloured, and which dissolve easily in water and can be washed away.

Some of the enzymes are lipases, which catalyse the breakdown of fats to fatty acids and glycerol. This is good for removing greasy stains.

To prevent these enzymes from digesting proteins and fats in the skin of people handling them, the enzymes are packed into microscopic capsules (Figure 21.6). The capsules break open when the washing powder is mixed with water.

The first biological washing powders only worked in warm, rather than hot, water, because the proteases in them had optimum temperatures of about 40 °C. However, proteases have now been developed which can work at much higher temperatures. These proteases have often come from bacteria which naturally live in hot water, in hot springs. This is useful, because the other components of washing powders – which get rid of grease and other kinds of dirt – work best at these higher temperatures.

Pectinase

Fruit juices are extracted using an enzyme called pectinase. Pectin is a substance which helps to stick plant cells together. A fruit such as an apple or orange contains a lot of pectin. If the pectin is broken down, it can be much easier to squeeze juice from the fruit. Pectinase is widely used commercially both in the extraction of juice from fruit, and in making the juice clear rather than cloudy.

Figure 21.6 Biological washing powder seen using a scanning electron microscope. The enzymes are packed inside the tiny granules of the powder.

Activity 21.1
Investigating biological washing powders

Skills
AO3.1 Using techniques, apparatus and materials
AO3.2 Planning
AO3.3 Observing, measuring and recording
AO3.4 Interpreting and evaluating observations and data

 Wear eye protection if available.
Whichever methods you use, do not let the enzymes come into contact with your hands any more than necessary. Remember, you contain a lot of protein and fat! If you do get the powders on your skin, wash with plenty of water.

Design and carry out an experiment to test one or more of the hypotheses listed.

a A biological washing powder removes egg stains from fabric better than a non-biological washing powder.

b The optimum temperature for biological washing powders is lower than that for non-biological washing powders.

c Lipases – enzymes which digest fats – help to remove grease stains from fabrics.

If you want to test the protease-containing powders on fabrics, you could first stain the fabrics with a protein-containing stain such as egg.

Your teacher will suggest suitable amounts of enzymes or washing powders to use.

Activity 21.2
Investigating the use of pectinase in making fruit juice

Skills
AO3.1 Using techniques, apparatus and materials
AO3.2 Planning
AO3.3 Observing, measuring and recording
AO3.4 Interpreting and evaluating observations and data
AO3.5 Evaluating methods

 Take care if using a sharp blade to cut the fruit. Since you are doing this investigation in a laboratory, and because the pectinase you use may not be food grade, you must not taste the fruit juice you make.

Design and carry out an experiment to test one of the hypotheses listed.

Your teacher will suggest suitable amounts of pectinase to use.

a   You can extract more juice if you add pectinase to the fruit than if you do not.

b   Juice is extracted more quickly if pectinase is added to the fruit than if it is not.

c   The effect of pectinase varies on different kinds of fruit – for example, apples and pears.

d   Pectinase has a greater effect on the amount of juice extracted from old fruit than from freshly picked fruit.

e   It is more difficult to extract juice, even when using pectinase, from Golden Delicious apples than from other varieties.

f   People cannot tell the difference between the appearance of juice extracted using pectinase and that of juice extracted without it.

g   Pectinase added to the extracted juice can make it clear.

h   Pectinase has an optimum temperature.

i   Bought fruit juice contains pectinase.

🄢 Lactase

Lactase is an enzyme that breaks down lactose, the sugar found in milk.

$$\text{lactose} \xrightarrow{\text{lactase}} \text{glucose + galactose}$$

All human babies produce lactase in their digestive systems. This is needed to help them to digest the lactose in the milk that is their only source of food for the first few months of their life. Some people – for example, those of European descent – continue to make lactase all of their lives. However, most people – for example those of Asian descent – stop making lactase when they are adults. These people cannot digest lactose. They may feel ill if they eat or drink milk products such as cheese or cream.

Milk can be treated with lactase to break down the lactose, so that people who don't make lactase themselves can drink milk or eat products made from the lactose-free milk. Another reason for treating milk with lactase is to produce glucose and galactose, which can be used for making sweets.

If you do Activity 21.3, you can try using lactase that has been immobilised. This means that lactase is trapped in tiny beads, rather than just being in solution.

Immobilised enzymes are useful because they do not get 🄢 mixed up in the product. The lactose-reduced milk that is made does not contain the enzymes. The little beads containing the enzymes can be reused many, many times.

21.4 Penicillin

Antibiotics are substances which kill bacteria without harming human cells. We take antibiotics to help to cure bacterial infections.

Penicillin is made by growing the fungus *Penicillium* (Figure 21.7) in a large fermenter (Figure 21.8 on page 286).

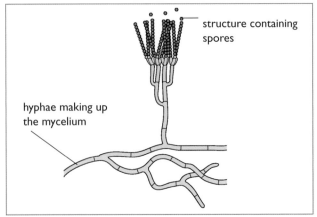

Figure 21.7 *Penicillium*, the fungus that makes penicillin.

Ⓢ Activity 21.3
Making lactose-reduced milk

Skills
AO3.1 Using techniques, apparatus and materials
AO3.3 Observing, measuring and recording

1 Measure 8 cm³ of sodium alginate solution into a small beaker.
2 Add 2 cm³ of lactase solution to the sodium alginate and mix them carefully.
3 Take a second clean beaker. Pour some calcium chloride solution into it.
4 Now you are going to make some sodium alginate/lactase beads. Take up some of the sodium alginate/lactase solution into a small syringe. Very carefully add some of the solution, drop by drop, to the calcium chloride solution. (Don't let the tip of your syringe touch the calcium chloride solution – just drop the liquid from somewhere roughly level with the top of the beaker.) You should see your drops forming little beads. The beads are formed by the sodium alginate, and they have lactase trapped in them.
5 Let the beads harden for a minute or two. Then wash your beads by tipping the calcium chloride solution with the beads in it into a sieve or tea strainer, and gently run clean (preferably distilled) water over them.
6 Take a clean syringe barrel, and put a small piece of nylon gauze at the bottom of it. Fill it with the washed beads, as shown in the diagram. Shake them gently so that they settle in and pack closely together. Don't push them!
7 Now you can try out your immobilised enzymes. Take some milk, and pour it gently over the beads in the syringe. Make sure you have something to catch it in as it drops out.
8 Dip a glucose test strip into some of the milk. Dip another glucose test strip into the liquid which drips out of the immobilised enzyme column. Record your results.

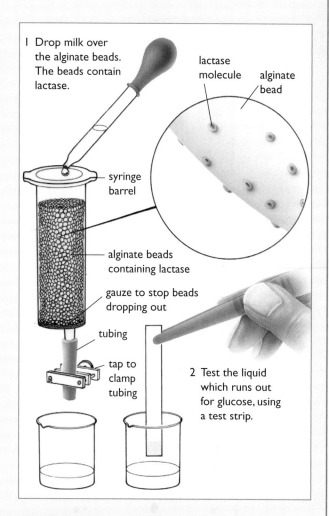

1 Drop milk over the alginate beads. The beads contain lactase.

lactase molecule   alginate bead

syringe barrel

alginate beads containing lactase

gauze to stop beads dropping out

tubing

tap to clamp tubing

2 Test the liquid which runs out for glucose, using a test strip.

❓ Questions

A1 Suggest why you needed to wash the beads before putting them into the syringe barrel.
A2 What was the purpose of the piece of nylon gauze in the syringe barrel?
A3 How quickly did the liquid move through the immobilised enzymes? Could you speed it up? Might this affect your yield of glucose? If you have time, you could test several different arrangements, to see how to get the fastest, highest yield of glucose.)

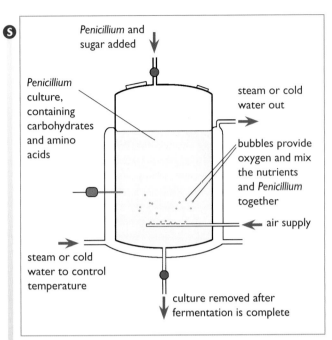

Figure 21.8 A fermenter used for producing penicillin.

Penicillium is grown in a culture medium containing carbohydrates and amino acids. The contents of the fermenter look a bit like watery porridge. They are stirred continuously. This not only keeps the fungus in contact with fresh supplies of nutrients, and mixes oxygen into the culture, but also rolls the fungus up into little pellets. This makes it quite easy to separate the liquid part of the culture – which contains the pencillin – from the fungus, at a later stage.

To begin with, the fungus just grows. This stage takes about 15–24 hours. After that, it begins to secrete penicillin. The rate at which it produces penicillin partly depends on how much sugar it has available. If there is a lot of sugar, then not much penicillin is made. If there is no sugar at all, then no penicillin is made. So small amounts of sugar have to be fed into the fermenter all the time that the fungus is producing penicillin.

The culture is kept going until it is decided that the rate of penicillin production has slowed down so much that it is not worth waiting any longer. This is often after about a week, although the exact time can vary quite a lot on either side of this. Then the culture is filtered, and the liquid is treated to concentrate the penicillin which it contains.

Questions

21.4 What are the advantages of using biological washing powder, rather than an ordinary detergent?

21.5 Explain why the enzymes in biological washing powders are trapped inside microscopic capsules.

21.6 How does pectinase help in the manufacture of fruit juice?

21.7 Explain why lactose-reduced milk is produced.

21.8 Look at the diagram of a fermenter in Figure **21.8**. Explain the reasons for each of the following.

    a   the addition of carbohydrates and amino acids to the culture

    b   the need to control the temperature in the fermenter

    c   the addition of air, containing oxygen, to the fermenter

21.5 Genetic engineering

We have seen that a gene is a length of DNA that codes for the production of a particular protein in a cell. We are now able to take genes from one organism and put them into another organism. This is called **genetic engineering**.

Genetic engineering was first carried out in the 1970s. Since then, many different uses have been found for this process.

♦ Insulin – needed regularly by people with type 1 diabetes (page **185**) – is now produced by bacteria. The human insulin gene was inserted into the bacteria, and they are now grown in huge vats. You can read more about how this is done on pages **288–289**.

♦ Crop plants have been genetically modified to be resistant to herbicides or insect pests. For example, soya plants have been genetically modified so

Key definition

genetic engineering – changing the genetic material of an organism by removing, changing or inserting individual genes

that they are not harmed when a herbicide called glyphosate is sprayed onto them. This means that farmers can spray a field of these plants with the herbicide, and only the weeds are killed. Cotton plants have been genetically modified so that they contain a substance called Bt, which is toxic to insects (Figure 21.9). Insect pests, such as the cotton boll weevil, are killed if they eat the cotton plants. This reduces the use of pesticides.

Figure 21.9 A scientist in India working with cotton plants that have been genetically modified to be resistant to insect pests.

♦ Rice has been genetically modified to produce much more vitamin A than normal rice. The rice grains are yellow, so it is called Golden Rice. Lack of vitamin A is a big problem for children in some parts of the world, particularly where their diet mainly consists of white rice. Severe vitamin A deficiency can cause blindness, and is thought to kill more than one million people each year. Growing and eating Golden Rice rather than ordinary rice could be a big help in solving this problem.

S There are some concerns about the use of genetically modified crops, and it is important that these are carefully considered.

For example, some people have argued that Golden Rice is not the way to solve problems caused by vitamin A deficiency. They say that it would be better to solve the real cause of these problems, which is that people do not have enough money or enough food in some parts of the world. Others argue that at least Golden Rice may be able to help some people now, whereas trying to get rid of poverty is not as easily done.

Growing GM (genetically modified) crops that are resistant to herbicides reduces the number of times that farmers need to spray herbicides onto their crops. This **S** reduces the number of occasions on which the herbicide might cause harm to other plants growing nearby. Growing herbicide-resistant crops can also increase yields, because the spray that is used is very effective at killing everything other than the crop plant. It also reduces labour costs, so it could mean cheaper food. However, farmers have to pay a premium to buy the seeds, so in the end costs do not fall by much, if at all.

There is also a concern that the herbicide resistance gene might spread from the crop plants into other plants growing nearby, producing 'superweeds' that can no longer be killed by herbicides. This could happen if pollen from the GM crop plant fell onto the stigma of a different plant, and the male gametes inside the pollen fertilised an ovule. This is very unlikely, however, because it is very unusual for pollen of one species to be able to grow on the stigma of another species. So far, despite millions of hectares of these GM crops being grown, no 'superweed' has yet appeared.

GM crops with resistance to pests have also been the source of concern. For example, some people think that eating these crops may harm their health, because the crops contain a toxin that kills insects. However, numerous tests have found absolutely no evidence that eating these crops causes any harm at all to people. It is also possible that these crops might harm insects other than those that eat the crop and cause damage – for example bees that eat nectar from the flowers, or ladybirds that are predators of insect pests such as aphids. However, studies show little or no effects on predators – the Bt toxin is specific and harms only herbivores that eat the plants. Indeed, the use of the GM crops may benefit biodiversity, because the farmer does not have to spray the crop with pesticides.

One issue that is emerging is that some pest insects are evolving to become resistant to the Bt toxin. This is not a new problem, as resistance to ordinary pesticides has evolved on many occasions. A possible way of avoiding this problem is to plant only certain areas with the Bt-containing crop, and grow non-Bt crops nearby. Insect pests will be able to feed on the non-Bt crop, and so the selection pressure for resistance to Bt will not be as great.

How genetic engineering is done

To explain the processes that are involved in genetic engineering, we will look at the way in which bacteria have been modified to produce insulin.

We have seen (page 185) that some people are not able to make the protein hormone insulin, resulting in type 1 diabetes. Many of these people need to inject insulin every day.

For a long time, our only source of insulin was from animals that had been killed for food, such as pigs. Now, almost all insulin used by people with diabetes is made by genetically-modified bacteria.

The process begins with the extraction of the gene for insulin from human cells (Figure 21.10). This is done using enzymes called restriction enzymes. These enzymes cut DNA molecules at particular points. They leave short lengths of unpaired bases at either end of the cut DNA, called sticky ends.

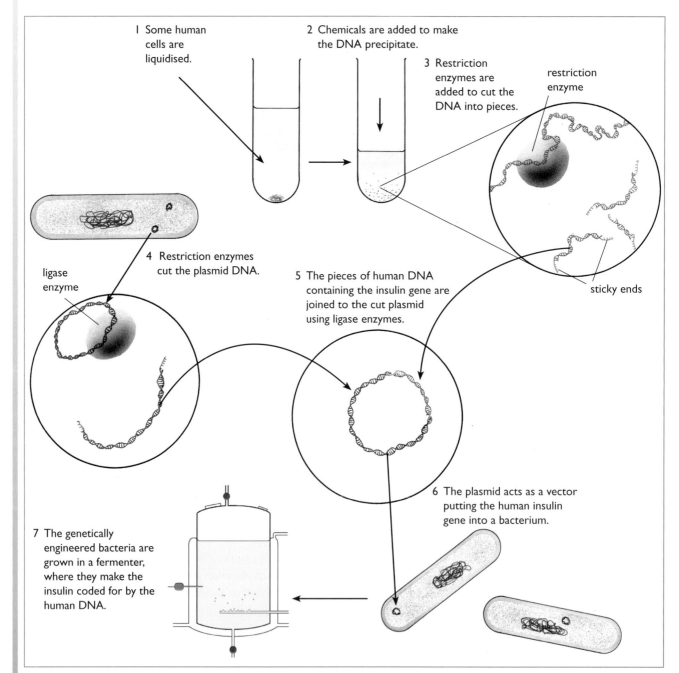

1 Some human cells are liquidised.

2 Chemicals are added to make the DNA precipitate.

3 Restriction enzymes are added to cut the DNA into pieces.

restriction enzyme

sticky ends

4 Restriction enzymes cut the plasmid DNA.

ligase enzyme

5 The pieces of human DNA containing the insulin gene are joined to the cut plasmid using ligase enzymes.

6 The plasmid acts as a vector putting the human insulin gene into a bacterium.

7 The genetically engineered bacteria are grown in a fermenter, where they make the insulin coded for by the human DNA.

Figure 21.10 How genetic engineering has been used to produce bacteria that express the human insulin gene.

(S) The particular length of DNA that is required – the insulin gene – is identified and extracted from all the other DNA. The next step is to insert it into a bacterium. This is not easy – you cannot just suck up some DNA with a syringe and inject it into a bacterial cell. One way of getting DNA into a bacterium is to use a plasmid. As we have seen, a plasmid is a ring of DNA, found in bacteria.

First, the ring of DNA in the plasmid is cut, using the same restriction enzymes that were used for cutting the human DNA. The reason for this is that these enzymes will leave sticky ends that are complementary to the ones on the human DNA. The human insulin gene and the cut plasmids are now mixed together. The sticky ends (unpaired bases) on the insulin genes pair up with the sticky ends on the plasmids. Another enzyme, called DNA ligase, links the two strands firmly together. Now we have plasmids that contain the human insulin gene. They are called recombinant plasmids, because they contain a combination of bacterial and human DNA. (S)

Next, these genetically modified plasmids are added to a culture of bacteria. Some of the bacteria take up the plasmids into their cells. These bacteria are put into fermenters, where they reproduce asexually to form large populations. They follow the instructions on the human DNA to make insulin, which can be extracted from the fermenters and purified.

Summary

You should know:
- ♦ the features of microorganisms that make them useful in biotechnology
- ♦ the use of yeast to make biofuel and bread
- ♦ how we use enzymes in biological washing powders
- ♦ the use of pectinase for making fruit juice
- (S) ♦ the use of lactase to make lactose-reduced milk
- ♦ how *Penicillium* is used to make penicillin
- ♦ some examples of genetic engineering
- (S) ♦ arguments for and against the use of genetically modified crops.

End-of-chapter questions

1 Copy and complete these sentences, using the words below. You may use each word once, more than once or not at all.

amylase	bacterium	biofuel	bread-making	catalase
enzyme	ethanol	carbon dioxide	fungus	glucose
oxygen	protease	starch	sulfur dioxide	

Yeast is a single-celled .... It can respire anaerobically, breaking down glucose to form .... and the gas ....

To make ethanol for use in .... , yeast is provided with sugars that have come from crops such as maize.

To make bread, yeast is mixed with flour and water. The enzyme .... breaks down starch in the flour, producing .... that the yeast uses in respiration. This forms .... which makes the bread rise.

S **2** Outline the roles of each of the following in genetic engineering.

    a   restriction enzymes
    b   DNA ligase
    c   plasmids

3 Selective breeding and genetic engineering can both be used to improve the yields of crop plants such as maize or soya.

    a   Explain the difference between selective breeding and genetic engineering.   **[5]**
    b   Outline one example of the use of genetic engineering to increase yields in a crop plant.   **[4]**
    c   Discuss the possible advantages and disadvantages of the example you have described in **b**.   **[5]**

4 Enzymes are used commercially to extract juice from apples.

    The diagram below shows two containers of apple juice. One contains juice extracted using an enzyme and the other without an enzyme.

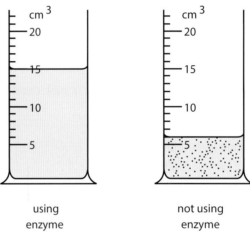

using   not using

enzyme   enzyme

    a   With reference to the diagram, compare the volume and appearance of the two juices extracted.   **[3]**

    Some students investigated the effect of pH on the production of apple juice using the same enzyme.
    • The apples were chopped up and formed into a smooth pulp.
    • The pulp was divided into samples. Each sample was adjusted to a different pH.
    • Enzyme was stirred into each sample of pulp and left to stand for 10 minutes for the enzyme to react.
    • The mixtures of pulp and enzyme were then filtered for 20 minutes to collect the juice. The volumes of apple juice collected, are shown in the table.

pH	Volume of apple juice collected / cm³
3	40
4	56
4	95
6	60
7	30

b   i   Construct a graph to show the effect of pH on the production of apple juice using this enzyme.   [4]

   ii   State the optimum pH for the action of this enzyme.   [1]

   iii   Describe and explain the effect of pH on the production of apple juice, using this enzyme.   [2]

c   Suggest the factors that need to be controlled in this investigation.   [4]

[Cambridge O Level Biology 5090/61, Question 1, October/November 2012]

22 Humans and the environment

In this chapter, you will find out about:

- ◆ agriculture and food production
- ◆ habitat destruction
- ◆ pollution
- ◆ conservation.

Saving a species on the brink

Black-footed ferrets used to be common on the prairies of North America (Figure **22.1**). But, as humans took over more and more land to graze cattle and grow crops, their habitat and food supply dwindled. Black-footed ferrets are predators that feed almost entirely on burrowing rodents called prairie dogs, and farmers killed large numbers of prairie dogs because they thought they competed with their cattle for grass. In 1974, the black-footed ferret was declared extinct in the wild.

But in 1981, in Wyoming, a dog brought a dead black-footed ferret to his owners. They notified wildlife officials, who leapt into action. Searches for the ferrets eventually discovered a small population of them living nearby.

The wild ferrets were given protection. But, as their numbers remained low, it was eventually decided that they needed more help. Some of the ferrets were taken to zoos, where they were given the right conditions to help them to breed. Many of the offspring were reintroduced into suitable habitats in several states, where their populations are gradually growing.

Today, the black-footed ferret is out of danger. Just in time, we have managed to reverse a population decline that would have resulted in extinction.

Figure 22.1   Black-footed ferrets are adapted to hunt their prey in their underground burrows.

22.1 Food production

Most of the world's supply of food is produced by growing crops or by keeping animals. During the last century, the quantity of food produced has greatly increased. Figure 22.2 shows the increase in one type of crop – cereal grains, such as wheat and rice – between 1950 and 2006.

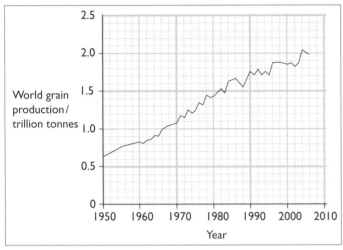

Figure 22.2 Increases in grain production since 1950.

Increasing food production

It is important that we increase the quantity of food that we produce, because the world's increasing population needs to be fed. There are several ways in which this has been achieved.

Agricultural machinery has made a very big difference. With machinery such as tractors and combine harvesters, one farmer can cultivate a much greater area of land in a much shorter time than using manual labour (Figures 22.3 and 22.4).

Figure 22.3 This farmer in the Philippines is preparing land for planting rice. His work is labour intensive, as people in this region cannot afford much machinery.

Figure 22.4 In the US, farmers have tractors and other machinery to work the land. This farmer is preparing the soil for sowing seeds.

Farmers are also using agricultural chemicals to help to improve the growth of their crops, so that they can get more yield from the same area of ground. Chemical fertilisers add more mineral ions – such as nitrate ions – to soils that do not contain enough of them. Insecticides are sprayed onto crops to kill insects pests that might reduce yields or make the crop look less appealing to buyers. Herbicides are sprayed to kill weeds, which would compete with the crop plants and reduce their growth. Although all of these chemicals are expensive, the cost is outweighed by the increased quantity and quality of the crops.

Selective breeding has also played an important part in increasing world food production. We have seen how breeders can choose parents, generation after generation, to produce new and improved varieties of animals and plants. For example, modern wheat varieties produce far more grain per plant than older ones ever did. Selective breeding has also produced crop plants that can grow in poor soils, or that are resistant to diseases (Figure 22.5).

Negative impacts of monocultures

As we increase the quantity of food that we produce, we reduce the habitat that is available for species other than ourselves.

Crop plants are usually grown as large areas of a single variety (Figure 22.6). This is called a **monoculture**. In a natural ecosystem, there are usually many different species of plants growing, which in turn support many different species of animals. We say that there is a high biodiversity (Figure 22.7). In a monoculture, biodiversity is low. Only a few species can live where the crop is growing.

Figure 22.5 The International Rice Research Institute in the Philippines breeds new varieties of rice to help farmers in developing countries to produce more food.

Figure 22.7 The natural ecosystem in much of Indonesia is rainforest. It contains an enormous number of different species of plants and animals.

Figure 22.6 This palm oil factory is in Indonesia. Huge areas of land are covered by the same kind of tree, which only supports a small number of different species of animals.

Another problem with monocultures is that they can lead to an increase in the populations of organisms that are pests of the crop. For example, leafhoppers feed on the sap of rice plants, and can greatly reduce yields. They also transfer plant viruses to the rice, which cause serious diseases in the plants. If a large area of land is covered with just rice plants, then leafhoppers have so much food available to them that their population can become enormous.

Farmers can try to reduce the quantities of these pests by spraying insecticides onto the crop. However, this kills not only the leafhoppers, but also other harmless insects – including predatory insects and spiders that would help to reduce the leafhopper population. It is also very expensive. And, in many places, leafhoppers have become resistant to the insecticides and are no longer killed by them.

Many farmers try to use other methods of controlling insect pests. One approach is to use mixed cropping, where only fairly small areas of ground are covered with the same crop at the same time of year. This makes it more difficult for insect pests to spread from one rice field to another.

Negative impacts of intensive livestock production

In many parts of the world, cattle and other livestock are kept outside. They graze on grass, or are fed by people bringing freshly-cut vegetation for them to eat (Figure 22.8).

Figure 22.8 A farmer in India feeding water buffalo calves.

In developed countries, livestock are often farmed intensively. This means that large numbers of livestock are kept in an area that would not normally be able to support more than a very small number (Figure 22.9). The farmer uses high inputs to increase the production of milk, meat, wool from his animals. For example, high-energy foods are bought to feed them. Regular medication may be given to stop the development of disease. The animals may be kept in temperature-controlled buildings to maximise their growth rates.

Intensive farming can help to provide more food, but there are some big disadvantages. For example, there can

Figure 22.9 An intensive production unit for chickens in England.

be welfare issues for the livestock, which may suffer in the crowded conditions in which they are kept. Disease can spread easily among them. In some countries, this is dealt with by giving the animals regular doses of antibiotics – which, as we have seen, increases the risk that bacteria will develop resistance to the antibiotics. The waste from the intensive farming unit can pollute land and waterways nearby.

World food supplies Ⓢ

It has been calculated that more than enough food is produced on Earth to provide every single person with more than enough for their needs. Yet many people do not get enough food. Each year, many people – both children and adults – die because they have an inadequate diet.

The fundamental problem is that, while some parts of the world produce more than enough food for the people that live there, in other parts of the world nowhere near enough food is produced. Food is distributed unequally on our planet. Although large amounts of food are transported from one area to another, this is still not sufficient to supply enough food to everybody. Also, if food prices rise too high, then even if there is plenty of food around, many people may not be able to afford to buy it.

Famines can occur for many different reasons. Often, the main cause is the weather. If an area suffers drought for several years in succession, then it becomes impossible for the people to grow crops. Their animals die, too. Sometimes, however, the problem is exactly the opposite – so much rain falls that it causes flooding, again preventing crops from growing (Figure 22.10). Sometimes, even though the weather remains normal, the human population may grow so large that the land on which they live can no longer provide enough food for them. Sometimes, wars raging in an area prevent people from working the land and harvesting their crops.

When the world becomes aware that an area is suffering from famine, other countries are usually very willing to donate food supplies to the people. Hopefully, this will only need to happen for a relatively short time, until things improve and people can plant their crops and become self-sufficient again. Most people would much prefer this, rather than having to rely on hand-outs of food.

Figure 22.10 These people, living near the village of Muzaffarpur in northern India, had no food for four days after flooding swept away their houses and drowned their farmland. These floods happened in 2007 and were the worst in living memory.

22.2 Habitat destruction

All living things affect the living and non-living things around them. For example, earthworms make burrows and wormcasts, which affect the soil, and therefore the plants growing in it. Rabbit fleas carry the virus which causes myxomatosis, so they can affect the size of a rabbit population, and perhaps the size of the fox population if the foxes depend on rabbits for food.

Perhaps the biggest ever effect of living organisms on the environment happened about 1500 million years ago. At this time, the first living cells that could photosynthesise evolved. Until then, there had been no oxygen in the atmosphere. These organisms began to produce oxygen, which gradually accumulated in the atmosphere. The oxygen in the air we now breathe has been produced by photosynthesis. The appearance of oxygen in the air meant that many anaerobic organisms could now only live in particular parts of the Earth which were oxygen-free, such as in deep layers of mud. It meant that many other kinds of organism, which used the oxygen for respiration, could evolve. All this oxygen excreted by photosynthetic organisms could be considered to be the biggest case of pollution ever!

Within the past 10 000 years or so, another organism has had an enormous impact on the environment. Ever since humans learnt to hunt with weapons, to domesticate animals and to farm crops, we have been changing the environment around us in a very significant way.

One of the greatest effects we have had, and the one that is most threatening to the existence of many different species of organisms, is that we have destroyed their habitats. We have seen that each species has adaptations that help it survive in its particular habitat. If we destroy that habitat, then it is difficult for many species to survive in a new kind of environment.

Habitats are destroyed when we use land for other purposes. Here are some examples.

♦ We cut down native vegetation to make land available for growing crops, for farming livestock, for building houses and factories, and for building roads.
♦ We damage habitats when we mine for natural resources, such as metal ores or fossil fuels (Figure 22.11).

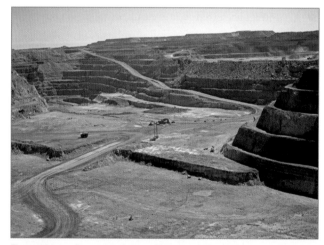

Figure 22.11 Open cast mining, such as here in Australia, can damage huge areas of land.

♦ We add pollutants to land and water, which can kill the plants that normally live there, and so change the habitat.

Habitats can also be damaged if we remove key species from them. For example, collecting live corals from coral reefs damages the whole coral reef habitat, endangering the hundreds of species of other animals that depend on corals (Figure 22.12). Corals contain tiny photosynthetic protoctists inside their bodies, which are the start of every food chain on the reef.

Figure 22.12 The fish on a coral reef are entirely dependent on the living corals to provide their habitat, and to support the complex food webs.

Deforestation

Humans have always cut down trees. Wood is an excellent fuel and building material. The land on which trees grow can be used for growing crops for food, or to sell. One thousand years ago, most of Europe was covered by forests. Now, most of them have been cut down. The cutting down of large numbers of trees is called **deforestation** (Figure **22.13**).

Rainforests occur in temperate and tropical regions of the world (Figure **22.14**). Recently, most concern about deforestation has been about the loss of tropical rainforests. In the tropics, the relatively high and constant temperatures, and high rainfall, provide perfect conditions for the growth of plants (Figure **22.15**).

Figure 22.13 When rainforest is cut down and burnt, as here in Brazil, habitats are destroyed, large amounts of carbon dioxide are released and soil nutrients are lost.

Figure 22.14 This rainforest is growing in a part of Chile where the climate is temperate (with cold winters and warm summers) and there is very high rainfall. It has an enormous species diversity.

A rainforest is a very special place, full of many different species of plants and animals. More different species live in a small area of rainforest than in an equivalent area of any other habitat in the world. We say that rainforest has a high **species diversity**.

When an area of rainforest is cut down, the soil under the trees is exposed to the rain. The soil of a rainforest is very thin. It is quickly washed away once it loses its cover of plants. This soil erosion may make it very difficult for the rainforest to grow back again, even if the land is left alone. The soil can also be washed into rivers, silting them and causing flooding (Figure **22.16**).

Figure 22.15 Unspoiled tropical rainforest in Sarawak, Malaysia.

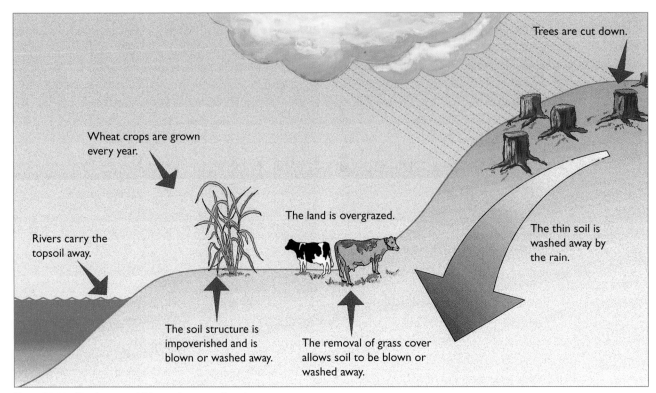

Figure 22.16 How human activities can increase soil erosion.

Labels in figure:
- Trees are cut down.
- Wheat crops are grown every year.
- The land is overgrazed.
- The thin soil is washed away by the rain.
- Rivers carry the topsoil away.
- The soil structure is impoverished and is blown or washed away.
- The removal of grass cover allows soil to be blown or washed away.

The loss of part of a rainforest means a loss of a habitat for many different species of animals. Even if small 'islands' of forest are left as reserves, these may not be large enough to support a breeding population of the animals. Deforestation threatens many species of animals and plants with extinction.

The loss of so many trees can also affect the water cycle (Figure 20.11, page 272). While trees are present and rain falls, a lot of it is taken up by the trees, and transported into their leaves. It then evaporates, and goes back into the atmosphere in the process of transpiration. If the trees have gone, then the rain simply runs off the soil and into rivers. Much less goes back into the air as water vapour. The air becomes drier, and less rain falls. This can make it much more difficult for people to grow crops and keep livestock.

When people in industrialised countries get concerned about the rate at which some countries are cutting down their forests, it is very important they should remember that they have already cut down most of theirs.

Most tropical rainforests grow in developing countries, and in some countries many of the people are very poor. The people may cut down the forests to clear land on which they can grow food. It is difficult to expect someone who is desperately trying to produce food, to keep their family alive, not to do this, unless you can offer some alternative. International conservation groups such as the World Wide Fund for Nature, and governments of the richer, developed countries such as the USA, can help by providing funds to the people or governments of developing countries to try to help them to provide alternative sources of income for people. Many of the most successful projects involve helping local people to make use of the rainforest in a sustainable way.

The greatest pressure on the rainforest may come from the country's government in the big cities, rather than the people living in or near the rainforest. The government may be able to obtain large amounts of money by allowing logging companies to cut down forests and extract the timber. A way of getting round this could be to allow countries to sell 'carbon credits' to other, richer countries. In 2009, Indonesia did this. The idea is that other countries give money to Indonesia to use in conserving their forests, and that these countries are then allowed to produce more carbon dioxide from their industrial activities.

Questions

22.1 List **four** reasons why the quantity of food produced by agriculture has increased enormously in the last century.
22.2 Explain what is meant by a monoculture.
22.3 Describe **two** problems caused by monocultures.
22.4 Describe **two** problems caused by intensive livestock farming.
22.5 Outline the main ways in which humans destroy habitats.
22.6 Explain how extensive deforestation can affect the amount of carbon dioxide in the air.
22.7 Explain how deforestation can cause soil erosion and flooding.

22.3 Pollution

Greenhouse gases

The Earth's atmosphere contains several different gases that act like a blanket, keeping the Earth warm. They are sometimes called greenhouse gases. The most important of these gases is carbon dioxide. Methane is also a significant greenhouse gas.

Carbon dioxide is transparent to shortwave radiation from the Sun. The sunlight passes freely through the atmosphere (Figure **22.17**), and reaches the ground. The ground is warmed by the radiation, and emits longer wavelength, infrared radiation. Carbon dioxide does not let all of this infrared radiation pass through. Much of it is kept in the atmosphere, making the atmosphere warmer.

This is called the greenhouse effect, because it is similar to the effect which keeps an unheated greenhouse warmer than the air outside.

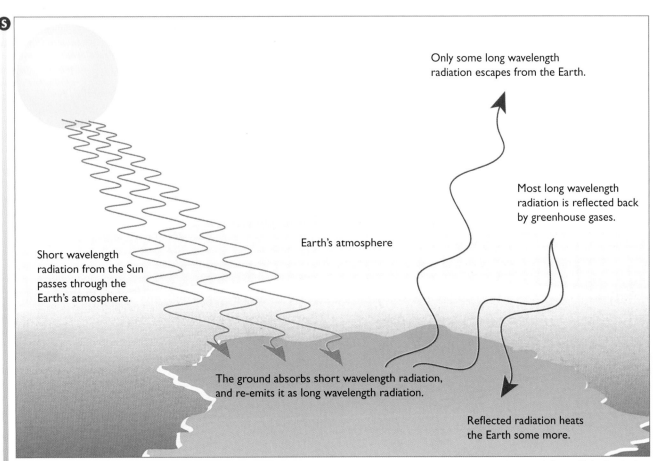

Only some long wavelength radiation escapes from the Earth.

Most long wavelength radiation is reflected back by greenhouse gases.

Earth's atmosphere

Short wavelength radiation from the Sun passes through the Earth's atmosphere.

The ground absorbs short wavelength radiation, and re-emits it as long wavelength radiation.

Reflected radiation heats the Earth some more.

Figure 22.17 The greenhouse effect. Short wavelength radiation from the Sun passes through the atmosphere and reaches the ground. Some of it is absorbed by the ground, and is re-emitted as long wavelength radiation. Much of this cannot pass through the blanket of greenhouse gases in the atmosphere. It is reflected back towards the Earth, warming the atmosphere.

S The glass around the greenhouse behaves like the carbon dioxide in the atmosphere. It lets shortwave radiation in, but does not let out the longwave radiation. The longwave radiation is trapped inside the greenhouse, making the air inside it warmer.

We need the greenhouse effect. If it did not happen, then the Earth would be frozen and lifeless. The average temperature on Earth would be about 33 °C lower than it is now.

However, the amount of carbon dioxide and other greenhouse gases in the atmosphere is increasing (Figure **22.18**). This may trap more infrared radiation, and make the atmosphere warmer. This is called the **enhanced greenhouse effect**, and its effect on the Earth's temperature is called global warming.

Over recent years, the amount of fossil fuels which have been burnt by industry, and in engines of vehicles such as cars, trains and aeroplanes, has increased greatly. This releases carbon dioxide into the atmosphere.

Other gases that contribute to the greenhouse effect have also been released by human activities. These include methane, nitrogen oxides and CFCs. Table **22.1** shows where these gases come from. The concentrations of all of these gases in the atmosphere are steadily increasing.

As the concentration of these gases increases, the temperature on Earth will also increase. At the moment,

we are not able to predict just how large this effect will be. There are all sorts of other processes, many of them natural, which can cause quite large changes in the average temperature of the Earth, and these are not fully understood. For example, every now and then the Earth has been plunged into an Ice Age. Perhaps we are due for another Ice Age soon. Perhaps the enhanced greenhouse effect might help to delay this.

But most people think that we should be very worried about the enhanced greenhouse effect and global warming. If the Earth's temperature does rise significantly, there will be big changes in the world as we know it. For example, the ice caps might melt. This would release a lot more water into the oceans, so that sea levels would rise. Many low-lying areas of land might be flooded. This could include large parts of countries like Bangladesh, almost the whole of the Maldive islands, and major cities such as London.

A rise in temperature would also affect the climate in many parts of the world. No-one is sure just what would happen where – there are too many variables for scientists to be able to predict the consequences. It would probably mean that some countries which already have low rainfall might become very dry deserts. Others might have more violent storms than they do now. This would mean that animals and plants living in some areas of the world might become extinct. People in some places might not be able to grow crops.

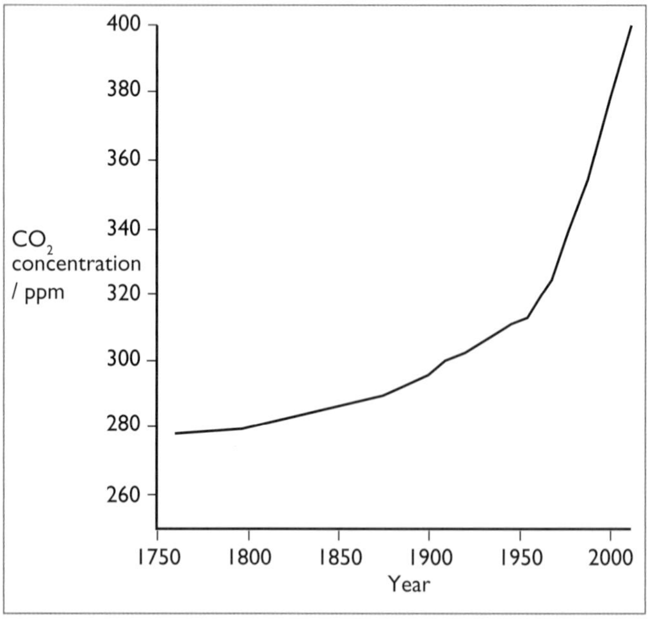

Figure 22.18 How carbon dioxide concentrations in the atmosphere have changed since 1750.

Gas	% estimated contribution	Main sources
carbon dioxide	55	burning fossil fuels
methane	15	decay of organic matter, e.g. in waste tips and paddy fields; waste gases from digestive processes in cattle and insects; natural gas leaks
CFCs	24	refrigerators and air conditioning systems; plastic foams
nitrogen oxides	6	fertilisers; burning fossil fuels, especially in vehicles

Table 22.1 Gases contributing to the greenhouse effect.

There might be some beneficial effects, too. For example, extra carbon dioxide in the atmosphere and higher temperatures might increase the rate of photosynthesis in some parts of the world. This could mean that higher yields could be gained from crops.

One obvious way to cut down the emission of greenhouse gases is to reduce the amount of fossil fuels that are burnt. This would reduce the amount of carbon dioxide we pour into the air. Agreements have been made between countries to try to do this, but they are proving very difficult to implement.

Deforestation has also been blamed for increasing the amount of carbon dioxide in the air. It has been argued that cutting down rainforests leaves fewer trees to photosynthesise and remove carbon dioxide from the air. Moreover, if the tree is burnt or left to rot when it is chopped down, then carbon dioxide will be released from it.

Methane is produced by farming activities (Figure 22.19). It is released by bacteria which live on organic matter, such as in paddy fields (flooded fields which are used for growing rice), by animals which chew the cud, such as cattle, and by some insects, such as termites. There is probably not much that we can do about this.

Methane is also produced by decaying rubbish in landfill sites. We can reduce this problem by decreasing the amount of rubbish we throw away, and by collecting

the methane from these sites. It can be used as fuel (Figure 22.20). Although burning it for fuel does release carbon dioxide, this carbon dioxide does not trap so much infrared radiation as the methane would have done.

Figure 22.20   Bacteria feeding on rubbish in landfill sites produce methane, which can be piped off and used as a fuel.

Figure 22.19   Methane is produced by anaerobic microorganisms growing in the mud in paddy fields.

Questions

22.8   Explain the difference between the greenhouse effect, the enhanced greenhouse effect and global warming.

22.9   Each of the following has been suggested as a way of reducing global warming. For each suggestion, explain why it would work.

   a   reducing the top speed limit for cars and trucks

   b   improving traffic flow in urban areas

   c   insulating houses in countries with cold climates

   d   increasing the number of nuclear power stations

   e   encouraging people to recycle more of their rubbish

⑤ Acid rain

Fossil fuels, such as coal, oil and natural gas, were formed from living organisms. They all contain sulfur; coal contains the most. When they are burnt, the sulfur combines with oxygen in the air and forms sulfur dioxide.

When fuels are burnt in vehicle engines, the high temperatures cause nitrogen in the air to combine with oygen, producing nitrogen oxides.

Sulfur dioxide is a very unpleasant gas. If people breathe it in, it can irritate the linings of the breathing system. If you are prone to asthma or bronchitis, sulfur dioxide can make it worse. Sulfur dioxide is also poisonous to many kinds of plants, sometimes damaging their leaves so badly that the whole plant dies.

Rainwater is usually slightly acidic, with a pH a little below 7. This is because carbon dioxide dissolves in it to form carbonic acid. Sulfur dioxide and nitrogen oxides also dissolve in rainwater. They form a more acidic solution, called acid rain. The pH of acid rain can be as low as 4.

Acid rain damages plants. Although the rainwater usually does not hurt the leaves directly when it falls onto them, it does affect the way in which plants grow. This is because it affects the soil in which the plants are growing. The acid rainwater seeps into the soil, and washes out ions such as calcium, magnesium and aluminium. The soil becomes short of these ions, so the plant becomes short of nutrients. It also makes it more difficult for the plant to absorb other nutrients from the soil. So acid rain can kill trees and other plants.

The ions which are washed out of the soil by the acid rain often end up in rivers and lakes. Aluminium ions, in particular, are very poisonous to fish, because they affect their gills. Young fish are often killed if the amount of aluminium in the water is too great. Other freshwater organisms are often killed, too. At the same time, the water itself becomes more acidic, which means that many kinds of plants and animals cannot live in it (Figure 22.21).

One of the biggest problems in trying to do anything about the problems of acid rain is that it does not usually fall anywhere near the place which is causing it. A coal-burning power station might release a lot of sulfur dioxide, which is then carried high in the air for hundreds of miles before falling as acid rain. Sulfur dioxide produced in England might fall as acid rain in Norway.

But acid rain is, in many ways, a much easier problem to solve than the enhanced greenhouse effect. The answer is simple – we must cut down emissions of sulfur dioxide and nitrogen oxides.

Coal-burning power stations have been the worst culprits. The number of coal-burning power stations in some European countries has been going down and

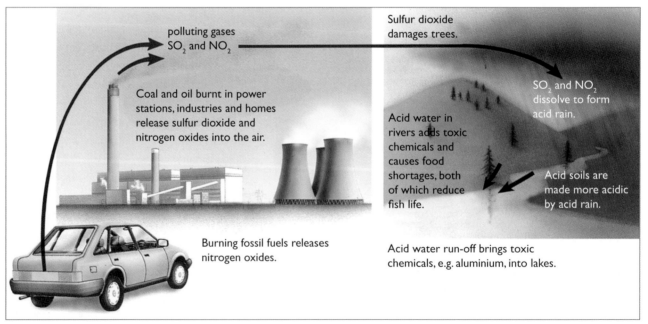

Figure 22.21 The causes and effects of acid rain.

more of them are burning oil which produces less sulfur dioxide. New ways of producing energy, which do not produce sulfur dioxide, are being used. These include using wind power, wave power, or solar energy.

Where fossil fuel is burnt in power stations or other industries, the waste gases can be 'scrubbed' to remove sulfur dioxide. This often involves passing the gases through a fine spray of lime.

We have seen that car engines also produce nitrogen oxides. These can be removed by catalytic converters fitted to the exhaust system. In most countries, all new petrol-burning cars now have to have catalytic converters.

❓ Questions

22.10 What causes acid rain?

22.11 How does acid rain damage trees?

22.12 How does acid rain damage fish?

22.13 Summarise what is being done to try to reduce the production of acid rain.

Nuclear fall-out

Accidents at nuclear power stations may release radioactive substances into the atmosphere. Exposure to large amounts of radiation from these substances can cause radiation sickness and burns. This type of radiation can also increase mutation rates in DNA in our cells, which may lead to cancer.

This happens because ionising radiation – such as alpha, beta and gamma radiation – damages the DNA molecules in living cells. Alpha is the most ionising and so causes the most damage, but only if it gets inside the body. This is because it is not able to penetrate the skin. Gamma is the least ionising but the most penetrating.

ⓈEutrophication

Many organisms live in water. They are called aquatic organisms. Aquatic habitats include fresh water, such as streams, rivers, ponds and lakes; and also marine environments – the sea and oceans.

Most organisms that live in water respire aerobically, and so need oxygen. They obtain their oxygen from oxygen gas which has dissolved in the water. Anything which reduces the amount of oxygen available in the water can make it impossible for fish or other aquatic organisms to live there.

There are two main sources of pollution which can reduce oxygen levels in fresh water. They are fertilisers and untreated sewage.

Farmers and horticulturists use fertilisers to increase the yield of their crops. The fertilisers usually contain nitrates and phosphates. Nitrates are very soluble in water. If nitrate fertiliser is put onto soil, it may be washed out in solution when it rains. This is called leaching. The leached nitrates may run into streams and rivers.

Algae and green plants in the river grow faster when they are supplied with these extra nitrates. They may grow so much that they completely cover the water. They block out the light for plants growing beneath them, which die. Even the plants on the top of the water eventually die. When they do, their remains are a good source of food for bacteria, which are decomposers.

The bacteria breed rapidly. The large population of bacteria respires aerobically, using up oxygen from the water. Soon, there is very little oxygen left for other living things. Those which need a lot of oxygen, such as fish, have to move to other areas, or die.

This whole process is called eutrophication (Figures **22.22** and **22.23**). It can happen whenever food for plants or bacteria is added to water. As well as fertilisers, other pollutants from farms, such as slurry from buildings where cattle or pigs are kept, or from pits where grass is rotted down to make silage, can cause eutrophication.

Untreated sewage can also cause eutrophication (Figure **22.24**). Sewage does not usually increase the

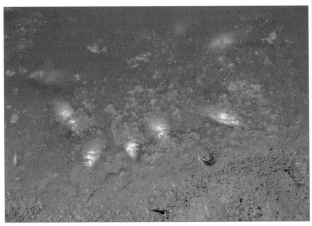

Figure 22.22 The huge growth of algae in this polluted pond has provided food for aerobic bacteria. These have used up most of the oxygen in the water, so the fish have died.

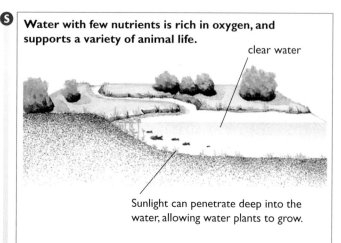

Water with few nutrients is rich in oxygen, and supports a variety of animal life.

clear water

Sunlight can penetrate deep into the water, allowing water plants to grow.

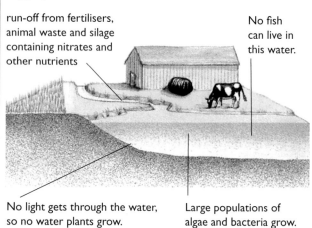

Water with high concentrations of nutrients is low in oxygen, so few animals can live in it.

run-off from fertilisers, animal waste and silage containing nitrates and other nutrients

No fish can live in this water.

No light gets through the water, so no water plants grow.

Large populations of algae and bacteria grow.

Figure 22.23 Eutrophication. Nutrients flowing into the water increase algal and bacterial growth. This reduces oxygen concentration, killing fish.

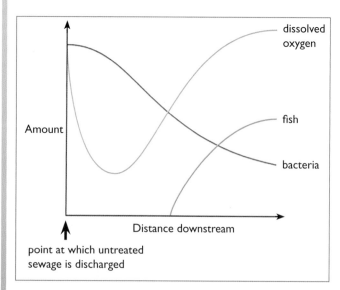

Figure 22.24 The effect of raw sewage on a stream.

growth of algae, but it does provide a good food source for many kinds of bacteria. Once again, their population grows, depleting the oxygen levels.

Could we stop using nitrate fertilisers? It is not really sensible at the moment to suggest that we could. People expect to have plentiful supplies of relatively cheap food. Although fertilisers are expensive, by using them farmers get so much higher yields that they make more profit. If they did not use fertilisers at all, their yields would be much lower and they would have to sell their crops for a higher price, in order to make any profit at all.

Some farmers use organic fertilisers, such as manure. Organic fertilisers are better than inorganic ones in that they do not contain many nitrates which can easily be leached out of the soil. Instead, they release their nutrients gradually, over a long period of time, giving crops time to absorb them efficiently. Nevertheless, manures can still cause pollution, if a lot is put onto a field at once, at a time of year when there is a lot of rain or when crops are not growing and cannot absorb the nutrients from them.

The yields obtained when using organic fertilisers are not usually as great as when using inorganic ones, so the crops are usually sold for a higher price. Many people are now prepared to pay this extra money for food from crops grown in this way, but many cannot afford to.

If nitrate fertilisers are used, there is much which can be done to limit the harm they do. Care must be taken not to use too much, but only to apply an amount which the plants can take up straight away. Fertilisers should not be applied to empty fields, but only when plants are growing. They should not be applied just before rain is forecast. They should not be sprayed near to streams and rivers.

Study tip

Effluent from properly treated sewage (page 309) does not cause eutrophication. It is raw (untreated) sewage that causes problems.

Pesticides

A pesticide is a substance that kills organisms which damage crops. Insects that eat crops can be killed with insecticides. Fungi that grow on crops are controlled with fungicides. Weeds that compete with crop plants for water, light and minerals can be controlled with herbicides. Pesticides may also be used to control organisms which transmit disease, such as mosquitoes.

We have seen that insects or fungi which can feed on a monoculture have an almost inexhaustible food supply. The usual limits on their population growth do not apply. The populations of the insects or fungi may grow very rapidly, until they are so big that they cause extensive damage to the crop (Figure 22.25).

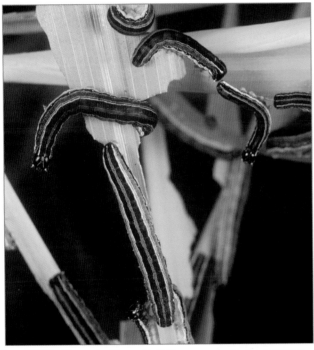

Figure 22.25 These caterpillars, called African army worms, can cause huge amounts of damage to a maize crop.

If nothing is done about this, then crop yields can be very badly reduced. It has been estimated that, in developing countries, at least one-third of potential crops are destroyed by pests. If farmers did not use pesticides, then this would be even worse.

By definition, a pesticide is a harmful substance. If they are not used with care, some pesticides can do a lot of damage to the environment. For example, DDT is a pesticide that kills insects. It is a persistent insecticide, which means that it does not break down, but remains in the bodies of the insects or in the soil. When a bird or other organism eats the insects, they eat the DDT too. The DDT stays in their bodies; each time they eat an insect, more DDT accumulates in their tissues. If a bird of prey eats the insect-eating bird, it too begins to accumulate DDT. Birds and other animals near the ends of food chains can build up very large concentrations of DDT in their bodies (Figure 22.26).

Unfortunately, as well as being persistent, DDT is also nonspecific. This means that it not only harms the insects it is meant to kill, but is also harmful to other living things. In high concentrations it is very harmful to birds, for example. In Britain, it affected the breeding success of peregrine falcons, by making their egg shells very weak, so that they very rarely hatched. The peregrine falcon population dropped very rapidly.

Once it was realised that DDT was doing so much harm, its use in Britain was stopped. Now DDT is banned in some parts of the world. However, it is still used in many developing countries, because without it, insects would be such a problem that more people would starve or die of diseases like malaria. Other insecticides need to be developed which are as cheap and effective as DDT, but that do not harm other living organisms.

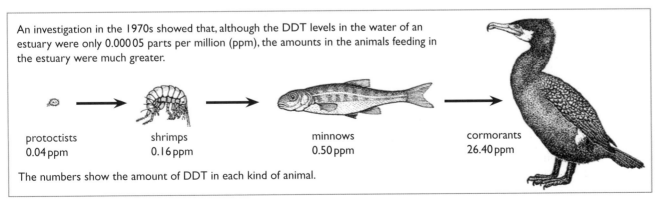

An investigation in the 1970s showed that, although the DDT levels in the water of an estuary were only 0.000 05 parts per million (ppm), the amounts in the animals feeding in the estuary were much greater.

| protoctists | shrimps | minnows | cormorants |
| 0.04 ppm | 0.16 ppm | 0.50 ppm | 26.40 ppm |

The numbers show the amount of DDT in each kind of animal.

Figure 22.26 DDT accumulation along a food chain.

Chemical waste

A very different kind of water pollution may result from the discharge of chemical waste into waterways. Chemical waste may contain heavy metals, such as lead, cadmium or mercury. These substances are very poisonous (toxic) to living organisms, because heavy metals stop enzymes from working. If they get into streams, rivers or the sea, they may kill almost every living thing in that area of water.

⑤ Non-biodegradable plastics

Plastics are man-made materials that we use for many different purposes. Most of them are made from fossil fuels. If you look around you now, you will almost certainly be able to see several items made from plastics. Plastics are cheap, lightweight and can be made into any shape and colour that we want.

One big problem with plastics is that most of them are non-biodegradable. This means that decomposers cannot break them down. When a plastic item is thrown away, it does not rot. Discarded plastic objects just accumulate (Figure 22.27).

Figure 22.27 Non-biodegradable plastics never rot away.

Litter is very unsightly. It can also be dangerous to other organisms. For example, plastic waste thrown away at sea is often mistaken for jellyfish by turtles. They eat it. As they eat more and more, it gradually collects up in their stomachs, because it cannot be broken down by their enzymes. Now they cannot eat their real food, and eventually die.

Animals can also get trapped inside plastic containers, or may get plastic cords or bags wrapped around their bodies, which can kill them.

Female contraceptive hormones

In Chapter **17**, we saw that hormones containing oestrogen can be taken by women to stop them producing eggs, as a method of birth control. Some of these hormones are excreted in the woman's urine, and eventually find their way into waterways, in sewage.

Fish and other animals, such as molluscs, that live in water can be affected by these hormones. They can prevent the male hormone, testosterone, working effectively in the animals' bodies. Male fish, for example, have been shown to produce fewer sperm if the water in which they live is polluted with female contraceptive hormones. In some cases, they can even make a male fish change sex and become female.

This might also be one of the reasons why, worldwide, the sperm count of many men is much lower now than it was 20 years ago. 'Sperm count' is a measure of the number of sperm produced, and their activity. A study involving 26 000 men found that, between 1989 and 2005, the average sperm count fell by one third. One possible explanation for this is exposure to female contraceptive hormones. Another is exposure to synthetic chemicals used for various purposes – such as making plastics – that behave in similar ways to these hormones. At the moment, however, no-one knows the full explanation for this fall in sperm count.

Table 22.2 summarises some of the damaging effects we have had on our environment. The rest of this chapter explains what we can do to limit further damage.

❓ Questions

22.14 List **two** substances that can cause eutrophication if they get into waterways.

22.15 Eutrophication reduces the concentration of a dissolved gas in a river or lake. Name this gas.

22.16 DDT is a persistent pesticide. Explain what is meant by this term.

Ⓢ 22.17 Explain why throwing away a plastic bag is likely to cause more harm to the environment than throwing away a paper bag.

22.4 Conservation

Conservation is the process of looking after the natural environment. Conservation attempts to maintain or increase the range of different species living in an area, known as biodiversity.

We have seen that one of the greatest threats to biodiversity is the loss of habitats. Each species of living organism is adapted to live in a particular habitat. If this habitat is destroyed, then the species may have nowhere else to live, and will become extinct.

Tropical rainforests have a very high biodiversity compared with almost anywhere else in the world. This is one of the main reasons why people think that conserving them is so important. When tropical rainforests are cut down or burnt, the habitats of thousands of different species are destroyed.

Damage	Example	Main causes	Possible solutions
air pollution	global warming	enhanced greenhouse effect, caused by release of carbon dioxide, methane, CFCs and nitrogen oxides	reduce use of fossil fuels; stop using CFCs; produce less organic waste and/or collect and use methane produced from landfill sites
	acid rain	sulfur dioxide and nitrogen oxides from the burning of fossil fuels	burn less fossil fuel; use catalytic converters on cars
habitat destruction	deforestation	destruction of forests, especially rainforests, for wood and for land for farming, roads and houses	provide alternative sources of income for people living near rainforests
	loss of wetlands	draining wetlands for housing and land for farming	protect areas of wetlands
water pollution	toxic chemicals	untreated effluent from industry; run-off from mining operations	impose tighter controls on industry and mining
	eutrophication	sewage and fertilisers running into streams	treat all sewage before discharge into streams; use fewer fertilisers
	oil spills	shipwrecks; leakages from undersea oil wells	impose tighter controls on shipping and the oil industry
species destruction	loss of habitat	see deforestation and wetlands above	see above
	damage from pesticides	careless use of insecticides and herbicides	development of more specific and less persistent pesticides; more use of alternative control methods, such as biological control
	damage from fishing	overfishing, greatly reducing populations of species caught for food; accidental damage to other animals such as dolphins	impose controls on methods and amount of fishing

Table 22.2 A summary of the harmful effects of humans on the environment.

We have already seen how and why deforestation occurs. Another kind of habitat that is under threat is wetland, such as swamps. People drain wetland so that it can be more easily farmed. We build roads and houses, destroying whatever used to grow on that land. We farm animals in large numbers on land that cannot really produce enough vegetation to support them, so that the land becomes a semi-desert.

Many governments and also world-wide organisations such as the World Wide Fund for Nature are aware of these problems and are attempting to make sure that especially important habitats are not damaged. Most countries have special areas where people's activities are carefully controlled, ensuring that wildlife can continue to live there. Often, the loss of money from agriculture in these areas can be regained by allowing tourists to visit them. The most successful projects actively involve local people, who are usually delighted to see their environment being cared for, so long as they can still make a living from it.

Sustainable resources

People will always need to use resources that we take from our environment. These include food, fuels (such as fossil fuels) and minerals (such as ores of copper or aluminium). If we are careful, then we can take and use these resources without doing too much harm to other organisms.

We say that a resource is sustainable if we can keep on using it, and it does not run out. For example, fish in the sea could be a **sustainable resource**, as long as we do not take so many that their populations fall to dangerously low levels. Wood for fuel could be a sustainable resource, so long as we replant trees to replace the ones we cut down, or make sure that plenty of young trees are allowed to naturally grow.

Unfortunately, many of the resources that we take from the Earth are not sustainable. Fossil fuels are a good example of a non-sustainable resource. These fuels were formed millions of years ago, from dead plants and bacteria that lived in the Carboniferous period. Their partially decayed bodies were compressed and formed coal, oil and natural gas. This took a very long time to happen. These fossil fuels cannot be replaced. Once we have used them, they are gone for ever. We therefore need to limit our use of fossil fuels, to ensure that there will still be some available for future generations.

One way that we can help to conserve non-sustainable resources is to recycle things that are made from them.

Recycling glass

Glass is made from sand (silicon oxide) and a few other chemicals, such as lime (calcium oxide) and soda (sodium oxide). These are non-sustainable resources. The best glass is made from especially pure sand, which is mined from deposits made long ago.

Making new glass involves heating these chemicals to very high temperatures. It releases a lot of carbon dioxide.

Used glass can be crushed, melted at high temperatures, and then used to make new glass objects (Figure 22.28). This releases much less carbon dioxide than making new glass. It also reduces our use of the raw materials, such as sand.

Recycling plastics

We have seen that plastics are made from fossil fuels. If we can reuse plastic objects, such as bottles, over and

Figure 22.28 This heap of crushed green bottles will be used to make new glass.

> ## Key definition
>
> **sustainable resource** – one which can be removed from the environment without it running out

over again, that will reduce the amount of fossil fuels we have to use to make them. If we cannot reuse things, then we can still recycle them. This means using the plastic from a used object to make a different object. Used plastic, for example, can be used to make fleece clothing, packaging and many other items.

Recycling paper

Paper is made of cellulose fibres from plants, usually trees. Waste paper can be mixed with water and chemicals that break it down to form a pulp. This is passed through filters that remove any glue that may have been stuck to it (for example, to hold together the pages of magazines) and then treated to remove the printing ink from it. This leaves clean cellulose fibres, which can be made into new paper.

Recycling paper does reduce the number of trees that have to be cut down to make new paper, but in fact most paper mills use trees that are specially grown for the purpose, and each time some are cut down new ones are planted to replace them. The main advantage of recycling paper is that it causes less water and land pollution than making new paper, and uses less energy. However, it is important to take into account the energy – usually from fossil fuels – used in collecting and transporting the used paper, which can be quite significant.

Recycling metals

We get metals from ores that are found underground. Mining metal ores uses a lot of energy – usually from fossil fuels – and damages habitats. Metal ores are also a non-renewable resource. Most metals can be recycled. Aluminium, copper, lead, steel (iron) and zinc are all recycled in many parts of the world. Recycling aluminium saves 95% of the energy that would be used in mining aluminium ore and extracting aluminium metal from it.

Sewage treatment

Water is a scarce resource in many parts of the world. Water that we have used can be recycled.

Sewage is waste liquid which has come from houses, industry and other parts of villages, towns and cities. Some of it has just run off streets into drains when it rains. Some of it

has come from bathrooms and kitchens in people's houses and offices. Some of it has come from factories. Sewage is mostly water, but also contains many other substances. These include urine and faeces, toilet paper, detergents, oil and many other chemicals.

Sewage should not be allowed to run into rivers or the sea before it has been treated. This is because it can harm people and the environment. Untreated sewage is called raw sewage.

Raw sewage contains many bacteria and other microorganisms, some of which may be pathogenic. People who come into contact with raw sewage, especially if it gets into their mouths, may get ill. Raw sewage also contains many substances which provide nutrients for plants and microorganisms. We have seen how this can cause eutrophication if it gets into waterways (page **303**).

It is therefore very important that sewage is treated to remove any pathogenic organisms, and most of the nutrients, before it is released as effluent. Microorganisms play an important part in all the most commonly used methods of sewage treatment.

When sewage has been treated, the water in it can be used again, so sewage treatment enables water to be recycled. It may not be a nice thought to know that the water you drink was once inside someone else's body, but if we did not recycle water in this way then significant water shortages would occur in many parts of the world.

Sewage is treated to make it safe. First, the raw sewage is passed through screens. These trap large objects such as grit which may have been washed off roads. The screened liquid is then left for a while in settlement tanks, where any other insoluble particles drift to the bottom and form a sediment (Figure **22.29**).

There are two different ways in which the resulting liquid can now be treated.

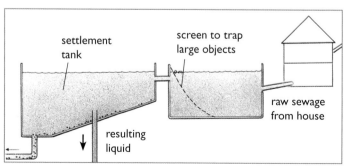

Figure 22.29 How sewage is treated.

Trickling filters

The liquid from the settlement tanks is sprinkled over a trickling filter bed. This is made of small stones and clinker (Figure 22.30). Many different aerobic microorganisms live on the surface of the stones. Some of them are aerobic bacteria, which feed on various nutrients in the sewage. Protoctists (single-celled animal-like organisms, such as *Amoeba*) feed on the bacteria. Fungi feed on soluble nutrients. These microorganisms make up a complex ecosystem in the trickling filter bed.

The liquid is trickled onto the surface of the stones through holes in a rotating pipe. This makes sure that air gets mixed in with the liquid. The liquid trickles quite slowly through the stones, giving the microorganisms plenty of time to work on it. By the time the water drains out of the bottom of the bed, it looks clear, smells clean, contains virtually no pathogenic organisms, and can safely be allowed to run into a river or the sea.

Activated sludge

In this method (Figure 22.31), the liquid from the settlement tanks runs into a tank called an aeration tank. Like the trickling filter bed, this contains aerobic microorganisms, mostly bacteria and protoctists. Oxygen is provided by bubbling air through the tank. As in the trickling filter bed, these aerobic microorganisms make the sewage harmless.

Why is this method called 'activated sludge'? 'Activated' means that microorganisms are present. Some of the liquid from the tank, containing these microorganisms, is kept to add to the next lot of sewage coming in. 'Sludge' means just what it sounds like! It is a word which describes the semi-solid waste materials in sewage.

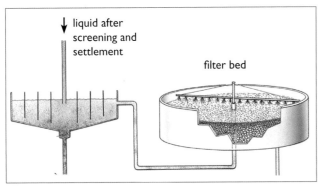

Figure 22.30　Filter bed treatment of sewage.

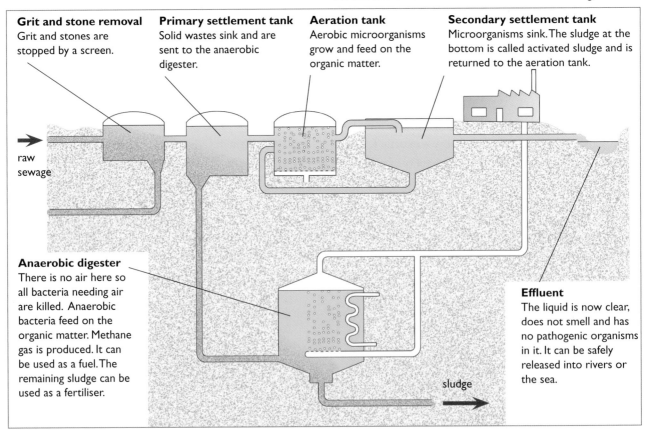

Grit and stone removal
Grit and stones are stopped by a screen.

Primary settlement tank
Solid wastes sink and are sent to the anaerobic digester.

Aeration tank
Aerobic microorganisms grow and feed on the organic matter.

Secondary settlement tank
Microorganisms sink. The sludge at the bottom is called activated sludge and is returned to the aeration tank.

raw sewage

Anaerobic digester
There is no air here so all bacteria needing air are killed. Anaerobic bacteria feed on the organic matter. Methane gas is produced. It can be used as a fuel. The remaining sludge can be used as a fertiliser.

Effluent
The liquid is now clear, does not smell and has no pathogenic organisms in it. It can be safely released into rivers or the sea.

sludge

Figure 22.31　Activated sludge treatment of sewage.

Both the trickling filter and the activated sludge methods can run into problems if the sewage contains substances which harm the microorganisms. These include heavy metals such as mercury, disinfectants, or large quantities of detergents. Heavy metals and disinfectants are toxic to many of the microorganisms. Detergents may cause foaming, which stops oxygen getting into the liquid. To solve these problems, the contaminated sewage can be diluted before being allowed to enter the trickling filter bed or the activated sludge tank.

So far, we have described how the liquid part of the sewage is treated. What about the solid part?

Solids – sludge – first drop out of the sewage in the settlement tank. The activated sludge method also produces sludge. This material contains lots of living and dead microorganisms. It contains valuable organic material. It is a pity to waste it.

The sludge can be acted on by anaerobic bacteria. The sludge is put into large, closed tanks. Inside the tanks, several different kinds of bacteria act on the sludge. Some of them produce methane, which can be used as a fuel. When they have finished, the remaining solid material has to be removed from the tank. It is often used as fertiliser – it is usually quite safe, because it is very unlikely that any pathogenic organisms will have survived all these processes.

S **Sustainable development**

As our population increases, we need to build more houses, roads and industries, and to produce more food. Achieving this without damaging the environment is called **sustainable development**.

Sustainable development requires the cooperation of many different people and organisations. In most countries, new developments such as housing, roads or industrial complexes, have to be submitted for approval by planning authorities. These authorities should take into account the needs of the environment, as well as the business interests of the developers.

> **Key definition**
>
> sustainable development – providing for the needs of an increasing human population without harming the environment

This can cause serious conflicts of interest. The developers will almost certainly be able to spend less, and make more profit, if they do not have to think about what they are doing to the environment. It is therefore important that there are strongly upheld regulations in place, in order to make sure that new developments are planned and constructed with the environment in mind. National governments are usually responsible for producing and upholding these regulations. Local people and authorities are also very important – they are the ones who will be living close to the new development, and they often feel strongly about their environment and do not want it to be damaged. International organisations can also help out. For example, many countries have signed up to agreements such as the Ramsar Convention, in which they have promised to take particular care of wetlands. Wetland habitats are under threat worldwide, and international efforts are needed to try to conserve them.

Conserving forests and fish stocks

Forests and fish populations could be sustainable resources, if we use them carefully. Unfortunately, in many places, we are taking too many of these resources from the environment, so that they are being reduced to dangerously low levels.

Conserving forests

We have already seen how deforestation in many parts of the world has caused severe problems. But it is possible to use forests sustainably.

- ♦ Governments can refuse to grant licences to companies who want to cut down valuable forests. This can be difficult, however, because governments can make large amounts of money from selling the rights to harvest timber from forests.
- ♦ Instead of cutting down all the trees in a forest (called clear-felling), just a small proportion of the trees are cut down. This is called selective felling. The remaining trees will hold the soil in place, and will continue to provide habitats for animals. New trees can regrow to replace those which have been cut down. In practice, however, selective felling often does a lot of damage to the forest because of the roads that are built to allow access, the large machinery that is used to drag the timber out, and also the

disturbance caused by the people working in the forest.

- Many deciduous trees will regrow after they are cut down. Trees can be cut down to about 1 metre or less, and then left to regrow. This is called coppicing. If only part of a wood or forest is coppiced at any one time, then the rest of it remains untouched for many years. The coppicing can be done in a cycle over, say, twelve years, with different parts of the forest being coppiced each year.

- Where large numbers of trees are cut down, new ones should be planted to replace them. This is what happens with most of the trees used to make paper. However, planting new trees cannot replace primary forest. Primary forest is forest that has never been cut down. In the tropics, primary forest contains huge numbers of different species of trees, which provide habitats for many different species of animals. Primary forest should be conserved.

- Education can help to make sure that people understand how important it is to conserve forests. For example, in some places, local people cut down trees to use as fuel for cooking. If they understand the importance of conserving trees, then they can make sure that they replant new trees to replace the ones that they cut down. Better still, they may be able to use renewable sources of energy, such as solar energy, to reduce their need for wood (Figure 22.32).

Conserving fish stocks

Humans have probably always used fish as a source of high-protein food. However, there is increasing concern about the threat to fish populations from the large numbers of fish that are being caught. Figure 22.33 shows how fish catches have increased since 1950. The figures on this graph only include fish caught by people who then sell their catch. There are probably tens of millions of tonnes more that are caught by people who eat it within their own family or community.

As a result of the great numbers of fish being caught, the populations of most of the species that are used for food are getting less. If we do not reduce catches, the populations will get so small that there will not be enough adult fish left to breed and sustain the population.

Reducing the number of fish that are caught is not

Figure 22.32 Solar cookers focus the Sun's rays at the centre of a parabolic reflector. A pan placed in the middle of the reflector gets hot enough to cook food.

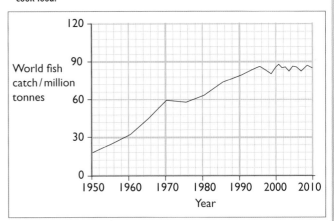

Figure 22.33 World fish catches since 1950.

easy. Each country wants to make sure that it gets a fair share of the fish catch, so any international regulations are very difficult to draw up and to enforce. Everyone is worried that other countries are getting more fish than they are. Moreover, fish do not stay in one place in the sea. Even if a country manages to reduce fishing to reasonable levels around its own shores, the same fish may be under threat when they move to the seas around other countries.

One system of controlling the number of fish caught is to impose quotas. These allow countries, regions or fishermen to catch only a certain quantity of fish. Most quota systems specify different amounts for different species. For example, fishermen might be given quotas to catch large amounts of fish that are not under threat, but very low quotas – or none at all – for species whose

(S) populations have fallen to dangerously low levels. The rules are enforced by inspectors who visit boats at sea, and also check the catches that are brought in to land. This is expensive to do, and is unpopular with fishermen. It is also difficult for fishing boats to catch only one particular species of fish. They may accidentally catch fish of a different species, for which they have already passed their quota. They will not be allowed to land these fish, and will have to throw them back into the sea. It is unlikely that these fish will survive. Nevertheless, imposing and enforcing quotas can be very helpful in conserving threatened fish species.

Another way of trying to keep up the numbers of a particular species of fish is to breed large numbers of them in fish hatcheries, and then release them. This is called restocking. Restocking is done more frequently with freshwater fish than with marine fish. However, some fish, such as salmon, which spend part of the lives in the sea and then go back to fresh water to breed, have been restocked in this way (Figure **22.34**). For example, over 50 million young fish, belonging to several different native species, have been released into the Murray river in Australia in the last 30 years.

Endangered species

A species whose numbers have fallen so low that it is at risk of becoming extinct is said to be endangered. Once a species has become extinct, it is gone for ever.

(S) We have seen (Chapter **19**) how important genetic variation is to a population. If there is variation between individuals, then the population as a whole has a better chance of surviving if they are threatened by a pathogen, or if their habitat changes in some way. At least some of the individuals may have variations that allow them to survive and reproduce, even if others are killed.

When the numbers of a species drop to very low levels, so that only a few individuals survive, then much of this genetic variation is lost. This makes the species much more likely to become extinct.

Through the history of life on Earth, millions of species have become extinct. Palaeontologists (people who study fossils) have identified several periods in the past when huge numbers of species seem to have become extinct. These are called mass extinction events (Figure **22.35**).

Figure 22.34 These tiny trout are about to be released into the Adige river in Italy.

Each of these mass extinctions was caused by a major change in the conditions on Earth. The most catastrophic event occurred about 251 million years ago, when 96% of all species disappeared. We are not sure what caused this event, but major climatic change may have played a part, perhaps brought about by the continuous eruption of huge volcanoes in Siberia. It is also possible that an asteroid hit the Earth at this time.

Another major extinction event is happening now. This time, no asteroid is involved. The cause of the mass extinction is us.

Habitat destruction

We have seen how human activities can destroy habitats. Species with no habitat cannot survive.

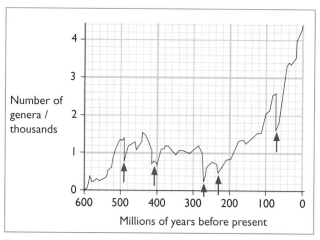

Figure 22.35 Mass extinction events have occurred five times in the last 500 million years.

Hunting

Humans have always hunted animals for food, but sometimes this hunting is so severe that it can destroy an entire species. There is much evidence that mammoths finally became extinct 5000 years ago because of hunting by humans. The dodo, a giant flightless pigeon that used to live on Mauritius (Figure 22.36), was destroyed by humans in the late 17th century, when its eggs were eaten and adults killed.

Figure 22.36 The dodo was hunted to extinction only 80 years after it was discovered.

Pollution

We have seen that the addition of extra carbon dioxide and methane to the atmosphere is causing climate change. As temperatures rise on Earth, organisms with adaptations that allow them to live in a particular environment may no longer be so well adapted. This is especially true of species that require cold conditions, such as polar bears. Polar bears need large areas of sea ice on which to hunt seals. As the ice caps melt, they may be left without a habitat. Climate change is one of several factors that are thought to have brought about the extinction of the golden toad (Figure 22.37).

Introduced species

New species that are introduced by humans into an ecosystem can threaten the existence of native species. For example, New Zealand has long been isolated geographically from the rest of the world. No major predators ever evolved there, and so native species did not evolve adaptations that helped them to avoid predation. Humans introduced rats and other predatory mammals into these islands when they first arrived in the late 18th century. Since then, almost half of the native vertebrate species in New Zealand have become extinct.

Figure 22.37 A pair of golden toads mating. These toads, which used to live in the cloud forests of Costa Rica, are now extinct.

Conserving endangered species

In the 1970s, the Mauritian green parakeet, also known as the echo parakeet, was said to be the most endangered bird species in the world (Figure 22.38). Only about 10 birds were known to exist. These parakeets live in forests and scrub habitats, but by 1996 only 5% of Mauritius was still covered with its native vegetation. The parakeets, which feed on fruits of native trees, had little to eat. They were also threatened by introduced species such as rats and monkeys, which took eggs from nests and competed with the parakeets for food. And the loss of old trees meant that there were few suitable nest sites available.

In 1973, an intensive conservation programme began. At first, it concentrated on helping the parakeets to survive and breed in their habitat. Nest boxes were put up, predators were controlled, and non-native trees and weeds were cleared from the forest. This helped, but numbers still remained very low, so some of the eggs were taken to be reared in captivity. Many captive-reared birds have now been released into the wild. The

Figure 22.38 Mauritian green parakeets in their natural habitat.

population stood at almost 600 birds in 2012, so it looks as though this parakeet is now out of immediate danger.

Many local organisations and individuals have been involved in this conservation project. Visits to schools and other education initiatives have helped to make young people aware of the importance of taking care of this endangered species, and how their actions can help it to survive.

S There is still concern, however, about the loss of genetic diversity in the green parakeet population. All the individuals now alive were bred from the 10 birds that remained in the 1970s, so they are all quite closely related and share many of the same alleles. The breeding programmes are being organised to try to keep as much genetic diversity as possible.

This conservation success story illustrates many of the different tactics that can be used to conserve endangered species. They include:

♦ monitoring and protecting the species in its natural habitat

♦ using captive breeding programmes

♦ educating local people about the importance of conservation, and what they can do to help.

Animals are not the only organisms that are in danger of extinction. Many plant species are also under threat. We can use all of the same techniques that are used to conserve threatened animal species, but there is also another possibility – building up seed banks (Figure 22.39).

Seeds are often able to survive for many years in a dormant state, and then germinate when conditions are right. We can make use of that by collecting and storing seeds of as many different plant species as possible. These can be kept safe for long periods of time. In the future, if a species is threatened with extinction, we will have some of their seeds that can be used to grow into new plants, either to be kept 'in captivity' or reintroduced into their natural habitat.

S Reasons for conservation programmes

Conservation programmes are expensive. They can cause conflict with people who want to use an area of land for a different purpose. So what are the arguments for spending money and effort on trying to conserve endangered species and their habitats? Here are just a few of these arguments.

Figure 22.39 The Svalbard Seed Vault, in Norway, stores more than half a million different kinds of seeds deep under the ice.

♦ For many of us, it is clear that we have no right to make any species extinct. We share the Earth with a whole range of different species, and we have a responsibility to make sure that they can live successfully in their habitats. We are keeping them safe so that future generations can enjoy them.

♦ If we damage ecosystems, we can be doing harm to ourselves. Cutting down large numbers of trees, for example, can reduce the amount of water vapour that goes back into the air, which in turn can reduce rainfall. People who depend on locally-collected wood for fuel may no longer be able to heat their homes or cook food. Taking care of the environment helps to make our own living conditions more pleasant and safe.

♦ Losing species from an ecosystem can have wide-reaching effects. For example, if we catch too many fish, then we will no longer be able to use them as food. Moreover, the loss of one species may have harmful effects on other species that are part of the same food web.

♦ Many plant species contain chemicals that can be used as drugs. If we lose plant species, we may be losing potential new medicines.

♦ We have seen how selective breeding has been used to produce new varieties of crop plants. Wild relatives of our crop plants contain different alleles of genes that could be useful in future breeding programmes. Conserving wild plants, as well as all the different varieties of crop plants, is important if we are not to lose potentially useful alleles (Figure **22.39**).

End-of-chapter questions

1 a i   Plants need a supply of nitrate ions.
            State the use made of nitrate ions in plants.   [1]
       ii   Many farmers regularly add nitrate fertilisers to their fields.
            Explain why this is necessary.   [2]
    b   A farmer spreads a nitrate rich fertiliser over his fields. Each time he does this, he washes out his
        spreading equipment in a farm pond.
        Suggest and explain what the likely effects of such pollution will be on the plants and
        animals in the pond.   [5]
    [Cambridge IGCSE® Biology 0610/02, Question 4, October/November 2003]

2   The graph below shows the effect on the number of insects present on the crops when
        an insecticide is used in each of the five years.

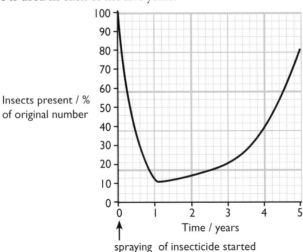

a State **one** way an insect might be
  i helpful to the crops
  ii harmful to the crops. [2]
b Explain why the percentage of insects began to rise in the second year until almost reaching its original level. [5]
c Suggest three methods of improving the yield from the crops without the use of an insecticide. [3]

[Cambridge O Level Biology 5090/22, Question 2, October/November 2010]

S 3 The graph shows the amount of dissolved oxygen in the water of a river in a city.

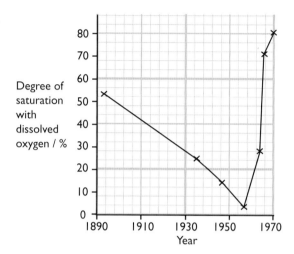

In the 19th century, sewage from the city drained directly into the river. At the beginning of the 20th century sewage treatment plants were installed, which removed some of the organic material from the sewage before it entered the river. These plants have gradually become more efficient.

a Give **two** ways in which water obtains dissolved oxygen. [2]
b Explain how pollution by sewage causes dissolved oxygen levels to decrease. [4]
c Suggest why dissolved oxygen levels in the river:
  i decreased until 1948 [2]
  ii have increased since the 1950s. [2]
d What effect would you expect a decrease in dissolved oxygen to have on the fish population in the river? [1]
e Apart from affecting the levels of dissolved oxygen, what other harmful effects can the discharge of untreated sewage into rivers have? [2]

Answers to questions

Chapter 1 Classification

1.1 **a** Distantly related, because they belong to the same kingdom but different phyla.

   b *Manis*

   c

Kingdom	animal
Phylum	vertebrates
Class	mammals
Order	primates
Family	Hominidae
Genus	*Homo*
Species	*Homo sapiens*

1.2 **a** They do not move very much (although, in fact, they are able to move from place to place). Their tentacles look rather like flower petals.

   b You would see that their cells never have cell walls, large vacuoles or chloroplasts.

1.3 Look at its cells under a microscope. You would see that they have cell walls, large vacuoles and chloroplasts.

1.4 They both have cell walls. They both have a nucleus, cytoplasm and a cell membrane. Possible differences include the following. A plant cell may have chloroplasts, but fungal cells do not. The cell wall of a plant cell is made of cellulose, the cell wall of a fungal cell is not.

1.5 They do not have a nucleus.

1.6 They cannot carry out any of the characteristics of living things. They are not made of cells. They can only reproduce when they are inside a living cell.

1.7 They have hair, not feathers. They suckle their young. Their young develop inside the female's body, attached to a placenta, rather than inside a shelled egg. They do not have a beak. (There are other possible answers you may have given – but do make sure they apply to all mammals and all birds.)

1.8 They have hair and they suckle their young on milk.

Chapter 2 Cells

2.1 about 1500 times

2.2 10 mm (1 cm)

2.3 10 000 (10^4)

2.4 1000 (10^3)

2.5 **a** 74 mm (to be checked)

   b 74 000 µm

   c real size = 74 000 ÷ 20 000
      = 3.7 µm

   d 1 mm = 10^3 µm
      So you could fit 10^3 ÷ 3.7
         = 270 of them into 1 mm

2.6 all cells

2.7 cellulose

2.8 It will allow all substances to pass through.

2.9 It will allow some substances to pass through, but not others.

2.10 water

2.11 It is a space inside a cell, surrounded by a membrane, containing a liquid.

2.12 It is a liquid containing sugars and other substances dissolved in water, found inside a vacuole in a plant cell.

2.13 It absorbs energy from sunlight.

2.14 DNA, in the form of chromosomes; this is the genetic information of the cell.

2.15 They are usually too long and thin, but become shorter and fatter just before the cell divides.

2.16 All cells except bacterial cells.

2.17 Mitochondria are the site of aerobic respiration, where energy is released from glucose.

2.18 All cells.

2.19 They are the site of protein synthesis.

Chapter 3 Movement in and out of cells

3.1 It is the net movement of molecules from a region of their higher concentration down a concentration gradient to a region of their lower concentration, as a result of their random movement.

3.2 Oxygen diffusing into an organism across a gas exchange surface; carbon dioxide diffusing out of an organism across a gas exchange surface; absorption of products of digestion (for example, amino acids) across the wall of the small intestine; diffusion of carbon dioxide into the air spaces of a leaf.

3.3   a   It increases kinetic energy.
      b   It will increase the rate of diffusion, because the molecules move faster.

3.4 A sugar molecule is larger.

3.5 a membrane that allows some particles to pass through, but not others

3.6 Visking tubing, a cell membrane

3.7 It is a dilute solution (or it has a high water potential).

3.8 It absorbs water by osmosis, swelling until it bursts.

3.9 The plant cell absorbs water by osmosis just like an animal cell, but the strong cellulose cell wall prevents it bursting.

3.10 a   the cell wall
       b   the cell membrane

3.11 a cell that has taken up water so that the cell contents are pressing outwards onto the cell wall

3.12 the condition of a plant cell when it has lost so much water that the cytoplasm and vacuole have shrunk, pulling the cell membrane away from the cell wall

3.13 by putting a plant cell into a solution that is more concentrated than the cytoplasm and cell sap

3.14 The same solution as is outside the cell – the cell wall is fully permeable, so both water and solute molecules can diffuse freely through it.

3.15 In Figure 3.5, the solution outside the cell has a higher water potential than the cytoplasm or cell sap. Water therefore diffuses down the water potential gradient, into the cell, through the partially permeable cell membrane.
In Figure 3.6, the solution outside the cell has a lower water potential than the cytoplasm or cell sap. Water therefore diffuses down the water potential gradient, out of the cell, through the partially permeable cell membrane.

Chapter 4 The chemicals of life

4.1 the chemical reactions that take place inside the body

4.2 Cells will lose water. Reactions take place in solution in the cytoplasm. If there is not enough water, this cannot happen. Water is also required for transport (for example, substances dissolve in the water in blood plasma), and cooling (sweating and transpiration).

4.3 carbon, hydrogen, oxygen

4.4 There are 6 carbon atoms, 12 hydrogen atoms and 6 oxygen atoms in one glucose molecule.

4.5 a   simple sugar (monosaccharide)
      b   polysaccharide
      c   polysaccharide

4.6 a   glucose
      b   glucose
      c   glycogen
      d   sucrose
      e   starch

4.7 carbon, hydrogen, oxygen

4.8 heat insulation, energy store

4.9 The oils are an energy store for the embryo plant to use when germination begins, before it can photosynthesise.

4.10 nitrogen, sometimes sulfur

4.11 about 20

4.12 They are made of long chains of smaller molecules linked together.

4.13 haemoglobin, any enzyme, antibodies, other suitable example

4.14 For example: transporting oxygen (haemoglobin); the formation of new cells (for growth or repair); in active transport (in cell membranes); destroying pathogens (antibodies); forming hair (keratin); providing elasticity to skin (collagen).

Chapter 5 Enzymes

5.1 a substance that speeds up a chemical reaction without itself being changed

5.2 enzymes

5.3 all of them

5.4 an enzyme that acts on carbohydrates

5.5 amylase, maltase, sucrase

5.6 For amylase, the substrate is starch and the product is maltose.
For maltase, the substrate is maltose and the product is glucose.
For sucrase, the substrate is sucrose and the products are glucose and fructose.

5.7 the temperature at which an enzyme works at its fastest

5.8 40 °C

5.9 The enzyme molecule loses its shape at high temperature, so the substrate will no longer fit into the active site.

Chapter 6 Plant nutrition

6.1 any suitable organic substance – for example, sugar

6.2 carbon dioxide and water

6.3 the green pigment, found in chloroplasts, that absorbs energy from sunlight, used to drive photosynthesis

6.4 petiole

6.5 epidermal cells

6.6 to prevent water loss from leaf cells

6.7 small holes, mostly on the lower surface of a leaf, through which gases can diffuse

6.8 sausage-shaped cells surrounding a stoma, which can change their shape and open or close the stoma

6.9 Palisade mesophyll cells, spongy mesophyll cells and guard cells contain chloroplasts. Epidermal cells (and xylem vessels and phloem sieve tubes) do not.

6.10 carbon dioxide and water

6.11 about 0.04%

6.12 by diffusion, through the stomata

6.13 Water is brought to the leaf in xylem vessels.

6.14 More sunlight can be absorbed; more carbon dioxide can diffuse into the leaf at the same time.

6.15 Sunlight can reach all the cells in the leaf. Carbon dioxide can diffuse quickly to all the cells in the leaf.

6.16 Glucose is soluble and fairly reactive.

6.17 nitrogen (in a reactive form, such as nitrates)

6.18 Nitrate is needed for making proteins, and proteins are needed for growth.

6.19 Sucrose, produced by photosynthesis in the leaves, is supplied to them through phloem sieve tubes.

6.20 A limiting factor is something present in the environment in such short supply that it restricts life processes.

6.21 light intensity, carbon dioxide concentration

6.22 Stomata often close if the weather is very hot and dry, to prevent too much water being lost. This means carbon dioxide cannot diffuse into the leaves, so photosynthesis may slow down or even stop.

Chapter 7 Animal nutrition

7.1 a Carbohydrates, fats, proteins and vitamins are organic. Minerals and water are inorganic.
b carbohydrates, fats and proteins
c stimulate peristalsis and prevent constipation

7.2 heart disease, diabetes, stroke

7.3 a disease of the coronary arteries of the heart, which become partially blocked by deposits of cholesterol, preventing sufficient oxygen reaching the heart muscle

7.4 Starvation means not getting enough food. Malnutrition means having an unbalanced diet, perhaps a diet lacking in one nutrient or containing too much fat.

7.5 a disease caused by a lack of a particular nutrient in the diet

7.6 scurvy (lack of vitamin C); rickets (lack of vitamin D); brittle bones (lack of calcium); anaemia (lack of iron)

7.7 the breakdown of large, insoluble food molecules into small molecules using mechanical and chemical processes

7.8 vitamins and minerals (and water)

7.9 a simple sugars (glucose)
b amino acids
c fatty acids and glycerol

7.10 breaking down large molecules of food into small ones, using enzymes

7.11 the teeth at the front of the mouth, used for biting off pieces of food

7.12 they have different types of teeth (incisors, canines, premolars and molars); they have two sets of teeth (milk teeth and permanent teeth)

7.13 a mix of food remnants and bacteria coating the teeth

7.14 a Bacteria in plaque can breed and penetrate between the tooth and the gums, causing inflammation and eventually even loss of the tooth.

b Bacteria in plaque produce acids when they metabolise foods. The acid dissolves enamel, producing a hole through which bacteria can reach the living part of the tooth.

7.15 a circular muscle that can contract to close a tube

7.16 where the oesophagus enters the stomach; where the duodenum joins the stomach; at the anus

7.17 Mucus is secreted throughout the alimentary canal. It provides lubrication, so food does not damage the cells lining the alimentary canal. It protects these cells from attack by enzymes.

7.18 The mouth (in saliva); the duodenum (in pancreatic juice). It breaks down starch to maltose.

7.19 a flap that covers the trachea when swallowing

7.20 The acid provides the optimum pH for pepsin to work, and destroys bacteria in the food.

7.21 duodenum and ileum

7.22 pancreatic juice and bile

7.23 Bile salts emulsify fats, making it easier for lipase to come into contact with them and digest them.

7.24 Diarrhoea is the loss of large amounts of watery faeces. It can be treated by drinking fluids containing small amounts of salt and sugar.

7.25 The bacterium attaches to the wall of the small intestine and secretes toxins. These cause chloride ions to move from the cells into the lumen of the intestine. This causes water to follow, by osmosis, which results in large amounts of water being present inside the intestine. This is passed out with the faeces.

Chapter 8 Transport in plants

8.1 water and inorganic ions such as nitrate

8.2 lignin (and cellulose)

8.3 sucrose and amino acids

8.4 Phloem tubes are alive but xylem is dead; phloem tubes have cellulose cell walls, while xylem vessels contain lignin; phloem tubes end in sieve plates, but xylem vessels are open-ended.

8.5 a collection of xylem vessels and phloem tubes

8.6 It protects the tip of the root as it grows through the soil.

8.7 Water moves into root hairs by osmosis, down its water potential gradient (or from a less concentrated solution to a more concentrated one), through the partially permeable cell membrane of the root hair cells. Minerals enter by diffusion (or active transport).

8.8 evaporation of water from the surfaces of mesophyll cells followed by loss of water vapour from plant leaves, through the stomata

8.9 small holes, mostly on the lower surface of a leaf, each surrounded by a pair of guard cells, through which gases can diffuse into and out of the leaf

8.10 measuring the rate at which a shoot takes up water (and therefore the rate at which it loses water by transpiration)

8.11 a An increase in temperature increases the rate of transpiration. (This happens because at higher temperatures, water molecules have more kinetic energy. They are more likely to turn from liquid to gas, and will diffuse more rapidly out of the leaf.)

b An increase in light intensity increases the rate of transpiration. (This happens because the plant is more likely to open its stomata when it is light, to allow carbon dioxide to enter for photosynthesis. If stomata are open, more water vapour can diffuse out of the leaf.)

Chapter 9 Transport in animals

9.1 a system of blood vessels with a pump and valves to ensure one-way flow of blood.

9.2 blood containing a lot of oxygen

9.3 in the lungs

9.4 left

9.5 In a double circulatory system, blood flows from the heart to the lungs, and then back to the heart again before travelling to the rest of the body. In a single circulatory system, blood flows directly from the lungs or gills to the rest of the body.

9.6 It means oxygenated blood is transported to body cells faster, at higher pressure.

9.7 a left atrium
b right atrium

9.8 between the atria and the ventricles

9.9 septum

9.10 a right ventricle
b left ventricle

9.11 They contain more cardiac muscle, which can therefore provide a greater force when they contract. This is needed to pump the blood around the body.

9.12 It contains more cardiac muscle, needed to produce more force to pump blood all around the body rather than just to the lungs.

9.13 With an ECG, by measuring pulse rate, listening to the sounds of valves closing.

9.14 The pulse is the regular expansion of arteries, caused by blood surging through at high pressure each time the ventricles contract.

9.15 a three
     b about 0.7 seconds

9.16 To move oxygenated blood to the muscles more quickly, to supply the oxygen they need to release energy from glucose, by respiration.

9.17 It is a patch of muscle in the right atrium which sets the pace for the beating of the rest of the heart muscle.

9.18 Extra CO_2 (from respiring muscles) dissolves in blood plasma, reducing its pH. This is sensed by receptors in the brain, which increases the frequency of nerve impulses sent to the pacemaker.

9.19 The valves are pushed closed by the high pressure of the blood in the ventricles. This prevents blood flowing back into the atria.

9.20 a arteries
     b veins

9.21 The pressure of the blood in arteries is high and pulsing, so the strong walls are needed to withstand this pressure.

9.22 The elastic walls allow the arteries to expand with each pulse of pressure (produced by the heart) and then recoil in between pulses; if they could not do this they might burst.

9.23 Capillaries deliver blood, containing oxygen and nutrients, very close to every cell in the body.

9.24 A large lumen provides less resistance to blood flow, needed because blood pressure in the veins is low.

9.25 Skeletal muscles in the legs squeeze inwards on the veins when the muscles contract, pushing blood along inside them.

9.26 It is supplied with blood by two vessels – the hepatic artery and the hepatic portal vein.

9.27 Five from: water, glucose, vitamins, minerals (inorganic ions), urea, hormones, fibrinogen, antibodies (and others).

9.28 They transport oxygen.

9.29 They have no nucleus, and contain haemoglobin. They have a biconcave shape.

9.30 a red pigment that absorbs and releases oxygen; a protein found inside red blood cells

9.31 tiny fragments of cells that help with blood clotting

9.32 It contains oxyhaemoglobin, which is bright red. Blood in (most) veins is deoxygenated, and therefore contains haemoglobin, which is purplish red.

9.33 hepatic portal vein

9.34 dissolved in blood plasma

9.35 sealing wounds by clotting; destroying pathogens

9.36 fluid that has leaked out of capillaries and fills the spaces between cells in the body

9.37 providing a medium through which nutrients, gases and waste products can diffuse between blood and cells; helping to maintain a constant temperature around cells

9.38 tissue fluid that has drained into lymphatic capillaries

9.39 There is no heart in the lymphatic system, so lymph moves only slowly through the vessels, pushed by the contraction of nearby muscles. The valves are needed to keep it flowing in the right direction.

9.40 Two from: armpit, groin, neck, thorax.

9.41 White blood cells proliferate and help to destroy pathogens and their toxins.

Chapter 10 Pathogens and immunity

10.1 an organism that causes disease

10.2 for example, rabies, malaria, influenza, polio, cholera, AIDS, food poisoning

10.3 by direct contact; in droplets in the air (into the respiratory passages); in food or water; via a vector

10.4 for example, layer of dead cells covering the skin; blood clotting; cilia and mucus in the respiratory passages; hydrochloric acid in the stomach

10.5 a The hat stops hairs falling into the food; hairs could have bacteria on them.

 b The white clothes show that they are clean and therefore less likely to have harmful microorganisms on them – if they get dirty, they should be changed. Simple clothing is less likely to harbour microorganisms in out-of-the way places.

10.6 To prevent animals such as houseflies or rats getting to it; these animals can pick up pathogens from the food and transmit them to other, fresh, food that might be eaten.

10.7 a To prevent harmful substances from the waste getting into water, where it might harm drinking water.

 b To ensure that the rubbish ends up taking up a relatively small amount of space, and so that it can be covered with soil at a later stage

 c To prevent microorganisms in the rubbish infecting humans, or being taken back into people's homes.

 d To allow gases produced by the decomposition of the rubbish to escape, rather than building up underground; so that useful gases such as methane can be collected and used as fuel.

 e so that the land can be used for another purpose

10.8 It may contain pathogens, such as the bacteria that cause cholera or the viruses that cause polio.

10.9 It takes time for the lymphocytes to recognise the bacterium, and for the lymphocytes that can make the appropriate antibody to produce a clone of themselves. Only then is the antibody produced in large quantities.

10.10 The number of bacteria stays very low. This is because memory cells are already present in the person, so the appropriate antibody is made almost immediately, preventing the bacteria from reproducing.

10.11 This would be the first infection with that bacterium, so the person would probably get ill. The memory cells produced for the infection with the other bacterium can only make antibodies against that one, not against this new kind of bacterium.

Chapter 11 Respiration

11.1 to release energy from glucose for cells to use

11.2 active transport; driving chemical reactions such as protein synthesis; movement; producing heat; transmitting nerve impulses; cell division

11.3 the release of a relatively small amount of energy by the breakdown of food substances in the absence of oxygen

11.4 yeast, humans (for short periods of time)

11.5 It produces lactic acid. It does not produce CO_2. It releases less energy.

11.6 It produces lactic acid, not ethanol. It does not produce CO_2.

11.7 They sweep mucus, which contains trapped bacteria and dust particles, up to the top of the trachea and into the throat, where it can be swallowed.

11.8 the voice box

11.9 across the walls of the alveoli

11.10 two

Chapter 12 Excretion

12.1 carbon dioxide and urea

12.2 respiration and deamination

12.3 It is broken down into amino acids. These are absorbed through the walls of the small intestine and transported to the liver in the blood, where – if they are surplus to requirements – they are broken down, producing urea which is carried to the kidneys to be excreted.

12.4 one of thousands of tiny tubes in the kidney which produce urine from filtered blood

12.5 renal arteries

12.6 a tangle of blood capillaries in the cup of a renal capsule

12.7 The vessel supplying blood to the glomerulus is wider than the one taking it away.

12.8 It helps to push the components of the blood through the filter, into the nephron.

12.9 red blood cells; proteins (or any named protein, such as fibrinogen)

12.10 water; glucose; some ions such as sodium or potassium ions

12.11 a solution of urea and other substances in water

Chapter 13 Coordination and response

13.1 any muscles or glands

13.2 nerves and hormones (the nervous system and the endocrine system)

13.3 They have a nucleus, cell membrane and cytoplasm.

13.4 They have a long axon (or dendron) to transmit impulses rapidly from one part of the body to another. They have nerve endings to pass the impulses onto another nerve cell or an effector. They (may) have a myelin sheath around the axon (or dendron) to speed up the impulses. They have dendrites to receive nerve impulses from other cells.

13.5 The CNS receives inputs from different receptors, which it integrates, and produces nerve impulses to send to appropriate effectors.

13.6 **a** in a small swelling just outside the spinal cord
     b in the central nervous system – either the brain or the spinal cord
     c in the central nervous system – either the brain or the spinal cord

13.7 They produce very quick, automatic responses with no time wasted in making decisions. This can enable escape from danger.

13.8 There are many possibilities. Answers should state the stimulus and the response.

13.9 a change in the environment that is detected by a receptor

13.13 tongue and nose

13.11 retina

13.12 There are many cone cells packed closely together at the fovea, so they can produce an image made of many tiny 'spots' of information in a small space (that is, with a high resolution).

13.13 When you look straight at an object, the image is focused on the fovea, where the receptor cells are all cones. These cannot respond to dim light. If you look to one side, the image is focused elsewhere on the retina, where there are more rods, which are sensitive to dim light.

13.14 It is a black layer that absorbs light so it does not continuously reflect inside the eye.

13.15 conjunctiva, cornea, aqueous humour, pupil, lens, vitreous humour, retina

13.16 cornea and lens

13.17 changing the shape of the lens to focus light rays from different distances onto the retina

13.18 **a** contract
     b This reduces tension on the suspensory ligaments, which allows the lens to become its natural, rounded shape.

13.19 pancreas – insulin (and glucagon); adrenal gland – adrenaline; testis – testosterone; ovary – oestrogen.

13.20 dissolved in blood plasma

13.21 any situation in which you are nervous, frightened or angry

13.22 It increases glucose concentration in the blood, so muscles can use more for respiration; it increases heart rate, increasing the supply of glucose and oxygen to muscles; it increases breathing rate – similar effect.

13.23 the tip

13.24 just behind the tip

13.25 Auxin made in the tip diffuses down into the part just below the tip. Auxin is like an animal hormone, a chemical that is made in one part of the body and moves to another where it has an effect. However, auxin is not made in an endocrine gland like animal hormones, and it is not transported in the blood.

13.26 It moves the leaves towards a light source, maximising the amount of light available for photosynthesis.

13.27 It grows towards it; this is positive gravitropism.

13.28 tall, thin, yellow or white

Chapter 14 Homeostasis

14.1 Advantages: allows the organism to be active in all seasons, and at all times of day and night, even when external temperatures are lower or higher than the optimum for the enzyme-catalysed reactions of its metabolism. Disadvantage: much more food required, to generate heat to keep the body warm.

14.2 Stores fat as an energy reserve, which can be used in respiration to release energy for cells to use. Acts as a heat insulator, preventing loss of heat from the body to the external environment.

14.3 The water in sweat evaporates. This requires energy, which is taken from the skin, thus cooling it.

14.4 hypothalamus

14.5 Vasodilation is the widening of the arterioles supplying the blood capillaries near the surface of the skin. It allows more blood to flow through these capillaries, losing heat by radiation through the skin surface.

14.6 When a parameter changes in a particular direction, this is sensed and measures are put into place to change it back towards the norm.

Chapter 15 Drugs
There are no quick-check questions in this chapter.

Chapter 16 Reproduction in plants
16.1 In asexual reproduction, cells divide by mitosis. This produces genetically identical cells, so the offspring are genetically identical to their parent and to each other.

16.2 to produce many more plants that have identical characteristics to the parent plant

16.3 a swollen part of a stem, which stores food (generally in the form of starch)

16.4 a haploid cell that fuses with another haploid gamete to produce a zygote – for example, an egg or a sperm

16.5 a diploid cell formed by the fusion of the nuclei of two gametes

16.6 so that when their nuclei fuse at fertilisation, the new cell formed will have the normal two sets of chromosomes

16.7 a cell with two complete sets of chromosomes

16.8 any part of the body

16.9 a cell with one set of chromosomes

16.10 egg or sperm

16.11 during the formation of gametes

16.12 to produce haploid cells from a diploid cell

16.13 sexual reproduction

16.14 anthers

16.15 ovules

16.16 the transfer of pollen grains from the male part of the flower (anther of stamen) to the female part of the flower (stigma)

16.17 Much of the pollen of wind-pollinated flowers will not land on the stigma of a flower of the same species and will be wasted. The pollen of insect-pollinated flowers is more likely to be delivered to an appropriate flower.

16.18 down a tube that grows out of the pollen grain, through the style and into the ovule

16.19 a tiny gap in the integuments of the ovule, through which the pollen tube grows

16.20
  a they fall off
  b they fall off
  c develops into an embryo plant
  d develops into a seed, which contains the embryo plant
  e develop into the testa (the tough covering of a seed)
  f develops into a fruit containing seeds

16.21 starch and protein – food reserves for the growing seedling

16.22 inactive; metabolism has slowed down almost to a stop

16.23 It allows the seed to survive through adverse conditions such as low temperatures or drought, when an adult plant would not survive.

16.24 the uptake of water

16.25 They break down the food reserves into smaller molecules that can travel to the embryo and be used to fuel its growth.

16.26 It is likely to result in more variation, as it is likely that different plants will have different characteristics (alleles of genes) that will be brought together in the zygote. Self-pollination can only produce mixing of genes already present in the parent.

16.27 Advantages: the plant can reproduce sexually and form seeds even if it is the only one of its species in an area; the relatively small amount of variation amongst its offspring means that, if the parent plant was well adapted to conditions, then the offspring will be also. Disadvantages: the small amount of variation amongst offspring means that there are less likely to be individuals able to cope well in new environmental conditions than if cross-pollination had taken place.

Chapter 17 Reproduction in humans
17.1 cervix

17.2 where the two sperm ducts join the urethra; it produces fluid for sperm to swim in

17.3 An egg bursts out of an ovary, and is caught in the funnel of the oviduct.

17.4 in the testes

17.5 Cilia in the wall of the oviduct waft it along.

17.6 in the oviducts

17.7 Sperm are much smaller than eggs. Sperm can swim but eggs cannot. Sperm have a head, a long tail, and enzymes in a vesicle in the head. Eggs have none of these, but do have a layer of jelly surrounding them.

17.8 when the embryo sinks into the lining of the uterus

17.9 a developing baby in the uterus from about the 11th week after fertilisation

17.10 by the umbilical cord, which contains two arteries and a vein

17.11 oxygen; glucose; any other soluble nutrients; water

17.12 a contract and relax rhythmically
 b widens
 c detaches from the uterus wall some minutes after the baby has been born

17.13 Advantages: breast milk is sterile; it is free; it contains the perfect balance of nutrients for the baby's needs; it changes its composition as the baby grows; it contains antibodies which give the baby protection from infections; breast-feeding promotes close bonding between mother and baby. Disadvantages: the father cannot help with feeding the baby; the mother may not be well enough or have a good enough diet to produce sufficient milk; some mothers find it difficult to breast-feed.

17.14 So that it is prepared for the arrival of an embryo if an egg is fertilised.

17.15 It is lost through the vagina.

17.16 a the stage in a person's life as they approach puberty
 b the point at which sexual maturity is reached

17.17 the male sex hormone, produced by the testes

17.18 deep voice; broad shoulders; hair growth on face, under arms and around genitals

Chapter 18 Inheritance

18.1 DNA

18.2 a pair of chromosomes that carry the same genes in the same positions

18.3 different forms of a gene

18.4 a B and b (or any other upper and lower case versions of the same letter)
 b brown eyes

18.5 a condition in which both alleles of a gene have an effect on the phenotype of a heterozygous organism

18.6 codominance and the existence of more than two alleles of the gene

18.7 $I^A I^o$ group A
 $I^B I^o$ group B
 $I^o I^o$ group O

18.8 23

18.9 a Nn
 b N or n

18.10

P's phenotypes	normal wings	normal wings
P's genotypes	NN	Nn
Gametes	Ⓝ	Ⓝ ⓝ
Offspring genotypes and phenotypes	Ⓝ	ⓝ

	NN	Nn
Ⓝ	normal wings	normal wings

All the offspring would have normal wings.

18.11

P's phenotypes	brown hair	brown hair
P's genotypes	Bb	Bb
Gametes	Ⓑ ⓑ	Ⓑ ⓑ
Offspring genotypes and phenotypes	Ⓑ	ⓑ

	BB	Bb
Ⓑ	brown hair	brown hair
ⓑ	Bb brown hair	bb red hair

If both parents were heterozygous, then both can produce gametes containing the b alleles. If two such gametes fuse to form a zygote, the resulting child will have the genotype bb and have red hair. The chance of this happening is one in four each time they have a child. By chance, this has happpened three times out of five.

18.12 She could breed the black-spotted dog with a liver-spotted dog. If the dog is heterozygous:

P's phenotypes	black spots	liver spots
P's genotypes	**Bb**	**bb**
Gametes	(B)	(b)

Offspring genotypes and phenotypes

	(b)
(B)	**Bb** black spots
(b)	**bb** liver spots

If the black-spotted dog is homozygous, all of its gametes will have the allele **B**, so all the offspring will have the genotype **Bb** and will have black spots. Therefore, if any of the offspring have liver spots, the breeder knows that the genotype of the black-spotted dog is **Bb**.

18.13 If the parents have a child with blood group O, then they must each have allele I^o.

P's phenotypes	group A	group B
P's genotypes	$I^A I^B$	$I^A I^o$
Gametes	(I^A) (I^o)	(I^B) (I^o)

Offspring genotypes and phenotypes

	(I^B)	(I^o)
(I^A)	$I^A I^B$ group AB	$I^A I^o$ group A
(I^o)	$I^B I^o$ group B	$I^o I^o$ group O

18.14 Person 1 (male) has a child with blood group O, so he must have the allele I^o. His genotype is therefore $I^A I^o$.

Person 2 (male) is married to person 3 (female) who is blood group B. One of their children has blood group AB so person 2 must be blood group A with genotype $I^A I^o$. Their other child has blood group O so must be genotype $I^o I^o$ having inherited an I^o allele from each parent.

So person 3 must be genotype $I^B I^o$.

18.15 a

P's phenotypes	colour-blind man	woman with normal vision
P's genotypes	$X^b Y$	$X^B X^b$
Gametes	(X^b) (Y)	(X^B) (X^b)

Offspring genotypes and phenotypes

	(X^B)	(X^b)
(X^b)	$X^B X^b$ girl with normal vision	$X^b X^b$ colour-blind girl
(Y)	$X^B Y$ boy with normal vision	$X^b Y$ colour-blind boy

There is a one in four chance that any child will be a colour-blind boy. There is also a one in four chance of a colour-blind girl, but this has not happened.

b one in four (25%)

Chapter 19 Variation and natural selection

19.1 **a** discontinuous
b continuous
c continuous
d discontinuous

19.2 **a** and **d** genes only
b and **c** genes and environment

19.3 Large eyes take in large amounts of light, to help the tarsier to see at night when there is little light available.
Large ears help to detect sounds made by prey.
Eyes and ears are forward-facing, making it possible to judge distance.
Grasping fingers help the tarsier to move easily among trees.
Accept other adaptations and sensible suggestions about how they help the tarsier to survive.

19.4 Variation: most peppered moths were pale, but a few dark ones were born in each generation.
Over-production: only a few moths from each generation survived to adulthood.
Struggle for existence: most moths were eaten by predatory birds.
Survival of the fittest: only the best camouflaged moths survived. As pollution increased, dark moths were better camouflaged against the dark tree bark than pale ones.
Advantageous characteristics passed on to offspring: more dark moths bred than pale moths, so more alleles producing dark colouring

were passed on to the next generation. Gradual change: each generation, the proportion of dark moths increased and the proportion of pale moths decreased.

19.5 The more that populations of bacteria are exposed to an antibiotic, the more likely that bacteria resistant to this antibiotic will gain an advantage over non-resistant bacteria. These will breed and pass on their resistance genes to the next generation.

19.6 This is selection that maintains the same characteristics in a population, if the individuals in that population are already well adapted to the conditions in which they live. There are many examples, e.g. the coelacanth.

19.7

P's phenotypes	normal	normal
P's genotypes	Hb^AHb^S	Hb^AHb^S
Gametes	Hb^A Hb^S	Hb^A Hb^S

Offspring genotypes and phenotypes Hb^A Hb^S

	Hb^A	Hb^S
Hb^A	Hb^AHb^S normal	Hb^AHb^S normal (carrier)
Hb^S	Hb^AHb^S normal (carrier)	Hb^SHb^S sickle cell anaemia

19.8 Choose sperm from a bull whose female offspring and other female relatives have high milk yields. Choose a cow that has a high milk yield, and fertilise her eggs with sperm from the chosen bull. Continue for several generations.

19.9 a Grow wheat in conditions where it gets infected by rust. Collect seed from any plants that are not infected, or that are not harmed. Grow this seed and repeat for several generations, each time picking out seed from plants that are least affected by rust.
b It reduces the need to spray fungicides onto the crops.
c Some of the rust organisms may have a variation that allows them to infect the resistant wheat plants. These will have a selective advantage, and be more likely to survive and reproduce, passing on the genes for this characteristic to the next generation of rust fungi. Over time, most of the rust fungi may have this gene and be able to infect the previously resistant wheat plants.

Chapter 20 Living organisms in their environment

20.1 the study of organisms in their environment

20.2 a group of organisms of the same species, living in the same area at the same time

20.3 There are many possible answers, ranging from a seashore to the surface of an orange.

20.4 Almost all the energy in living organisms on Earth originates from sunlight. (There are deep-sea ecosystems that are based on energy from geothermal vents on the ocean floor, but the vast majority of life on Earth is ultimately driven by solar energy.)

20.5 a One example might be: Sun → maize (grown for fodder) → cattle → human.
b One example might be: Sun → phytoplankton → zooplankton → fish → seal → shark.
c One example might be: Sun → grass → grasshopper → rat → snake → hawk.

20.6 because, in photosynthesis, they use energy from sunlight to produce the food that then powers the rest of the food chain

20.7 The further up the food chain you go, the less energy is available from the original energy provided by the Sun. This is because at each trophic level, the organisms use up a lot of energy as they live and grow, so there is less available to pass on to animals that eat them. Beyond about five links in a chain, the energy has effectively run out.

Chapter 21 Biotechnology

21.1 They reproduce very quickly. They can be kept easily, in controlled conditions, anywhere in the world. There are no ethical issues associated with using them. They share the same genetic material as us (DNA) so can use our genes to make substances.

21.2 ethanol

21.3 carbon dioxide

21.4 Biological powders are able to break down stains made from proteins or fats – such as haemoglobin from blood – which are not removed by ordinary detergents. They can be used at lower temperatures, which saves energy.

21.5 They contain proteases and lipases, which could harm skin if they come into direct contact with it.

21.6 It breaks down pectin, which holds cells together. This makes it easier to extract the juice, and also clarifies the juice.

21.7 Most people in the world do not make the enzyme lactase, so cannot digest lactose in milk.

21.8
a The carbohydrates provide the fungus with an energy source, for respiration. The amino acids provide it with materials for reproduction and growth.
b The metabolic reactions of the fungus produce heat, which would cause the temperature to rise. This might go above the optimum temperature of its enzymes. Cooling helps to keep the temperature at the optimum.
c Oxygen is required for aerobic respiration by the fungus.

Chapter 22 Humans and the environment

22.1 More mechanisation – e.g. using tractors instead of animals to pull machinery; using fertilisers; using herbicides; using pesticides; selective breeding.

22.2 a large area on which a single variety of crop is grown

22.3 They reduce biodiversity. They can lead to increases in sizes of pest populations.

22.4 It requires high inputs (e.g. a lot of money has to be spent on buying food for the animals). It is easy for disease to spread among the animals, so antibiotics may be used, increasing the risk of antibiotic-resistant strains of bacteria developing. The animals may be kept in conditions in which they are not happy (e.g. overcrowding). High volumes of waste produced in a small space can pollute waterways.

22.5 by cutting down forests; by polluting land and water; by mining, especially open-cast mining; by building houses, roads or industries; by taking over land for agriculture; by removing key species such as corals

22.6 Growing trees take carbon dioxide from the air for photosynthesis. If trees are removed, then less carbon dioxide is removed. If the trees are burnt, this produces carbon dioxide that goes into the air.

22.7 Tree roots help to hold soil in place, especially on sloping land. Without trees, rain can easily wash the soil down the slope. Trees intercept raindrops as they fall, reducing the force with which they hit the soil. Without trees, rain hits the ground harder, so that soil is loosened and washed away. Trees absorb water from the soil. Without trees, less water is absorbed and more runs off the surface of the land, increasing soil erosion and flooding.

22.8 The greenhouse effect is an important natural phenomenon in which gases such as carbon dioxide in the atmosphere trap heat, keeping the Earth warmer than it would otherwise be. The enhanced greenhouse effect is an increase in this effect, caused by an increase of carbon dioxide and methane in the atmosphere. Global warming is a consequence of the enhanced greenhouse effect, in which the temperature on Earth increases.

22.9
a This could reduce the amount of carbon dioxide emitted in car exhausts.
b This could reduce the time cars and trucks are on the road, reducing the emissions of carbon dioxide from their exhausts.
c This could reduce the amount of fuel that is burnt, either in the home itself or in power stations generating electricity that is used for heating the home. Burning fuels produces carbon dioxide.
d This could reduce the amount of fossil fuel that is burnt in power stations. Nuclear power stations do not produce carbon dioxide.
e This could reduce the amount of fuel used in factories where the materials in the rubbish are made, or in the generation of electricity to supply these factories.

22.10 sulfur dioxide and nitrogen oxides

22.11 It reduces the pH of soil, which makes it more difficult for trees to absorb the ions they need from the soil.

22.12 It reduces the pH of lakes, and increases the amount of aluminium ions, which adversely affects the function of the gills.

22.13 Governments are trying to reduce the quantity of sulfur-containing fossil fuels that are burnt, especially in power stations. Gases from the burning of coal can be 'scrubbed', removing the sulfur dioxide from them.

22.14 untreated sewage, fertilisers

22.15 oxygen

22.16 It is not broken down in an animal's body. It increases in concentration in animals' bodies as you go up the food chain.

22.17 Plastic bags are not able to be decomposed by organisms. Instead, they remain in the environment, where they can cause problems such as being eaten by animals and staying, undigested, in their alimentary canals. Paper bags are easily broken down by decomposers.

Glossary

absorption the movement of digested food molecules through the wall of the intestine into the blood or lymph

accommodation the change of shape of the lens, in order to focus on objects at different distances

active immunity defence against a pathogen by antibody production in the body

active site the part of an enzyme molecule into which its substrate fits

active transport the movement of molecules and ions in or out of a cell through the cell membrane, from a region of their lower concentration to a region of their higher concentration against a concentration gradient, using energy released during respiration

adaptation (adaptive feature) a feature of an organism that helps it survive in its environment

adaptive features the inherited functional features of an organism that increase its fitness

adipose tissue tissue made up of cells in which fat is stored

adrenaline a hormone secreted by the adrenal glands, which prepares the body for 'flight or fight'

adult stem cell a cell in an adult that can give rise to a limited range of specialised cells

aerobic respiration the release of a relatively large amount of energy in cells by the breakdown of nutrient molecules in the presence of oxygen

allele any of two or more alternative forms of a gene

alimentary canal part of the digestive system; a long tube running from mouth to anus

alveolus (plural: alveoli) an air sac in the lungs, where gas exchange occurs

amino acids molecules that can link together in long chains to form proteins; they contain carbon, hydrogen, oxygen and nitrogen, and sometimes sulfur

amniotic fluid fluid secreted by the amnion, which supports and protects a developing fetus

amylase an enzyme which breaks down starch to maltose

anaerobic respiration the release of a relatively small amount of energy by the breakdown of nutrient molecules in the absence of oxygen

anatomy the detailed body structure of an organism

anther the part of a stamen in which pollen is produced

antibiotic a drug that kills bacteria in the human body, without damaging human cells

antibodies chemicals secreted by lymphocytes, which attach to antigens and help to destroy them

antigens chemicals on the surfaces of pathogens, which are recognised as foreign by the body

artery a blood vessel that carries blood away from the heart

artificial selection the choice by a farmer or grower of only the 'best' parents to breed, generation after generation

asexual reproduction the process resulting in the production of genetically identical offspring from one parent

assimilation the movement of digested food molecules into the cells of the body where they are used, becoming part of the cells

atrioventricular valves valves between the atria and ventricles in the heart that prevent blood flowing from the ventricles into the atria

auto-immune disease a disease caused by a person's own immune system attacking parts of their body

auxin a plant hormone which causes cells to elongate

axon a nerve fibre that conducts impulses away from the cell body

balanced diet a diet containing some of each of the different types of nutrients, in a suitable quantity and proportions

base in DNA, one of four substances (A, C, G and T) that make up the genetic code

bile a liquid made in the liver, stored in the gall bladder and emptied into the small intestine, where it helps to emulsify fats

binomial a two-word Latin name for a species of organism

biuret test a test for protein

breathing muscular movements which cause air to move into and out of the lungs

bronchioles the small tubes into which the bronchi branch

bronchus (plural: bronchi) one of the two tubes into which the trachea branches, carrying air into each lung

capillaries a tiny blood vessel that delivers blood to tissues

carbohydrase an enzyme that catalyses the breakdown of carbohydrates

carbohydrates starches and sugars

carcinogen a substance which increases the risk of a person's body developing cancer

cardiac muscle the muscle of which the heart is made

carnivore an animal that gets its energy by eating other animals

carpel the female part of a flower

catalase an enzyme found in almost all living tissues, which catalyses the breakdown of hydrogen peroxide to water and oxygen

catalyst a substance that speeds up a chemical reaction and is not changed by the reaction

cell membrane a very thin layer of fat and protein that surrounds every living cell

cell sap a solution of sugars and other substances inside the vacuole of a plant cell

cellulose a polysaccharide carbohydrate which forms fibres and is found in the cell walls of plant cells

central nervous system the brain and spinal cord

chemical digestion the breakdown of large molecules of food into smaller ones, done by enzymes

chlorophyll a green, light-absorbing pigment found inside chloroplasts in plant cells

chloroplast an organelle found in some plant cells, which contains chlorophyll and where photosynthesis takes place

chromosome a thread-like structure of DNA, made up of a string of genes

cholera a disease caused by a water-borne bacterium, which causes severe diarrhoea

chyme the partly-digested food, that moves from the stomach into the small intestine

cilia tiny extensions on the surface of a cell, which can wave in unison and cause fluids to move

ciliary muscle a ring of muscle around the lens, which can change its shape

cirrhosis a disease of the liver in which the cells are permanently damaged

clone a group of genetically identical organisms

codominance a situation in which both alleles in a heterozygote have an effect on the phenotype

common ancestor a species that lived long ago that is thought to be a distant ancestor of two or more species living today

community all the organisms, of all the different species, living in an area at the same time

cone cell a light-sensitive cell in the retina, which responds to light of a particular colour

consumer an organism that gets its energy by feeding on other organisms

continuous variation differences in the features of a group of organisms in which there are no definite categories; each individual's features can lie anywhere between two extremes

coronary heart disease a condition in which the coronary arteries become partly blocked

corpus luteum the structure that forms in an ovary after an egg has been released; it secretes progesterone

cortex in a kidney, the outer layer; in a plant stem or root, a tissue made of typical plant cells (usually, however, without chloroplasts)

cotyledons food storage structures in a seed, which sometimes come above ground during germination and begin to photosynthesise

cross-pollination the transfer of pollen from the anther of one plant to the stigma of another plant of the same species

cuticle a layer of wax on a leaf

cytoplasm jelly-like material that is found in cells

deamination a metabolic reaction that takes place in the liver, in which the nitrogen-containing part of amino acids is removed to form urea, followed by the release of energy from the remainder of the amino acid

death phase a stage where the number in a population falls rapidly towards zero

decomposer an organism that gets its energy from dead or waste organic matter

deforestation the destruction of large areas of forest

denatured an enzyme is said to be denatured when its molecule has changed shape so much that the substrate can no longer fit into it

denitrifying bacteria bacteria that obtain their energy by converting nitrate ions into nitrogen gas

deoxygenated blood blood containing only a little oxygen

depressant a drug that inhibits the nervous system and slows it down

dialysis exchange of substances between two solutions through a partially permeable membrane; dialysis machines are used in the treatment of people with kidney failure

diastole the stage of a heart beat in which the muscles in the heart relax

dichotomous branching into two

diffusion the net movement of molecules from a region of their higher concentration to a region of their lower concentration down a concentration gradient, as a result of their random movement

digestion the break-down of large, insoluble food molecules into small molecules using mechanical and chemical processes

diploid having two sets of chromosomes

disaccharide a complex sugar; a carbohydrate whose molecules are made of two sugar units

discontinuous variation differences in the features of a group of organisms where each fits into one of a few clearly defined categories

DNA the chemical from which genes and chromosomes are made

dominant an allele that is expressed if it is present (e.g. T or G)

dormant a condition in which an organism shuts its metabolism down, so that it can survive in adverse conditions

double circulatory system a system in which blood passes twice through the heart on one complete circuit of the body

drug any substance taken into the body that modifies or affects chemical reactions in the body

ecosystem a unit containing all of the organisms and their environment, interacting together, in a given area e.g. decomposing log or a lake

ectothermic unable to regulate body temperature physiologically; the organism's temperature varies with that of its environment

effector a part of the body that responds to a stimulus, e.g. a muscle or a gland

egestion the passing out of food that has not been digested, as faeces, through the anus

egg a female gamete

embryo a young organism before birth, and before all the body organs have formed

embryonic stem cell a cell in an embryo that is capable of giving rise to all types of specialised cell

emphysema a disease in which the walls of the alveoli in the lungs break down, reducing the surface area for gas exchange

emulsification breaking large globules of fat into tiny droplets, so that they mix easily with water

endocrine glands the ductless glands that secrete hormones into the blood and together make up the endocrine system

endothermic able to internally regulate body temperature; the body temperature is independent of the temperature of the environment

enhanced greenhouse effect the increase in the greenhouse effect casused by the addition of more greenhouse gases to the atmosphere

enzymes proteins that function as biological catalysts

epidermis (mammal) the outer layer of the skin

epidermis (plant) a tissue made up of a single layer of cells which covers the top and bottom of a leaf, and the outside of the stem and root

excretion removal from organisms of the waste products of metabolism (chemical reactions in cells including respiration) toxic materials and substances in excess of requirements

exponential phase (log phase) the stage in population growth when numbers increase exponentially

evolution the change in adaptive features of a population over time, as a result of natural selection

F1 generation the offspring from a parent homozygous for a dominant allele and a parent homozygous for the recessive allele

fermentation the breakdown of glucose by yeast, using anaerobic respiration; it produces carbon dioxide and alcohol

fertilisation the fusion of the nuclei of two gametes

fetus a young organism before birth, once all the body organs have formed

fibrin an insoluble protein that forms fibres that help in blood clotting

fibrinogen a soluble protein that is converted to insoluble fibrin when blood clots

filament the stalk of a stamen

fitness the probability of an organism surviving and reproducing in the environment in which it is found

flaccid a term used to describe a cell that has lost a lot of water, becoming soft

follicle a space inside an ovary in which an egg develops

food chain a chart showing the flow of energy (food) from one organism to the next beginning with a producer (e.g. mahogany tree → caterpillar → song bird → hawk)

food web a network of interconnected food chains showing the energy flow through part of an ecosystem

fovea the part of the retina where cones are most tightly packed

fruit an ovary of a plant after fertilisation; it contains seeds

FSH follicle stimulating hormone; a hormone secreted by the pituitary gland which causes the development of eggs in the ovaries

fully permeable able to let most substances pass through

gametes sex cells, e.g. eggs and sperm

gas exchange the entry of oxygen into an organism's body, and the loss of carbon dioxide

gene a length of DNA that is the unit of heredity and codes for a specific protein.

gene mutation a change in the base sequence of DNA

genetic diagram the conventional way to set out a genetic cross

genetic engineering taking a gene from one species and putting it into another species

genotype the genetic makeup of an organism in terms of the alleles present (e.g. Tt or GG)

genus (plural: **genera**) a group of similar and related species

glomerulus a tangle of blood capillaries in a Bowman's capsule in the kidney

glucagon a hormone secreted by the pancreas, which increases blood glucose level

glycogen the polysaccharide that is used as an energy store in animal cells and fungi

goblet cells cells which secrete mucus

gravitropism a response in which a plant grows towards or away from gravity

greenhouse effect the warming effect of carbon dioxide, methane and other greenhouse gases, on the Earth

growth a permanent increase in size and dry mass by an increase in cell number or cell size or both

guard cell one of two sausage-shaped cells in the epidermis in plants, between which there is a hole called a stoma; the guard cells can change shape to open and close the stoma

habitat the place where an organism lives

haploid having one set of chromosomes

hepatic portal vein a blood vessel that transports blood from the digestive system to the liver

herbivore an animal that gets its energy by eating plants

heterozygous having two different alleles of a gene (e.g. Tt or Gg), not pure-breeding

hilum the scar where a seed was attached to a fruit

homeostasis the maintenance of a constant internal environment

homologous chromosomes the two chromosomes of a pair in a diploid cell; they have genes for the same features at the same positions

homozygous having two identical alleles of a particular gene (e.g. TT or gg). Two identical homozygous individuals that breed together will be pure-breeding

hormone a chemical substance produced by a gland, carried by the blood, which alters the activity of one or more specific target organs and is then destroyed by the liver

hydrophyte a plant adapted to live in wet conditions

hyperglycaemia having too much glucose in the blood

hypertension high blood pressure

hypoglycaemia having too little glucose in the blood

hypothalamus a part of the brain that helps to regulate body temperature

immune able to fight off a particular type of pathogen before it causes any symptoms in the body

implantation the movement of a young embryo into the lining of the uterus, and its attachment there

ingestion taking substances (e.g. food, drink) into the body through the mouth

inheritance the transmission of genetic information from generation to generation

inorganic substances that are not made by living organisms

insulin a hormone secreted by the pancreas, which reduces blood glucose level

intercostal muscles muscles between the ribs, which help to produce breathing movements

involuntary action an action taken automatically, without conscious thought

iris the coloured part of the eye, which controls the amount of light allowed through to the lens and retina

islets of Langerhans groups of cells in the pancreas which secrete insulin and glucagon

key a series of questions whose answers lead you to the identification of an organism

kingdom one of the five large groups into which all living organsisms are classified

kwashiorkor a deficiency disease caused by lack of protein in the diet

lactation production of milk by mammary glands

lag phase the early stage of population growth, when numbers scarcely change

lamina the main part of a leaf

LH luteinising hormone; a hormone secreted by the pituitary gland which causes an egg to be released from an ovary

light microscope a microscope that uses light to produce images

lignin a tough, waterproof material that makes up the walls of xylem vessels; wood is mostly lignin

limiting factor something present in the environment in such short supply that it restricts life processes

lipase an enzyme that digests fats (lipids) to fatty acids and glycerol

lipids fats, oils and waxes

log phase (exponential phase) the stage in population growth when numbers increase exponentially

lymph the fluid found inside lymph vessels, formed from tissue fluid

lymph nodes organs in which large numbers of white blood cells (which can destroy bacteria or toxins) collect

maltase an enzyme that breaks down maltose to glucose

marasmus a disease resulting from a severe lack of energy in the diet

maltose a disaccharide produced by the digestion of starch

mechanical digestion the breakdown of large pieces of food to smaller ones, increasing their surface area; it is done by teeth in the mouth and by the contraction of muscles in the stomach wall

medulla (in kidney) the central area in a kidney

meiosis reduction division in which the chromosome number is halved from diploid to haploid

memory cells cells produced by activated lymphocytes, that remain in the body and are able to respond quickly to a pathogen

menstruation the loss of the uterus lining through the vagina

mesophyll the tissues in the centre of a leaf, where photosynthesis takes place

metabolic reactions the chemical reactions that take place inside a living organism

micrometre 1×10^{-6} metres

micropyle a tiny hole in the testa of a seed

mineral an inorganic ion required in small quantities by living organisms

mitochondria organelles in which aerobic respiration takes place, releasing energy for use by the cell

mitosis nuclear division giving rise to genetically identical cells in which the chromosome number is maintained by the exact duplication of chromosomes

monoculture a large area of the same crop plant

monosaccharide a simple sugar; a carbohydrate whose molecules are made of one sugar unit

morphology the overall shape and form of an organism's body

movement an action by an organism or part of an organism causing a change of position or place

mutagen a substance that causes mutations

mutation a change in a gene or a chromosome

myelin a fatty substance surrounding the axons of many neurones, enabling the nerve impulse to travel faster

natural selection the greater chance of passing on of genes by the best-adapted organisms

nectary a gland producing a sugary fluid, found in many insect- or bird-pollinated flowers

negative feedback a mechanism used in homeostasis, in which a change in a parameter brings about actions that push it back towards normal

nephron one of the thousands of tiny tubules in a kidney, in which urine is produced

nerve a bundle of axons or dendrons belonging to many different neurones

nerve impulse an electrical signal that sweeps along a neurone

neurone a nerve cell; a cell specialised for the rapid transfer of electrical impulses

nicotine an addictive drug found in tobacco smoke

nitrifying bacteria bacteria that obtain their energy by converting ammonia or nitrite ions to nitrate ions

nitrogen fixation changing unreactive nitrogen gas into a more reactive nitrogen compound such as nitrate or ammonia

nitrogenous waste excretory products containing nitrogen – for example, ammonia, urea, uric acid

non-biodegradable not able to be broken down by microorganisms

normal distribution a curve in which the largest number occurs near the midpoint, with approximately equal quantities on either side of this point and a gradual decrease towards the extremes

nucleus a large organelle in which chromosomes are found

nutrition taking in materials that are required for energy, growth and development

oesophagus the part of the alimentary canal along which food travels from the mouth to the stomach

oestrogen a hormone secreted by the ovaries that helps to control the menstrual cycle

optimum temperature the temperature at which something happens most rapidly

organ a structure made up of a group of tissues, working together to perform specific functions

organ system a group of organs with related functions, working together to perform body functions

organelle a structure within a cell

organic a term used to describe substances that have been made by living organisms, or whose molecules contain carbon, hydrogen and oxygen

organism a living thing

osmosis the diffusion of water molecules from a region of high water potential to a region of lower water potential, through a partially permeable membrane

ovary an organ in which female gametes are made

oviduct the tube leading from an ovary to the uterus

ovulation the release of an egg from an ovary

ovule a structure in the ovary of a flower which contains a female gamete

oxygen debt the extra oxygen that must be taken in by the body following strenuous exercise, when anaerobic respiration took place; the oxygen is needed to break down the lactic acid that accumulated as a result of anaerobic respiration

oxygenated blood blood containing a lot of oxygen; in humans, blood becomes oxygenated in the lungs

palisade layer the upper mesophyll layer in a leaf, made up of rectangular cells containing many chloroplasts

pancreas an organ lying close to the stomach, which is both an endocrine gland (producing insulin and glucagon) and an exocrine gland (producing pancreatic juice)

pancreatic juice the liquid secreted into the pancreatic duct by the pancreas; it flows into the duodenum where its enzymes help with digestion of fats, proteins and carbohydrates

partially permeable allowing some molecules to pass through, but not others

passive immunity having antibodies provided from another organism, that temporarily protect against a pathogen

pathogen a disease-causing organism

pelvis (in kidney) the part from which the ureter emerges

penicillin an antibiotic which destroys bacteria by damaging their cell walls

pepsin a protease enzyme found in the stomach

peripheral nervous system all the nerves and receptors in the body, not including the brain or spinal cord

peristalsis rhythmic contractions of muscles that ripple along a tube – for example, peristalsis pushes food through the alimentary canal

petiole a leaf stalk

phagocytes white blood cells that surround, engulf and digest pathogens

phenotype the physical or other features of an organism due to both its genotype and its environment (e.g. tall plant or green seed)

phloem tubes long tubes made up of living cells with perforated end walls, which transport sucrose and other substances in plants

photosynthesis the process by which plants manufacture carbohydrates from raw materials using energy from light

phototropism a response in which a plant grows towards or away from the direction from which light is coming

placenta in mammals, an organ made up of tissues of both the mother and embryo, through which the mother's and embryo's bodies exchange nutrients and waste materials

plaque a sticky film, containing bacteria, that builds up on teeth

plasma the liquid part of blood, in which the cells float

plasmolysed the condition of a plant cell that has lost so much water that its cytoplasm shrinks and pulls the cell membrane away from the cell wall

platelets tiny fragments of cells found in blood, which help with clotting

plumule the young shoot in an embryo plant

pollen grains tough, resistant structures containing the male gametes of a flower

pollination the transfer of pollen from the male part of the flower (anther of stamen) to the female part of the plant (stigma)

polysaccharide a carbohydrate whose molecules are made of hundreds of sugar units linked in long chains – for example, starch, glycogen and cellulose

population a group of organisms of one species, living in the same area at the same time

predator an animal that kills and eats other animals

primary consumers herbivores

process of adaptation the process resulting from natural selection, by which populations become more suited to their environment over many generations

producer an organism that makes its own organic nutrients, usually using energy from sunlight, through photosynthesis

product the substance formed in an enzyme-controlled reaction

progesterone the pregnancy hormone; a hormone secreted by the ovaries and placenta which maintains the lining of the uterus

prostate gland a gland close to a male's bladder, that secretes fluid in which sperm can swim

protease an enzyme that catalyses the breakdown of proteins

puberty the stage of development during which sexual maturity is reached

pulmonary relating to the lungs

pure-breeding homozygous

pyramid of biomass a sideways-on graph, in which the size of the boxes represents the dry mass of organisms in each trophic level of a food chain

pyramid of numbers a sideways-on graph, in which the size of the boxes represents the number of organisms in each trophic level of a food chain

radicle the young root in an embryo plant

receptor a cell that is able to detect changes in the environment; often part of a sense organ

recessive an allele that is only expressed when there is no dominant allele of the gene present (e.g. t or g)

reducing sugar a sugar that turns Benedict's solution brick red when heated

reflex action a fast, automatic response to a stimulus

reflex arc the arrangement of neurones along which an impulse passes during a reflex action

renal relating to the kidneys

respiration the chemical reactions in cells that break down nutrient molecules and release energy for metabolism

retina the part of the eye that contains receptor cells

ribosome tiny organelles where protein synthesis takes place

rod cell a light-sensitive cell in the retina, that responds to dim light

root cap a tough, protective covering over the tip of a root

rough endoplasmic reticulum a network of membranes inside a cell, on which ribosomes are present

secondary consumers carnivores that eat herbivores

seed an ovule after fertilisation; it contains an embryo plant

selection pressure an environmental factor that causes organisms with certain characteristics to have a better chance of survival than others

self-pollination the transfer of pollen from the anther to the stigma on the same plant (but not necessarily the same flower)

semen a mixture of sperm and fluids from the prostate gland and seminal vesicles

seminal vesicles glands that secrete fluid in which sperm can swim

sense organs groups of receptor cells responding to specific stimuli: light, sound, touch, temperature and chemicals

sensitivity the ability to detect or sense changes in the environment (stimuli) and to make appropriate responses

sex-linked characteristic characteristic in which the gene responsible is located on a sex chromosome, which makes it more common in one sex than in the other

sex-linked gene a gene found on the X chromosome but not on the Y chromosome

sexually-transmitted infection an infection that is transmitted via bodily fluids through sexual contact

sexual reproduction the process involving the fusion of haploid nuclei to form a diploid zygote and the production of genetically dissimilar offspring

sickle cell anaemia a condition caused by a codominant allele of the gene that codes for haemoglobin, in which a person has two copies of the gene and suffers serious health problems

simple sugar a monosaccharide; a carbohydrate whose molecules are made of one sugar unit

sink a place to which substrates are transported in phloem

solvent a liquid in which another substance is dissolved

source a place from which substances are transported in phloem

species a group of organisms with similar characteristics, which can interbreed with each other to produce fertile offspring

species diversity the number of different species living in a habitat

sperm a male gamete

sphincter muscle a muscle surrounding a tube, which can contract to close the tube

spongy layer the tissue beneath the palisade layer in a leaf; it is made up of cells that contain chloroplasts and can photosynthesise, with many air spaces between them

stamen the male parts of a flower

starch the polysaccharide that is used as an energy store in plant cells

stationary phase a stage when the numbers in a population remain approximately constant

stem tuber a swollen part of a stem, which stores food

stigma the part of a flower that receives pollen

stimulant a drug that makes the nervous system work faster

stimulus a change in an organism's surroundings that can be detected by its sense organs

stoma (plural: **stomata**) a gap between two guard cells, usually in the epidermis on the lower surface of a leaf

style the connection between the stigma and ovary of a flower

substrate the substance on which an enzyme acts

sucrase a carbohydrase found in the small intestine, which breaks down sucrose to glucose and fructose

sucrose a disaccharide, non-reducing sugar, made of a glucose molecule and a fructose molecule linked together; the form in which carbohydrates are transported in the phloem of plants

suspensory ligaments a ring of ligaments linking the ciliary muscles to the lens

sustainable resource one which can be removed from the environment without it running out

sustainable development providing for the needs of an increasing human population without harming the environment

synapse a point at which an impulse can be passed from one neurone to another

synaptic cleft a tiny gap between two neurones

systole the stage of a heart beat in which the muscles in the walls of the heart chambers contract

target organ an organ that is affected by a hormone

tendons strong, inelastic cords of tissue, which attach muscles to bones; they are also found in the heart, where they attach the atrioventricular valves to the wall of the ventricle

test cross breeding an offspring with the dominant phenotype with an organism with the recessive phenotype; the offspring of the cross can help to determine the genotype of the parent with the dominant phenotype

testis (plural: testes) an organ in which sperm are made

testosterone a hormone secreted by the testes, which causes male characteristics

tissue a group of cells with similar structures, working together to perform a shared function

tissue fluid the fluid that surrounds all the cells in the body, formed from blood plasma that leaks out of capillaries

toxin a poisonous substance

trachea the tube that carries air from the nose and mouth down to the lungs

translocation the movement of sucrose and amino acids in phloem, from regions of production to regions of storage, or to regions of utilisation in respiration or growth

transmissible disease a disease caused by a pathogen that can be passed from one person to another

transmitter substance a chemical that carries a nerve impulse across a synapse

transpiration evaporation of water at the surfaces of the mesophyll cells followed by loss of water vapour from plant leaves, through the stomata

transpiration stream the pathway of water from the root hairs of a plant, up the root and stem and out of the leaves into the atmosphere

trophic level the position of an organism in a food chain, food web or pyramid of biomass, numbers or energy

tropism a plant growth response to a stimulus, in which the direction of growth is related to the direction of the stimulus

trypsin a protease enzyme found in pancreatic juice

turgid a term used to decribe a plant cell that has absorbed water and has cytoplasm that is pressing outwards on the cell wall

type 1 diabetes a condition in which the pancreas is unable to make insulin

umbilical cord an organ linking an embryo to the placenta, containing blood vessels

unicellular made of one cell

urea the main nitrogenous excretory product of mammals, produced in the liver from excess amino acids

ureter a tube that leads from a kidney to the bladder

urethra a tube that leads from the bladder to the outside

urine a solution of urea and other excretory products in water, produced by the kidneys

uterus the organ in a mammal in which the embryo develops

vaccination the introduction to the body of dead or weakened pathogens, to make a person immune to an infectious disease

variation differences between individuals of the same species

vascular bundle a vein in a plant, containing xylem vessels and phloem tubes

vasoconstriction narrowing of blood vessels

vasodilation widening of blood vessels

vein a blood vessel that carries blood towards the heart

vesicle a very small vacuole (space inside a cell)

villus (plural: **villi**) a tiny, finger-like process on the inner wall of the small intestine; villi increase the surface area for digestion and absorption

vitamins organic substances required in small quantities in the diet

voluntary action an action taken as the result of a conscious decision

water potential a measure of the tendency for water to move out of a solution; the more water in the solution, the greater its water potential

xerophyte a plant adapted to live in dry conditions

xylem vessels long hollow tubes made up of dead, empty cells with lignified walls, which transport water in plants and help to support them

zygote the diploid cell produced when two gametes fuse

Index

absorption 78, 85–6
accommodation 169
acid rain 302–3
activated sludge 310–11
active immunity 135
active site 50–1
active transport 35–6, 100
adaptation 13, 61–3, 250–3
adaptive features 250–3
addictive drugs 190–5
adipose tissue 44, 181
adrenaline 171
adult stem cell 234
aeration tank 310
aerobic respiration 141
age pyramid 274–5
AIDS and HIV 224, 225–6
alcohol, effects of 190–1
alcoholism 191–2
alimentary canal 82–8
alleles 235
alveoli 145
amino acids 23, 40, 45–6, 50, 64, 78, 85, 154–5
amniotic fluid 217
amphibians 10
amylase 49, 50, 51, 84, 206, 282
anabolic steroids 192
anaerobic respiration 141, 143, 149, 282
anatomy 3
animal cells 20, 21, 33
animal hormones 170–1
animal kingdom 6, 9–12
animal nutrition 73–90
ante-natal care 218–19
anther 199, 201, 202, 204
antibiotics 7, 188, 189, 257, 276, 284–6, 295
antibodies 45–6, 118, 127, 130, 133–4, 135
antigens 133
arachnids 11
arteries 109–12, 113, 116, 121
arthropods 11–12
artificial fertilisers 259, 271, 293, 303–4
artificial insemination 223

artificial photosynthesis 58
artificial selection 259
asexual reproduction 198, 208–9
assimilation 89
atrioventricular valves 113
atrium (atria) 108–9
auto-immune diseases 137
auxin 172–4
axon 162

bacteria 8, 18, 281
    antibiotics destroying 188
    human insulin production 286, 288–9
    nitrifying 272
    in the nitrogen cycle 271–2
    sewage and 310–11
balanced diet 74–7
bases 3–4, 47, 243
Benedict's test for sugars 42
beta cells 137
bile/bile salts 85
binomial naming system 4, 5
biodiversity 293
bioethanol 281–2
biofuels 281–2
biological drawings, making 13
biological washing powders 283
biotechnology 280–9
birds 10, 153, 179
birth control methods 222–5
birth process 218
birth rates 273, 276
biuret test for proteins 46
black-footed ferret 292
bladder 156, 157
blind spot 167
blood 120
    filtration by kidneys 157
    how the heart pumps 113
    oxygenated and deoxygenated 107
    substances transported by 121
    sugar levels, regulation of 184
blood clotting 119–20
blood groups 236, 237
blood pressure 113, 114
blood vessels 113–17

body defences 129–33
    chemical barriers 130
    mechanical barriers 129–30
body temperature, control of 179–83
brain, damage caused by alcohol 191
bread-making 282
breast milk, advantages of 219
breathing 146–50
bronchi and bronchioles 145
butterflies 247

cacti 251–2, 254
cancer 192–5, 303
capillaries 113, 114, 116, 122
carbapenem 188
carbohydrases 50, 85
carbohydrates 41–3, 47
    digestion of 79
    photosynthesis 59, 64–5, 102
    tests for starch and sugar 42–3
carbon credits 298
carbon cycle 271
carbon dioxide
    blood transporting 121
    diffusion of 29
    in expired and inspired air 148, 149
    and global warming 299–301
    limiting factor for photosynthesis 69, 70
    in photosynthesis 59, 62
    product of respiration 141, 143, 148
    waste product of metabolism 154
carbon monoxide 193
carcinogens 192
cardiac muscle 108
carnivores 267
carpel 201
catalase 50, 52
    effect of pH on activity of 53–4
catalysts, enzymes as 50–1, 52
cell division 231–4
cell membrane 20
cell sap 21
cell wall 20–1
cells 18–26
cellulose 20–1, 42, 154

central nervous system 163
chemical digestion 79
chemical methods, birth control 222
chemical waste, toxins in 306
chinchillas 230
chlorophyll 21, 58, 67
    absorption of sunlight 59, 63
chloroplasts 20, 21, 60, 62–3
cholera 88
cholesterol 76
choroid 167
chromosomes 3, 21, 47, 198, 199,
    208, 231
chronic obstructive pulmonary disease
(COPD) 193
chyme 84
cilia 26, 130, 145, 215
ciliary muscle 169–70
circulatory system 107–8
cirrhosis of the liver 191
classification of living organisms
    3–14
clear-felling 311
climate change 314
clones 133, 208
codominance, alleles 236, 237
coelacanths 257
cohesion 98
colon 86
colour blindness 241–2
common ancestor 3, 4
community 265
concentration gradients 28, 29, 30–1
cone cells, retina 167–8
conjunctiva 166
conservation 307–16
    of rainforests 307
conservation programmes, reasons
    for 315
constipation, preventing 76
consumers 267
continuous variation 248, 249
contraception 222–5, 276
contraceptive hormones as pollutant
    306
contraction of muscles 147, 149–50,
    162–4, 168–70
controls for investigations 66
cooling experiments 183
coordination and response
    in animals 162–71
    in plants 172–5
coppicing 312

cornea 169
coronary arteries 109
coronary heart disease 76, 109–12
corpus luteum 221
cortex 156
cotyledons 205, 206
cross-pollination 204
crustaceans 11
cuticle, leaves 60, 252, 253
cystic fibrosis 231
cytoplasm 20, 21, 33, 34

Darwin, Charles 253–5
deamination 155
death phase 273
death rates 273, 276
decomposers 270
deforestation 297–8, 301
denatured enzymes 53
denitrifying bacteria 272
dentine 80, 82
deoxygenated blood 107
depressant drugs 190–1
dermis, human skin 181
desert plants 251–2
development 233
diabetes, type I 137, 185, 234, 286,
    288
dialysis, kidneys 158–9
diarrhoea 88
diastole 113
dichotomous key 15
diet 74–7, 110, 218
diffusion 28, 29–30, 32, 62, 64, 97,
    107, 117, 121, 122, 144, 146
digestion 78–9
diploid cells/nuclei 199, 231, 232
disaccharides 41
discontinuous variation 248
DNA 3–4, 21, 47, 231, 243, 281,
    288–9
    bases 3–4, 47, 243
dodo 314
dominant alleles 236
dormant, plants/seeds 102, 206
double circulatory system 107–8
Down's syndrome 249–50
drugs 188–95
    misuse of 190–2
    see also antibiotics
duodenum 84, 85, 86

ecology 265
ecosystem 265–8
ectothermic animals 179
effectors 163–4
egestion 86, 154
egg 200
electron microscope 19
embryo
    human 216, 217, 220
    plant 50, 205
embryonic stem cells 234
emphysema 193
emulsification 85
endangered species 313
endocrine glands/system 162, 170–1
endoscope 73
endothermic animals 179
energy
    from a balanced diet 74
    in an ecosystem 266–9
    efficiency 269
    flow 266–9
    from foods 42, 44, 141
    released by respiration 141
enhanced greenhouse effect 300
enterobacteria 188
environment
    adaptation to 250–3
    organisms and 264–76
environmental variation 249
enzymes 49–55
    in biotechnology 280, 282–4
    lock and key mechanism 50–1
    effects of pH on 52, 53–4
    properties 52–4
    and temperature 52, 53
    uses of 282–4
epidermis
    flowering plants 96
    human skin 180
    of a leaf 60, 61
epiglottis 84, 145
ethanol emulsion test for fats 44
etiolated plants 175
eutrophication 303–4
evolution, Darwin's theory 253–5
excretion 2, 153–9
exercise
    and breathing rate 149–50
    effect on heart rate 112
    and oxygen debt 150
expiration 147–8, 149
exponential phase 273

extinction 292, 313, 314
extremophiles 18
eyes
    focusing by 169–70
    iris 168
    protection of 166
    retina 166–8
    structure of 166

F1 generation 239
famine 295
fats 44, 47
    danger of saturated 76, 110
    digestion and absorption 79, 85
    testing foods for 44–5
fatty acids 44
fermentation 281
fermenters producing penicillin 282, 284, 286
ferns 12
fertilisation 198
    in flowering plants 28, 200–2, 205, 208
    and genetic variation 249, 250
    in humans 215–16
    and inheritance 237
fertilisers, artificial 259, 271, 293, 303–4
fertility drugs 224
fetus, placenta supplying 216–17
fibre, dietary 74–6
fibrin 120
fibrinogen 120
filtration in kidneys 157
fish 9, 76
    respiration in 140
    stocks, conservation of 312–13
fitness 251
flaccidity of plant cells 34, 99
flowering plants 12
    attracting pollinators 28
    fertilisation in 205
    pollination 202–4
    sexual reproduction in 200–8
    transport systems in 93–103
fluoride 82
focusing by the eye 169–70
follicle
    hair 180, 233
    ovarian 216, 220, 221

food
    digestion by enzymes 50
    energy content of 74
    transport by the blood 121
food chains 264, 266, 269
    harm caused by DDT 305
food hygiene 128, 130–1
food poisoning 130–1
food production 293–6
    use of enzymes 283–4
    use of hormones 175
    intensive 295
food supplies, global 295–6
food webs 266
forests
    conservation 311–12
    deforestation 297–8, 301
fossil fuels 58, 300–3, 308
fossils 313
fovea 166
fruit 205
FSH 221, 224
fungi 7, 189

gametes 199–200, 200–2, 237
    produced by meiosis 233, 249
gas exchange in humans 143–6, 148
Gaucher disease 280
genes 110, 198, 231
genetic code 243
genetic diagrams 238
genetic diversity 315
genetic engineering 280, 281, 286–9
genetic variation 248, 249
genetically modified (GM) crops 287
genotypes 235–40
genus (genera) 4
geotropism 172
germination of seeds 206–7
gills 140
glass recycling 308
glasshouses, crop growing 69–70
global warming 58, 299–303
glomerulus 157
glucagon 184
glucocerebroside 280
glucose 29, 32, 33
    liver controlling level of 184
    and photosynthesis 12, 50, 123–4
    uses of, by plants 55–6
    in respiration 141, 149
    test sticks 185
glycerol 34, 72

glycogen 21, 22, 33, 81, 89, 184
glyphosphate 286
goblet cells 82, 84, 145
gonorrhoea 223
gravitropism 172
gravity 172, 173, 174
greenhouse effect 299–303
greenhouse gases 299–301
growth 2
    cell 233
    responses by plants 172–5
guard cells, leaves 60, 61
gum disease 81

habitats 265, 272, 292, 293, 303
    destruction 296–9, 307–8, 313
haemoglobin 117, 258, 283
haploid cells/nuclei 199, 231
heart 108–13
heart beat 112
heart disease 76, 109–12
heart valves 113
heat, blood transporting 121
    see also energy; temperature
hepatic portal vein 89, 115, 116, 117
herbicides 285–6, 293
herbivores 264, 267
hermaphrodite 200–1
heroin 190
heterozygous 235, 236, 237–9
hilum 205
HIV 224, 225–6
homeostasis 178–85
homologous chromosomes 231, 233, 234
homozygous 235, 236, 238, 239
homunculus theory 212
hormones 162, 170, 221
    female contraceptive, as pollutant 306
    for increasing fertility 224
    and the menstrual cycle 221–2
    transport of 121
human population 275–6
humidity, and transpiration rate 99
hunting 314
hydrochloric acid 73
hydrogen peroxide 50, 53–4
hydrophytes 252–3
hygiene
    food 130–1
    personal 131
hyperglycaemia 185

hypoglycaemia 185
hypothalamus 181, 182–3

iguanas, marine 178
ileum 29, 84, 85, 86
immune response 134
immune system 112, 133–7, 158, 159, 225
immunity 134
    active 135
    passive 135
implantation 216, 217
in vitro fertilisation (IVF) 224–5
infections 82, 88
    and antibiotics 188, 189
    sexually transmitted 225–6
ingestion 80
inheritance 231, 235–43
inorganic substances 59
insecticides 293, 294
insects 11, 200, 273
    pollination by 202–4
inspiration 147, 148, 149
insulin 137
    controlling blood sugar levels 184, 185
    genetically engineered 286, 288–9
intensive farming 295
intercostal muscles 146, 147
involuntary action 164
iodine test for starch 43, 65–6
ionising radiation 250, 303
ions, uptake by plants 100
iris of the eye 168
islets of Langerhans 184

keratin 129
keys 15–16
kidneys 156–9
kingdoms of living organisms 4
knee jerk reflex 164
kwashiorkor 77

lactase 284, 285
lactation 219
lactic acid 141, 150
lactose 284
lactose-reduced milk 284, 285
lag phase 273
lamina 60
landfill 132–3
large intestine 86
larynx 145

leaves
    adaptation for photosynthesis 62–3
    structure of 59–63
    surface loss of water 99
lens of the eye 169–70
LH 221
light
    cells in retina receptive to 166–7
    controlling in glasshouses 69–70
    cornea and lens focusing 169
    effect of darkness on plants 175
    intensity and transpiration rate 99
    part of shoot sensitive to 173
    photosynthesis investigations 66, 68
    response of iris to 168
    shoot response to 172, 174
    sunlight for photosynthesis 59, 62–3
light microscope 19–22, 231
lightning 271
lignin in xylem vessels 93, 94
limiting factors
    photosynthesis 69–70
    population size 274
lipase 50, 84, 85, 283
lipids (fats) 44, 47
liver 82, 85, 89, 117, 121, 155
    control of blood sugar level 184
    damage by alcohol 191
log phase 273
lumen 111, 114, 115, 116
lungs 107–8, 121, 140
    and breathing 146–8
    damage from smoking 192, 193, 194–5
    and gas exchange 143–6
lymph 123
lymph nodes 123
lymphocytes 133–4, 137

magnesium, plant nutrition 64
magnification 14
malaria 129, 258
malnutrition 77
maltase 50, 85
maltose 41, 50, 84, 282
mammals, classifying 1, 3, 4, 10
marasmus 77
measles 136–7
mechanical birth control methods 223

mechanical digestion 78
medicinal drugs 189
medulla 156
meiosis 199, 233, 249, 250
membrane of cells 20
    partially permeable 20, 30, 32, 33–4
memory cells 134
menstrual cycle/menstruation 220–2
mesophyll cells/layer 60, 62
messenger RNA 243–4
metabolic reactions/metabolism 21, 41
    enzymes 50
    and excretion 154
    and temperature 180, 182
metals, recycling of 309
meteorite 40
methane 133, 299, 300, 301
micrometres 23
microorganisms
    enzymes obtained from 282–4
    methane produced from 301
    and sewage treatment 310–11
micropyle 205, 206
microscopes 19
milk, breast versus formula 219
milk teeth 81
mimicry 247
minerals 64, 74, 76, 102
    uptake by plants 100
mitochondria 22
mitosis 232, 233
monocultures 293–4
monosaccharides 41, 78
morphology 3
motor neurones 162–4, 164
mouth 83–4
    breathing through 145
movement 2
    growth in plants 172–5
    in and out of cells 28–36
    see also muscles
mucus 82, 84, 130, 145, 222
muscles
    and breathing 146–7
    respiring anaerobically 141, 149
mutagen 250
mutation 249–50
myelin 162
myriapods 12
myxomatosis 274, 296

natural methods of birth control 222
natural selection 253–9
nectar/nectaries 201, 202
negative feedback, temperature control 182–3
nephrons 156
nerve impulses 162
nerves 162
nervous system 171
   human 162–5
neurones 162
niche 265
nicotine 192
nitrates in fertilisers 271, 293, 303–4
nitrifying bacteria 272
nitrogen, plant nutrition 64, 65
nitrogen cycle 271–2
nitrogen fixation 271–2
nitrogen oxides, acid rain 302–3
nitrogenous waste 154–5, 272
non-biodegradable plastics 306
normal distribution 248
nose, breathing through 145
nuclear fall-out 303
nucleus 20, 21
nutrient cycles 270–2
nutrients needed in diet 74
nutrition 2
   animal 73–90
   plant 58–70

obesity 76–7, 110
oesophagus 84
oestrogen 221
orbit 166
optimum temperature 53, 283
organ 25
organ systems 25
organ transplants 112, 158–9
organelles 20
organic fertilisers 304
organic substances 59, 64
organisms
   characteristics of 2
   classification of 1, 3–14
osmosis 30–1, 33–4, 97
ovaries 201, 202, 205
oviducts 213, 214, 215, 216, 220, 222, 224, 237
ovulation 214, 215, 220, 221, 222
ovules in flowers 200, 201–2, 205, 287

oxygen 41, 45
   depletion in water 303–4
   diffusion of 29
   in inspired and expired air 148
   photosynthesis 59, 67
   transport by blood 107–8, 117, 121
oxygen debt 150
oxygenated blood 107
oxyhaemoglobin (oxyHb) 121

pacemaker, heart rate 112
palisade cells/layer 60
pancreas 84, 137, 184
pancreatic juice 84
paper recycling 309
passive immunity 135
pathogens 118–19, 127–37, 309–11, 313
   direct transmission 128
   indirect transmission 128–9
pectin 283–4
pectinase 283–4
pelvis, of kidney 56
penicillin 7, 189, 257
peppered moths 255–8
pepsin 84
peripheral nervous system 163
peristalsis 76, 82, 83, 215
permeability of cells 20, 30, 32, 33
personal hygeine 131
petiole 60
pH
   of acid rain 302
   changes in blood 150
   effect on enzyme activity 52, 53–4
phagocytes 118–19
phagocytosis 119, 130
phenotypes 235–6, 237–40
phloem tubes 61, 94, 95, 102
photosynthesis 21, 59
   adaptation of leaves for 63
   importance of 70
   investigations 65–8
   limiting factors 69–70
   uses of glucose 64–5
phototropism 172, 173
placenta 216–17, 218
plant cells 20, 20–1, 33–4
plant hormones 172–4
plant kingdom 6–7
   classification 12
plaque and tooth decay 81, 82

plasma, blood 30, 41, 89, 117, 118, 120–1
plasmolysis, plant cells 34
plastic
   non-biodegradable 306
   recycling 308–9
platelets and blood clotting 117, 119–20
platypus 1
plumule 205
polio vaccine 136
pollen 201–2
pollen grain 200
pollination 202–4
pollution 299–307, 314
polysaccharides 42, 45
population 58, 131, 134, 188, 239, 253, 257, 265
   factors affecting 273
   human 275–6
population size 222, 272–6
potometers 98, 99
predator 274
primary consumers 267
process of adaptation 253
producers 267
product 50
progesterone 221–2
prokaryotes 8
prostate gland 214
proteases 50, 85, 206, 283
proteins 45–6
   digestion of 79
   excretion of excess 155
   made by plants 64
   synthesis 243–4
   testing food for 46
   see also amino acids; enzymes
Protoctista 8
puberty 221
pulmonary artery and vein 108
pulmonary embolism 115
pulse rate 112
pure-breeding 239
pyramid of biomass 268
pyramid of numbers 267, 268

rabies 127, 129
radiation, ionising 250, 303
radicle 205
rainforests 294, 297–8, 301, 307
Ramsar Convention 311
raw sewage 133, 309

reabsorption by kidneys 157
reaction time 161, 166
receptors 162, 165–70
recessive alleles 236
rectum 86
recycling
   glass 308
   metals 309
   paper 309
   plastics 308–9
   water 309
red blood cells 117, 120, 121, 258
reducing sugar 42, 43
redwoods, giant (*Sequoia sempervirens*) 93
reflex action 163–4
reflex arc 163–4
rejection, transplant 159
relay neurones 163, 164
renal (relating to kidneys) 156–9
rennin 84
reproduction 2
   asexual 198, 208–9
   in humans 212–26
   in plants 197–209
   sexual 198–200, 200–8, 208–9
reproductive organs, human 213–14
   female 213
   male 213–14
reptiles 10, 153
respiration 2, 141
   aerobic 22, 141
   anaerobic 141
   in plants 35, 42, 53, 70
   releasing energy from food 141
   yeast for baking and brewing 141
retina 166–8
rib cage and breathing 147
ribosomes 22–3
rod cells 167, 168
root cap 96
roots of plants 96–7
   desert plants 252
   response to gravity 173, 174
rough endoplasmic reticulum 22

saliva, role in digestion 83–4
saturated fat 76, 110
sclera 166
scuba diving 140
secondary consumer 267
seeds 44, 50, 172–5, 205–7
selection pressure 189, 257, 287

selective breeding 259, 293, 315
selective felling 311
selective weedkillers 175
self-pollination 204
semen 215
seminal vesicle 214
sense organs 165
sensitivity 2
sensory neurones 163, 164
septum, heart 108
sewage treatment 133, 309–11
sex chromosomes 239–40
sex linkage 241–2
sexlinked genes 241–2
sexual reproduction 198–200, 208–9
   advantages and disadvantages 208–9
   in flowering plants 200–8
   in humans 199
sexually transmitted diseases 225–6
shoots of plants
   effect of auxin on 175
   response to gravity 172, 173
   response to light 172–3
sickle cell anaemia 258
sieve tubes 95
sigmoid growth curve 273
simple sugars 41
sinks and sources, translocation 102, 103
skin 129–30, 131–2, 180–1
small intestine, digestion in 84, 85–6
smallpox 136
smoking, effects on health 110, 192–5
snottites 18
soil erosion 297–8
solar energy 58
solvent 30
sources and sinks, translocation 102, 103
species 4, 231, 239
   conserving 314–15
   diversity in rainforests 297
   ecology 265
   endangered 313
   introduced 314
species diversity 297
sperm 22, 198, 199, 200, 212, 213–14, 215, 221, 233, 237, 249
   donation 223–4
spermicides 222
sphincter muscles 82, 84

sphygmomanometer 113, 114
spongy layer 60
stabilising selection 257
stalactite 18
stamen 201
starch 42
   amylase digesting 50–1, 84, 282
   stored in plants 64, 102, 198
   testing foods for 43
   testing leaf for 66–7
starvation 77
statins 111
stationary phase 273
stem cells 233–4
stem tubers 102, 198
steroids, anabolic 192
stigma 201, 202, 204, 205, 287
stimulant drugs 192
stimuli 162
stomach 53, 84
stomach acid 73
stomata 60, 61, 62, 69, 97, 98
   and transpiration rate 99, 252
   on water hyacinth leaves 253
stress, heart disease and 110
style, flowers 201, 205
substrates 50–1, 52, 53
sucrase 50
sucrose 41
   role in plant nutrition 64–5
   translocation of 102
sugars 41, 42, 282
sulfur dioxide 302–3
sunlight and photosynthesis 6, 21, 59, 62–3, 69, 99, 172
surgery
   for birth control 223
   organ transplants 112, 158–9
suspensory ligaments 169
sustainable development 311
sustainable resources 308
swamps 308
sweat 131–2
sweat glands/sweating 181, 182
synapses 165
synaptic cleft 165
systole 113

tar in cigarettes 192
target organs 170
teeth 80–2

temperature
 of body, regulation of 179–83
 effect on enzymes 52, 53
 effect on transpiration rate 99
 and rate of photosynthesis 69
tendons 113
test crosses 239
testa 205, 206
testes 213, 214, 215, 221
testing foods 42–3, 44–5, 46
testosterone 221
thorax 145, 147
tissue 25
 adipose 44, 181
 fluid 122
 rejection after transplants 158,
  159
tobacco, damage from 192–5
tooth decay 82
toxin 88
trachea 84, 145
translocation, plants 102
transmissible diseases 128, 131
transmitter substance 165
transpiration 97
transpiration rates 98–101
transpiration stream 97–8
transport systems
 in animals 106–23
 in flowering plants 93–103
tree felling 297–8, 311–12
trickling filter 310, 311
tricuspid valve 113
trophic levels 267, 268, 269
tropisms 172
trypsin 84
tubers (potato) 102, 198
turbinal bones 145
turgid cells 34

umbilical cord 216
urea 121, 154–5, 157, 158
ureter 156, 157
urethra 157, 158, 213–14, 215, 226
urine 157
uterus 193, 212, 213, 215–17, 218,
 220–4

vaccination 130, 134–5, 136–7
vaccine 135
vacuoles 21
valves
 in heart 113
 in lymph vessels 122
 in veins 115
variation 248–60
 artificial selection 259
 environmental 249
 genetic 248–9
 and natural selection 253–9
vascular bundles 60, 95
vasoconstriction 182
vasodilation 182
vector 129
veins
 blood vessels 114–17
 leaves 60, 61
ventricles of the heart 108–9
vertebrates 9–10
vesicle 21, 165
villi
 intestinal 85
 placental 216
viruses 9, 189
Visking tubing 30, 32
vitamins 74, 76, 77
vocal cords 145
voice box 145
voluntary action 164

washing powders, biological 283
waste disposal 132–3
water 41
 absorption by plants 96–7
 photosynthesis equation 59
 uptake by leaves 62
 uptake by seeds 206
water cycle 272, 298
water pollution 303–4
water potential gradient 31, 98
water recycling 309
weedkillers 175
wetlands 308
white blood cells 117, 130
 in lymph nodes 122
 role in killing pathogens 118–19
wind-pollination 204
World Wide Fund for Nature 298,
 308

xerophytes 251–2
xylem 93, 94, 102

yeast
 for baking and brewing 141
 in biotechnology 281–2
 experiments 273–4

zygote 198, 205, 216

Terms and conditions of use for the CD-ROM

This is a legal agreement between 'You' (which means the individual customer or the Educational Institution and its authorised users) and Cambridge University Press ('the Licensor') for *Cambridge IGCSE Biology Coursebook CD-ROM*. By placing this CD in the CD-ROM drive of your computer, You agree to the terms of this licence.

1 Limited licence

a You are purchasing only the right to use the CD-ROM and are acquiring no rights, express or implied, to it, other than those rights granted in this limited licence for not-for-profit educational use only.

b The Licensor grants You the licence to use one copy of this CD-ROM.

c You shall not: **(i)** copy or authorise copying of the CD-ROM, **(ii)** translate the CD-ROM, **(iii)** reverse-engineer, alter, adapt, disassemble or decompile the CD-ROM, **(iv)** transfer, sell, lease, lend, profit from, assign or otherwise convey all or any portion of the CD-ROM or **(v)** operate the CD-ROM from a mainframe system, except as provided in these terms and conditions.

d Permission is explicitly granted for use of the CD-ROM on a data projector, interactive whiteboard or other public display in the context of classroom teaching at a purchasing institution.

e If You are an Educational Institution, once a teacher ceases to be a member of the Educational Institution, all copies of the material on the CD-ROM stored on his/her personal computer must be destroyed and the CD-ROM returned to the Educational Institution.

f You are permitted to print reasonable copies of the printable resources on the CD-ROM. These must be used solely for use within the context of classroom teaching at a purchasing institution.

2 Copyright

a All original content is provided as part of the CD-ROM (including text, images and ancillary material) and is the copyright of the Licensor or has been licensed to the Licensor for use in the CD-ROM, protected by copyright and all other applicable intellectual-property laws and international treaties.

b You may not copy the CD-ROM except for making one copy of the CD-ROM solely for backup or archival purposes. You may not alter, remove or destroy any copyright notice or other material placed on or with this CD-ROM.

3 Liability and Indemnification

a The CD-ROM is supplied 'as is' with no express guarantee as to its suitability. To the extent permitted by applicable law, the Licensor is not liable for costs of procurement of substitute products, damages or losses of any kind whatsoever resulting from the use of this product, or errors or faults in the CD-ROM, and in every case the Licensor's liability shall be limited to the suggested list price or the amount actually paid by You for the product, whichever is lower.

b You accept that the Licensor is not responsible for the availability of any links within or outside the CD-ROM and that the Licensor is not responsible or liable for any content available from sources outside the CD-ROM to which such links are made.

c Where, through use of the original material, You infringe the copyright of the Licensor, You undertake to indemnify and keep indemnified the Licensor from and against any loss, cost, damage or expense (including without limitation damages paid to a third party and any reasonable legal costs) incurred by the Licensor as a result of such infringement.

4 Termination

Without prejudice to any other rights, the Licensor may terminate this licence if You fail to comply with the terms and conditions of the licence. In such an event, You must destroy all copies of the CD-ROM.

5 Governing law

This agreement is governed by the laws of England, without regard to its 'conflict of laws' provision, and each party irrevocably submits to the exclusive jurisdiction of the English courts. The parties disclaim the application of the United Nations Convention on the International Sale of Goods.